Film Bodies

'In this challenging and provocative book, Katharina Lindner tackles the problems that film phenomenology has skirted around for years. What is a queer feminist phenomenology? What about female bodies that are in movement, that disrupt, that display themselves and unsettle? Who can speak about them and for them? Lindner looks at filmic female bodies that dance and play sport, and that are performatively queer, and examines the thrilling spaces and affective timeframes in which they move. The result is a new realm of queer feminist embodiment that enables different kinds of non-normative lived bodies to become visible and active, from tango dancers to tomboys, and boxers to ballerinas. A vital and significant development of film phenomenology'.

**Lucy Bolton, Senior Lecturer in Film Studies,
Queen Mary University of London**

'*Film Bodies* vibrantly explores the intersections between film phenomenology and queer and feminist theories. Through a series of agile textual analyses, Lindner draws out the potential of the gendered body to trouble both cinema's sensory experience and film theory's critical categories. *Film Bodies* is an essential contribution to queer film scholarship'.

**Rosalind Galt, Head of Department of Film Studies,
King's College London**

'I cannot think of a single other scholar in the world who combines such an integrated approach to philosophical phenomenology, queer theory and feminist theory while also examining contemporary films in such insightful detail. It therefore follows that the book makes a startlingly original contribution to the field'.

**Jenny Chamarette, Senior Lecturer in Film Studies,
Queen Mary University of London**

Library of Gender and Popular Culture

From Mad Men to gaming culture, performance art to steampunk fashion, the presentation and representation of gender continues to saturate popular media. This series seeks to explore the intersection of gender and popular culture, engaging with a variety of texts – drawn primarily from Art, Fashion, TV, Cinema, Cultural Studies and Media Studies – as a way of considering various models for understanding the complementary relationship between 'gender identities' and 'popular culture'. By considering race, ethnicity, class and sexual identities across a range of cultural forms, each book in the series adopts a critical stance towards issues surrounding the development of gender identities and popular and mass cultural 'products'.

For further information or enquiries, please contact the library series editors:

Claire Nally: claire.nally@northumbria.ac.uk
Angela Smith: angela.smith@sunderland.ac.uk

Advisory Board:
Dr Kate Ames, Central Queensland University, Australia
Dr Michael Higgins, University of Strathclyde, UK
Prof Åsa Kroon, Örebro University, Sweden
Dr Andrea McDonnell, Emmanuel College, USA
Dr Niall Richardson, University of Sussex, UK
Dr Jacki Willson, University of Leeds, UK

Published and forthcoming titles:

The Aesthetics of Camp: Post-Queer Gender and Popular Culture, by Anna Malinowska

Ageing Femininity on Screen: The Older Woman in Contemporary Cinema, by Niall Richardson

All-American TV Crime Drama: Feminism and Identity Politics in Law and Order: Special Victims Unit, by Sujata Moorti and Lisa Cuklanz

Are You Not Entertained?: Mapping the Gladiator Across Visual Media, by Lindsay Steenberg

Bad Girls, Dirty Bodies: Sex, Performance and Safe Femininity, by Gemma Commane

Beyoncé: Celebrity Feminism in the Age of Social Media, by Kirsty Fairclough-Isaacs

Conflicting Masculinities: Men in Television Period Drama, edited by Katherine Byrne, Julie Anne Taddeo and James Leggott

Fat on Film: Gender, Race and Body Size in Contemporary Hollywood Cinema, by Barbara Plotz

Fathers on Film: Paternity and Masculinity in 1990s Hollywood, by Katie Barnett

Feel-Bad Postfeminism: Impasse, Resilience and Female Subjectivity in Popular Culture, by Catherine McDermott

Film Bodies: Queer Feminist Encounters with Gender and Sexuality in Cinema, by Katharina Lindner

From the Margins to the Mainstream: Women in Film and Television, edited by Marianne Kac-Vergne and Julie Assouly

Gay Pornography: Representations of Sexuality and Masculinity, by John Mercer

Gender and Austerity in Popular Culture: Femininity, Masculinity and Recession in Film and Television, edited by Helen Davies and Claire O'Callaghan

Gender and Early television: Mapping Women's Role in Emerging US and British Media, 1850–1950, by Sarah Arnold

The Gendered Motorcycle: Representations in Society, Media and Popular Culture, by Esperanza Miyake

Gendering History on Screen: Women Filmmakers and Historical Films, by Julia Erhart

Girls Like This, Boys Like That: The Reproduction of Gender in Contemporary Youth Cultures, by Victoria Cann

'Guilty Pleasures': European Audiences and Contemporary Hollywood Romantic Comedy, by Alice Guilluy

The Gypsy Woman: Representations in Literature and Visual Culture, by Jodie Matthews

Love Wars: Television Romantic Comedy, by Mary Irwin

Male and Female Violence in Popular Media, by Elisa Giomi and Sveva Magaraggia

Masculinity in Contemporary Science Fiction Cinema: Cyborgs, Troopers and Other Men of the Future, by Marianne Kac-Vergne

Paradoxical Pleasures: Female Submission in Popular and Erotic Fiction, by Anna Watz

Positive Images: Gay Men and HIV/AIDS in the Culture of 'Post-Crisis', by Dion Kagan

Postfeminism and Contemporary Vampire Romance: Representations of Gender and Sexuality in Film and Television, by Lea Gerhards

Queer Horror Film and Television: Sexuality and Masculinity at the Margins, by Darren Elliott-Smith

Queer Sexualities in Early Film: Cinema and Male-Male Intimacy, by Shane Brown

Screening Queer Memory: LGBTQ Pasts in Contemporary Film and Television, by Anamarija Horvat

Steampunk: Gender and the Neo-Victorian, by Claire Nally

Television Comedy and Femininity: Queering Gender, by Rosie White

Tweenhood: Femininity and Celebrity in Tween Popular Culture, by Melanie Kennedy

Women Who Kill: Gender and Sexuality in Film and Series of the post-Feminist Era, edited by David Roche and Cristelle Maury

Wonder Woman: Feminism, Culture and the Body, by Joan Ormrod

Young Women, Girls and Postfeminism in Contemporary British Film, by Sarah Hil

Film Bodies
Queer Feminist Encounters with Gender and Sexuality in Cinema

KATHARINA LINDNER

BLOOMSBURY ACADEMIC
LONDON • NEW YORK • OXFORD • NEW DELHI • SYDNEY

BLOOMSBURY ACADEMIC
Bloomsbury Publishing Plc
50 Bedford Square, London, WC1B 3DP, UK
1385 Broadway, New York, NY 10018, USA
29 Earlsfort Terrace, Dublin 2, Ireland

BLOOMSBURY, BLOOMSBURY ACADEMIC and the Diana logo
are trademarks of Bloomsbury Publishing Plc

First published in Great Britain 2017
Paperback edition published 2023

Copyright © Katharina Lindner, 2017, 2023

Katharina Lindner has asserted her right under the Copyright, Designs and Patents Act, 1988, to be identified as Author of this work.

For legal purposes the Acknowledgements on p. xv constitute an extension of this copyright page.

Cover design: Tango Media
Cover image: Blurred Hand Movements (© M.Sobreira / Alamy)

All rights reserved. No part of this publication may be reproduced or transmitted in any form or by any means, electronic or mechanical, including photocopying, recording, or any information storage or retrieval system, without prior permission in writing from the publishers.

Bloomsbury Publishing Plc does not have any control over, or responsibility for, any third-party websites referred to or in this book. All internet addresses given in this book were correct at the time of going to press. The author and publisher regret any inconvenience caused if addresses have changed or sites have ceased to exist, but can accept no responsibility for any such changes.

A catalogue record for this book is available from the British Library.

A catalog record for this book is available from the Library of Congress.

ISBN: HB: 978-1-7845-3624-4
PB: 978-1-3502-5836-5
ePDF: 978-1-8386-0855-2
eBook: 978-1-8386-0854-5

Series: Library of Gender and Popular Culture

Typeset by Deanta Global Publishing Services, Chennai, India

To find out more about our authors and books visit www.bloomsbury.com and sign up for our newsletters.

For Laura

Contents

List of Illustrations	xiii
Acknowledgements	xv
Series Editors' Foreword	xvii
Foreword to the Paperback Edition	xix

	Introduction: Starting Points, Directions, Tendencies	1
1	**Gender and the Body in Feminist and Queer Film Criticism**	**10**
	Feminism and Film: What Body?	10
	Women's Cinema? Countering Dominant Habits	14
	Grounding Butler: Queer (Theory), Identity, Politics	21
	Women and/in Queer Cinema: (In)visibility and Appearance	28
2	**Film and Embodiment: Queer-ing Film Phenomenology**	**39**
	Grasping Cinema: Tactile, Muscular and Kinaesthetic Encounters	41
	Bodies, Movement and Cinematic Empathy	50
	Countering Normative Tendencies: Gender and/in Phenomenology	55
	Touchy-Feely? The Gendering of Film Phenomenology	67
3	**Queer Encounters with Feminist Politics: Dancing Bodies in *The Tango Lesson* and *Black Swan***	**73**
	Dance/Film	76
	Why Dance? Gender and Sexuality and/as/in Motion	78
	Turning Tables: Feminist Reorientations in *The Tango Lesson*	85
	Out of Your Skin, Out of Your Mind: Unnervingly Visceral Encounters with the Dancing Body in *Black Swan*	116

Contents

4	**Queering the Sports Film: Failure and Gender (Tres)Passing in *2 Seconds* and *Offside***	141
	Towards a Queer Feminist Sports/Film Phenomenology	144
	A Waste of Time? Bad Timing and Queer Failure in *2 Seconds*	150
	On Being *Offside*: Lines and (Tres)passing	173
5	**Céline Sciamma's 'Queer' Cinema: Affirming Gestures of Refusal in *Tomboy* and *Girlhood***	194
	Trans, Lesbian or Queer? Passing, (Mis)Recognition and (Dis)Appearance in *Tomboy*	197
	Queer Shape-Shifting: Embodied Trajectories of Transformation and Resistance in *Girlhood*	223

Conclusion: Collectivities, the Familiar and (Un)Common Sense   246

Notes   251
Bibliography   278
Index   289

List of Illustrations

3.1	Sally's Writing Table (*The Tango Lesson*, Adventure Pictures, 1997)	90
3.2	Dancing Reorientations (*The Tango Lesson*, Adventure Pictures, 1997)	98
3.3	Gendered Tension (*The Tango Lesson*, Adventure Pictures, 1997)	109
3.4	Queer Tango (*The Tango Lesson*, Adventure Pictures, 1997)	115
3.5	Nina Sayers/Natalie Portman (*Black Swan*, 20th Century Fox, 2010)	124
3.6	Mirror/Skin (*Black Swan*, 20th Century Fox, 2010)	126
3.7	Mirror/Skin (*Black Swan*, 20th Century Fox, 2010)	126
4.1	Laurie (*2 Seconds*, Max Films Production, 1998)	163
4.2	Life as a Bike Courier (*2 Seconds*, Max Films Production, 1998)	169
4.3	Smoking Girl (*Offside*, Jafar Panahi Film Productions, 2006)	174
4.4	First Girl, (tres)passing (*Offside*, Jafar Panahi Film Productions, 2006)	178
4.5	Soldier and Smoking Girl in Touching Distance (*Offside*, Jafar Panahi Film Productions, 2006)	185
4.6	Embodied Engagements (*Offside*, Jafar Panahi Film Productions, 2006)	189
4.7	Embodied Engagements (*Offside*, Jafar Panahi Film Productions, 2006)	189
4.8	Embodied Engagements (*Offside*, Jafar Panahi Film Productions, 2006)	191

List of Illustrations

5.1	Lisa and Laure/Mikaël Watching the Football Game (*Tomboy*, Hold up Films, 2011)	213
5.2	Touching the Body/Image (*Tomboy*, Hold up Films, 2011)	215
5.3	Laure/Mikaël in the 'World of Boys' (*Tomboy*, Hold up Films, 2011)	219
5.4	Laure/Mikaël in 'Drag' (*Tomboy*, Hold up Films, 2011)	220
5.5	Marieme (*Girlhood*, Hold up Films, 2014)	224
5.6	Celebrating Female Physicality (*Girlhood*, Hold up Films, 2014)	231
5.7	Laughter and 'Diamonds' (*Girlhood*, Hold up Films, 2014)	238
5.8	Twisting Binary Gender (*Girlhood*, Hold up Films, 2014)	242

Acknowledgements

There are a great number of people who have contributed to and influenced this project, in one way or another, knowingly or not, through their scholarly brilliance, unconditional kindness, incisive questioning, invigorating curiosity, awe-inspiring vision and fearless convictions:

Jennifer Barker, Lucy Bolton, Jenny Chamarette, Cristina Johnston, Felicity Colman, Lucy Fife Donaldson, Rosalind Galt, Christine Geraghty, Catherine Grant, Skadi Loist, So Mayer, Lisa Purse, Miriam Ross, Catherine Wheatley.

Sara Ahmed's work has inspired this book, from beginning to end. We have never met but I am enormously grateful to her for giving me the intellectual, emotional and political tools that allowed me to even begin to think about writing this book.

I also want to thank my colleagues at the University of Stirling for suffering me, Lisa Goodrum and Arub Ahmed at I.B.Tauris for their patience and editorial support, and the anonymous reviewers for their insightful comments.

Finally, I am massively indebted to Karen Boyle for reading a draft of the book. And for everything else.

Series Editors' Foreword

Katharina Lindner's book offers a fresh approach to analysing films by putting the body (in and of film) at the centre of inquiry. It builds on the conceptual tools and enabling possibilities of feminist and queer theory, as many of the books in this library do, including Darren Elliott-Smith's *Queer Horror Film and Television*. In this particular study, Lindner engages with questions of gender and sexuality by accounting for the kinaesthetic, corporeal and phenomenological engagements that cinema might evoke. Through an exploration of the female body in a selection of contemporary films, including dance films (*The Tango Lesson, Black Swan*), sports films (*2 Seconds, Offside*) and queer cinema (*Tomboy, Girlhood*), Lindner develops a framework that accounts for the troubling potential of the female body and the cinematic modes of embodiment it gives shape to. Struggles around identity (politics) are at the heart of this book, as with so many in this series. How those struggles are played out in relation to a queer feminist phenomenology (of cinema) is one of the key issues this study sheds light on.

In *Film Bodies*, Lindner brings together bodies of theory, film and politics and begins to work through, and to work out, the various tensions, alignments, directions, frictions, orientations and tendencies that emerge from the ensuing points of contact. The book uses white Anglophone feminist film theory as a starting point, before turning towards a phenomenological engagement with ageing, the geopolitics of gender, gender fluidity and black girlhood. The book thus takes the reader from the centre to the margins – conceptually, geographically, cinematically – while asserting the possibilities for thinking and feeling the relations between gender, the body and cinema differently.

Angela Smith and Claire Nally

Foreword: A (Queer) Place from Which to Speak

Jenny Chamarette

As you read this book, *Film Bodies*, you might not know how you are also time travelling through the author's writing process. What first sentence began the long journey to publication? All writers know this question and the nature of time embedded in it: the time of writing that could have begun years, decades even, prior to the book being published. Drafting and redrafting blur the edges of those beginnings. What scratchings of an itch first created a research question, a problem to be solved, to then become an essay, a chapter, a monograph? It is not my place to speculate on an answer, but the questions are important. Because strange things happen when you write. Words come from a place you don't recognize. Through fingertips, hands, voice notes emerge a familiar–unfamiliar location, person, axiom, feeling-tone. On occasion, these words find kinship with the words of another writer, and for a moment there is room to breathe.

When I read the work of Katharina Lindner – when I read and re-read *Film Bodies* – these spacious sensations of familiarity–unfamiliarity arise for me. Lindner – Kat – is not concerned with any or all bodies in film. She focuses her lens specifically on queer feminist bodies, feminine bodies in movement, female and more-than-female human bodies that range across race and ethnicity, sexuality and gender expression. She is concerned with, as she writes in the Introduction, the 'affirmatively troubling potential of the female body and the cinematic modes of embodiment to which it gives shape'.[1]

When you see the word 'female' in this book, this is not at all an essentialist claim. This clarification should not be necessary, and yet the turn in recent culture wars, particularly in the UK, seems to necessitate it. The deeply embedded and embodied knowledge of queer feminist theory and queer feminist praxis in *Film Bodies* knows not to assume universal definitions of femininity, since the very concept of gender is entangled with a bewilderingly wide array of sociocultural, historical and motile contexts. Katharina Lindner knew this, not just from her perspective as an academic but also as an ex-professional footballer. Kat – and I hope the reader will forgive me in this shift from surname to first name, because I want and need to recognize her first and foremost as the person I knew – was an admirably temperate and discerning commentator on gender and sport, publishing on the wider cultural ramifications of, for instance, the introduction of women's boxing into the 2012 Olympics, in which she diagnoses how women athletes' ways of being in the world 'unhinge, in the most fundamental of ways, binary understandings of the gendered body'.[2]

Kat was therefore not interested in upholding gender binaries, knowing that to do so would ultimately return queer bodies, and bodies of all kinds, to a heteropatriarchal stranglehold.

Film Bodies' overt engagements with queer femininity provide a ground to describe in detail covert models of gender fluidity and gender non-conformity. And these models are multiple: from temporary vehicles of cross-dressing that critique Iranian subject positions for women in public spaces in Jafar Panahi's *Offside* (2006) to complex and subtle re-formations of tomboyism through the lens of queer gender-nonconformity in Céline Sciamma's *Tomboy* (2011). With the exception of *Black Swan* (Darren Aronofsky, 2010) which grossed some $300 million at the box office (some way smaller than the largest grossing US films that year, which reached $1 billion in box office receipts), Kat deliberately and specifically chose critically acclaimed films which were not blockbuster hits. Her description of this choice to frame 'minor' cinema in this way is itself subversive, aiming to 'infiltrate (major) conceptions of the minor' – to show how the queer feminist embodiments she traces with such care are not simply marginalized pursuits, but dissenting undercurrents in a broader milieu of filmmaking and film cultures.[3] What is 'minor' is a shifting relation, not an absolute designation. The 'minor' is fluid; fitting for a book that expresses at every stage discomfort with and refusal of normative delineations of gender and sexuality.

I sense in my writing here that I am deflecting from the felt sense-making of Kat's prose. It is true that *Film Bodies* is an exceptionally deft work of theory, which understands deeply its relationships to the queer feminist archive (to quote Robyn Wiegman) and wider indebtedness to phenomenology.[4] But this book is more than a vehicle for a specific array of concepts about embodiment. The first two chapters of *Film Bodies*, theoretically dense and methodologically intricate, identify tensions in the not-quite-enoughness of either discourse. That is, neither frameworks of queer and gender theory nor queer(ed) film phenomenologies are enough to contend with the fleshy being of polyvalently gendered, gender fluid and non-binary people, women and girls onscreen in contemporary 'minor' cinema. And Kat's fine-grained apperception of this not-quite-enoughness, this insufficiency in the theoretical canon to explore or elucidate genderfluid or gender non-conforming queer femininity, is what makes this book so outstanding.

It is not enough to write *about* film bodies or *about* gender and sexuality on screen: Kat explicitly states this throughout *Film Bodies*. Theoretical models tend to enact a strange kind of Cartesian body–mind split, where the high-level cognitive processing of prose disconnects from the felt, sensed, experienced world of film and film-watching: a head without a body watching in a darkened room. *Film Bodies* gently but firmly places that head back on its shoulders, reconnects to its connective tissue: muscle and bone and skin, and queer movement through the world. Kat re-appraises historical phenomenological writing on bodily empathy through Edith Stein, Iris Marion Young and Maurice Merleau-Ponty, while interrogating the muscularity of contemporary writing on cinematic embodiment through Jennifer M Barker, Elena del Rio and Adriano D'Aloia. Equally, she traces the various lineages of queer film theory by grounding and affirming the heady, literary-philosophical, conceptual frameworks of Judith Butler within the context of more historically applied, theoretical scholarship from Patricia White, Richard Dyer and Annemarie Jagose. This technique of grounding is deeply embedded in *Film Bodies*: it is humorous and kind, and it is also deeply political. When responding to Jagose's articulation of queerness as the fundamentally ambivalent combination of identity formation and strategies that disassemble identity formations, I can hear Kat's dry wit when she responds, 'we can be queer *and* paranoid, or so it seems.'[5]

Foreword

Queer and paranoid. The fleshy body of my being recognizes this itching in-betweenness of what is queer, what is queer 'enough', what is 'too' queer. There is body-knowledge in this phrase. It seems so obvious that the embodied knowledge Kat brought with her from her decades as a professional athlete contributes to the speaking voice of this book. The term she uses for this voice, with which she opens and closes *Film Bodies*, is a queer feminist vernacular. What does this mean, a *queer feminist vernacular*? When I turn to etymological dictionaries, I am surprised that the word 'vernacular' does not come from the Latinate root I had anticipated – *vermis*, the little worm – but from *vernaculus*. This curious root marries concepts of the home-grown, the indigenous and indentured slavery in some kind of pre-emptively queer descriptive triumvirate.[6] The vernacular contains sustained relationships to land and sustained relationships to suffering. In this is it most apposite: How to live the complexities of a queer body, committed to polygendered fluidity and to challenging constrictive heteropatriarchal norms, in a world hostile to the footfall of queer feet on occupied land? I see this question reflected, revolved, shattered and rebuilt in *Film Bodies*, which examines how global minor cinema uniquely demonstrates the consequences of this question.

Kat was always scrupulously honourable in her citational praxis, honouring every seed of every idea planted in her prose. This skilful act of literary craft is as demonstrative of her brilliance as a scholar and thinker as it is testament to her life's work as a queer feminist. It is not inconsequential that Sara Ahmed's book *Living a Feminist Life* was published just a year before *Film Bodies*. Nor is it unconnected that citation as a mode of scholarly doing has since then, once again, come to wider feminist prominence. Kat's copy editor, So Mayer, confirms this constellation of queer feminist citational praxis. From So I learn that they and Kat 'spoke extensively about Ahmed's citational and emphatic practices (italicisation in particular) when approaching the copy edit' to *Film Bodies*.[7] While Ahmed's reflections on citational praxis were visible since the publication of *Queer Phenomenology* a decade previously, in *Living a Feminist Life* her 'strict citation policy' sparked both applause and condemnation: 'I do not cite any white men.'[8] Ahmed clarifies that this is an anti-institutional statement, not a personal one.[9] And yet, I have seen rolled eyes (from white men) and bunched up faces (from white men), who misconstrue this as a sudden and strategic exclusionary insult, not an ongoing praxis of self-care from those who have endured decades of exclusion.

I cannot make claims regarding Kat's own intentions for *Film Bodies*, but my intuition as a critic and a scholar and a reader is that *Film Bodies'* own citational praxis pre-emptively tests Ahmed's methods with a softer queer(ying) edge. Explicitly and implicitly, *Film Bodies* examines the citational entanglements between scholars who exist on the borderlines of the white heteropatriarchal male institution (gay white men) and feminist women. The *queer feminist vernacular* to which *Film Bodies* inclines, which it identifies at the beginning and the end of the book, and which aptly describes the praxis of embodied knowing that Kat analyses with such nuance and delicacy, is an adaptive strategy of exactly this kind. To rework Ahmed's metaphorical lexicon, one queer brick upon which this book's *queer feminist vernacular* is built is Brett Farmer's term 'vernacular queerness', as Kat identifies in the opening section of *Film Bodies*.[10] Farmer's terminology describes queer formations of relational desire in contemporary Thai cinema, which do not require strict assignations of gender or sexual identity, and moreover, which resist the specific Euro-Western vocabularies associated with non-normative sexuality.[11] And yet, Farmer also uses this term adaptively, connectively, drawing on Miriam B. Hansen's analysis of popular cinema as a 'vernacular modernism' which accounts for the 'localised contingency of cinema's negotiations of modernity'.[12] What circulates, therefore, are citational entanglements of the queer, and the feminist, and the cinematic. This is Kat's mode of encountering entanglement: resisting oversimplification, making space for both nuance and discomfort.

Giving the body a place from which to speak was a central concern for Kat's scholarship. Particularly the non-fitting, mis-fitting body: the feminine body that is 'too' masculine, the cross-dressing female body trying to 'pass' (*Offside*), the trans-masculine, non-binary body of a child and adolescent (*Tomboy* and *Girlhood*, Céline Sciamma, 2015), the ageing dancing and athletic body (*The Tango Lesson,* Sally Potter, 1997, *Black Swan*), endlessly scrutinized for any perceived physical or choreographic imperfection, but also always in stages of creative movement. The ageing body of the female athlete is a central concern of *2 Seconds* (Manon Briand, 1998), but so are failure, and the queer scrambling of the film's temporal co-ordinates, and of film narratives more broadly. In this mis-fitting of time and space, I am reminded of Rosemarie Garland Thomson's concept of *mis-fitting* 'as a shifting spatial and perpetually temporal relationship [that] confers agency and value on disabled subjects'.[13] Though *2 Seconds* is not a film about disability, nor is disability a feature of *Film Bodies*, my own sense of reading Kat's prose is that she would have been radically open to considering the queer relationships between athletic and disabled bodies (particularly since disabled athletes have become increasingly prominent in public discourses of sport over the last decade); that her work sought to question the ableist and eugenicist cultural pressures that enforce gendered boundaries upon the embodied practices of athletes, on- and off-screen; and that her hyperacuity to those insistent demands of gendered and racialized performance would have likely forged renewed alliances with the body-oriented feminist materialist research of disability scholars like Garland Thomson.

This is more than a question of alliances, however. *Film Bodies* supports the interrogation of contemporary lesbian cinema which Clara Bradbury-Rance takes up in *Lesbian Cinema after Queer Theory*.[14] In *Film Bodies*, lesbians are given room to breathe, to expand, to falter. And my intuition is not just that Kat would have openly welcomed the emerging field of scholarship on trans cinema, but that in effect, *Film Bodies* is a work of trans cinematic scholarship *avant-la-lettre*, sharing affinities with the more structural-materialist work of Eliza Steinbock's *Shimmering Images: Trans Cinema, Embodiment, and the Aesthetics of Change*, while also retaining an emphatically powerful emphasis on *bodies* and embodied knowledge as the site of Kat's analysis.[15] Considering *Film Bodies* within this trinity of works builds a chorus of resonant contemporary voices in the struggle to articulate queer, lesbian and trans cinematic bodies, filled with the weighty embodiment of living, as well as the discursive social formations of gender fluidity and non-binary being.

Writing comes from an embodied place – the mutable, changing, shimmering body of the writer – but its embodied destinations, in readers and interlocutors, the chorus of writers who stand behind and beside the work, are infinitely more dispersed across time zones and linear temporalities, enmeshed in forces of past, present and future. This is the nature of writerly kinship. What moves you might have been written a month ago or ten years ago. Writing and scholarship carry deep within them their own temporal drag, their own queerly mis-fitting time. Trailing gloriously in the wind behind *Film Bodies* are all the beginnings, the experiences that shape it, the visceral connections that give the book a body–mind from which to speak. And also the endings: Kat's death on Saturday, 9 February 2019.

I don't know how to give space to my fervent longing for Kat to have read this foreword and given her permission for it, correcting it where it needs correcting. Despite the guise of assurance in this essay, my re-reading of *Film Bodies* feels in so many ways like swimming in the dark. Reading, especially scholarly reading, is always a matter of drifting through the darkness, making tiny bioluminescent signals from time to time that others might just see. I know that the integrity Kat upheld would have welcomed this queer oscillation between clarity and confusion, while always pressing still further, getting to the heart of things. Her bioluminescence remains: in her scholarship, in this book, in those of us touched by the grace of her writing and being. The queer feminist vernaculars she builds in this book that you are reading are continuously entangled with the queer, intersectional feminist and trans scholarship on cinema and embodiment published since her passing, and the queer, ambivalent, intersectional ways of being that she unwaveringly supported. I can feel her here in the new edition of this book, to which I am honoured to contribute this foreword. But as a friend of mine once said, conversation with the dead is lonely when all you hear is your own voice in return.

If a queer feminist vernacular is not a language, but a place from which to speak, or to rephrase another queer feminist thinker, a place for making kin to speak with,[16] then this queer embodied place from which to speak is what *Film Bodies* is for.

Notes

1 Katharina Lindner, *Film Bodies: Queer Feminist Encounters with Gender and Sexuality in Cinema* (London: IB Tauris, 2017), p. 1.
2 Katharina Lindner, 'Women's Boxing at the 2012 Olympics: Gender trouble?', *Feminist Media Studies* 12/3 (2012), p. 467 (464–7).
3 Lindner, *Film Bodies*, p. 21.

4 Robyn Wiegman, 'The times we're in: Queer feminist criticism and the reparative "turn"', *Feminist Theory* 15/1 (2014), pp. 4–25, p. 6, cited in Lindner, *Film Bodies*, p. 3.
5 Lindner, *Film Bodies*, p. 27.
6 'vernacular'. *The Concise Oxford Dictionary of English Etymology*. Edited by T. F. Hoad (Oxford: Oxford University Press). *Oxford Reference*. https://www.oxfordreference.com/view/10.1093/acref/9780192830982.001.0001/acref-9780192830982-e-16619 (accessed 3 February 2022).
7 Email correspondence with So Mayer, 9 February 2022.
8 Sara Ahmed, *Living a Feminist Life* (Durham: Duke University Press, 2017), p. 15.
9 Ibid., p. 15 and 270n8.
10 Ibid., p. 15 and Lindner, *Film Bodies*, p. 6.
11 Brett Farmer, 'Loves of siam: Contemporary Thai cinema and vernacular queerness', in Peter A. Jackson (ed.), *Queer Bangkok: 21st Century Markets, Media, and Rights* (Hong Kong: Hong Kong University Press, 2011), pp. 81–98 (82).
12 Miriam B. Hansen, 'The mass production of the senses: Classical cinema as vernacular modernism', *Modernism/Modernity* 6/2 (1999), pp. 59–77 cited in Farmer, 'Loves of siam', 81–98.
13 Rosemarie Garland-Thomson, 'Misfits: A Feminist Materialist Disability Concept', *Hypatia* 26/3 (Summer 2011), pp. 591–609.
14 Clara Bradbury-Rance, *Lesbian Cinema after Queer Theory* (Edinburgh: Edinburgh University Press, 2019).
15 Eliza Steinbock, *Shimmering Images: Trans Cinema, Embodiment, and the Aesthetics of Change* (Durham: Duke University Press, 2019).
16 Donna Haraway, *Staying with the Trouble: Making Kin in the Chthulucene* (Durham: Duke University Press, 2016).

Introduction

Starting Points, Directions, Tendencies

It is a fascination with the multifaceted entanglements between cinema, gender and the body, and their continuously shifting and teasingly uncontainable critical allure, that 'cleare[d] a space' for this book to 'surface' and to take 'shape' in the way it does.¹ It coheres around the female body in cinema, with a particular focus on those contexts in which it appears to disrupt, unhinge or gesture beyond normative incarnations of gender and cinema. It is concerned with the ways in which the female body might allow for variously queer modes of embodiment to 'appear' in and through film.² The 'point' of this book – from its starting point to what it attempts to point towards – is to develop a framework that accounts for the affirmatively troubling potential of the female body and the cinematic modes of embodiment to which it gives shape.

The coming together of 'queer', 'female' and 'body' (in cinema) opens up into a wide, complex and inherently contradictory network of theories, debates and philosophical considerations. Each of these terms carries a whole range of historical, symbolic, political and conceptual baggage. They are also relatively open and malleable concepts, however, that, when brought into contact with each other, open up productive, and productively different, ways of thinking (about) our variously queer encounters with film. This is precisely what this book does: it brings together bodies of theory, film and politics, and begins to work through, and to work out, the various tensions, alignments, directions, frictions, orientations and tendencies that emerge from the ensuing points of contact.

The work presented here is not only *about* cinematic embodiments – it also has specifically embodied (tactile, muscular and kinaesthetic) beginnings. It emerges from a slowly burning sense of frustration with the conceptual tools and possibilities provided by existing (feminist and queer) approaches to gender, sexuality and the body in film. It is also motivated by the ways in which some of the recent work on cinema's affective, sensuous and corporeal dimensions seems to resonate, in some sense profoundly, both with my frustrations (with theory) and with those films (some of which are explored in this book) that appear to escape the reach and grasp of more conventional ways of accounting for the queer, feminist and queerly feminist resonances of the body in and of film. We might also say that the book 'takes the shape' of its aboutness and its beginnings: it constitutes a series of affective, tactile, muscular and kinaesthetic encounters – with theories, concepts, ideas and films – that might leave a certain impression on the reader who is willing to make contact.

Some of the most groundbreaking work on cinema and embodiment, most notably the writing of Vivian Sobchack and Laura U. Marks, was developed quite specifically in response to the normative (Western, white, male, heterosexual) underpinnings of conventional, especially psychoanalytic, semiotic and ideological/Marxist, approaches to film.[3] In subsequent work on embodiment, however, the concern with gender, and with difference more generally, seems to have been relegated to the margins and a suspiciously unmarked body/mode of embodiment appears to have made a sneaky reappearance in various accounts of the sensuous, affective, haptic, kinaesthetic, emotional, corporeal and muscular dimensions of, and encounters with, film.[4]

At the same time, the work of feminist, gender and queer studies scholars – including, in particular, Sara Ahmed, Judith/Jack Halberstam, Ann Cvetkovich and Elizabeth Freeman – has produced vital contributions to our understanding of the embodied, affective, spatial and temporal dimensions of gender, sexuality and queerness.[5] They provide a sense of the potentialities of the gendered body that allows us to be mindful of the affective and spatio-temporal specificity of lived experience, without,

Introduction

importantly, falling into the traps of a potentially debilitating essentialism – which is, in part, why Robyn Wiegman refers to this body of work as a specifically 'queer feminist archive'.[6] These accounts, especially when brought into contact with *film* phenomenology, also allow us to get a better grasp of the convoluted entanglements of gender, queerness and the body that take shape in and through cinema.

In the broadest sense, then, the conceptual work this book does is tied to its working through of the resonances and synergies between debates around film, sensuousness and embodiment on the one hand, and queer (and) feminist engagements with embodiment and affect on the other. What happens when film phenomenology meets queer/feminist phenomenology? What kind of queer feminist film phenomenology might surface in this encounter?

These questions are explored through a 'textural analysis' of films that variously foreground the workings of embodiment in, of and through film in relation to their variously troubled and troubling female protagonists.[7] They include *The Tango Lesson* (Sally Potter, UK, 1997), *Black Swan* (Darren Aronofsky, US, 2010), *2 secondes* (*2 Seconds*, Manon Briand, Canada, 1998), *Offside* (Jafar Panahi, Iran, 2006), *Tomboy* (Céline Sciamma, France, 2011) and *Bande de filles* (*Girlhood*, Céline Sciamma, France, 2014).

The films emerge from a range of generic contexts – the dance film, the sports film and queer cinema – all of which centre, albeit to varying extents, on the gendered display and appearance of the body that ground questions of identification, agency and (in)visibility. The textural encounters with these films in what follows take place in relation to the representational and critical landscapes – marked in particular by the coming together of a post-feminist sensibility and the legacy of the New Queer Cinema and queer theory – that they emerge from and that have profoundly reorientated precisely the questions around (in)visibility, (dis)appearance, identity (politics), representability, legibility, recognisability and intelligibility of gender and sexuality that the films themselves centrally invoke.

What connects the otherwise fairly diverse selection of films are their queer feminist resonances that hinge on, and take shape through, the female body's multifaceted cinematic incarnations. The centrality of the female body in the context of various kinds of (highly gendered) bodily performances – dance (*The Tango Lesson*, *Black Swan*, *Girlhood*),

3

cycling (*2 Seconds*), football/soccer (*Offside, Tomboy*), American football (*Girlhood*) and fighting (*Tomboy, Girlhood*) – functions to magnify, and to make strange, the (hetero)normatively gendered processes of embodiment that normally take shape in, through and around film.

My own affective, embodied engagements with these films – as well as with the debates around film phenomenology and queer/feminist embodiment – constitute initial points of departure. This is not to say, however, that the book takes an autobiographical approach (conceptually or methodologically) and somehow substitutes 'subjective' for 'objective' analysis – a charge often directed at this kind of work.[8] In fact, I would argue that this move (the writer being drawn to and turning towards certain bodies of film and theory) is the starting point for most academic writing – although the situated and supposedly 'subjective' nature of these starting points tends to only be acknowledged, and become an issue, when they differ from those normative and unmarked (white, male, heteronormative) starting points that go unnoticed and pass under the mantel of objectivity. I engage with these tensions in more detail in Chapter 2 but they are usefully flagged here in relation to Rosi Braidotti's reminder not to confuse the process of subjectivity with individualism or particularity, and to acknowledge that 'subjectivity is a *socially mediated* process.'[9] My own embodiedness, inescapable as it is, makes me part of a wider network of embodied connections and relations (human, cinematic, theoretical, affective), rather than the detached and disembodied voice of authority. It is the socio-cultural situatedness, embeddedness and relationality of embodiment – and the ways in which modes of embodiment circulate and take shape in and around film – that enable meaning and affect to surface. This project aims to explore these variously corporeal entanglements – and to make them graspable, intellectually and sensuously.

The encounters with/of films and theory in this book are marked by what Eve Kosofsky Sedgwick has referred to as a reparative, rather than paranoid, mode or sensibility.[10] The intention here is not to expose 'hidden' meanings that might linger beneath the surface of bodies and texts, but to engage (with) bodies and texts in a way that is open to and expectant of 'surprise'. Rather than staging the 'drama of exposure' of what might be beneath, behind or beyond, the mode of inquiry employed in this book is one of *besideness* – of reading, and encountering, *beside*.[11] What happens

Introduction

when we allow, or enable, bodies, ideas, films and politics to encounter each other in a manner that resists the linear, teleological logics of beneath, behind and beyond – and the 'dualistic thinking' of 'cause versus effect' and 'subject versus object' intrinsic to it? That said, I also want to resist the kind of (paranoid) dualistic thinking that posits reparative and paranoid modes as binary opposites.[12] In this sense, the mode of inquiry that shapes this book is best thought of as having reparative orientations and tendencies (while a healthy dose of paranoia is kept within reach and close to hand).

For Sedgwick, '[b]eside comprises a wide range of desiring, identifying, representing, repelling, paralleling, differentiating, rivalling, leaning, twisting, mimicking, withdrawing, attracting, aggressing, warping and other relations.'[13] Engaging theories, ideas, politics, films and bodies in a mode, or orientation, of *besideness*, as I do here, opens up *spaces of possibility* (in the spatial, rather than teleological sense) for queerly non-normative modes of embodiment to surface, take shape and make (pleasurable, troubling) contact. '*Sensation*, we might say, displaces the authority of suspicion' – a conceptual turn, which, for Wiegman, marks the formation of a specifically 'queer feminist scholarship.'[14]

This book fore-grounds, in the phenomenological sense, the *spatiality* of gender and sexuality, which is why relations of depth and surface, foreground and background, proximity and distance are central to the ways in which the reshaping of gender and sexual norms and tendencies is accounted for. Relations of beneathness, behindness and beyondness therefore do underpin the argument that takes shape throughout – but *not* primarily in the paranoid sense of discovery and exposure. Probing beneath the surface (of the gendered contours of the body; of the 'skin of the film')[15] and engaging the muscular and kinaesthetic dimension (of gender and of cinema), as I do in this book, aims *not* to unearth what is hidden or covered up. It is a decidedly sense-ational endeavour that aims to reorientate and dehabituate our perceptual tendencies and to make more acutely graspable what is (potentially) always already within our bodily horizons. Methodologically, this manifests itself, following Barker's 'textural analysis' model, through a focus on the haptic, muscular, kinaesthetic, and spatio-temporal dimensions of embodiment in and of film (see Chapter 2) and their various resonances, alignments, frictions and synergies with surrounding modes of embodiment.

Brett Farmer's notion of 'vernacular queerness' posits an understanding of queer cinema/queerness in cinema in terms of its 'interactive "embeddedness" in broader socio-historical contexts,' and 'not so much [as] a set of textual representations of predetermined content and value.'[16] Farmer's formulation provides a useful way of pulling together one of the things this book does: by situating the engagement with cinema within the 'broader constellation of discourses, practices and institutions in and through which [gender and sexual norms] are realized and take effect' in specifically embodied terms (in this case in dance, sport and queer culture), I am able to trace the connections between cinematic and everyday, lived modes of embodiment and their variously entangled resonances.[17]

'Chapter 1: Gender and the Body in Feminist and Queer Film Criticism' begins to work through and give shape to the broad conceptual underpinnings of the book as they relate to questions of gender, sexuality and the body in film (criticism). It explores the resonances and tensions between 'feminist', 'lesbian' and 'queer' in the context of cinema, with a specific focus on how feminist, lesbian or queer might manifest themselves in and through film. Tracing feminist film criticism's relatively recent conceptual reorientation towards corporeality and sensuousness, it foregrounds *how* the body, and what *kind* of body, appears in these debates. It is within this context that I highlight how existing scholarship around women's cinema, female authorship, enunciation and spectatorial address, as well as around queer theory, identity politics, queer cinema and the 'minor', might benefit from an encounter with phenomenonologically grounded understandings of both gender and cinema.

After bringing feminist, lesbian and queer in touch with cinema, I turn my attention to the kinds of embodied and affect-based approaches to cinema that allow for an understanding of the visceral, muscular and kinaesthetic dimensions of the cinematic entanglements of feminist, lesbian and queer. 'Chapter 2: Film and Embodiment: Queer-ing Film Phenomenology' suggests ways in which queer/feminist critiques of phenomenology might usefully be integrated into film phenomenological debates in order to displace the strangely neutral and unmarked body that has made an uncanny appearance in recent explorations of cinematic embodiment and embodied, muscular and kinaesthetic empathy in particular. A necessarily detailed unpacking of the ways in which gender appears within phenomenology, and of how we might conceive of a phenomenology of gender that does not fall back onto notions of an unmarked 'human' subjectivity and a constituting transcendental consciousness in the last instance, asserts the grounds on which a queer feminist film phenomenology might surface.

'Chapter 3: Queer Encounters with Feminist Politics: Dancing Bodies in *The Tango Lesson* and *Black Swan*' explores the multi-layered intertextu(r)ality that takes shape when the (female) dancing body encounters the filmic body. Dancing provides a space in which gender relations are displayed and worked out in specifically muscular, kinaesthetic and spatial terms. It is also a context in which questions around muscular and kinaesthetic empathy have become crucial critical concerns. My discussion of *The Tango Lesson* traces the film's act of turning its back on an 'outdated' feminist film criticism and its simultaneous taking shape as the protagonist's/filmmaker's embodied performance of both tango *and* cinema. The film provides a corporeal space in which cinema, feminism and tango encounter each other in a way that enables the performative incarnation of a queerly corporeal feminism. This is contrasted with *Black Swan*'s viscerally intense and thrillingly disturbing trajectory, which traces its dancing protagonist's mental and physical disintegration in a way that unhinges our normative perceptual habits and expectations. With the female ballet body as its 'zero point of orientation' and *dis*orientation, *Black Swan* makes graspable the agonising pressures that crush and tear apart the female body in the heteropatriarchal context of contemporary mainstream cinema.[18]

'Chapter 4: Queering the Sports Film: Failure and Gender (Tres)Passing in *2 Seconds* and *Offside*' moves towards cinematic incarnations of a different kind of public physical display – from dance to sport – with a specific focus on two films with female protagonists who variously disrupt generic sports film conventions. Both *2 Seconds* and *Offside* make strange sport's normative significance and function (in cinema and beyond) and offer a visceral, graspable reshaping of the ways in which ideologies of gender, success and the nation normally surface in and through sport. I explore the ways in which *2 Seconds*' foregrounding of 'the phenomenology of the sporting body'[19] conveys a sense of the unravelling of what Freeman calls 'chrononormativity' and Halberstam refers to as 'straight time'.[20] It is the cyclist-protagonist's continuous failure to be 'on time', not to 'waste time' and to incorporate the rhythms and directionality of normative temporal registers that not only disrupt assumptions of the givenness of 'straight time' but allow for different kinds of temporalities (that might be twisted or backwards) to surface. The textural encounter with Jafar Panahi's *Offside* foregrounds the 'temporary space of political and agential potential' that manifests itself in relation to the film's gender (tres)passing protagonists: a group of women, disguised as men, who try to gain access to a football stadium.[21] The discussion highlights how the spectator's alignment with the perceptual possibilities and limitations of being 'offside' (spatially, symbolically, politically) reorients the perceptual habits and expectations that normally underpin our encounters with both cinema and football.

Following the explorations of the variously 'twisted' and 'twisting', troubled and troubling, dis- and reorientating incarnations of female bodies and modes of embodiment and perception in the dance and sports film, the final chapter returns to questions around the queerness of queer cinema – and feminism's place within it.[22] With a specific focus on Céline Sciamma's queer feminist body of films, 'Chapter 5: Céline Sciamma's "Queer" Cinema: Affirming Gestures of Refusal in *Tomboy* and *Girlhood*' proposes that *Tomboy*'s and *Girlhood*'s variously queer resonances emerge not so much (only) from a making visible of 'queer' identities but through the films' sensory, tactile, muscular and kinaesthetic 'working out' of tensions and conflicts around (in)visibility and (dis)appearance as they relate to gender, sexuality and the body. While *Tomboy* offers an affirmative opening-up of the conventions that tend to shape the intersections of tomboy, trans and gender disguise tropes, *Girlhood* makes graspable its female protagonist's shape-shifting journey of corporeal transformation as well as the ways in which female solidarity and collectivity might give shape to a 'gestural code of women's bodies' that disrupts normatively heteropatriarchal systems of language and signification.[23]

The trajectory of the book as a whole thus uses predominantly white and Anglophone feminist film theory as a point for departure (*The Tango Lesson*, *Black Swan*), before turning towards a phenomenological engagement with ageing and the geopolitics of gender (*2 Seconds*, *Offside*) and eventually culminating in encounters with gender fluidity, tomboyism and black girlhood (*Tomboy*, *Girlhood*). In other words, the directionality of this journey is one that takes us away from the centre and towards the margins – conceptually, geographically, cinematically and politically.[24]

Introduction

Overall, what takes shape through the multiple encounters in this book is a queer feminist film phenomenology, a conceptual frame that allows us to grasp, and make sense of, the variously unruly, sticky, numbing, exhilarating, frustrating, agitating and affirming resonances that emerge from the textural entanglements of bodies in, through and around film. The originality of this project lies in its cultivation of the synergies between embodied film theory and queer/feminist accounts of embodiment. The ensuing encounters (between bodies, ideas, theories, films and politics) suggest that, in a cultural landscape characterised by post-feminist discourses as well as increasing queer visibility, it is in the realms of embodiment, corporeality and sensuousness that questions of gender and sexuality are most affectingly worked out.

1

Gender and the Body in Feminist and Queer Film Criticism

Feminism and Film: What Body?

The orientations of this book, and the cinematic encounters it makes graspable, are situated in relation to the broader historical trajectory of feminist film criticism, especially with regard to the kinds of bodies that have, often implicitly, underpinned these debates. I want to briefly trace this rather twisted and certainly not straightforward trajectory – we might think of it as a tentative turn towards corporeality – in order to make sense of the kinds of bodies that surface in this book. This is not a matter of providing a simplistic account of feminist film criticism's teleological progress towards greater insight. Rather, the aim here is to map a number of critical tendencies and their alignments, tensions and synergies in relation to wider social, political and cinematic shifts and drifts, in order to contextualise the broadly phenomenological approach employed here.

It might be tempting to draw on established models of 'waves' of feminism, and other 'movements' for that matter, in order to account for contemporary (theoretical, cinematic, political) tendencies in terms of how previous concerns have 'lined up' what's next 'in line'.[1] However, as Freeman argues so eloquently, the notion of waves, and associated understandings of history and temporality, are useful only if we consider that the relation between waves is 'neither one of continuity nor one of complete repudiation but instead a story of *disjunctive, sticky entanglements and dissociations*.'[2] As Meryl Altman puts it, 'every wave has its undertow.'[3]

Freeman suggests we should consider the 'gravitational pull', or 'deadweight effect', that certain moments, stances or styles have on others – even, or perhaps especially, if they appear anachronistic. This includes, for instance, 'the gravitational pull that "lesbian", or even more so "lesbian feminist", sometimes seems to exert on "queer"' – and it is precisely the continuing pushing, pulling, brushing up against each other and colliding of lesbian, feminist and queer critical and filmic tendencies that have shaped the directions and orientations of this book.[4] Freeman has similar concerns around the notion of 'generations' of feminists, because it draws on 'repronormative' (heteronormative and reproductive) teleologies, or on what she calls 'chrononormativity, the interlocking temporal schemes necessary for genealogies of descent.'[5] The engagement with the historical tendencies of feminist film criticism that follows is therefore not meant to (re)affirm the repronormative line of feminist film criticism, but to invoke a sense of preparedness for the push and pull between feminist and queer habits that re-surfaces throughout.

It is also worth pointing to Freeman's notion of 'temporal drag' here, which links 'the queenier kind' of drag 'celebrated in an early 1990s influenced by deconstruction' with the more specifically temporal dimensions of the term, especially 'the associations the word "drag" has with retrogression, delay and the pull of the past on the present.'[6] We might additionally think of the corporeal and kinaesthetic implications of drag and the ways in which they are linked (metaphorically and phenomenologically) to intentionality: when we 'drag our feet' or when we are 'dragged along' we embody a hesitant and resistant directionality as we move towards what we do not want to 'face'.[7] And, of course, we can also 'drag someone with us'. It is the temporal drag that feminist (film/criticism) and queer (film/criticism) mutually exert on each other, in all of these senses, that underpins the ways in which the conceptual and analytical dynamics of this project take shape. While I explore the sticky entanglements and dissociations between 'feminist' and 'queer' as well as 'lesbian' in more detail below, they are usefully flagged here in order to foreshadow the uneasy, and at times volatile, entanglements of feminist, queer and lesbian approaches to film and the pull they exert on each other (and) across time.

Critiques of stereotypes and of women's roles in film in the early 1970s are often used as a starting point for considerations of feminist film criticism's history.[8] Feminist concerns with film emerged very specifically from the activist context of the Women's Liberation Movement and the stereotypes or 'images of...' approach reflected what is now perceived to be a simplistic understanding of the relationship between representation and social reality. Within the larger context of theoretical shifts in film studies towards psychoanalysis, semiotics and apparatus theory, an additional, psychoanalytically informed body of work, with Laura Mulvey's 'Visual pleasure and narrative cinema' as its cornerstone, emerged and pushed questions of ideology, spectatorship and the unconscious to the fore.[9] Mulvey argued that the patriarchal unconscious structures cinema and inscribes to-be-looked-at-ness onto the female body in order to satisfy the needs of the male psyche. This work was primarily concerned with classical Hollywood cinema. It identified Woman as an effect of the apparatus, as signifying lack and passivity (via representations of an abstracted, objectified body) and as central to the scopophilic pleasures on offer for a spectator that was addressed as, and assumed to be, male (and, of course, heterosexual).

This broadly psychoanalytic approach, based on 'Freudian and Lacanian concepts of the constitution of the subject, the entry into language, and sexual difference,'[10] has subsequently been criticised for relying on an inherently patriarchal paradigm, essentially reinforcing what it aims to critique, namely the equation of 'women = lack = cinematic image'.[11] For Mary Ann Doane, this was problematic in that early feminist film theory 'mimicked this cinematic construction [of generalised, abstracted and idealised femininity] and reinscribed the abstraction of woman through its use of the apparatus of cinema as its frame of reference.'[12] Feminist film criticism appeared to be 'in strange complicity with its object.'[13]

Accounting for cinema via a Freudian/Lacanian constitution of the subject (as Mulvey and others have done) means that spectatorial engagements with cinema are conceived of as occurring along a binary split of identification and desire, of narcissism and voyeurism, of wanting to *be* and wanting to *have*. This split is mapped onto, and reasserts, the binary of sexual difference that underpins psychoanalysis, which, while rooted in physiology (having or not having a penis), posits a model of gender, and of spectatorship, that fails to account for the specific, lived materiality of the body (on and off-screen). The foundational binarisms (including male/female, subject/object, identification/desire), as well as the disembodied and universalising tendencies of psychoanalytic and semiotic feminist film criticism, have been addressed from a range of theoretical and conceptual angles, some of which I trace here. It is precisely in relation to this larger (winding and twisted rather than straightforward) historical trajectory, *away* from essentialising understandings of sexual difference yet *towards* the body, that the motivations for and concerns emerging from this book can be situated.

Mulvey's initial polemic was of course developed and reworked in more or less immediate responses to some of the key questions it raised, especially around female spectatorship. However, the problematic binaries underpinning a broadly psychoanalytic frame remained in place and largely unchallenged throughout the 1970s, 80s and most of the 90s – although Linda Williams' work on body genres, Jackie Stacey's work combining theories of spectatorship with ethnographic research, as well as Barbara Creed's and Carol Clover's explorations of the horror genre, while variously grounded in psychoanalysis, began to move beyond the confines of spectatorship theory's narrow conceptual underpinnings.[14]

In general, however, 'feminist film theory of the 1970s and 1980s was marked by a deep suspicion of the female body as source of aesthetic and erotic pleasure,' as feminists employed theoretical models in which 'the body is not so much a material entity in itself as it is a written and spoken sign.'[15] Elena del Rio usefully contextualises the abstraction of the female body in early feminist film theory that we might perceive as restrictive and short-sighted from the vantage point of contemporary critical concerns. Feminist critics were drawn to psychoanalysis and semiotics because the realms of language and the unconscious were perceived as central to women's oppression – as well as to potential strategies for liberation. 'The notion of the body as linguistic or symbolic sign accorded well with the feminist efforts to revalorize woman's speech and to promote her integration within symbolic social and cultural systems,' while also countering binary equations of female/body – male/mind.[16]

The reliance on psychoanalytic and semiotic frameworks and the resultant 'strategic erasure of the body' in feminist film criticism made sense, within the larger, social, political and theoretical contexts of its time.[17] It was born of 'urgent necessity', argues del Rio – a necessity that 'relegate[d] the sensual and bodily aspects of female subjectivity to a practically irrelevant status' due to a failure to 'sufficiently account for the differences between the fetishized body (the product of a specific form of patriarchal representation) and the lived-body.'[18] For the purposes of this book, one of the key questions emerging here concerns the 'urgent necessities' of the contemporary context: What are they? And what are the implications of addressing these with a particular 'analytic stress'?

The lived-body has made a (re)appearance in some of the more recent feminist film scholarship, giving materiality and substance to the 'speechless and thoughtless' body examined in earlier feminist work. For del Rio, this is linked to the realisation that 'the antidote to the male equation of woman with body may not so much lie in the repression/omission of the body, as, perhaps, in the *construction of a different one.*'[19] One of the key objectives here is therefore to allow for such a different kind of body to appear. Specifically, what takes shape throughout is a kind of body with graspably sensuous, tactile, muscular and kinaesthetic capacities and dimensions; one that is capable of embodying variously twisted habits, tendencies, orientations, directions, leanings and possibilities.

Women's Cinema? Countering Dominant Habits

These overarching tendencies are also reflected in feminist debates about the need for, and significance of, a women's cinema – an oppositional, counter or minor cinema – as well as in related concerns about authorship and spectatorial address. These debates constitute an important initial reference point, especially in terms of how questions about 'women's cinema' intersect with those about 'lesbian' or 'queer cinema' – labels variously applicable to the films discussed in this book – as well as with larger ontological and epistemological questions about gender, sexuality and cinema. I hope to show that a broadly phenomenological approach (to gender, sexuality and cinema), along with a focus on corporeality, sensuousness and affect, provides a particularly fruitful framework given the contemporary 'necessities' that emerge from the intersections of theoretical, political and aesthetic concerns – especially with regard to the frictions between, and conflicting demands and expectations around, identity (politics), (in)visibility, feminism and queerness (including trans). What is foregrounded in what follows, therefore, are the limitations of conventional conceptions of 'women's cinema', in particular their inability to fully grasp the queer feminist orientations that take shape in, through and around the films discussed in this book, in order to highlight how a phenomenologically grounded approach might emerge from this critique.

Alison Butler observes important historical shifts in how a women's cinema has been conceived of: *away* from the kind of avant-garde and constructivist feminist aesthetics advocated (and put into practice) by Laura Mulvey, which was characterised by a decidedly negative stance and the negation of visual and narrative pleasure, and *towards* discursive conceptions of a counter-cinema that might be articulated from within the mainstream (for instance in Claire Johnston's work on Dorothy Arzner).[20] This is, broadly, a shift from negation to affirmation. As Teresa de Lauretis wrote in 1984:

> The present task of women's cinema may not be the destruction of narrative and visual pleasure, but rather the construction of another *frame of reference*, one in which the measure of desire is no longer just the male subject. For what is at stake is not so much how to 'make visible the invisible' as how to produce the *conditions of representability* for a different social subject.[21]

While this account links desire, visibility and representability to a *specific* subject in ways I go on to challenge, it usefully complicates questions of (in)visibility and posits a *social* cinematic subject, rather than the abstract and ahistorical subject of more conventional psychoanalytic accounts. This constitutes an important shift in (feminist) conceptions of women's cinema and of spectatorship. 'The spectator is addressed as *a* woman, not as Woman, taking into account the intersections of gender with class, race, age and sexuality, acknowledging differences among women as well as differences between women and men.'[22] Identity is posited here as multiple, intersecting and in terms of positionality.[23]

This type of argument is indicative of a strand of feminist thinking that increasingly sees women's cinema in a dialogical relation to patriarchal traditions, rather than as a separate, alternative art form – and it is precisely this dialogical relation to heteropatriarchal norms that variously characterises the films that I encounter in this book. Judith Mayne, for instance, argues that women's cinema can be understood as a 'feminist reinvention of film which reworks conventions of narrative and narration, authorship and spectacle, to create the formal conditions for inscriptions of female desires and points of view.'[24] This is precisely the focus of Lucy Bolton's recent exploration of *Film and Female Consciousness*.[25] Bolton's analysis of three contemporary films by and about women – *In the Cut* (Jane Campion, US, 2003), *Lost in Translation* (Sofia Coppola, US, 2003) and *Morvern Callar* (Lynne Ramsay, UK, 2002) – links questions of representation, authorship and spectatorship with a particular focus on how the films represent female subjectivity and interiority. The concern, via Luce Irigaray's philosophy, with the *embodied* nature of consciousness makes Bolton's study an important reference point for this book.

In very general terms, the debates I have briefly sketched here are based on assumptions, however tenuous, about the relationship between authorship, content and address (for instance the links between female directors, the representation of female consciousness, subjectivity and desire and the address of a female subject in Bolton's work). They raise complex questions about authority, agency and intent, and highlight feminist criticism's contradictory relation to notions of authorship. I therefore want to embark on a brief detour of critical feminist engagements with authorship, both in order to trace conceptual twists and turns and to gesture towards points of contact with queer theoretical tendencies. In doing so, the aim is to respond, here and elsewhere in the book, to Freeman's call for a criticism that is not necessarily straightforward, but that 'turns us backward to prior moments' as well as sideways, and that requires 'dragging a bunch of cultural [and critical] debris around us and stacking it in idiosyncratic piles "*not necessarily like any pre-existing whole*," though composed of what pre-exists.'[26] Freeman aligns her assertion with Sedgwick's notion of reparative criticism, 'because we can't know in advance, but only retrospectively if even then, what is queer and what is not.'[27] This lack of guarantee also holds for what is, or is not, 'feminist' or 'lesbian' (or as we will see in Chapter 5, trans).

Venturing into authorship territory is not about locating or predicting manifestations of feminism (in the form of female subjectivity, consciousness and desire) – or of queerness, lesbianism, or trans for that matter. It is, instead, about attempting to grasp the intermingling of critical, socio-political and filmic relations from which meaning and affect emerge – and this provides an essential inroad for grappling with questions of authorship and address in relation to *The Tango Lesson* in particular, a film that engages with authorship head on, but also with regard to *Black Swan*, *Offside*, *Tomboy* and *Girlhood*, films that continue to be surrounded by extra-filmic discourses concerned with the significance of their directors – not all of whom are women and/or feminist and/or queer.

The question of female authorship gained critical currency at a time when auteurism came under increased scrutiny due to larger theoretical shifts (including structuralist and post-structuralist influences; the 'death of the author') that made the existing concept of the auteur untenable within film studies and beyond.[28] There are important tensions, therefore, between this more general anti-auteurist stance on the one hand and feminist critiques of the oppressive image of women in mainstream cinema on the other, especially in in terms of assumptions that this image is oppressive, at least in part, because it is 'an image created by men.'[29] An implicitly auteurist stance also underpins feminist concerns with how this oppressive image might be transformed and by whom, as the 'death of the author' coincided, rather contradictorily, with the demands of previously marginal (female, black, queer) groups to authorial roles.

There is also a strand of feminist film criticism, however, that engages notions of authorship and auteurism critically – and in ways that resonate productively with the broader concerns of this book. It is marked by a shift away from concerns with authorial volition and intentionality and towards the text itself and an understanding of meaning as somehow residing in the text and/or emerging in its relationship with the reader/viewer. The notion of 'enunciation', for instance, allows for conceptualisations of cinematic meaning-making through a focus on discourse and voice. While, as Kaja Silverman argues, many post-1970s film theorists were 'at pains to distinguish cinema's enunciating agency from the figure of the director or scriptwriter,' the relationship between the two remains unclear, and there is a need for a further reconceptualisation of the relationship between meanings residing 'outside' and 'inside' the text.[30] Cinematic enunciation does open up ways of accounting for a female or feminist, or even lesbian or queer or trans, discourse or voice in film – as well as for variously female, feminist, lesbian, queer or trans modes of address – but it does not fully resolve the conceptual tensions surrounding the relationship between cinematic discourse/voice and the author/filmmaker/director. Where does the female, feminist, lesbian, queer or trans discourse/voice come from? What makes it 'authentic'? Is it possible for a male director to make a film with a female voice? How and under what circumstances? Can a straight author produce queer filmic discourses and/or queer enunciation? Who is able to do so, and why? Are all films by female filmmakers characterised by a female or feminine or feminist discourse? Clearly, they are not. Is there any relationship between the kinds of discourses and voices articulated in film and the filmmaker? There probably is.

What is crucial here is that the complexities and contradictions in these debates hinge on conceptualisations of gender itself and how we understand it (biologically, symbolically, psychologically, psychoanalytically, socially, experientially, performatively, affectively), as well as on how we understand cinema. It seems to me that understandings of female authorship, as varied as they are, tend to be based on understandings of both gender *and* cinema as symbolic, specular, psychological, linguistic and discursive; in other words, as abstract and disembodied, based on 'psychic structures' and 'libidinal econom[ies]'.[31] In the light of contemporary developments in theories of cinema *and* gender, a consideration of their material, visceral, embodied and affective dimensions promises to be highly productive. Rather than thinking about gendered subjectivity via voice or discourse, we might conceptualise subjectivity (and cinema) relationally, in terms of embodiment, stance, contact and orientation and their variously visceral, corporeal and affective dimensions. This is one way to tackle the 'disembodiment and disembeddedness' that Catherine Grant observes in relation to textually and theoretically focussed work – not, importantly, by tying a film's corporeal dimensions to a specific author, but to the ways in which modes of movement and gesture, spatiality and temporality, orientations and tendencies are embodied and circulate within the wider socio-cultural context. In other words, it not only allows us to account for the relationship between how meaning is *embodied* inside and outside the text. It also challenges the inside-outside distinction itself. It offers opportunities to grasp the ways in which cinematic embodiments are variously entangled with the modes of embodiment that take shape in and around film.

Questions of authorship are not the primary concern of this book, but a consideration of these debates and their developments constitutes an important conceptual context because they provide insights as to the wide-reaching complexities and contradictions that inevitably 'gather around' (to use Ahmed's term) explorations of gender and/in film.[32] This also applies to the debates around spectatorship discussed earlier. They highlight that, in the context of an exploration of the female body in film, the bodies surrounding the film (behind the camera, in front of the screen – and this includes the body of the critic) do matter. As I elaborate below, various contemporary approaches to cinema conceptualise the film itself as a body and as being characterised by particular modes of embodiment. The initial concern with the female body *in* film in this book thus serves as a starting point for thinking through the web of relations (embodied and affective) that enfold and unfold (around) this body – and that might challenge the givenness of its being 'female' altogether (as we will see in relation to *Tomboy* in particular).

I want to briefly engage with here with one final approach that takes questions of authorship in a slightly different, more affectively grounded, direction: Gilles Deleuze and Félix Guattari's notion of 'minor literature'. It has enabled alternative understanding of women's, feminist as well as queer cinema that I variously draw on throughout. In *Kafka: Towards a Minor Literature*, Deleuze and Guattari write that 'a minor literature doesn't come from a minor language; rather it is that which a minority constructs within a major language.'[33] A minor literature is characterised by three key features: deterritorialisation, politicising and collectivity. Nick Davis explains that 'in this schema, culturally marginalised members of a "major" culture internally recalibrate its expressive forms and grammars.'[34] It involves '*deterritorializing* sense and syntax from their usual frameworks; *politicizing* these renegotiated structures; and endowing them with a *collective* value, less on behalf of existing "minorities" than for new coalitions they catalyse among the oppressed and invisible, along previously unrecognisable lines.'[35]

The notion of the minor has been used to conceptualise (some) women's cinema and has also been put to efficient use in relation to queer and lesbian cinema, as discussed below. As Meaghan Morris points out, while the minor refers to the experience of immigrants and colonised people, its central tenets echo:

> the concerns of early feminist criticism and [in particular] Johnston's work on 'women's films made *within the system*' of Hollywood's social and cinematic codes. A minor literature is not "marginal," it is what a minority constructs *in a major language*, and so it is a model of action from a colonised position *within* a given society. In this it differs from theories that propose, like Laura Mulvey's early work in film, to found an alternative system.[36]

For purposes of framing the argument taking shape in this book, the concept of the minor is productive in a number of ways. It refrains from positing a strict separation between the minor (women's, feminist, lesbian or queer cinema) and the major (dominant, mainstream cinema), but rather suggests a 'mediated and contestatory' relationship, not one of subjugation of the minor by the major, but of 'infiltration' and 'potency'.[37] It is in this sense that *The Tango Lesson, Black Swan, 2 Seconds, Offside, Tomboy* and *Girlhood* are characterised by minoritarian dimensions, albeit in very different ways and to varying extents. The minor takes an affirmative, rather than negating and deconstructive, stance. It also does not – certainly not as a matter of principle – separate (visual) pleasure from the potentially political implications of film. Most importantly, perhaps, it posits an understanding of collectivity that does not absorb people 'into major-culture structures of identity, alliance and power, which frequently perpetuate key inequities.'[38] Instead, it provides a way of thinking through and mobilising particular groupings in a decidedly non-essentialising way. As Butler notes, 'the notion of a minor literature as involved in the *projection* of a community rather than its *expression* is especially useful to the argument that the existence of a woman's cinema need not be premised on an essentialist understanding of the category "women."'[39] This turning away from conventional understandings of identity also gestures towards the queer implications of the minor and/or the minor implications of queer.

The sense that a minor cinema can bring certain collectivities and solidarities into existence and that it can 'express another possible community and [...] forge the means for another consciousness and another sensibility' is particularly seductive in that it allows for a conceptualisation of the queer feminist resonances of the films discussed in this book that is *not* underpinned by binary and essentialist understandings of identity.[40] However, it also raises some very complicated questions about the viability of the category 'woman', or any other identity category for that matter, in a way that resembles queer post-structuralist accounts of gender – Judith Butler's in particular.[41]

What I hope to add to the existing body of work around gender (as well as sexuality and queerness) in cinema – or, perhaps more daringly, how I want to infiltrate (major) conceptions of the minor – is a foregrounding of the embodied, visceral and sensuous dimensions of the communities and collectivities as well as the new sense-ibilities a minor literature/cinema is said to express. This is an attempt to put the senses (back) into sensibility, as it were, and to grasp the significance of corporeality in our sense-making, while keeping hold of the affirmative potency of Deleuze and Guattari's collectivities.

Grounding Butler: Queer (Theory), Identity, Politics

Some of the issues and questions raised in relation to women's cinema resonate, as I have already gestured towards, with key aspects of debates around queer cinema. There are also important differences, however, based largely on the very different relationships that 'gay', 'lesbian' and 'queer' have (and have had) with identity, visibility and politics. While gender is, or is presumed to be, in some way stable and related to specific bodily characteristics – that is, it is inscribed on, and visible at the level of, the body – sexuality is not, or at least much less visibly so (although sexuality is, of course, made visible through stereotypes, for instance). The relations between women and feminist theory (and politics) also play out slightly differently than the relation between gays/lesbians and queer theory, not to mention the precarious links between gay/lesbian (identity) politics and queer politics. And there are also, of course, the more recent tensions and conflicts between feminist and trans identity/politics that further complicate the relations between sex, gender, sexuality and the body.

Throwing cinema into the mix adds further complexity because of its unstable and often contradictory ties to (in)visibility, representability and (dis)appearance. While women have been visible in cinema – hypervisible even – gays and lesbians have not. While women have been identifiable as a fairly stable identity category, 'gay' and 'lesbian' had to emerge *as* identities. The history of homosexuality in mainstream cinema is primarily one of invisibility and 'negative' stereotyping, largely due to the Production Code and its legacy. However, there is an important body of literature that explores how, despite, or perhaps because of, the (relative) absence of explicitly gay and lesbian characters or narratives, the cinema and its stars significantly aided the formation and cultivation of gay and lesbian identities and communities.[42] Patricia White, for instance, notes that while the Production Code forbade depictions of 'sex perversion' such as homosexuality, 'motion picture practitioners recognised censorship as a set of codes for producing meaning, and particularly sexual meaning, and indeed for producing readings.'[43] While this argument gestures towards a not entirely helpful notion of intent (on part of the practitioners), it also highlights the impossibility of clearly separating visibility from invisibility. How does what is 'visible' on screen (absence, gaps, ambiguity) relate to what we 'see' (lesbianism)?

In their work on camp, Richard Dyer and Andy Medhurst suggest that the 'camp sensibility' of certain classical Hollywood films and stars provided a shared reference point, that gay men in particular could be orientated toward and that put them in touch with each other.[44] This echoes arguments about the crucial role played by cinema and certain female stars in the formation of lesbian identities in the 1930s and 40s in particular.[45] Clare Whatling, for instance, highlights the *reciprocal* relations between the cinema and lesbian identity put forward in this work through her assertions of 'lesbian desire [as] constituted within and by exposure to a filmic culture,'[46] while also reminding her readers that '[i]dentification can only be made through *recognition*, and all recognition is itself an explicit confirmation of an existing form.'[47]

Although these authors work with conventional and psychoanalytically based understandings of spectatorship, identity, identification and desire, they also foreground the *reciprocal* relations between film and viewer and, perhaps incidentally, gesture towards the significance of lived experience. As Ahmed suggests, '"becoming lesbian" [is] a very social experience.'[48] She links her own 'becoming lesbian' to her contact with lesbian literature, especially Radclyffe Hall's novel *The Well of Loneliness* (1928), the 'lesbian bible' that 'acquired its sociality by being passed around, by *changing hands*', and by providing lesbian women an object to 'gather around' and 'tend toward'.[49] Such an understanding of lesbian tendencies, orientations and contact, and the ways in which they shape and are shaped by '*what is reachable within the body horizon of the social*' allows us to rethink notions of 'recognition', 'appeal' and 'cultivation' as they feature in (some) writing on gay and lesbian film spectatorship.[50] They encourage us to go beyond disembodied conceptualisations of subjectivity and looking, and to account for the tactile, spatial, kinaesthetic and sensuous dimensions of our encounter with film. I elaborate further on the significance of embodied, phenomenological approaches to gender and sexuality below. However, I want to gesture, along the way as it were, towards the resonances and potential alliances between existing work on film and contemporary queer (and) feminist approaches to embodiment and affect in particular.

The simultaneous emergence of queer theory and (the new) queer cinema in the early 1990s links in important ways to what are often perceived to be heteronormative and essentialising tendencies within gay and lesbian politics at the time. The hard-fought social and political recognition of gay and lesbian identities was increasingly seen as counterproductive and unhelpful from the vantage point of queer concerns. It is important to provide some context here for the arrival of queer theory and its complex relations to gay and lesbian identity and politics (as well as to identity more generally), as these tensions continue to resonate within contemporary debates and practices. A working through of, rather than straightforward resolution to, these tensions is a key aspect of the embodied and affective work this books does.

The Gay Liberation movement, which started to take shape in response to the Stonewall riots of June 1969, was in part a reaction against the quietism of earlier groups and subcultures. It emerged within the wider context of other identity-based movements (Women's Liberation, Civil Rights) and stressed that tolerance and acceptance were insufficient aims. What was needed was not acceptance within an unjust system, but a critique of social structures and heterosexual dominance. Gay Liberation was also a response to the wide reach of pathologising medical and psychoanalytic discourses around homosexuality. It was an identity-based movement by/for 'homosexuals' and, in this sense, similar to the feminist movement and its concern with the marginalisation and oppression of a particular and *identifiable* identity group: women.

Gay Liberation, *un*like Women's Liberation, provided a publicly visible assertion and, to a certain extent, bringing into being, of a marginalised and largely invisible identity. It provided a sense of community, a recognisable social identity and a political voice. It also created a space for gay and lesbian culture to emerge *visibly*. Lesbian feminism sits rather awkwardly between these movements and one might say that lesbian women found themselves in a decidedly minor position in relation to already marginalised groups/movements – one gender-based, one sexuality-based – whose aims were, and are, underpinned by often conflicting concerns. Lesbians did not clearly belong to either group due to the shifting and inherently unstable allegiances and alliances with 'other'/straight women and 'other' homosexuals/gay men. Shared experiences of oppression, and a desire to tackle that oppression, are part of what brings identity-based movements into being, and assumptions about what is (not) shared and about who has what 'in common' can privilege certain experiences of oppression and marginalise others. The resultant tensions lead to critiques of both the (white) heterosexist bias of Women's Liberation and the (white) male-centredness of Gay Liberation. They also foregrounded the importance of (at)tending to the specificity of gender in relation to sexuality and the specificity of sexuality in relation to gender.

The conflicts and pressure points gestured towards here are indicative of some of the key criticisms of identity-based movements more generally. Although they provide a sense of community, culture and recognisability, rigid identity categories can become too restrictive and exclusive, glossing over differences within groups and similarities between groups/individuals. These various processes of inclusion and exclusion manifest themselves in new hierarchies of power and oppression. The inability to account sufficiently for multiple oppression and marginality (and for intersections of identity) was one of the downfalls of Gay Liberation as an identity-based movement. Its largely white, middle-class, able-bodied, male tendencies meant that women, working-class, non-white, disabled, older, rural and less affluent 'homosexuals' did not necessarily always recognise themselves *as* 'homosexuals' and/in the ways in which that identity category was being politically mobilised. In essence, what started out as an oppositional movement in the 1960s and 1970s took a conservative turn towards more assimilationist strategies by the 1990s, including the striving for societal integration and acceptance into heteronormative structures (for instance through gay marriage) – which is when 'queer' appeared at the political, theoretical, cultural and cinematic horizon. This is linked with a shift, within the context of film studies, from concerns with (in)visibility and gay and lesbian film history, towards queer theory, aesthetics and (gender) trouble.

In her account of the emergence of queer theory, Annamarie Jagose argues that '[i]nstead of assuming that collective identities simply reflect differences among persons that exist prior to mobilisation, we need [...] to look closely at the process by which *movements remake identities*.'[51] It is precisely this unmooring of identity from essentialising assumptions around gender and sexuality in particular that is at the heart of queer theory, which also, in turn, means that the relations between 'queer' and gender and sexuality are inherently unstable. Queer sits uneasily with the perceived givenness not only of 'male' and 'female' but also of 'homosexuality'. Homosexuality as self-evident and easily defined is the result of a system of binary sexual difference that is, by definition, hierarchical and oppressive. 'Queer' therefore developed as an increasingly inclusive term (from the early 1990s) encompassing all kinds of variations of sex/gender/sexuality. Gender and sexual 'minorities' are now not only 'gay' and 'lesbian' but LGBTQIA, which variously stands for lesbian, gay, bisexual, trans, queer/questioning, intersex, asexual/allies/alternative and also includes practices like drag, cross-dressing and transvestism. However, while this all-inclusivity challenges binary figurations of sex/gender/sexuality, it also means that queer acquires a certain vagueness, which has a range of contradictory implications.

'Queer' is perhaps most easily defined in negative terms (in terms what it is *not* or *against*) in the sense that queer is non-, anti-, contra-(hetero)normative – although such an understanding carries the risk of including certain marginalised behaviours that, like paedophilia or snuff practices, are highly problematic. Nonetheless, where to 'draw the line', and why, become seemingly impossible questions to answer if 'queer' is, indeed, queer (fluid, open, uncontained). What is additionally problematic about queer is that it passes itself off as (gender) neutral, while, as feminist and lesbian feminist critics have argued, it is a space in which a certain generic maleness/masculinity manifests itself as an invisible norm. These tensions (between queer, lesbian and feminist) are very much alive and kicking in the contemporary context and particularly tangible in relation to tensions between (some) radical feminists and (some) trans theorists and activists.[52]

Questions also remain around the extent to which queer can be political – mainly because queer appears to take away the grounds for a more traditional identity politics, which aims to achieve change on behalf of/for a particular identity group with particular kinds of identifiable interests. This is related to a concern that queerness might be more about style, surface and play, rather than (political) substance. Queer theory, especially perhaps in its Butlerian incarnations, is also often accused of inaccessibility, elitism, pretentiousness and an increased disconnect from social reality as well as from the political and activist context. Moreover, queer theory has become relatively mainstream within academic institutions (at least in the context of the humanities), creating some obvious tensions with queer's aim to be anti- or contra- the norm. Larger questions about institutionalisation and its consequences become important here and I want to be mindful of these wider issues around the status, function and circulation of queer (theory), which might be quite different from how/why it was initially conceived, especially with regard to how it functions vis-à-vis feminist theory in the context of film criticism.

For Jagose, queer's potency lies precisely in its 'conceptually unique potential as a necessarily unfixed site of engagement and contestation,'[53] meaning that, as David Phillips notes, 'its sudden and often uncritical adoption has at times foreclosed what is potentially most significant – and necessary – about the term.'[54] So we might ask, as Jagose does, what happens 'when queer does little more than function as a shorthand for the unwieldy lesbian and gay, or offer itself as a new solidification of identity, by kitting out more fashionably an otherwise unreconstructed [and male-focussed] sexual essentialism'?[55] And 'does queer become defunct the moment it is an intelligible and widely disseminated term?'[56] I do believe there is a sense in which queer has lost some of its critical edge and I want to argue, perhaps controversially, that, within the context of film criticism in particular, queer has come to stand for a kind of 'sophisticated' engagement with gender and sexuality in film, which distances itself, more or less explicitly, from an anachronistic, unsophisticated and paranoid feminist film criticism. This tendency relates, rather poignantly, to previously discussed debates around (political and theoretical) waves and progress – and my use of queer in the title of the book arguably makes make me complicit (choosing a title is as much a marketing decision as it is about reflecting intellectual content).

That said, the aim of this chapter in particular, as well as the book as a whole, is to put feminist and queer (back) in touch with each other, to foreground alignments and points of contact and to work through tensions and frictions. Jagose points to the resonances between queer and more conventional notions of identity politics, in a way that usefully encapsulates how I want to engage 'feminist', 'gay', 'lesbian' and 'queer' in this book:

> Instead of theorising queer in terms of its opposition to identity politics, it is more accurate to represent it as ceaselessly interrogating both the preconditions of identity and its effects. Queer is not outside the magnetic field of identity. Like some postmodern architecture, it turns identity inside out, and displays its supports exoskeletally. If the dialogue between queer and more traditional identity formations is sometimes fraught – which it is – that is not because they have nothing in common. Rather, lesbian and gay [and we might add feminist] faith in the authenticity or even political efficacy of identity categories and the queer suspension of all such classification energise each other, offering [...] the ambivalent reassurance of an unimaginable future.[57]

So we can be queer *and* paranoid – or so it seems.

In the context of some of the early, Butlerian incarnations of queer theory, debates around gender and sexuality took place primarily in relation to language and discourse as well as citations, recitations and style – and, importantly, these are also the preoccupations of the New Queer Cinema that emerges at roughly the same time (the early 1990s). One of the key criticisms levelled at queer theory's preoccupation with language and discourse is a seeming disregard for the 'material conditions' in and through which gender is lived.[58] Butler does draw on a broadly phenomenological frame in her thinking about gender, as Ahmed highlights: 'For Judith Butler, it is precisely how phenomenology exposes the "sedimentation" of history in the sedimentation of bodily action that makes it a useful resource for feminism.'[59] However, Ahmed also notes that the kind of queer theory founded upon Butler's early work only scratches the surface of the corporeal and sensuous realm and is based on an account of subject formation with largely immaterial tendencies:

> Butler, following Louis Althusser, makes 'turning' crucial to subject formation. One becomes a subject through 'turning around' when hailed by the police. For Butler, this "turning" takes the form of hearing oneself as the subject of an address: it is a turning that is not really about the physicality of the movement [...] But we can make this question of direction crucial to the emergence of subjectivity and the 'force' of being given a name. In other words, we could reflect on the difference it makes *which way subjects turn.*[60]

It is precisely this turn towards the corporeality of performativity that I return to with reference to Ahmed's *Queer Phenomenology* as well as other queer/feminist interventions concerned with the sensuous and visceral dimensions of embodiment and affect. First, however, I want to turn toward queer cinema; toward the ways in which (gender and sexual) identity and politics manifest themselves in this context; and to the questions it raises about how exactly queerness might take shape and 'appear' on screen.

Women and/in Queer Cinema: (In)visibility and Appearance

I continue to draw and touch upon the key tensions and frictions that continue to 'gather around' (again using Ahmed's term) notions of queer and its relation to gender, sexuality, feminism, politics and identity in the remainder of the book. For one, they provide a useful starting point for a slightly more detailed consideration of (the new) queer cinema and queer film studies as well as the ways in which the unstable alignments of gender and sexuality, identity and desire and politics and aesthetics continue to play out in these contexts.

New Queer Cinema (NQC) was the name famously given by B. Ruby Rich to what she identified as a new movement or wave of films (although Rich later conceded that the NQC might have been more of a moment than a movement).[61] As with any cinematic wave (keeping in mind my earlier discussion of Freeman's conception of waves and generations), to provide an agreed-upon definition of its (temporal) boundaries, and/or a list of films that 'belong' to it, are impossible, and not very useful, endeavours, especially in retrospect and with hindsight. Suffice it to say here, then, that the movement was named, and brought into being, in response to a range of films that appeared on the festival circuit in 1991 and 1992, and that seemed to engage with questions of gender and sexuality in a new, exciting and rebellious manner.[62] No longer concerned with positive images and 'realistic' representations of gays and lesbians, these films were 'both radical and popular, stylish and economically viable.'[63] It was, as Rich argues, 'a flock of films that were doing something new, renegotiating subjectivities, annexing whole genres, revisiting histories in their image.' In an attempt to identify key characteristics of the NQC, Rich writes:

> Of course, the new queer films and videos aren't all the same, and don't share a single aesthetic vocabulary or strategy or concern. Yet, they are nonetheless united by a common style. Call it 'Homo Pomo': there are traces in all of them of appropriation and pastiche, irony, as well as reworking of history with social constructionism very much in mind. Definitely breaking with older humanist approaches and the films and tapes that accompanied identity politics, these works are irreverent, energetic, alternatively minimalist and excessive. Above all, they're full of pleasure.[64]

What these films share, in other words, is an *attitude* – an attitude that is 'queer' because it challenges, and troubles, heteronormative understandings of gender and sexuality.

There are a few important points to be made about NQC and the critical discourses surrounding it in terms of how they shape the orientations of this book and its tending towards notions of cinema and queerness as embodied. Firstly, there is a turning away from modernist understandings of identity and representation as well as from earlier conceptions of gay and lesbian film. Barbara Mennel explains that:

> '[g]ay' and 'lesbian' refers to men-loving-men and women-loving-women. It applies to characters, their sexual desires and political identities, whether explicit or implicit, to films that address them and to self-identified directors, actors and producers. An approach committed to homosexual rights suggests that conventional representations of gays and lesbians in film constitutes societal acceptance and indicates political and social progress. Queer Film Studies, however, proposes that non-normative desire undermines cinematic conventions because the subversion of coherent identity also *questions the possibility of its mimetic representation* in film. Queer film aesthetics challenges the cinematic conventions based on gender-normative heterosexuality.[65]

This raises larger questions, which I have touched upon already, about how queer film and queer film scholarship might negotiate the tensions between the possibilities provided by (postmodern, poststructuralist) queer approaches on the one hand, and the specificity of experience and of gendered forms of sexuality, desire and oppression on the other. A broadly phenomenological approach, along the lines of Ahmed's queer phenomenology, that acknowledges the embodied and affective dimensions of queerness, is one way of negotiating these tensions affirmatively, especially when it comes to cinema and spectatorship.

Secondly, and related to the previous point, there is the precarious position of women in the context of new queer cinema, both on and off-screen. As Rich, Anneke Smelik and Anat Pick have highlighted, women have been marginalised in queer cinema (in ways not too dissimilar to their marginalisation in popular/mainstream cinema).[66] White asserts that 'the lesbian feature is the most persistently elusive of programming elements' at queer film festivals, and that 'the number of feature films by and about lesbians, though increasing, still lags behind, in correlation with the minority percentage of women feature filmmakers.'[67] Of course, this concern with the specificity of lesbianism and lesbian desire sits very uneasily with the anti-identitarian tropes of queer.

Nonetheless, such a critique seems necessary. Pick notes that 'while "queer" ideally signals an emancipated (and potentially limitless) range of sexual and social relations, most of the products identified as "new" and "queer" were in contrast overwhelmingly male.'[68] Questions arise, therefore, as to whether queer comes to stand for 'the reintroduction of male hegemony, through the back door as it were,' and risks 'becoming yet another false universal masking a peculiarly masculine ethos.'[69] White's observation about the 'paucity of viable lesbian features' asserts the tendency for conflations of queerness and maleness/masculinity within the queer cinema context.[70]

However, White also suggests that Deleuze and Guattari's notion of the minor is one way of coming to terms with the kind of 'queer' work that *has* been undertaken by women. 'If major is to minor as film is to video, feature to short, cinema to television, fiction to documentary, women – and thus lesbians and often transpeople – tend to labour in the latter category of each of these pairs.'[71] White also links the minor to the ephemeral (films made explicitly only for festival networks) and to the intentional/forced deployment of a certain ' "poverty" – in terms of means of production and aesthetic approach – in order to deflect audience demand for familiar stories, happy endings, repeatable pleasures, identity assurances.'[72] The work of Chantal Akerman (*Portrait d'un jeune fille de la fin des années 60s à Bruxelles/Portrait of a Young Girl at the End of the 60s in Brussels*, Belgium/France, 1994) and Sadie Benning (*Flat is Beautiful*, US, 1998), two 'lesbian "auteurs" ', provides two very different key examples for White, as both filmmakers 'embrace the insignificant – stillness, sparseness, solitude – in works marked by a refusal of conventional formats.'[73] Importantly, while White traces the ways in which ' "minor" resonates with but is not a cognate for "queer," ' she refrains from 'aligning the minor with queer cinema *tout court*,' and instead argues for the usefulness of conceiving of *lesbian* as minor in the hope of 'bring[ing] forward the gendered and pejorative associations with the former term [queer].'[74]

While such an understanding (of lesbian as minor) appears to remain trapped within and restricted by normative and essentialising conceptions of identity, White also notes that the notion of lesbian (cinema) as minor (cinema) helps to emphasise the 'materiality of the minor and to keep in play dimension of gendered sexuality and subjectivity that are not obviously compatible with Deleuze and Guattari's anti-identitarian models of flux or with reflexive uses of queer.'[75] White refers to the materiality of production conditions (such as underfunding), but the notion of the 'materiality of the minor' has important wider implications that I want to pursue here, especially in relation to the materiality of how the minor might be *embodied cinematically*. It opens up a space for considering how cinema might bring together queer and feminist tendencies and attitudes (in the phenomenological sense) and how they might materialise in and through film.

Lesbian cinema, in this sense, is not straightforwardly defined in terms of content or subject matter (films 'about' lesbians), or, indeed, by conditions of production (films 'by' lesbians), but in terms of what it *does*. It is a cinema that 'inflects rather than opposes the dominant, one that "deterritorializes" sexuality and expression [and that] "express[es] another possible community and [forges] another consciousness and another *sensibility*."'[76] White's account opens up a number of conceptual and analytical possibilities that are acutely relevant to the key concerns of this book, particularly in relation to how the tensions between 'queer', 'lesbian' and 'feminist' are played out in and around cinema. In highlighting the 'intersection[s] of authorship and audience, form and subject matter, and desire and identification' and how they might be enacted by certain films and filmmaking practices, White conjures, perhaps inadvertently, questions about what exactly it is that might be 'queer' or 'lesbian' in or about (a) film – questions that a queer feminist film phenomenology can begin to answer.[77]

White's conception of lesbian minor cinema also usefully resonates with Pick's suggestion that lesbian films are best understood not only in relation to subject matter, but as articulations of a particular 'stance' – a poignantly embodied, muscular, and orientated way of describing films to which I shall return.[78] Importantly, Pick also asserts that the precarious (minor) significance of lesbian film within the context of queer cinema can be grasped more efficiently when taking into account the postmodern commodification and co-opting of 'queer' and 'lesbian' by the mainstream. Understanding lesbian film within the context of the NQC and its legacy requires a consideration of the increase in mainstream lesbian visibility and the specificity of how 'lesbian' has been co-opted. This is the third point I want to draw attention to with regard to issues raised by the NQC and surrounding discourses that are particularly relevant here: mainstream lesbian and queer female visibility.

In her exploration of 'the politics of lesbian appearance', Amy Villarejo asks important questions about the 'costs' of visibility and of 'making lesbians *appear*.'[79] She also suggests that 'the demands to make lesbians visible, whether as ammunition for anti-homophobic campaigns or as figures for identification, renders lesbian static, makes lesbian into (an) image and forestalls any examination of lesbian within context.'[80] Recalling Butler's suggestions about the unpredictability of signification, Villarejo complicates the perceived boundaries between visibility and invisibility, and asks poignant questions about the 'grounds' on which we might determine why certain people, things, places, images or films signify (as) lesbian, ultimately suggesting that 'there is no final ground.'[81] This means that 'there remains no ultimate certainty with which one can pronounce the content of that image or film lesbian. Instead, something in a context allows viewers to produce a ground for their readings, to make an image or narrative work as "lesbian" even, sometimes, against the will of those who created it.'[82] Conversely, one might say that certain explicit lesbian representations do not 'work' as lesbian because they are removed from the *grounds* on which such a reading might be produced and from which the lesbian *figure* might emerge. In other words, making lesbians visible (in the mainstream) does not necessary mean that 'lesbian' appears. This links in fundamentally important ways to larger questions about how gender and sexuality might be 'present', how they might 'appear' and how/why films, characters or narratives are recognised, identified and perceived as 'lesbian' or, indeed, as queer, feminist or trans.

Villarejo's reference to 'gaydar' (as a mechanism the enables certain people to be recognised and identified *as lesbian*) is particularly insightful in this context:

> Call it what you will, 'gaydar', recognition, or identification remains one of the most elusive, and therefore provocative, procedures of modern queer life. Founded on vision, but suggesting, through the reference to radar, something that flies beneath the visible or the screen, this procedure nonetheless falters before the demands of visual evidence.[83]

This account of the limitations of vision in relation to recognition and identification (of somebody or something *as lesbian*) is tantalisingly suggestive of the potentialities of a more fully embodied, sensuous and affective approach to lesbian appearance and lesbian presence in film. Villarejo's argument remains within the realms of an ocularcentric paradigm, and for good reasons, while also highlighting the limits of vision in ways that gesture towards the significance of embodied perception.

It is worth quoting an additional passage from Villarejo's critique of visibility at length here:

> [It] seems that it is on the terrain of the visible that gender binarism is most strictly enforced. At the same time, one tends to rely most heavily on visual cues to extrapolate sexual difference from gender representation, so that one can [for instance] read Hepburn or Garbo in trousers as lesbian. Although many have long marked the tyrannical companionship between gender and sexuality, gay and lesbian and queer peoples have not fought hard politically to delink gender codes and sexual orientation, although queer and transgender politics have incipient potential and the right to insist upon such a cleavage. Rather, it has been crucial to gay and lesbian history to solidify a certain guarantee that the visual evidence of cross-dressing in the past, say, means that there were gays and lesbians 'just like us' then, or enough like 'us' to ensure that we, too, will survive. In gay humour, in art, in rituals, and in everyday lives, there is a certain *common-sense knowingness* about appearance. While [...] cinema depends upon this common sense, it also has the potential to challenge it.[84]

Villarejo links visibility and the guarantees it seemingly provides (for instance of a lesbian presence in the past) to a certain common-sense understanding of how 'lesbians' appear – and she also suggests, in a similar manner to White and Whatling, that cinema has the potential to trouble and undermine our common sense. What I want to provide here is an attempt to grasp more fully the phenomenological and affective dimensions of our common and *un*common 'sense', by linking it to a certain 'knowingness about appearance' that is based not just on visibility/vision/looking, but on conceptions of knowledge, and of apprehension, as embodied and sensuous.[85]

Gender and the Body in Feminist and Queer Film Criticism

Before moving on to a discussion of the kind of approaches to cinema that are concerned with the embodied and sensuous dimensions of film and our encounter with it, I want to make reference to one recent study of queer cinema, Davis's *The Desiring-Image: Gilles Deleuze and Contemporary Queer Cinema*, which speaks particularly poignantly to the aims of this book. While taking a slightly different, specifically Deleuzian, approach, Davis's intentions mirror my own: to construct 'new frameworks for understanding what is "queer" about recent queer cinema, including films rarely classified this way.'[86] Rich asks a very similar question when she revisits her initial NQC argument in 2000, conceding that the wide range of queer films that followed the initial wave of NQC complicated her initial conceptualisation.[87] Recent developments in film theory, as well as gender and queer theory, provide an important context for these questions – what is a queer film? what is or can be queer about (queer) film? – as do filmmaking practices and patterns of reception and circulation.

While acknowledging the resonances between the NQC and queer theory in relation to their simultaneous emergence, Davis also reminds us that the 'New Queer *Cinema* never aligned as closely as it might have with contemporaneous tenets of queer *theory*.'[88] He writes that 'the enshrining of universally gay- or lesbian-identified auteurs as leaders of the New Queer movement, telling stories almost exclusively about LGBT characters, signals an embrace of identity logics, however qualified in other respects, that queer theory typically challenges.'[89] While the aesthetic and stylistic unruliness of NQC films was crucial to their critical acclaim and commercial success, the significance of LGBT characters, and the gender and sexual identities they 'have', remains ambiguous. Would NQC have been 'queer', or maybe just 'new', had its aesthetic and stylistic rebelliousness not been tied to LGBT characters and stories? I would concur with Davis's assertion that 'the furor around New Queer Cinema – conceived, after all, as a journalistic meme, not a scholarly rubric – exposed its ill-preparedness to travel beyond its situated responses to the hit films, emergent auteurs and historical contexts of its early 1990s moment.'[90]

To be prepared for a consideration of films outside of and/or succeeding this 'new' and 'queer' moment requires a profound rethinking of queer vis-à-vis film. The discussions of *Tomboy* and *Girlhood* in particular (Chapter 5) speak directly to this context, but a more general rethinking of the convoluted entanglements of queer and film is a key aspect of the overall work this book does. Queer's struggles and tensions with 'lesbian' and 'feminist', as well as with recognisability, representability, (in)visibility and (dis)appearance are crucial and I have started to explore them here. However, there is a sense in which the conventional approaches that tend to be used – psychoanalytic and Marxist frameworks in particular – are not best equipped to grasp what 'queer' is, how it functions and what it can do.

Davis seizes the possibilities provide by a Deleuzian approach and asserts that questions of *desire* (in the Deleuzian rather than psychoanalytic sense) are key for coming to terms with what is queer about (queer) cinema. Revisiting NQC with Deleuzian desire in mind, we can see that it 'emerges less as a discrete phenomenon than as a signal of wider shifts in film's relation to desire.'[91] These wider shifts mean that cinematic queerness is not confined to those films that tend to be defined, and marketed, as 'queer cinema' in the contemporary context (i.e., those films that engage with LGBT characters, stories and themes). In fact, these films might not at all be queer in the sense in which Davis conceives of queerness and how it manifests itself in 'profound formal, thematic and political transformations in how [cinema] reflects and indeed *produces* non-normative desire.'[92] Importantly, there is no guarantee that these transformations emerge from a particular position: 'Neither the "innermost" [dominant, popular, mainstream] not the most "marginal" positions provide exclusive bases from which to assail the castle-keeps of Oedipus, capitalism, heteronormativity and artistic cliché.'[93]

Similar to Alison Butler's account of women's cinema as minor cinema and White's conceptualisation of a lesbian minor cinema, Davis draws on understandings of queer cinema as minor – as opposed to on binary distinctions between heteronormative mainstream cinema and its queer 'other' – as this allows for an acknowledgement of mutual infiltration (of the minor by the major and vice versa).[94] Understanding queer cinema as minor allows Davis to resist identifications of queer cinema as 'the exclusive enterprise of gay or lesbian artists or stories' or in relation to 'star directors, canonised films or bracketed historical periods' and enables, instead, an analysis of how queer desire circulates and functions in and through certain films.[95] The encounters with *The Tango Lesson, Black Swan, 2 Seconds, Offside, Tomboy* and *Girlhood* in this book are, in a sense, modelled on

Gender and the Body in Feminist and Queer Film Criticism

Davis's questions and underpinning premises (around complicating queerness vis-à-vis film) – but they are orientated differently in their pursuit. They are not turned towards and do not follow the directions of Deleuzian desire; instead, they are aligned with the embodied tendencies of the queer feminist film phenomenology that takes shape throughout. The films discussed here emerge from 'positions' that range from the 'innermost' (*Black Swan*) to the variously 'marginal' (*2 Seconds, Offside*) and also occupy various positions 'in between' (*The Tango Lesson, Tomboy, Girlhood*). They all have minor 'tendencies' and take shape in a contestatory relation to the major, in the sense of major modes of normatively gendered embodiment – a relation of infiltration and potency that might bring new (queer feminist) collectivities into being.

Deleuzian desire, understood as intensity, as impersonal, and as mutable and multifaceted, allows Davis to provide a profoundly insightful account of the queerness of a very diverse range of films (including *Dead Ringers* (David Cronenberg, Canada/US, 1988), *Shortbus* (John Cameron Mitchell, US, 2006), *Naked Lunch* (David Cronenberg, Canada/UK/Japan, 1991), *The Watermelon Women* (Cheryl Dunye, US, 1996), *Brother to Brother* (Rodney Evans, US, 2004), *Beau travail* (Claire Denis, France, 1999) and *Velvet Goldmine* (Todd Haynes, UK/US, 1998)), not all of which might be identified as queer otherwise. He is concerned not with the achievement of a certain (identity) politics by, in and through films, but with fostering 'the conditions for perceiving and producing escapes from habits of recognition, or of thought, or of desire broadly construed.'[96]

I hope to take the debates so usefully opened up by Davis in a slightly different direction through a more specific acknowledgement of the corporeal and embodied dimensions of perception, habits, recognition and desire in an attempt to grasp how certain films resonate (in tactile, muscular and kinaesthetic terms) with particular modes of embodiment and sense-bilities as they take shape in a range of corporeally affective scenarios: from tango to tomboyism, ballet to football fandom and cycling to (tres)passing. I approach both 'cinema' and 'queer' from a broadly (rather than exclusively) phenomenological angle, in order to account for the ways in which queerness is embodied, while also working with and through some of the fertile resonances and tensions between phenomenological, Deleuzian, cognitive and psychoanalytic frameworks, always keeping the lived-body (organs, the lot) in mind and 'close to hand'. Rather than clinging to a narrow theoretical approach, I want to remain open to the reverberations between theories (of gender, sexuality, the body and cinema), between films, and between theories and films. One way of engaging with and encountering this book, therefore, is as an attempt to make graspable the affective entanglements of certain bodies (cinematic and theoretical, human and social) that are enabled by their queer feminist orientations, resonances and tendencies.

2

Film and Embodiment: Queer-ing Film Phenomenology

Each time I watch, I am moved and affected in my body and in my senses.[1]

While an interest in the sensuous implications of cinema, from a broadly, though not always explicitly acknowledged, phenomenological perspective, reappears through the history of film and film criticism, a focused and sustained concern with the embodied and visceral dimensions of cinema and the cinematic experience is a relatively recent phenomenon. These conceptual tendencies – away from the ocularcentric and towards more fully embodied approaches – are linked both to shifts in filmmaking practices and technologies, as well as to larger philosophical paradigm shifts.[2] As del Rio reminds us, the prevailing critical frameworks in film studies from the mid-1970s to the mid-1990s drew on semiotic and psychoanalytic models in their focus on visual representations and structures of meaning, while more recent developments in film studies, and in media studies more broadly, include a concern with 'the film image as moving materiality/corporeality.'[3] I have already gestured towards the implications of this turning towards corporeality for feminist film criticism in Chapter 1.

One of the reasons for this conceptual shift was the realisation that 'the representational model proved either unwilling or insufficient to address the way in which the experience of the moving image can at times escape binary determinations and established signifying codes.'[4] While semiotic, psychoanalytic and ideological approaches generated important 'investigations into the power relations concerning binaries of race, gender, and other power-differential situations', del Rio highlights that they also 'unwittingly furthered oppositional binaries that the cinema itself has consistently proven quite capable of undoing, binaries such as reality/illusion, subject/object, thought/emotion, activity/passivity.'[5] The representational model brings with it 'the imposition of a totalising picture of reality as structured meaning' and fails to fully account for, and grasp, 'the unstructured sensations that are likewise set in motion in the film-viewing experience.'[6] While I share del Rio's broadly Deleuzian-inspired suspicions of the representational model, I also do not want to lose sight of the ways in which the sense-ational dimensions of cinema and the cinematic experience might not be entirely unstructured, but grounded in, and resonate with, socially-situated sense-ibilities and modes of embodiment. 'Tending toward' film phenomenology, as I do here, is one way to keep hold of the situatedness of corporeality, its entanglements with our perceptual habits as well as its broader socio-cultural reverberations and resonances.[7]

Del Rio acknowledges film phenomenology's potential despite the primarily Deleuzian orientations of her more recent work. She writes:

> A phenomenology of film experience emphasises the radical openness and unfinished nature of both the film medium and the spectator. Instead of the subject-object relations that prevail in other theoretical accounts of spectator and film, phenomenology considers both medium and spectator as *always already enworlded*, always mutually implicated and inclusive of each other.[8]

It is for these reasons, especially its assertions of the *enworldedness* of film and spectator, that a broadly phenomenological approach provides potentially groundbreaking possibilities to grasp the complex entanglements of gender, sexuality and the body in film that I have already gestured towards. I therefore want to make the case for a queer feminist film phenomenology, one that (at)tends towards and is sense-itive to the potentialities of the (troubled and troubling, twisted and twisting) female body in cinema, the cinematic modes of embodiment it gives shape to, and the embodied encounters it invites.

Grasping Cinema: Tactile, Muscular and Kinaesthetic Encounters

Sobchack's *The Address of the Eye: A Phenomenology of Film Experience* laid the groundwork for film studies' more sustained engagement with embodiment, materiality and sensuousness, and functions as a reference point for many subsequent explorations. Sobchack introduces a different kind of body into film criticism – a lived-body that is 'a sentient, sensual and sensible ensemble of materialized capacities and agency that literally and figurally makes sense of, and to, both ourselves and others.'[9] Her work instigated a shift in focus on 'what it is to *live* one's body, not merely *look* at bodies.'[10]

Sobchack contextualises and justifies her own turn towards phenomenology – considered a 'suspect' and 'naïve' move at the time – by articulating her frustrations with the dominant theoretical paradigms, Lacanian psychoanalysis and neo-Marxism.[11] She acknowledges the significance of and need for these frameworks' domination of cinema studies in the 1970s and 80s as they 'dynamize[d] the rigorous structuralism' that had turned film studies into a set of inanimate 'formal abstractions' that was ill-equipped to deal with the 'increasingly contentious and fractured social world.'[12] As del Rio will do, Sobchack also sees the taking up of Lacanian psychoanalysis by feminist theorists as necessary in relation to acute concerns with the patriarchal functions of Hollywood narrative and the gendered structures of a cinematic spectatorship implicitly assumed to be (gender) neutral.[13]

Feminist concerns very obviously underpin Sobchack's 'perverse' foray, as a film scholar, into the realms of phenomenology and the lived-body – a perversity that she describes as 'profound' given the state of film studies at the time.[14] However, Sobchack exhibits a strangely ambiguous hesitation to posit this work as explicitly feminist. She notes, for instance, that although *The Address of the Eye* 'is not an overtly feminist work, it is written by a *woman* who has *felt constrained* by contemporary theoretical analysis, who wants to speak of more possibilities than either psychoanalytic or Marxist theory currently allows.'[15] Clarifying her reasons for her conceptual reorientation, she writes:

> My move to phenomenology emerges not from my desire to exercise transcendental phenomenology's capacity for describing 'essences' or demonstrating 'universal' structures, but rather from my desire to cry out my *inherent qualification* of the world of essences and universals, to allow for my *existential particularity* in a world I engage and share with others.[16]

It seems that phenomenology, or rather certain aspects of it, are appealing because they acknowledge the specificity of embodiment and lived experience, including those experiences that are routinely marginalised – and Sobchack is keen to distance herself explicitly from those strands of phenomenology that turn a blind eye. She is critical of the notion of the 'transcendental ego' put forward by Edmund Husserl (the 'father of phenomenology') as well as his concern with the 'essence' of 'the things themselves' and with the process of 'bracketing' of all psychic and social qualifications.[17] These tendencies within phenomenology are profoundly antithetical to Sobchack's concerns, as are phenomenology's more general associations with 'transcendental, religious "mysticism"' and the kind of 'naïve realism' also found in André Bazin's film theory, for instance.[18]

Instead, Sobchack is drawn to Maurice Merleau-Ponty's existential phenomenology, particularly his notion of the lived-body, precisely because it accounts for our inherent enworldedness and existential particularity. She turns towards phenomenology because feminist film theory, with its neo-Freudian psychoanalytic underpinnings, 'has not exhausted [her] experience, although it has often exhausted [her] patience.'[19] Phenomenology is appealing because of its potential to enable 'another *kind* of look' at the 'women's film' or the 'family melodrama',[20] for instance – one that locates identification *not* in relation to the correlation of psychic structures (of femininity) on and off screen, but in relation to the 'correlated *postural schemas*, *motility* and *spatiality* of both the spectators watching the film and the film itself.'[21] In other words, we might consider the film experience in terms of the sensuous and affective intensity that arises from the

Film and Embodiment: Queer-ing Film Phenomenology

resemblances and affinities between the bodies, and modes of embodiment, of the film and of the spectator.

The example Sobchack uses here, interestingly, draws correspondences between the particularly feminine modes of embodiment identified by Iris Marion Young – which include an inhibited intentionality and a restricted and restricting taking up and moving through space, experienced as threatening and/or unavailable – and the kind of inhibited and restricted spatiality articulated in *Stella Dallas* (King Vidor, US, 1937), the quintessential maternal melodrama. In the final scene of the film Stella (Barbara Stanwyck) – whose maternal instincts have led her to sacrifice her life and happiness for her unappreciative daughter, Laurel (Anne Shirley) – looks in on Laurel exchanging her wedding vows through a window from behind a fence on the street. Stella is physically close to, yet infinitely removed from, the scene of happiness and fulfilment.

Accordingly, as Sobchack argues, for women whose lived experience of space is marked by constraint, self-conscious inhibition and separation, 'how much more *moving* and significant cinematic images of exclusion and longing become when they are articulated as the looking from a constricted "here" into another "yonder" space, which they can intend but cannot inhabit.'[22] The look here is *not* read as the disembodied, ahistorical gaze of psychoanalysis. It is conceived of as the sensuous, affective articulation of the lived and situated experience of a restricted mode of spatiality – one that might resonate with, and 'move' those spectators who embody similar modes of spatiality off-screen. This, for Sobchack, is what a film criticism that exhausts her experience, but not her patience, might look like: a 'more concrete and less deterministic way of describing cinematic "identification."'[23] (More on the role of gender in Sobchack's account later.) In a way, my motivations for this book are born from a similar sense of exhaustion and frustration – in my case with the ways in which an endeavour that emerged, however hesitantly, with feminist concerns and questions of gender and sexual difference in mind, has come to reconvene around a weirdly non-specific, standardised and neutral lived-body in some of its recent manifestations.

That said, the work of Jennifer Barker in particular, but also some of the more recent neuro-phenomemological accounts by Adriano D'Aloia and Vittorio Gallese, for instance, are invaluable in building on Sobchack's writing. They add an intriguing sense of energy and dynamism in their making even more specifically graspable the tactile, muscular and kinaesthetic dimensions of cinema and the cinematic experience.[24] It is the understanding of the cinematic experience as an *embodied encounter* put forward in this work that broadly underpins the conceptual and methodological tendencies of this book – and it is precisely this body of work that I want to (re)connect with the feminist concerns that shaped its emergence and with the queer concerns that might (re)shape its current and future incarnations.

I am particularly drawn to those conceptualisations that account for the tactile, muscular and kinaesthetic dimensions of the cinematic experience via conceptions of corporeal, sensuous empathy and embodied simulation. In her groundbreaking book, *The Tactile Eye*, Barker explores in intricate detail the various bodily 'levels' of our engagement with film through the concept of *cinematic tactility*, which she defines as:

> a *general attitude* towards the cinema that the human body enacts in particular ways haptically, at the tender surface of the body; kinaesthetically and muscularly, in the middle dimension of muscles, tendons, and bones that reach toward and through cinematic space; and viscerally, in the murky recesses of the body, where heart, lungs, pulsing fluids, and firing synapses receive, respond to, and re-enact the rhythms of cinema. The film's body also adopts towards the world a *tactile attitude* of intimacy and reciprocity that is played out across its nonhuman body: haptically, at the screen's surface [...]; kinaesthetically, through the contours of on- and off-screen space and of the bodies, both human and mechanical, that inhabit and escape those spaces.[25]

It is precisely this understanding of the parallels between, and (phenomenological) likeness of, the film's and the viewer's embodiment of time and space, that allows Barker to explore the 'resonances and reverberations of tactile patterns between the human body and the cinema' through notions of tactile and muscular empathy.[26]

This notion of the cinematic experience as a tactile, muscular encounter is usefully illustrated via the reciprocal bodily gesture of the 'handshake'.[27] A handshake usually involves an encounter of two bodies that mimic and

Film and Embodiment: Queer-ing Film Phenomenology

respond to one another's muscular movements: one body's movements are meaningful only in relation to the other's. A handshake can express agreement and mutuality, but it can also, of course, be awkward, insincere or threatening, depending on the compatibility of the encountering bodies' stances, attitudes, orientations and intentions. For Barker, the encounter between film and viewer takes shape in *phenomenologically* similar ways: 'Our empathy with the film's body can be considered a kind of handshake. We extend our bodies to the film, and it extends its body to us simultaneously, and in doing so, we agree on certain terms.' The handshake can be enacted by the film in a number of ways, including 'inclusive blocking and inclusive camera movements, close-ups, match-cuts – in short, nearly any cinematic device that makes it easy for us to move with the film's body.' The viewer, in turn, might engage in the encounter 'by leaning close, by relaxing our shoulders, or by stretching or straightening in response to [...] expansive camera movements for example.'[28]

Barker uses the physicality of slapstick and the 'comedy of kinetics' of Buster Keaton's silent films – including *The General* (US, 1925), *Steamboat Bill, Jr.* (US, 1928), *College* (US, 1927), *One Week* (US, 1922) and *Sherlock Jr.* (US, 1924) – as key examples to illustrate the workings of the phenomenology of the (cinematic) handshake. From an embodied, muscular standpoint, the gesture of the handshake can be perceived as shaping both Keaton's encounters with the worlds *in* his films as well as our encounters *with* his films. In *Sherlock Jr.*, in particular, a film in which Keaton plays a projectionist, who, in a dreamlike state, tries to enter the film that he is screening, the *character's* encounter with the *film's* body is additionally made explicit. Importantly, as Barker notes, the bodily encounters *in* and *with* Keaton's films mirror each other (phenomenologically), which is why they constitute particularly poignant examples of how the cinematic handshake works. The central humour and comedy in Keaton's films arise from the staging of the 'handshake gone wrong', that is from the *mis*matching of bodily gestures and movements: Keaton is an outsider and wants to 'fit it' (with the physical and socio-cultural worlds depicted *in* his films and, in *Sherlock Jr.*, with the world *of* the film), but he seems to have no real grasp of (bodily) conventions. As a result, he trips up, is jolted, runs into people and things, and thus his body ends up in peculiar positions, misshapen and, well, twisted. Barker argues that these variously corporeal and sensuous *mis*encounters (with bodies, objects and films) *in* Keaton's films might draw 'a muscular response from the audience' and thus allow us to experience muscular empathy with Keaton's attempts to 'fit in' physcially and socially.[29]

Through the seemingly simple gesture of the handshake, Barker provides a vivid illustration of the (physical, sensuous and affective) mechanisms at work in our encounter with cinema – and also of how these might be explicitly foregrounded through the various bodily encounters enacted in the diegesis. Dance, of course, is a similar, yet infinitely more complex, embodied encounter, in which relations of reciprocity, alignment, tension, proximity, desire and conflict are enacted via the coming together of two (and sometimes more) bodies in motion. I will explore the complexities of dance, and of our encounter with the dance film, in much more detail in Chapter 3. I do want to flag here, however, the conceptual and methodological debt to Barker's account for the explorations of bodily mutuality and muscular empathy in the remainder of the book. It underpins the engagement with *The Tango Lesson* and *Black Swan* (Chapter 3) as well as the encounters with other kinds of bodily performances in the chapters that follow.

D'Aloia's assertion that 'watching a film is an experience of a relationship between bodies [of characters, spectators and film] in space' conjures a similar understanding of the cinematic encounter.[30] D'Aloia's is a useful supplement to Barker's account in that it unpacks specifically the mechanisms underlying the relationship between these bodies. What kinds of relationships are they? How exactly do they work? And how and why do we experience them?

In his exploration, D'Aloia draws heavily on Merleau-Pontyan ideas about the human 'sense' of space (that is formed *before* our eyes) and the ways in which 'our relation to space is bodily, rather than primarily reflective.'[31] We only 'know' what space is, because we live and experience it – and not because we can somehow 'think' it independently of living it. Our film experience is grounded in the fact that the world of the viewer and the world of the film (even though different in nature) 'both have the same basic orientation: head up, feet down, as in ordinary life.'[32] Highlighting the parallels between human and cinematic orientation, D'Aloia reminds us that:

[t]he character walks along a street that is *under* his feet; a car runs along a road that passes *under* its wheels; a superhero soars *upwards*; in the face in the close-up, the forehead is *above* the chin, and the nose is *under* the eyes [...] In short, [cinema] offers an orientation that can be called 'natural', because it is 'common', 'usual', 'habitual', 'ordinary', 'normal' and readable without any effort, and because it obeys the laws of nature [i.e., gravity].[33]

But not only that; this standard orientation is also a 'good' orientation because the spectator's body is always already 'geared into the world', meaning that the relationship between our bodies and the world is always '"already constituted" in that way, at a preliminary spatial level, and *that* way is a *good* one.'[34] 'Bad' orientations are the ones that throw us off balance. For instance, for an upside-down close-up of a face to make sense to us – for it to be *good* – it needs to be readable, and recognisable, as the '*inversion of an image*'.[35] This might be enabled by spatial markers surrounding the face (buildings, objects, other bodies) that reassure us of the 'natural' orientation, for instance; or by a rectification of the 'unnatural' orientation (i.e., when the face is turned upside-up). In the prolonged absence of any correction or reaffirmation of the 'normal' orientation, the upside-down face becomes unreadable as a 'face': it becomes, instead, an '*image of inversion*', its significance and resonances entirely altered (i.e., 'bad').[36]

Of course, the cinematic play with the spectator's assumptions, expectations and experiences of various kinds of ordinary and exceptional, normal and twisted, familiar and unexpected orientations can also conjure (kinaesthetic) excitement or arousal. The action genre, for instance, is often used as an example of the 'thrills' (variously enjoyable and threatening) that cinema might provide us with, especially in relation to action sequences where bodies (of characters *and* of the film) variously defy the laws of gravity and normative spatiality, at least temporarily. Barker's discussion of the cinematic 'chase' is insightful in this regard (as chase sequences are often constitutive of the spectacular action of the action genre).[37] Like the handshake, the chase is an example of the muscular and kinaesthetic dimensions of the film experience. Unlike the handshake, the chase is not a coming together, or coming towards each other, of two bodies; it is, instead, the seduction and teasing of one body (the spectator's) by another (the film's). We might say that the chase is the incarnation of a different kind of filmic orientation, one that challenges the spectator to hold on tight and keep up the pace. During chase sequences films and viewers 'enter into a relationship of mimicry of sorts,' but one where the films 'push the connection to its breaking point [...] They invite us along for a ride, but once we've jumped on, they threaten to outrun us, push us too far or too fast, or throw us off completely.' Our bodies might:

> tense and swerve, lean forward or jump back, fingers clenching the armrests of our seats as we try to hang on. A chase film cuts us loose from our moorings altogether for minutes at a time only to return us safely to them at the end, leaving us exhilarated, exhausted, and shaken.[38]

For the purposes of illustration – not only of the chase but more generally of the proprioceptive dimensions of the 'natural' and 'good' orientation we share with cinema and the provides the grounds for empathy – we might think of *Gravity* (Alfonso Cuarón, UK/US, 2013) here, a film that engages directly with questions of spatial orientation, in part because of its subject matter. The film is set almost entirely in space, a context where the laws of gravity do not apply and where the directionality of 'up' and 'down' no longer makes 'sense'. Part of the sensuous, kinaesthetic thrill of the film is tied to its making tangible the exhilarating yet terrifying experience of being unanchored, ungrounded and not 'geared into the world' in any familiar way, especially in sequences where the bodies of astronauts Ryan Stone (Sandra Bullock) and Matt Kowalski (George Clooney) drift and spin through space in an entirely disorientated and disorientating manner. This is a potentially risky endeavour and a question of balance: there is a fine 'line' between thrilling and losing the spectator. It is a matter of reintroducing spatial markers (the space shuttle, pieces of space debris, glimpses of the earth and other stars and planets) that reaffirm a sense of spatiality that is recognisable and familiar, one that makes (spatial) 'sense', in order to not untether the film's and the spectator's bodies entirely. And, of course, *Gravity* lets us 'come back down to earth' in the end.

The kinds of embodied, sensuous and affective experiences gestured towards here – thrill, (im)balance, (dis)orientation, exhilaration, being (un)anchored, threat – are possible precisely because of the fundamental underlying parallels and resonances between the spectator's and the film's modes of spatiality and embodiment that 'ground' our corporeal encounters with film. As Barker notes, 'film and viewer share certain *deep-seated muscular habits*, beginning with the very tendency to move through the world in an upright position. We and the film are both inclined that way, as we are inclined to move and look forward, to *face* things directly.'[39] And crucially, the parallels between human and cinematic orientations and habits are highlighted when we consider moments in which the film's and the viewer's bodies are *not* aligned. As we have seen, in those moments of *dis*orientation, human and cinematic bodies tend to 'rectify the situation with a gesture, such as the twisting of the neck and camera.'[40] Other examples of how we share gestures and modes of comportment with film (in addition to the handshake and the chase) include the shot-reverse-shot pattern that tends to be used in the filming of conversations, mirroring our habit of turning our head from speaker to speaker when following a discussion, or the close-up as the cinematic equivalent of our habit of leaning forward to get a 'closer look'.

Overall, what is highlighted here then is that 'the film adopts our proprioception, the sense we have of our bodies in space; it may confirm it or thwart it by its own movements, but always it is indebted to it.'[41] And that is how we make kinaesthetic, muscular 'sense' of cinema. There are 'standard' bodily orientations and tendencies (upright, straightforward) that we share with film and that film shares with us, and that provide the 'grounds' for muscular empathy and kinaesthetic identification. These (and similar) arguments are based on Sobchack's notion of the 'common structures of embodied existence [and the] similar modes of being-in-the-world [...] that provide the *intersubjective* basis for cinematic communication' – including cinematic empathy.[42] Before I move on to a more detailed unpacking of how and in which contexts (cinematic) empathy might arise, I also want to flag the opportunities opened up here – those that go largely unacknowledged, but that I pursue herein – to explore more specifically the resonances between the modes of embodiment that take shape in, though and around film, and the different orientations, habits and tendencies that characterise these modes, especially in terms of their *gendered* dimensions.

Bodies, Movement and Cinematic Empathy

Opportunities for corporeally empathetic spectatorial engagements are foregrounded and heightened in the filmic encounters that shape this book. It is one of the key reasons for having chosen this particular body of films (*The Tango Lesson*, *Black Swan*, *2 Seconds*, *Offside*, *Tomboy*, *Girlhood*) that might otherwise seem fairly eclectic and perhaps idiosyncratic. The 'situations with the most potential for empathy', according to D'Aloia, tend to be those 'in which a strong kinesthetic intensification is invited (for instance acrobatics, falling, sports, performance, dance, etc.).'[43] Physical, athletic performances of various kinds (dancing, cycling, football/soccer, American football, fighting) are central to all the films encountered in this book – thematically, narratively, sensuously and affectively – and these performances are, as we will see, what the films' textural fabric and associated modes of spatiality and perception cohere around. They also provide the corporeal ground for the variously empathetic modes of queer feminist engagement on offer in and through the films.

D'Aloia notes that the human body in motion has been central to cinema from its very inception because of the 'intensified nature of cinematic perception' and the 'enhanced forms of sensory experience' cinema can provide of the skilled bodily action (of the acrobat, the dancer, the juggler, the athlete) that 'humanity has [always] been thrilled by.'[44] In order to provide a broader historical context for his concern with the body in motion and the role of kinaesthetic empathy in the film experience, D'Aloia returns to some of the early attempts to theorise cinema's 'draw' or 'appeal', particularly those by Jean Epstein (*Bonjour Cinema*) and Béla Balázs (*The Visible Man*) in the 1920s.[45] Balázs, for instance, writes that:

> [i]f it is true that film is concerned exclusively with the visible, that is bodily, human action, then it follows that sporting and acrobatic performances can constitute extremely enhanced expressions of human physical life [...] In reality, we see only a moment, a fragment of movement. In film, however, *we accompany a runner.*[46]

For D'Aloia, this suggests that cinema 'is capable of including the spectator in the totality of a particular intense movement, experienced at first hand and through "accompanying" the characters.' He also, importantly, points to the significance of an 'apparent genuineness' and 'perceived "authenticity"' of the bodily performance, as they impact on the 'immediacy' of the cinematic experience.[47] The inclusion of *The Tango Lesson*, *Black Swan*, *2 Seconds*, *Offside*, *Tomboy* and *Girlhood* in this book is, in no small part, related to the 'authenticity' of the embodied performances that take shape in, and in turn shape, the films. In particular, it is the palpably visceral corporeality of the female characters/actors that lends a heightened sense of immediacy to the cinematic encounter.

Questions of kinaesthetic empathy, as a way of accounting for intersubjectivity and our ability to relate to others, have developed as a key aspect of research primarily in the context of dance and other creative bodily practices on the one hand, and in relation to cinema on the other. Dee Reynolds notes that the current conceptual and analytical focus on kinaesthetic empathy in dance studies arises from 'a concern with how the body, and particularly the body in movement can evoke affect, and with how empathic understanding is linked with simulation on the part of the observer.'[48] With regard to film, the presence of the cinematic image, which signifies the body's absence, further complicates questions about how the spectator might relate to the moving bodies of performers and actors. The workings of kinaesthetic empathy are thus amplified, and complicated, in the context of the dance film, which is why the textural analysis work in this book begins with a focus on *The Tango Lesson* and *Black Swan* (in Chapter 3).

D'Aloia describes the film experience as an '"as if" experience [that] is an imaginary act that activates the spectator's kinesthetic sensation in a motor imitation [i.e., simulation] of movement perceived in the film, which can be that of a character or of the film itself, as in the movement of the camera.'[49] What is significant, for the purposes of the argument developed here, is the role the acrobat plays in this account and how it informs D'Aloia's understanding of kinaesthetic empathy in cinema. For one, D'Aloia draws centrally on Edith Stein's phenomenological writing in *On the Problem of Empathy* (1917), which consistently invokes the case of the acrobat. Ahmed highlights that orientation is crucial to Stein's notion of empathy in that 'empathy involves switching orientations.'[50] Empathy, for Stein, involves obtaining 'a new image of the spatial world and a new zero point of orientation.'[51]

The distinction between primordial experience ('whose content is present, bodily given') and non-primordial experience ('such as memory, expectation and fancy [...] that do not have their object bodily present before them') is particularly important in this context because 'the act of empathising consists in primordially experiencing something that is non-primordially given, since the content belongs to another.'[52] D'Aloia explains this with reference to Stein's account:

> In the empathic relation, 'I am not one with the acrobat but only "at" him. I do not actually go through his motions but only *quasi*' [...] In watching an acrobat, 'I put myself into the perceived body as if I were his vital centre, and perform an impulse "quasi" of the same type as that which could cause a movement' [...] The 'quasi' describes the 'imperfect substitution' of the empathising subject with the empathised subject, a proximity and accompaniment that does not result in a fusion or replacement and that preserves a distance, a 'unity in distinction'.[53]

Importantly, Stein's phenomenological conception of empathy as an accompaniment, rather than a projection or fusion, where the 'empathising subject is *side-by-side* with the empathised subject,' implying a 'paradoxical *proximity at a distance*,' displays crucial structural parallels with the film experience.[54] An understanding of empathy as a form of accompaniment 'implies the structure of a mediated experience, where mediation consists both in an inevitable distance and an opportunity for contact. In this sense, the debate on *Einfühlung* seems to provide a phenomenological description that relates closely to the spectator's experience of watching a film.'[55] For D'Aloia, this means that '[i]n the light of phenomenological and filmological accounts of empathy, the film experience can be described as the relationship between the spectator and a series of *quasi*-bodies with which he or she interacts'.[56] These quasi-bodies include the cinematic bodies that 'express vitality thanks to their *movements* and the *resemblance* to human bodies and movements.'[57] This resemblance is also described in some detail in Barker's account of the phenomenological similarities between human and cinematic skin, musculature and viscera (as discussed in the previous section).

The filmic body, then, is most usefully conceived of as *quasi*-body 'capable of expressing a vital essence that the spectator can *innerly accompany*,'

Film and Embodiment: Queer-ing Film Phenomenology

with the 'meta-movements of the camera and the depicted movements of objects and subjects' capable of eliciting sensory responses and 'an internal *kinesis* in the spectator.'[58] The body of a film character is an additional kind of quasi-body that constitutes a 'paradoxical "otherness"' as it cannot be said to embody the subjectivity of real-life bodies.[59] What additionally complicates our relations to bodies on screen is that we experience those bodies as fictional bodies (of characters), which are, however, 'inseparable from the performers' bodies (those of the actors).'[60] That said, although the bodies of characters and performers on screen 'cannot be considered as ontologically analogous to [the spectator's] lived-body, they are, *phenomenologically similar* (in their movements, postures and gestures)' – just as the filmic body is phenomenological similar to the spectator's body.[61]

Drawing once again on the figure of the acrobat (the body in motion, on display for spectatorial pleasure, defying gravity in spectacular fashion), D'Aloia illustrates the quasi-relations between quasi-bodies (a 'circuit of empathies') that constitute the film experience via the prologue of *Trapeze* (Carol Reed, US, 1956).[62] The sequence shows the acrobat Mark Ribble (Burt Lancaster) performing a triple somersault in front on an audience in a circus tent (*in* the film) and in front of the cinematic audience (*of* the film). The situation is infused with a sense of suspense, danger and risk and has a tragic outcome: Ribble falls from a significant height and the sequence ends with his motionless body on the ground, surrounded by the shocked spectators in the film, framed by a high-angle shot providing a bird's-eye view of the scene. The similarities and differences between the spectators *in* and *of* the film usefully illustrate the specificity of embodied, affective empathy in the cinematic experience. Firstly, as a narrative film, *Trapeze* makes a 'fictional pact' with the filmic spectator. We know the events in the film are not 'real', even if they are 'realistic': the bodies and actions 'obey the physical rules that the [filmic] spectators use to interpret the real world (for instance the acrobat does not fly).'[63] But that does *not* mean we cannot experience the events *as if* 'real'. We are also removed from the corporeal presence of the acrobat who is 'up there in the flesh' for the spectators *in* the film, who gasp and gather around the motionless body to help. The spectators *of* the film do not, of course, get up, try to help or phone an ambulance as we experience the events 'only' *as if* really happening.

D'Aloia describes this 'peculiar psychological structure' of the film experience as follows. The spectators *of* the film:

> can experience the character's sense of vertigo, loss of balance and impact with the ground vicariously. Their sensorimotor and affective activations are realised by varying degrees of empathy. The degree and quality of motor activation and emotional involvement depend on the effectiveness of the forces and tension created by the movement inherent in the film's body itself. [The spectator *of* the film] is positioned 'in the middle' of events, so that he/she in a way *participates* in the performance, rather than only *witnessing* it. Through a series of techniques (for instance camera angle, shot scale, point-of-view), the spectator [*of* the film] is brought closer to the action. In *Trapeze*, thanks to the alternation of long shots and close-ups, only spectators in front of the screen can see the fatigue on Ribble's face and the sweat on his forehead, or watch the action from above or just under the safety net, behind the trapeze or even clinging to the trapeze artist's belt. In addition to camera shots, camera movements also have to be considered. Conceived as film's body movement, camera movements do not simply produce a motor activation, but rather are capable of generating and implicitly suggesting a relation between the movement perceived on screen and the movement that is internally experienced by the spectator [*of* the film ...] the camera follows the acrobat and sways, on both the horizontal and vertical axes alternately, in order to keep him in the centre of the visual frame. This film body movement *simulates* the character's movement, but is also different and autonomous. Through this solution, the spectator can perceive the loss of balance, elicited by the movements of the camera as it follows the acrobat. In this sense, he/she has an experience that is only available through film.[64]

We can see then, that the film experience is best conceived of as '*quasi*-intersubjective relation in which the spectator, can empathise with the bodies in and of film.'[65] Importantly, these conditions, as Sobchack notes, are based on whether the quasi-bodies' embodiments are 'resonant' and whether they are 'sufficiently comprehensible' to a viewer 'who might "possibly" inhabit [them] (even if in a differently inflected and valued way).'[66] It

Film and Embodiment: Queer-ing Film Phenomenology

is precisely this understanding of the cinematic experience – albeit with a queer feminist twist – that centrally underpins the various encounters that take shape in what follows.

Overall, these accounts provide the kind of conceptual frame that makes movement, embodiment and perception central to an understanding of the cinematic experience, without 'closing the gap', as it were, between the body of the film and the body of the spectator. It resonates with Ian Garwood's and Lucy Donaldson's emphasis on the *distance* between spectator and film, even in the context of phenomenological approaches that foreground proximity and contact.[67] Donaldson, for instance, highlights the importance of acknowledging 'a simultaneously close and distant, but no less sensorial, relationship to film.'[68] What kinaesthetic empathy does, then, is *fill*, rather than close, the gap 'between bodily presence of the spectator and bodily absence of the character thanks to the film's *mediation* (in the double sense of keeping separate and putting into contact) between the two lived-bodies, although that of the character [like that of the film] is only a *quasi*-body.'[69] The film's mediation nonetheless leads to an *immediate* form of experience in the sense that it occurs 'when we observe what someone else is doing and we ourselves live in it in some sense, rather than understand it [only] at an intellectual level.'[70]

Countering Normative Tendencies: Gender and/in Phenomenology

In the wide range of work, some of which I have traced here, that draws on broadly phenomenological approaches (in a variety of ways and often in conjunction with other theoretical frames: Deleuzian, cognitive, neuroscientific), there appears to be a strange disjunction between the intense focus on the specific materiality of the body (skin, musculature, viscera, synapses) and a seeming disregard for how this materiality is lived. We might say that the 'neutral' body that appears in this work is a kind of reincarnation of the Merleau-Pontyan lived-body that has been identified by queer and feminist critics as being underpinned by very specific heteronormative, white, Western, able-bodied modes of embodiment. It tends to be based on assumptions of a very particular *kind* of lived experience that is so normative and 'habitual' as to be invisible and unfelt.[71] Queer and feminist scholars' critiques of phenomenology's straightforward, heteronormative tendencies have not been taken up within film studies – or at least not to the extent that they might be. Hence the overarching aim of this book is to put these vibrant areas of debate in touch with each other – not merely in order to explore how the issues raised (for instance around gendered and sexual embodiment) are represented *in* film, but in order to infiltrate the very fabric of film theory and to grasp more comprehensively the embodied, sensuous and affective tendencies, orientations and possibilities of cinema and our encounter with it.

This is not to say that concerns around gender (as well as race) have been absent from phenomenological engagements with film. They do come to the fore in Sobchack's, as well as other scholars', work and I want to trace where and how these concerns appear in order to provide a context for the queer feminist film phenomenology taking shape here. What follows is a section that is conceptually dense and thick – and necessarily so – as it attempts to crack and begin to dislodge the seemingly solid foundations of conventional (film) phenomenology. I hope the reader can stick with me in this endeavour and get his/her queer feminist teeth into this body of theoretical work.

In Chapter 2 of *The Address of the Eye*, a book that Sobchack retrospectively describes as a 'historically necessary polemic,' she briefly returns to questions of gender and sexual difference in a section entitled 'Whose body? A brief meditation on sexual difference and other bodily discriminations.'[72] Sobchack opens the section, which also contains the fleeting reference to *Stella Dallas* mentioned above, by stating that she has 'avoided particularizing the body in terms of gender (or, for that matter, race),' and that 'this neglect has been purposeful,' for the following reasons.[73] Firstly, since one of the aims of her overall project is to circumvent the 'constraints of binary thinking,' avoiding the terminology of 'sexual difference' was key to eluding 'the ground staked out by dominant theoretical discourse' around gender.[74] Secondly, 'insofar as any discussion of the body's specificity "outside" of the terms provided by dominant discourse calls for a new mode of articulation,' it seemed important to first highlight the relations between phenomenology and language and focus on 'the body's activity of visual perception and visual expression.'[75]

Thirdly, gender, Sobchack argues, is the result of the 'coding' and 'containing' of the body's 'excessive, mobile, and "wild" significations,' taking place through 'cultural and historical activity that stakes out upon the body's broader meaning-producing field a limited and mutable circumscription of significance.'[76] In other words, gender is perceived as being layered 'on top' of a neutral, unmarked body and its neutral, unmarked phenomenological capabilities. This is why, for Sobchack, it 'seemed important to introduce the lived-body in terms of its essential ontological functions – that is, those functions that do not precede, but do provide the grounds for, the marking of and discrimination against the lived-body and its excessive, ambiguous, and over-running semiosis.'[77] For Sobchack, it is on these grounds that we can conceive of gender in non-essentialising terms. The only 'essential' aspects of the body are its ontological functions, which all lived-bodies are said to have in common:

> all lived bodies are material, intentional, motile, and infinitely and perspectivally situated. Correlated with intentional consciousness, all lived-bodies constitute an 'orientational point, "O", from which spatio-temporal coordinates organize and structure the milieu.' All lived-bodies are 'organs of perception' or 'that by means of which' there is access to a world that can be said to exist; as perceptive organs, all lived-bodies also synthesize several sensory fields and are the material 'that on and in which [...] fields of sensation are spread out' and synoptically experienced in their modality as 'mine'. And, to varying degrees, all lived-bodies actualize both the operative and deliberative 'strivings of consciousness.'[78]

Bodies that are not normative, which, for Sobchack, include not only female, but 'colored', 'diseased', 'impaired', 'fat', 'old' and 'deprived' bodies, are grounded in an ontology and intentional capacity common to all bodies, while they 'are also synecdochically marked, disfigured, defaced, and incapacitated – made particularly, rather than individually, significant and generalized as a category.'[79] The lived-body is therefore '[t]he ground of discrete, strategic, and contested areas of value, differentiation, and discrimination,' and 'never merely or wholly male or female, white or black.'[80] This distinction is fundamental to Sobchack's hesitation to engage more specifically with gender in *The Address of the Eye* and she re-emphasises that 'to initially take it [the lived-body] up in those terms [male or female] is an essentializing act that confuses epistemological qualifications with ontological conditions.'[81] There is, for Sobchack, a clear firstness and secondness to embodiment, which 'is, first, always an essential set of *ontological* functions that enable "being-in-the-world" at all, and, second, always a qualified and specific set of *epistemological* functions that determine "being-in-a-particular-world" in a particular modality.'[82]

Some of the more recent queer/feminist engagements with 'conventional' phenomenology have questioned the binary distinction between ontology and epistemology asserted in Sobchack's account (which takes a strong stance against binary distinctions otherwise) by highlighting how our being-in-the-world is always already a *particular* being-in-the-world and that there is, in fact, only ever a being-in-a-*particular*-world in a *particular* modality – although, in certain cases, this particularity passes itself of as foundational and unmarked.

In their 'Introduction' to the *Continental Philosophy Review* special issue on Feminist Phenomenologies, Sara Heinämaa and Lanei Rodemeyer note that despite a recent shift towards an acknowledgement of intersubjectivity and intercorporeality as the constitutive grounds of consciousness (a turn away from the individualist tendencies in engagements with Husserl in particular), the subjects at the heart of these debates 'are usually characterized as simply human.'[83] They observe that:

> most contemporary commentators in phenomenology take human subjectivity as a unitary starting point and proceed in their description and analyses, as if mentioning men and women would risk slipping into empirical or merely mundane concerns. Gender is taken as a factual issue, an empirical problem, which belongs to the sciences of anthropology, psychology, and biology, far from transcendent phenomenology or fundamental ontology.[84]

This account resonates rather poignantly with Sobchack's initial hesitation to engage with gender in her development of a phenomenology of film.

Heinämaa and Rodemeyer assert the importance of challenging 'the standard view of the sexless subject of transcendental and existential phenomenology,' because 'problems of sexual difference and gender are

Film and Embodiment: Queer-ing Film Phenomenology

relevant, and even crucial, to phenomenological analyses concerning the constitution of sense and the meaning of being.'[85] While a phenomenological discourse on sexual difference is 'not a completely new invention' and dates back to the 1930s and 40s – including 'the excursions of Sartre, Merleau-Ponty, or Levinas,' the work of Stein, Simone de Beauvoir and Hannah Arendt as well as the writings of Irigaray and Julia Kristeva (who merged phenomenological with psychoanalytic approaches) – Heinämaa and Rodemeyer see an urgent need for a 'creative rediscovery' of this earlier work in order to 'question the perceived notion that the groundbreaking subject of phenomenology is a sexless pure ego or a neutral *Dasein*.'[86]

The key challenges of conceiving of a phenomenology of gender hinges on the status of ontology, epistemology, the transcendental and the empirical/mundane in the discourse and method of phenomenology. Johanna Oksala argues that, in its traditional manifestations, 'phenomenology cannot address the question of gender or sexual difference at all', due to the distinction between, on the one hand, a constituting transcendental, pre-reflective perceptual consciousness (which contains a 'neutral' and 'unmarked' corporeal component: an 'anonymous bodily subjectivity'), and, on the other, mundane and embodied subjectivity.[87] While this perspective – Oksala calls this the 'classical reading' in her wonderfully insightful piece on the 'phenomenology of gender' – allows for a feminist engagement with gender, it does so only at the 'mundane level of sexed bodies,' which are nonetheless constituted and structured by a transcendental, unmarked consciousness.[88] This is because 'transcendental subjectivity cannot be understood as sexed, otherwise we would have to argue that there are, in fact, two different types of transcendental subjectivities.'[89] On this 'classical' basis, feminist phenomenology would be an oxymoron. Heinämaa and Rodemeyer concur, noting that sexual difference, from this perspective, is the characteristic of the mundane subject, a difference that is 'completely alien' to the transcendental self/*Dasein*.[90]

Oksala's 'corporeal reading' is based more specifically on the Merleau-Pontyan, rather than the 'classical', Husserlian, version of phenomenology and on the premise that a 'complete reduction to transcendental consciousness is impossible' – we can never leave the mundane behind completely.[91]

It is therefore linked to a shift in phenomenological investigations from a focus on transcendental consciousness to the lived-body. This shift has led to various feminist appropriations of Merleau-Ponty's work, including, perhaps most famously, Young's phenomenology of feminine body comportment, motility and spatiality in 'Throwing like a girl.'[92] Importantly, this is also the key text that Sobchack draws on extensively, and almost exclusively, in her short section on gender in *The Address Of The Eye* mentioned above. In the context of this 'corporeal' approach, a phenomenology of gender comprises of 'a study of the basic modalities or structures of female embodiment that are typical of feminine existence.'[93] There is an assumption here, then, about a 'distinct mode of corporeal being in the world that is female or feminine' – which is why phenomenological inquiry should simply aim 'to describe the eidetic structures of the living body' that characterise 'feminine ways of being.'[94]

While this approach provides a much-needed engagement with the neglected experiences of women, it also, in Oksala's view, 'threaten[s] to push us back into defending a form of corporeal essentialism that potentially precludes political changes in the situation of women,' since these kinds of accounts tend to rely on first-person descriptions by women which are then turned into generalised and essentialising accounts of eidetic female embodiment (i.e., the 'essence' of being a woman).[95] This charge does not hold true in relation to Young's account of feminine movement and motility (which will make various appearances throughout this book), as it draws on ethnographic, empirical observations of bodily movement and takes an overt stance against biological essentialism. It does so by highlighting the ways in which feminine ways of being and moving in the world, and their relation to embodied perception, are acculturated and learned. Oksala concedes that the charge of essentialism might not always be justified since a general account of female embodiment 'need not be equivalent to the absolutist sense of generic, but should be understood rather as a thread of invariance; not a model that fits all, but structural invariance *within* variance, that gives shape and coherence to it.'[96] On this basis, feminist phenomenology should not be understood as 'a form of reifying and homogenizing essentialism that suppresses any variations,' but as an attempt to articulate 'the tension of general and specific.'[97]

Overall, however, Oksala considers this 'corporeal' approach to be limited and limiting. While it provides insights as to how gender might be lived as a particular mode of being-in-the-world, it is too narrowly focused on the body and does not engage with the question of ontology. Pointing to the significance of larger linguistic, socio-cultural and historical conditions of possibility, and aligning her argument with the kinds of post-structuralist criticisms of feminist phenomenology put forward perhaps most notably in Butler's *Gender Trouble*, Oksala asserts that a 'philosophical study of gender therefore cannot be limited to a description of the difference between two types of living bodies [male and female], but must also encompass a study of the ontological schemas in which those bodies and experiences gain value and meaning.'[98]

This assertion leads to a third phenomenological position on gender, the 'intersubjective reading', which opens up questions of gender to a much wider perspective that can account for the importance of 'shared normative structures such as language and historicity.'[99] The move towards intersubjectivity is linked to a shift in Husserl's later writing, which is marked by 'a decisive rethinking of the relation between the transcendental and the mundane that ultimately forced him to consider the transcendental significance of issues such as generativity, tradition, historicity and normality.'[100] Oksala usefully highlights variations in the ways in which the notion of intersubjectivity is understood and taken up. Most commonly, it is conceived of as a 'concrete relation between subjects,' while an additional, and perhaps more fundamental, interpretation is to understand it as an '*a priori* structure of subjectivity.'[101]

Most significant in relation to questions of gender, however, is an understanding of intersubjectivity as 'effective at the level of handed-down normality.'[102] It assumes that we are 'always already situated in an intersubjective, historical nexus of sense' and acknowledges 'the constitutive importance of the cultural sphere, or the *homeworld* of which the transcendental subject is a member.'[103] One of the attractive implications of such a reading is that a conception of gender based on a system of handed-down normality, rather than eidetic structures of embodiment, also leaves this system open to change. Oksala uses the example of intersex and transgender individuals to highlight ways in which the system of normality might already be changing. In the context of cinema, this leads to questions, variously underpinning the textural encounters in subsequent chapters, about how an 'intersubjective, historical nexus of sense' might be articulated or evoked in and through film; about how the 'homeworld' might be embodied cinematically; and also about the role cinema might play in challenging and reshaping the 'system of handed-down normality.'

In this third type of intersubjectivity, the constitutive conditions are not '*a priori* intersubjective structures,' as in the first two types, which are revealed by analysing the ahistorical and transcendental 'structures of perception as well as other intentional experiences.' Instead, constitutive conditions of intersubjectivity are 'historically and culturally changing norms.' In the context of the phenomenological method of reduction these norms 'are, in fact, exactly what distorts and clouds an investigation into *a priori* universal structures and must therefore be bracketed in the reduction.'[104] An understanding of intersubjectivity in relation to handed-down normality thus sits very uneasily with the methods that underpin phenomenology (and that distinguish phenomenology from other kinds of philosophical inquiry). Oksala reminds us that:

> the phenomenological method relies on prior ontological commitment to the universal, pre-linguistic validity of the transcendental structures of the ego. The method starts from the analysis of the first-person experience and moves from there to a transcendental inquiry into the constitution of sense by identifying apriori structures of transcendental subjectivity. This move can only be justified on the basis of an ontological commitment to the universal similarity of the subjects. The differences between them can only be understood on the basis of this more fundamental similarity and must be studied through empirical sciences such as anthropology, sociology or psychology.[105]

Therefore, a phenomenological concern with historically and culturally contingent norms leads to a rather unhelpful circularity. While, as Oksala shows, Husserl recognised 'the constitutive importance of the third type of intersubjectivity,' he also asserted that 'it must always be understood as dependent on a more primordial type – intersubjectivity as a universal *a priori* structure – and it is this primordial type that the phenomenological method can accommodate.' This means, importantly, that the phenomenological method cannot show 'both that the individual subjects of transcendental subjectivity are always furnished with identical *a priori* structures and that the concordance of their experiences is a relative accomplishment that has historical and cultural conditions of possibility.' In other words, phenomenology would need to abandon the reduction to transcendental consciousness in order to address 'the transcendental, constitutive significance of these mundane phenomena,' namely language and cultural normativity.[106]

However, giving up the method of phenomenological reduction takes us back to where we started. This is because of the impossibility of conceiving of 'transcendental subjectivity – now understood as comprising language and historicity – [as] constituted in experience if it is what ultimately makes individual constitution possible.' If we relate this more general paradox back to the question of gender, it manifests itself as follows: 'to start the analysis from a woman's experience when trying to understand what a woman is means already assuming that which we seek to explain.' One solution to this paradox put forward by Husserl is to return to a strict separation of the transcendental and the empirical – which, of course, includes gender. What this means is that either 'the question of gender cannot be investigated under the phenomenological method at all,' or that 'our investigation is doomed to a circularity that already presupposes that which it seeks to explain.'[107]

Rather than give in to this seemingly dead-end circularity, Oksala asserts the importance of modifying the phenomenological method itself so that it is 'better able to deal with the constitutive importance of the social and cultural world' – this is the final and 'post-phenomenological reading' (following the classical, corporeal and intersubjective).[108] Oksala argues that if we 'evaluate the relevance of phenomenology from the perspective of contemporary concerns, it is the method that is the driving force of phenomenology' – which is why an interrogation of the method itself should be our starting point. A post-phenomenological perspective asserts the impossibility of 'understand[ing] how gender is constituted through normative ontological schemas if we believe that we can, by some supreme methodological step such as the epoch, leave all our ontological commitments behind.' This means that we need to:

> accept the hermeneutical circle – at least in connection with our analysis of gender – and try to see to it that our method continuously turns back upon itself, questioning and modifying itself in an effort to articulate what it secretly thinks. This means understanding epoche not as total, universal and complete, but as an endless, circular and always partial task.[109]

This opening-up of the rigidity of the phenomenological reduction and a more explicit emphasis on the importance of radical self-reflection is also highlighted in Alia Al-Saji's account of the uses of Husserlian phenomenology for feminist theory. Al-Saji argues that the phenomenological reduction, which (cl)aims to bracket the empirical ego, including 'the concrete body, personal historicity, and, not mentioned by Husserl, gendered and racialized difference,' leads not to 'an empty, pure ego,' but to 'a universalized (masculine) consciousness.'[110] For Al-Saji, as for Oksala, this means that 'the phenomenological reduction's claim to "neutrality" thus appears rooted in a form of double forgetfulness that serves to normalize, and validate, the standpoint of the phenomenological observer.'[111] It is precisely an assertion of this 'double forgetfulness' as underpinning claims to neutrality and universality that also provides a starting point for Ahmed's queer phenomenology.

The double forgetfulness means not only that the empirical ego is 'explicitly put out of play,' but, perhaps more importantly, that 'this exclusion is based on a more *profound forgetting* of embodied dimensions of difference – dimensions of sex, race, gender, culture and class – which, without being universal, already structure subjectivity and potentially motivate the activity of reduction.'[112] For Al-Saji, this kind of self-forgetfulness essentially 'reinscribes Husserlian phenomenology within the "natural attitude" it has sought to bracket,' an assertion that further questions the rigid distinction between the transcendental and the empirical/mundane. The question, again, is what to do with this seemingly dead-end circularity and, like Oksala, Al-Saji suggests that 'depending on one's aim', this line of argument can be taken to show either 'the impossibility of reduction' or 'the need to carry the project further' – and if we were to carry the project further, 'the "true reduction would reveal such operative dimensions to be constitutive conditions of experience (without assuming their universality or ahistoricity).'[113] In this sense, Al-Saji's line of argument resonates with Heinämaa's and Rodemeyer's observation that recent feminist engagements with Husserl's work in particular highlight that 'the distinction between the transcendental ego and the empirical ego is methodological, without any ontological implications, and that the transcendental ego is not a separate being but a reflective modification or possibility of the mundane self.' Thus, they argue, instead of presuming that gender can only ever be disclosed as a 'worldly object' through the reflective attitude, we should 'not shy away from the idea that the reflective activity or practice itself may be gendered.'[114]

Al-Saji provides a useful elaboration of the intricacies of this kind of argument. 'In taking the transcendental ego to be its [the reduction's] ultimate discovery, what are left invisible are structures of experience that have been "naturalized" to this ego,' including naturalisations of maleness, whiteness and heterosexuality that manifest themselves more broadly elsewhere.[115] In relation to this naturalisation, it is crucial to bear in mind that, contrary to how this dilemma is often taken up:

> the point is not simply that the transcendental ego still carries traces of the empirical ego; it is that there is no ontologically prior level of subjectivity that can be so conceived. Thus the aim is not to try and find an ego unmarked by naturalizing historicizing processes, but to use the reduction to critically reveal the naturalization and contingency of subjectivity – the way in which structures, meanings and norms are being socially and historically sedimented so as to make our experience what it is.[116]

A post-phenomenological account can thus 'reveal something about the normative ontological schemas that are constitutive of our experiences' and functions as a study of different systems of normality.'[117] It is 'a form of reduction in the sense that it makes us aware of the hidden aspects of our own thought – it lifts the naïveté of the ordinary experience – and allows us to reveal and question its constitutive conditions, at least to some extent.' This is, importantly, not the familiar shift 'from natural attitude to the level of transcendental consciousness, but it is, nevertheless a shift to the level of transcendental discourse' – and thus bears similarities with Merleau-Ponty's conception of reduction as 'the interminable effort to break our familiar acceptance of the world and to see as strange and paradoxical what we normally take for granted.'[118]

In other words, a post-phenomenological reduction would reject a 'complete phenomenological reduction to transcendental subjectivity,' while, at the same time, it would 'attempt to accomplish a partial bracketing in order to reveal something about the ontological schemas underlying our ways of thinking, perceiving and acting.'[119] This means that in order to sidestep, as it were, the problematic implications of (aspects of) the 'classical', 'corporeal' and 'intersubjective' approach, we must, as Oksala argues, break away from the natural attitude understood as an attitude where our ontological pre-understanding of the world is not visible to us at all, to an attitude that is capable of problematizing it.' What it does not imply, however, is that we can somehow suspend ontology as it is 'irrevocably tied up with our language, methods of reflection and ways of seeing the world,' which leads Oksala to conclude that an 'analysis of experience that aims to be radical and transcendental can only every be fragmentary and incomplete.'[120]

With regard to gender, a broadly post-phenomenological approach can thus help us understand the ways in which gendered experiences are constituted and 'how their constitution is tied not only to embodiment, but also to the normative cultural practices and structures of meaning.'[121] The overall aim of such a phenomenological position on gender, therefore, 'is not to find eidetic structures of female experience that characterize all women […] it is rather to seek the structures that are constitutive of the sense of normal in *our* homeworld.' At the same time, the post-phenomenological method also allows us to study different systems of normality, as well as the function of the 'abnormal' and the 'alienworld', relative to the 'normal' in our 'homeworld'.[122] My aim here is to put these considerations in touch with *film* phenomenological concerns, in an attempt to make graspable how different systems of (ab)normality, different homeworlds/alienworlds and thus different figurations of gender (relations) might take shape in and through cinema and the embodied encounters it offers.

Touchy-Feely? The Gendering of Film Phenomenology

A broadly post-phenomenological approach appears to be taken up in Sobchack's later work, especially the collection of essays in *Carnal Thoughts: Embodiment and Moving Image Culture* – although it is never explicitly labelled as such. This work engages both autobiographical and anecdotal experience as well as a range of 'popular sources', including everyday speech, film reviews, advertisements and jokes, in order to foreground a 'certain common or general understanding of certain embodied experiences – and point to their broad resonances even as they never strike exactly the same chords in every body.'[123] The film analyses in the following chapters are underpinned by precisely such an understanding of the 'broad resonances' with embodied experiences that cinema might evoke, even without necessarily replicating or speaking to specific and individually grounded experiences. They turn, instead, to cinema's capacity to give shape to 'thread[s] of invariance' and 'structural invariance *within* variance' to account for the variously queer feminist encounters the films invite.[124]

Importantly, Sobchack also notes that, 'pathological' or abnormal embodiments might bring to the fore 'the usually transparent and normative aspects of being embodied.'[125] While she speaks specifically about the disabled body here, non-normatively gendered and queer embodiments might similarly bring to the fore the conventionally transparent aspects of heteronormative embodiments. This making visible and graspable of what is normally transparent is, or can be, heightened in the context of *cinematic* incarnations of gender and queerness – especially in relation to bodily performances such as sport or dance that are highly gendered to begin with and that put processes of embodiment on spectacular display.

Questions of gender are at the very forefront in *Carnal Thoughts*, which emerges from a much more 'subjective' starting point than *The Address of the Eye*. Sobchack is very much aware of the precisely gendered assumptions underpinning distinctions between touchy-feely, subjective analysis and rigorous, objective inquiry. Indeed, she argues that grounding analysis in autobiographical or anecdotal experience does not simply substitute subjective for objective analysis, but 'purposefully provides the phenomenological – and embodied – premises for a more processual, expansive and resonant materialist logic through which we, as subjects, can understand (and perhaps guide) what passes as our objective historical and cultural existence.'[126]

This is reminiscent of Rosi Braidotti's assertion that 'subjectivity is a socially mediated process,' and not to be equated with individualism and particularity, which also means that 'the emergence of new social subjects is always a collective enterprise, "external" to the self while it also mobilizes the self's in-depth structures.'[127] It is important, therefore, to account for both 'the *content* and *form* of embodied experience but also its *context*.'[128] It is a concern with cinema's role in this 'collective enterprise', especially in terms of how cinema might mobilise and reorient the 'self's in-depth structures' and clear the grounds for the emergence of 'new social subjects' and modes of subjectivity *in certain contexts*, that underpin the argument that takes shape throughout this book.

While this shift in Sobchack's approach to, and use of, phenomenology, especially around questions of gender, is a most welcome development, it is worth reflecting on the self-consciousness of its framing. While *The Address of the Eye* is, as mentioned, retrospectively posited as a historically necessary polemic that attempted, arguably successfully, to provoke a substantial paradigm shift within film studies, the collection of essays in *Carnal Thoughts* are, in contrast, introduced as 'relatively user friendly' (read: less sophisticated). The supposed user-friendliness is linked directly to the use of 'popular sources' as well as 'anecdotal' and 'subjective' experience, and Sobchack is quick to provide an elaborate justification of the use of the 'subjective' and an assertion of the rigour of such an approach.[129] While Sobchack's self-conscious acknowledgement of potential criticisms is, of course, understandable and necessary given the broader intellectual climate (in film studies and in the humanities and social sciences more generally), it is worth highlighting how the negative and often dismissive charge of phenomenological approaches to film as 'too subjective' plays out in relation to the wider theoretical and conceptual landscape in film studies, where certain kinds of analyses of films (psychoanalytic, semiotic, Marxist, cognitive, Deleuzian) are consider to be more 'objective', and certainly more generalisable, than others – even though they are, more often than not, carried out by individual subjects/scholars. Despite the more generally accepted postmodern suspicion towards grand narratives and notions of objectivity, there seems to be an eager suspension of suspicion when it comes to (academic) film criticism.

There is tendency for the position from which the scholar writes to be more explicitly acknowledged in feminist and queer film studies as well as in work on film concerned with race, for instance, areas which are more generally concerned with the 'politics of location' and the position from which we speak. However, what this does *not* mean, although it often seems to be interpreted that way, is that occupying specific 'locations' and 'positions' is something that only certain (marginalised) people/scholars do. In highlighting this discrepancy, my aim here is not to advocate the inclusion of elaborate autobiographical elements into film analysis, but to suggest that the kind of 'radical self-reflection' that Oksala demands should be at the heart of phenomenological inquiry (which shares concerns around perception and subjectivity with certain areas of film studies) might counter the 'double forgetfulness that serves to normalize, and validate, the standpoint of the phenomenological observer' as well as the film scholar.[130] In other words, concerns with the constitutive significance of the cultural sphere, of history and of 'handed-down normality', which normalise and universalise certain seemingly objective and transcendental experiences and perceptual habits, should not be the preoccupation of feminist or queer or postcolonial film criticism *only*.

Sobchack's account of what she considers to be 'proof of an adequate phenomenological description' is usefully adapted here to what I consider to be an 'adequate' phenomenological film analysis:

> [it] is not whether or not the reader [or viewer] has actually had – or even is in sympathy with – the meaning and value of [a film] experience as described – but whether or not the description is resonant and the experience's structure sufficiently comprehensible to a reader [or viewer] who might "possibly" inhabit it (even if in a differently inflected and valued way).[131]

This is precisely how I conceptualise the spectatorial resonances that cinematic embodiments of gender or queerness might evoke.

I believe it is significant, and perhaps not entirely surprising, that a number of the publications that constitute key reference points in film phenomenology, and that are constitutive of this relatively 'new' strand of film criticism, have been authored by women (most significantly Barker, Bolton, Marks and Sobchack as discussed, as well as Martine Beugnet, Jenny Chamarette and Kate Ince), while the foundational, canonical texts of most other areas in film studies tend to be written by men.[132] This is, I realise, a stark generalisation but I do believe it is important to draw attention to this tendency and also to provide a reminder that Sobchack was drawn towards phenomenology because psychoanalytic, semiotic and ideological approaches did not appear to speak to her experience of film (as a woman). This move mirrors, at least in part, the ways in which the myths of objectivity have been addressed in other disciplines (primarily by feminist scholars). It is equally unsurprising that, at least initially, the concern with embodiment, experience and sensuousness in relation to cinema was belittled in specifically gendered terms and mapped onto well-worn gendered binaries linking masculinity, mind, objectivity and reason on the one hand, and femininity, the body and emotions on the other (of course, race, class, age and other identity markers cut across and are mapped onto these binaries).

These larger tendencies, within film studies, of positing only *certain kinds* of (embodied) experiences *as* experiences, and opposing them to (disembodied, transcendental) thought or cognition, resonate with Richard Dyer's accounts of whiteness as a kind of non-race. Dyer's argument as to what this means for a critical analysis of whiteness as race is particularly relevant here:

> The colourless multi-colouredness of whiteness secures white power by making it hard, especially for white people and their media to see whiteness. This, of course, also makes it hard to analyse. It is the way that black people are marked as black (are not just 'people') in representation that has made it relatively easy to analyse their representation, whereas white people – not there as a category and everywhere everything as a fact – are difficult, if not impossible, to analyse *qua* white.[133]

The sense that whiteness is so normative as to be invisible as a particular racial category (particularly for those who are white, but also for those who

Film and Embodiment: Queer-ing Film Phenomenology

are not), resonates with Ahmed's suggestion that although (sexual/phenomenological) orientation is something we all 'have', 'when we are orientated, we might not even think "to think" about this point,' and that it is only '[w]hen we experience disorientation, we might notice orientation as something we do not have.'[134] Once marked as particular (rather than universal or as 'just' human), we lose 'the claim to speak for the commonality of humanity.'[135] In terms of race, this means that '[r]raced people can't do that – they can only speak for their race. But the non-raced people can, for they do not represent the interests of a race.'[136] This is one of the risks of identifying as a feminist and/or queer film scholar, in terms of taking on a particular identity, but also, and perhaps more importantly, in terms of identifying with a particular, broadly identity-based, kind of film criticism – and this is heightened in the context of a theoretical frame that foregrounds the embodied, sensuous and visceral dimensions of the film experience.

Overall, what I want to draw attention to here is the tendency for certain critical engagements with film to appear to be written on behalf of, or for, or in the interest of a particular identity group, while others appear as 'neutral' engagements with film because the particularity of their stance and orientation towards film is universalised and thus invisible. Invoking Oksala's call for radical self-reflection once more, '[i]t is ultimately *I* who' watch films, engage with theory and read film criticism. Again, this is not intended as a call for an autobiographical film criticism, but as an assertion of this importance 'to break our familiar acceptance of the world' and 'to seek the structures that are constitutive of our sense of normal' – and not only when embodying those structures becomes uncomfortable, but particularly when we those structures seemingly disappear and become common 'sense'.[137]

There is one final point I want to make here before turning to the dancing body in *The Tango Lesson* and *Black Swan* in the following chapter. Engaging with the muscular, kinaesthetic and spatial dimensions of cinema, their resonances with 'lived' experience and the ways in which they might make strange normative tendencies and orientations are what drives and shapes the textural encounters in this book. However, I want to reassert that this conceptual and methodological turning towards phenomenology should not be equated with a wholesale rejection of other critical approaches and concerns. I would like to align my endeavour with del Rio's:

Film Bodies

In acknowledging the central place the body should occupy within feminist film theory, I am not rejecting semiotic and psychoanalytic perspectives, which I find relevant at many junctures. Rather, I wish to combine these with a phenomenological approach [that identifies] bodily action as not only inherently significant, but also indivisible from symbolic and discursive structures.[138]

3

Queer Encounters with Feminist Politics: Dancing Bodies in *The Tango Lesson* and *Black Swan*

> *Dancing, perhaps the most highly complex and codified of kinesthetic practices, is one of the most important arenas of public physical enactment.*[1]

> *The dancer senses his [sic] dancing. The dancer does not see himself [sic] as an object in motion across space, but accompanies his [sic] body's movement.*[2]

> *[W]e are all potential dancers.*[3]

Dance, like sport, is a highly gendered bodily practice – and one with a long history in both mainstream and alternative/avant-garde cinema, which highlights the intricate entanglement of cinema and the moving and specifically *gendered* (human) body since the very inception of the 'moving image'.[4] Whether enacted socially or performed on stage, dance carries, and gives expression to, a wealth of meanings around a wide range of socio-cultural identity markers, including gender and sexuality as well as race, nation, religion, (dis)ability and age. Dance, like sport, displays and, in a sense, magnifies the processes, mechanisms and reifications of embodiment that tend to take shape more subtly elsewhere, through everyday bodily practices, habits and conventions. This is why the dance film, like the sports film (Chapter 4), offers particularly fruitful opportunities to explore the cinematic incorporations and incarnations of gender and sexuality as well as the embodied spectatorial resonances they might invoke.

At first glance, *The Tango Lesson* and *Black Swan*, the main foci of this chapter, might not appear to have very much in common, other than their subject matter: both are films about dance with white female dancing protagonists. Beyond that, the films are mainly marked by their differences.

The Tango Lesson is the third feature, following *The Gold Diggers* (UK, 1983) and *Orlando* (UK/Russia/Italy/France/Netherlands, 1992), by British filmmaker Sally Potter, one of the most prominent feminist auteurs of the last 40 years. Potter herself features as the central character, Sally, a filmmaker who learns how to dance tango. *The Tango Lesson* integrates elements of the dance film, the musical and the romantic drama and is structured around a narrative that interweaves Sally's attempts to write a film script/make a film and her encounters with the Argentine tanguero, Pablo (Pablo Verón), who becomes her dance teacher, romantic partner and artistic collaborator. The film offers a fairly explicit critique of gender norms and inequalities. It highlights both the obstacles facing women in the film industry (Sally struggles to get her script approved by a group of Hollywood producers, for instance; they want something more spectacular, flashy, sexy and violent) as well as the gendered power inequalities inherent in tango (the dance itself as well as the culture surrounding it).

Black Swan, on the other hand, is squarely situated within the cinematic mainstream. It features a star cast, including most notably Natalie Portman's Oscar-winning performance as Nina Sayers, as well as Mila Kunis as Lily and Winona Ryder as Beth Macintyre, dancers in variously rivalrous relationships with Nina. *Black Swan* draws much more directly on the fairly well-established conventions of the dance film, especially the cinematic history of ballet.[5] The dance sequences, moving from rehearsals to a climactic staged performance of *Swan Lake*, are integrated into the surrounding narrative and function as articulations of desire, jealously and female rivalry. The film also highlights the impossible bodily demands of ballet through a rather clichéd portrayal of Nina's body/image issues and eating disorder.

Queer Encounters with Feminist Politics

The Tango Lesson wears its representational politics on its sleeve and marks itself, fairly explicitly, as 'women's' or 'feminist' cinema and is frequently referred to in these terms. In contrast, *Black Swan* is much more muddled and less easily pinned down in this respect. In fact, critical responses to the film frequently highlight its phallocentrism and misogyny. Texturally encountering these films *side-by-side* foregrounds the affirmatively troubling resonances that surface through the muscular, kinaesthetic and spatial entanglements of the bodies of the *dancer*, the *dance* and the *film*.[6] In particular, there is a sense in which the turning away from a straightforward representational model, which variously shapes both films' corporeal trajectories, allows for questions around gender (relations) to surface in palpably touching, moving terms.

It is worth noting the wider cinematic context from which these films as well as my critical and conceptual concerns emerge. I have been drawn to *The Tango Lesson* and *Black Swan* in part because of the kinds of female bodies featured in these films – bodies that have been shaped by dance and that bear the cumulative marks of the dancer's labour. This kind of body also appears in *The Dancer* (Frédéric Garson, France, 2000), *The Company* (Robert Altman, US, 2003) and *Pina* (Wim Wenders, Germany, 2011), for instance. The ways in which dance moulds, reorientates and directs the body is given shape through Sally's/Sally Potter's tiny but toned and controlled frame in *The Tango Lesson*; Nina's/Natalie Portman's hard and bony yet variously disintegrating contours in *Black Swan*; India's/Mia Frye's long, muscular limbs and athletic, expansive movements in *The Dancer*; Ry's/Neve Campbell's strong, composed and compact physique in *The Company;* and Pina Bausch's emaciated and skeletal frame in *Pina*.

In this wider corpus of films, the female dancing body appears in relation to a variety of different types of dance (tango, ballet, hip hop/street dance and post-/modern dance) and in a range of different narrative and generic contexts (mainstream fiction, feminist independent cinema and documentary). What variously connects these cinematic incarnations of the female dancer, however, are the ways in which they disrupt normative habits of embodiment and perception and their gendered implications. Centred as they are around the performing and frequently exposed female body, these films articulate modes of embodiment that variously resist the recuperation of the body into normative structures (of gender, gender relations and cinema).

In what follows, I explore the ways in which variously twisted modes of gender and sexual embodiment take shape in, through and around *The Tango Lesson* and *Black Swan*. The textural analyses offer a sense of the films' corporeal registers and affective appeals that hinge on the cinematic incorporation of particular modes of spatiality, temporality, perception and orientation that extend through and around the dancing body and our encounter with it. It is through a focus on the tactile, kinaesthetic and muscular dimensions of *The Tango Lesson* and *Black Swan* that we might begin to grasp the films' queer feminist resonances.

Dance/Film

In many ways, a consideration of the female dancing body in film is a complex endeavour, entangled as this body is in a widespread and intricate network of signifying relations. It is this multi-layered intertextu(r)ality that also provides potentially rich insights as to how meaning and affect circulate through and around these bodies. There are a range of differences and similarities regarding the ways in which the body, and the female body in particular, is incorporated into cinema on the one hand and into (staged, theatrical) dance on the other. Similarities include the role of the body in relation to narrative, in relation to looking and agency on screen/stage and in relation to spectatorship. This has led to notable parallels in feminist critiques of the heteropatriarchal structures of both cinema and dance, built as they are around voyeurism, fetishism, lack, desire and abstraction and the privileging of an active male subject.[7] While both entertainment/art forms, especially with regard to their mainstream manifestations, depend on the erasure of the production process and apparatus that enable the ideally seamless spectatorial experience, one of the key distinctions between cinema and dance hinges on the corporeal absence/presence of the performer and the specific spatio-temporal dimensions that shape the encounters between the spectator and the body on screen and on stage.

There is a sense in which the three-dimensional body on stage is corporeally 'present', while the body on screen is an 'absent presence', in the sense that cinema 'makes absence presence.'[8] As Jane C. Desmond argues, '[t]he always-present body of the dancer presents special challenges and offers unique possibilities, different from those in film, painting, and literature, where the body may be represented but does not at the same time represent itself.'[9] While this assertion risks oversimplifying cinema's complex relationship to 'reality', it reminds us of the seemingly unmediated corporeal encounter with the dancer that live performances (as well as social dance) provide and also gestures towards the tenuous ontology of the body on screen and our encounter with it. In the dance film, these two contexts overlap and the pressures that shape the dancing body on screen and *how it means* are multiple.

There is long history of attempts to understand how meaning and affect circulate in and through dance. For Amelia Jones, the question driving much contemporary dance research is: 'How do bodies, particularly those creatively motivated to move intentionally towards the ends of communicating artistic meaning (however this might be defined), *come to mean* to others who encounter them?'[10] Some of the most exciting scholarship in this area has moved away from broadly psychoanalytic frameworks (and questions about what staged bodily performances symbolise or signify) and towards broadly phenomenological concerns with affect, embodiment and muscular, kinaesthetic empathy.[11] This corporeal turn in critical dance studies broadly parallels the conceptual reorientations in film studies that I trace in Chapters 1 and 2 – and this chapter explores the potential that the *intersections* of these debates hold for queer feminist concerns around gender and the body in film.

The notion of the 'body of the dance' – and its associations with the kinaesthetic and sensual (rather than discursive and rhetorical) implications of dance – is of particular relevance here. It opens up a conceptual space for grasping the corporeal resonances of the coming together of dance and cinema and the spectatorial engagements it invites. In fact, and as Dee Reynolds asserts, we might think of the similarities between:

> what Vivian Sobchack calls 'the film's body' [and what we might refer to as] 'the dance's body' to designate a body that is not identified with a fixed subject position of either performer or spectators, but which is both 'here' and 'there', invested as subject and object in the shared materiality and affective flow of choreographed movement.[12]

If we conceptualise, as I do in this book, the cinematic experience as an embodied encounter – as an 'experience of a relationship between bodies in space' – the presence of the 'dance's body' adds an additional layer of textural complexity.[13]

Susanne Langer's account of the dance's body is particularly relevant here: 'In watching a collective dance [...] one does not see *people running around*; one sees the dance driving this way. Drawn that way, gathering here, spreading there – fleeting, rising, and so forth.'[14] For Reynolds, this assertion raises a series of fundamental questions: 'What does it mean to "see" the dance driving, drawing, gathering, spreading, fleeing, rising? How do the senses work together and flow in and out of each other in perceiving the dance? And whose body are we watching and feeling: the dancer's, our own or the "dance's body"?'[15] And what about the body of the *film*?

What is crucial, however, is that in this complex entanglement of bodies (film, dance, human), the '[s]pectators' embodied, affective responses to the *dance's* body are grounded in responses to the *dancer's* body, which generates kinesthetic energies.'[16] Here, Reynolds reaffirms the significance of the physical, corporeal (human) body and its specifically sensuous and 'lived' dimensions as that which other kinds of bodies (the dance's, the film's, the spectator's) cohere around – and it is this living, breathing, orientated body that I do not want to lose sight of (as sometimes happens in some more Deleuzian-leaning encounters with film).

Why Dance? Gender and Sexuality and/as/in Motion

What is crucial for dance scholars like Desmond, is that dance is accounted for, and analysed, as an embodied social practice: '*embodied*, meaning lived physically, not just musings on the "idea" of dance; *social*, meaning embedded in specific material and ideological conditions of possibility; and *practice*, meaning a process in time and space, one of enactment, and articulation and materialisation of meanings and relationships.'[17] Dance is widely institutionalised, commercialised and rigidly structured along the lines of gender, sexuality, race and class. These structures are embodied and performatively reconstituted at the level of the body across a range of dance contexts. However, there is also a sense in which the lived-body in particular can never be fully contained and co-opted into normative identity structures (of gender, sexuality, race and class). This is precisely why this body 'has so much to offer to a feminist perspective interested in extricating the female body from phallocentric constraints.'[18] While larger linguistic and symbolic signifying contexts do, of course, inform how we might 'read' the dancing body (as male or female; as joyous or tormented; as controlled or animalistic; as strong or weak), its visceral and affective implications are much less easily grasped. Dance therefore also constitutes a context in which normative embodiments of time and space can be, and are, reorientated, in often spectacular manner – and it is precisely through cinema's corporeal, haptic and muscular qualities that we (as cinematic spectators) might be brought into contact with the ('lived') dancing body on screen.

In *Dancing Desires*, Desmond writes that dance history and dance practices can only ever be fully understood in relation to histories of gender and sexuality, and that 'the analysis of dance, as a form of material symbolic bodily practice, should be of critical importance' to gay and lesbian studies, to queer theory, and to concerns around gender more generally.[19] While the intersections between critical dance studies and gender/queer theory are underexplored, they provide fruitful ground for endeavours (such as this one) that might enhance both areas of inquiry. 'What happens to the writing of dance history and criticism when issues of sexuality and sexual identity become central? And what happens to our considerations of queer theory […] when a dancing body takes centre stage? *What do we see that we didn't see before?*'[20] When queer makes contact, dance, as a 'privileged arena for the bodily enactment of sexuality's semiotics', is said to be able to convey certain aspects, or dimensions, of gender and sexuality that we might not 'see' otherwise – a suggestion that resonates quite specifically with (some) queer approaches to film.[21] It also resonates rather crucially with my attempts to move beyond concerns about the gaze/what we *see/what is visible*, and towards an engagement with embodied perception and about what might 'appear' and become *graspable*.[22]

It is the concern with the constitutive importance of the physical body that allows critical engagements with dance to foreground the 'relationship between bodies and social categories' of gender and sexuality. As Desmond writes, dance provides a 'highly codified, widespread, especially visible, and privileged arena' to investigate these relations and to explore how gender and sexuality 'are inscribed, learned, rendered, and continually signified through bodily actions.' This is why analysing dance helps us understand how gender and sexuality are 'inhabited, embodied, and experienced.'[23] It is in this sense that the dance context also provides important insights as to the performative reconstitution of heteronormativity, by foregrounding how 'choreographed behaviors enact notions of romance, sex, physical expressivity, and sexual identity,' and how these 'motions gain their meanings in relation to dominant discourses about "male and "female", about "masculine" and "feminine", about "homosexual" and "heterosexual"', as well as in relation to 'movement conventions that have their own resonant histories on stage and in real life.'[24]

Both *The Tango Lesson* and *Black Swan* variously draw (more or less self-consciously) on these associations of dance with heterosexual romance and normatively gendered roles/movements, as well as the ways in which these conventions are routinely played upon in cinematic representations of dance. In the musical and in the dance film in particular, the articulation and eventual resolution of gendered oppositions in and through dance are key generic markers.[25] *The Tango Lesson* engages explicitly with the masculine/feminine, active/passive, leading/following binaries that appear to structure the choreography, steps and movement combinations of tango, while *Black Swan* foregrounds the damaging demands made of the female body in ballet, linked as it is to self-destructive tendencies. Both films critically engage with, and variously reconfigure the heteronormatively gendered histories and tendencies of tango and ballet, despite the heterosexual romance narratives that are entangled with the dance performances (although *Black Swan* does, of course, incorporate some explicitly lesbian tendencies as well). They do so through kinaesthetic, muscular and visceral cinematic renderings of dance that privilege the female characters' lived corporeality and embodied experiences/points of view.

Such an understanding of dance as a bodily practice means that we might analyse 'queer identifications and desires through their literal enactment on the dance floor' or stage, that is, in relation to same-sex partner dancing, which takes place in the final part of *The Tango Lesson*, for instance.[26] However, it also opens up possibilities, of the kind that I pursue here, to investigate questions of gender, sexuality and desire by paying attention to 'movement style, spatial negotiation, or relational positioning' and the ways in which they might contravene or rewrite social relations through particular 'kinesthetic renderings' of gender (relations).[27] So this is not only about analysing the literal reworking and manipulation of signifiers of gender and sexuality (for example women dancing male roles), but also about considering the embodied and affective implications of 'kinesthetic renderings' that are much less easily grasped (at least intellectually). In a way, we might think of this conceptual move as adding an important material dimension to Butler's notions of performativity and citation. Desmond, in fact, refers to certain kinds of movements as 'kinesthetic "speech acts."'[28]

In his thought-provoking piece on dance and 'queer kinesthesia' Jonathan Bollen elaborates on this idea. Responding to Ann Cvetkovich's call for a 'cultural politics of movement'[29] and Elspeth Probyn's suggestion 'to consider queer as movement,'[30] Bollen posits the notion of queer kinesthesia as 'an attempt to describe how the regulation of gender may be negotiated through movement, through a marshalling of kinesthetic resources that disarticulate ways of moving from the demand for consistently gendered performance.'[31] Crucially, he also notes that the aim of exploring the dancing body's choreographed 'kinesthetic capacities' is 'not so much to "see" kinesthetic habituation as *"feel* it."'[32] While we might attempt to read kinaesthesia (i.e., the feeling of movement) 'off the surface of the body in terms of matter, shape or form,' we need to be mindful that movement cannot, in fact, be 'read', but only *felt*. We can only 'make sense' of movement (and related notions of spatiality and temporality) because we 'live' movement – 'we are moving subjects.'[33] This conception of movement resonates rather poignantly with the Merleau-Pontyan ideas about the human 'sense' of space – we can only 'know' space because we 'live' it – that underpin the accounts of embodied/cinematic empathy explored in Chapter 2. The key, for Bollen, to 'registering the reality' of the performative effect of dance, is 'registering kinesthetic difference.'[34] Exactly what is meant by 'registering', how the registering process takes shape and who does the registering are important question that emerge from this turn towards the feeling of movement – especially if we add a further layer of complexity in trying to account for the ways in which kinaesthetic habituation and difference might be registered in the context of cinema. As we will see, notions of kinaesthetic, muscular empathy go some way towards unpacking these variously corporeal and affective entanglements.

I am additionally drawn to Bollen's call for a 'kinesthetic theory of subjectivity' that understands the body's capacity for movement 'not as evidence of an autonomous, independent agency, but as evidence of a body's enculturation, its training and participation in socialized and cultured ways of moving' – in other words, its various entanglements with and in the world.[35] This is an important move beyond Butlerian notions of performativity (of gender), where what 'matters' about the body are its surface, its contours, its morphology, rather than the ways in which bodily matter, including the body's capacity for movement and its 'choreographic repertoire', might be *experienced* and *felt*. Such a kinaesthetic approach to subjectivity might thus allow us to get a better sense of how the performance of gender might be queered kinaesthetically, as well as, importantly, of how we might '*experience* ways of moving and ways of desiring that are sometimes ambivalent, sometimes hyper-reflexive, about the morphological moorings of gender.'[36]

This kind of queer kinaesthesis locates the disruption of gender normativity in the *phenomenology* of movement, in ways that resonate productively with Ahmed's account, which links the unhinging of heteronormativity to differences in spatiality and modes of perception: different modes of embodiment and orientations shape 'what appears' within the horizon of the body and what becomes 'reachable'.[37] We might say that dance provides an amplified incarnation of Ahmed's phenomenological orientations – and, crucially, what *cinema* can provide is a foregrounding of the relationships between orientation and movement on the one hand, and experience and perception on the other. After all, film is, from a phenomenological perspective 'a sensuously and sensibly manifest[ed] expression of experience by experience,' that is embodied, cinematically, through specific manifestations of time and space.[38] The body of the film itself is orientated and moves (particularly through the orientations and movements of the camera), and has both perceptive and expressive qualities: what film makes available is an expression of (its) perception. Therefore, the coming together of dance and film provides exciting opportunities to grasp the sticky entanglements of movement, spatiality, temporality and perception as they relate to *embodiment*.

One final point about movement, performance, gender and queerness. The concept of queer kinaesthesis invites an analysis of gender and desire 'that is predicated not on the logic of morphological difference but on a choreography of kinesthetic engagement.'[39] In this sense, dance is doubly performative: it is always already intertwined with a performative rendering of gender and sexuality. When it comes to dance in film, especially fiction film, it takes on a triply performative dimension – via the performance of the actor – with gender variously cutting across all of these layers. That said, and as Bollen notes, quoting Biddy Martin, such an understanding also carries the risk that queerness 'is cast as a "mobile and fluid" kinesthetic *figure* against the *ground* of a "stagnant and ensnaring" morphological gender.'[40] We need to be mindful, therefore, to keep the body that 'matters' close to hand in our explorations of queer (as) movement if we want to challenge 'antifoundational celebrations of queerness [that] rely on their own projections of fixity, constraint, or subjection onto a *fixed ground* [...] in relation to which queer [becomes] figural, performative, playful, and fun.'[41] The figure/ground metaphor invoked here gestures, perhaps inadvertently, towards the phenomenological implications of 'queer' as well as the queer implications of phenomenology. They resonate with Ahmed's assertion that to queer phenomenology is to question what *grounds* us and our experiences, to consider the importance of the *background* in making certain things 'appear', and to reshape the common *ground* that clears the space for making contact with others.

The importance here is for queer approaches (to dance and to embodiment more generally) not to become overinvested in 'metaphors of kinesthetic mobility' that become abstract and disembodied, in an attempt to avoid the pitfalls of an essentialising 'morphological rigidity'.[42] My aim here is therefore to link questions of the corporeal body and its materiality to questions of movement and kinaesthetic 'habits' in a manner that is non-essentialising (with regard to the body's characteristics and capabilities), but that nonetheless, and centrally, acknowledges the reciprocal relations between the very specific material corporeality of the body (its properties) on the one hand, and its kinaesthetic capabilities, orientations and habits on the other. In doing so, I adopt a model of corporeal sedimentation, where bodily experiences and actions *shape and are shaped by* what we experience and how we act. Dance (like sport) is a context in which this kind of sedimentation is foregrounded, often in dramatic and spectacular fashion, through the ways in which bodily habits and repetitive actions shape the body (most visible in relation to musculature and injury). Moreover, 'our bodies *incorporate* dance, a pastness of movement that allows dance-already-danced to move through us. This is not a learning by heart'; instead, it is moving with and through 'the *already-felt*.'[43] Through the foregrounding of the dancers' corporeality, *The Tango Lesson* and *Black Swan* give the already-felt of the characters (and the actors!) a visceral presence, that informs how the dancing bodies 'come to mean' in the film and for the spectator.[44] In a way, this begins to address Desmond's concern that 'so few commentators on performativity actually talk about bodily enactment' and her assertion that we 'must keep the palpable presence of dancing, sweating, moving bodies very much alive'– which is precisely what *The Tango Lesson* and *Black Swan* manage to do.[45]

A broadly phenomenological approach therefore enables us to work through a series of pertinent questions: What makes a (movement) style 'queer'? '[W]hat would a category like "gay/lesbian/queer aesthetic" mean?' And, perhaps most crucially, 'How would we know it if we saw it?'[46] Or, as Jennifer DeVere Brody asks: where, 'in reading the [dance] performance [...] does one "mark" queerness *exactly*?'[47] More generally, we might ask what makes a movement style or performance non-heteronormative, non-patriarchal, non-phallocentric or feminist. What I want to foreground here is not the question about how queer (or) feminist styles/aesthetics might be made visible, and recognisable visually, but how they might register, and be recognisable, in embodied, tactile, muscular, kinaesthetic and affective terms. The aim is therefore to pursue a slightly modified version of Desmond's question: How would we know it if we *felt* or *sensed* it?

In this sense, my approach here broadly aligns with Susan Potter's account of the 'kinetic feminine aesthetic' and 'sexual kinaesthetics' articulated through and around the female dancers in Dorothy Arzner's *The Wild Party* (US, 1929).[48] Potter links shifts in dance styles (for women) and larger shifts in socio-cultural understandings of gender (in the 1920s) to the 'moments of intense kinesthetic identification' the film provides for female spectators in particular, a connection that begins to gesture towards what a more fully embodied account of cinema and spectatorship, one that accounts for social, cultural and historically shifting patterns of gendered embodiment and movement, might look (and feel) like.[49]

Turning Tables: Feminist Reorientations in *The Tango Lesson*

Sally Potter's *The Tango Lesson* is a perhaps (too) obvious starting point for this endeavour. Not only is it a film about dance and a female dancer, it is also a film about cinema and a film about a female filmmaker and her filmmaking, which includes a film about dance. It is also a film about women's writing, creativity and artistic expression. And it is a film about feminist film theory.

The Tango Lesson has been the subject of critical inquiry and reflection from a range of different perspectives, including most significantly (for the purposes of this discussion) accounts by Elena del Rio, So Mayer and Kate Ince.[50] What these writers share is a broad concern with feminism, embodiment and affect, albeit for very different reasons and with very different aims in mind. While del Rio moves from a phenomenological towards a Deleuzian frame in her fascinating reading of the affective-performative dimensions of the film, Ince's analysis is centred on aspects of de Beauvoir's phenomenological writing that foreground the situatedness of female embodiment. Mayer employs a broadly auteurist approach and situates *The Tango Lesson* within the broader context of Potter's collaborative feminist filmmaking practices, which she links to the patterns and themes that emerge across Potter's body of work. Drawing variously on Sobchack's and Marks's film phenomenology allows Mayer to include the embodied (living, breathing) viewer in this collaborative film-/meaning-making process and she variously touches upon how Potter's films 'reach out' to the viewer and/or 'pull us in'.

My textural encounter with *The Tango Lesson* takes this line of inquiry into a slightly different, even more corporeally grounded and palpably gritty direction. It adds a viscerally queer twist to these variously embodied/phenomenological/affective accounts in order to provide a more graspable sense of the film's variously troubling and reorientating resonances. A focus on tactility, muscularity and kinesthesis keeps the specific corporeality of the phenomenological body *in*, *of* and *around* the film (various dimensions of which tend to get lost or disappear into the background within existing work) at the very forefront of inquiry. This allows me to account for the specifically embodied spatio-temporal resonances and entanglements that circulate in and around the film – variously twisted, disorientated and backwards as they are.

'Should a feminist dance tango' ... and make a film about it?[51]

'Tango, of all popular dances, would seem to be the most extreme embodiment of traditional notions of gender difference.'[52] Why, then, would a self-proclaimed feminist filmmaker like Potter not only make a film about tango but also play the dancing protagonist in the film? I want to argue that *The Tango Lesson* incorporates the female dancing body in a manner that reorients the (hetero)normative conventions and tendencies of cinema, dance, authorship and their various entanglements. It is through the foregrounding of their material, corporeal dimensions, which enables a graspable reorientation of phenomenological (perceptive and expressive) habits, that *The Tango Lesson* 'dances its way confidently toward a feminist politics rooted in the [body].'[53]

At first glance, however, tango seems to be an odd choice of activity for reclaiming female subjectivity. Tango, as a type of dance, carries very specific associations with heterosexual desire and is based on very traditionally gendered forms of movement. Moreover, 'the appearance of the dancers [...] but also the lyrics of the music, and the codified interactions between dancers in salons (the venues where tango is danced) are all permeated by hyper-heterosexual and old-fashioned meanings of femininity and masculinity.' Tango, therefore, is 'the performance par excellence of gender inequality: feminine subservice and masculine machismo.'[54] Being a 'good' female tango dancer means following, not leading, and becoming the ground on which the male dancer 'figures', the ground on which the figure of the male dancer 'appears'. The masculine subject leads and controls the female object. Tango can be understood as a Butlerian gender performance that 'imitates heteronormativity, calling attention to hierarchical differences between the sexes, literally with every step the dancers take. Women, already immobilised by impractical clothing and uncomfortable stiletto heels, are forced to follow their partner's lead.'[55]

However, what such a feminist critique of the gender politics of tango is unable to grasp, as Kathy Davis notes, are the implications of tango as an 'affective, embodied and lived' practice and the 'embodied, visceral experience of passion' it might enable.[56] A self-confessed tango fanatic *and* feminist, Davis notes the acute jarring between (feminist) politics and (embodied) experience in this context and asserts the need for considering dance as a practice that 'emerges as an *invisible* constellation of sensations, meanings, and actions.'[57] What Potter manages to achieve with *The Tango Lesson* is to make this invisible constellation graspable. One way of accounting for the 'problematic passions' of tango, is via the 'body of the dance' and the 'unique kinaesthetic connection which tango produces where two bodies move in synchrony with the music and which generates a feeling of becoming one.'[58] Notably, the dancing protagonists' 'becoming one' through tango – Sally and Pablo are 'equalized' as the film bears out its 'doppelgänger motif' – is read by Lucy Fischer as an indication of Potter's 'interest in gender fluidity' and in producing 'gender melts'.[59] It is not through abandoning dance, therefore, but through a reshaping of the gendered dimensions underpinning tango's manifestations that *The Tango Lesson* becomes an incarnation of an embodied queer feminist politics.

Rage-*ing against feminist film (theory)*

The Tango Lesson is structured around 12 Lessons (rather than, say, chapters) that are separated by black title screens. The film takes place across three main geographical locations – London, Paris and Buenos Aires (and also a very short sequence that takes place in Hollywood) – all of which have very specific ties and resonances with cinema, tango and feminism. These different geographical locations are tied to different modes of spatiality, temporality, movement and perception – and these take shape as different phenomenological stances on and orientations towards cinema, tango and feminism. Sally's movement between and dwelling in these locations is thus linked to phenomenological shifts and reorientations that are articulated through the protagonist's variously corporeal entanglements with tango and cinema.

The primary focus of the first three Lessons is Sally's attempt to write a script for a film called *Rage*. *Rage* becomes a film-within-a-film, seen as a series of glimpses as Sally pursues her vision of a murder mystery set in the context of the fashion industry. It is a film, as Sally notes in her later conversation with the (unimpressed) Hollywood producers, about 'beauty and the glamorization of death'. It appears loosely structured around a photo shoot that includes a number of female fashion models – Red Model (Morgane Maugran), Yellow Model (Géraldine Maillet) and Blue Model (Katerinea Mechera) – all of whom mysteriously and violently die; a male Fashion Photographer (George Yiasoumi); and a male Fashion Designer who has no legs (David Toole): ingredients that scream psychoanalytic feminist film criticism.[60] However, there is also a sense in which the 'highly stylized postures, costumes, colours and surrounding settings' of *Rage* are so excessive as to be conspicuous and del Rio reads this very convincingly as putting feminist film theory itself 'at an ironic distance and a historical remove.'[61]

Sally's visions of *Rage* appear in colour, while the rest of *The Tango Lesson* is shot in black and white. The film thus embodies a range of (queerly) contradictory temporalities and directionalities. The engagement with an outdated, backwards feminist film (theory) appears in colour, while the move (forward) towards an embodied, corporeal feminist criticism and the entanglements of cinema and tango appear in cinematically anachronistic monochrome – with one important exception, about which, more below.

Sally's turning her back on 'modern' London and the kind of feminist film (criticism) associated with it in order to move *forward*, 'abandoning intellectual abstraction for embodied expression,'[62] is also, and at the same time, a move *back* in time (to Buenos Aires, tango's 'birthplace').[63] Moreover, tango itself, underpinned as it is by old-fashioned gender ideals, constitutes a contradictory embodiment of directionality for the female dancer who is forced 'to follow [her] partner's lead, *dancing backwards*, with their *eyes closed*.'[64] Notably, it is simply walking backwards that Sally, in her first lesson with Pablo, seems unable to do – a point I return to shortly.

This first part of the film, which engages explicitly with questions of female authorship and feminist film (theory), is primarily tied to London and specifically to Sally's apartment, which is where she writes. Sally does travel to Paris (which is where she meets Pablo and also where *Rage* is situated) as well as to Buenos Aires (a journey that resonates rather problematically with notions of the privileged, European tourist wanting get a taste of tango's 'authentic' manifestations in a traditional dance hall)[65] – but London is the (phenomenological) centre of Sally's (and our) world in the first three Lessons. It is where she continually re-turns to. London as a location seems tied to an outdated, 'backwards' feminism, especially the kind of psychoanalytic feminist film criticism that evolved around Mulvey's 'Visual pleasure and narrative cinema' – and I want to trace Sally's frustrated and frustrating encounter with this 'wave' or 'generation' of feminist film (criticism) and the turning away from disembodiment and abstraction that her engagement with tango precipitates.

The Tango Lesson opens with a bodily gesture as Sally wipes the surface of a round table (that fills the entire screen) with a cloth to prepare it for writing. Sally turns the table into a writing table – the kind of writing table that also makes various appearances in Ahmed's *Queer Phenomenology*.[66] The large bright room with big windows is only sparsely furnished and decorated. It contains very few objects, including a dark wooden chair in the corner and a black piano that is partially visible on the left side of the frame. The round writing table and a matching small round stool, as well as the white sheets of paper and a pencil on the table, are the only other objects in the room. The opening scene thus looks much like the one that Ahmed envisages as the primal scene of phenomenology. Her queer concern with the objects *in* and *of* philosophy (tables, chairs, pens and paper) leads her to 'imagine philosophy beginning here, with the pen and the paper, and with the body of the philosopher who writes insofar as he [in this case Husserl] is "at home" and insofar as home provides a space in which he does his work.'[67]

The room is an abstract and empty space with a cold and sterile feel: no clutter, no dust, no unnecessary objects. It is a hard and rigid space of solid

Figure 3.1 Sally's Writing Table (*The Tango Lesson*)

and impenetrable surfaces (the floor, the table, the stool). Sounds, even minimal ones, echo in this space, highlighting its rigidity and bareness. The 'feel' of the space resonates with psychoanalytic film criticism's concern with abstraction and surface. It is a space that seems 'unoccupied' and certainly not 'lived in'. It is a space that does not invite a sense of anyone being 'at home' in it. Ahmed's queer phenomenology of 'feeling at home' (and its relation to 'occupation') is a useful entry point for grasping *The Tango Lesson's* corporeal trajectory, intimately tied as it is to the sense of dis- and reorientation that is grounded in the female dancing body and the perceptual and expressive habits that cohere around it. Throughout, Sally's coming to 'feel at home' is articulated via her 'turning towards' tango, which is linked, in the first part of the film, to an unravelling of Sally's *homeworld* in specifically phenomenological terms. Her London apartment, her *home*, is literally falling apart.

For Ahmed 'feeling at home' is about 'knowing which way we are facing'; it is about 'becoming orientated', which 'involves the disorientation of encountering the world differently.'[68] It is Sally's encounter with tango that precipitates, and is intimately intertwined with, a journey from dis- to reorientation, which, in turn, reorientates our encounter with cinema, feminism and authorship in and through the film. Ahmed notes that spaces 'take the shape of bodies that occupy them' and that 'bodies also take the shape of the spaces they occupy and of the work they do.'[69] In the opening sequence, the writer's (Sally's/Potter's) physical body fits within the space of her apartment and is, at least initially, not out of place – it is all surface, disembodiment, abstraction. Like the space, Sally seems *unoccupied*, even as she attempts to be occupied by her occupation (as a writer/filmmaker). Ahmed notes that we can only be occupied 'when things are orientated'; when bodies extend, and occupy, space comfortably; 'when they are facing the right way.'[70] Sally's body, however, is rigid and tightly controlled, an object amongst others as she sits on the stool, back straight, legs pressed together, knees, ankles and feet touching, upper body, thighs, lower legs and arms all at 90 degree angles as she places her palms on the surface of the table on either side of the impeccably aligned empty sheets of paper, with the pencil also resting at a perfectly straight angle. Sally is preparing to work. Initially, her softly flowing blouse provides the only textural contrast within this space, although it does not manage to counter the sense of the writer's body as tightly contained. The blouse's collar and cuffs are buttoned up and so is Sally. If anything, the blouse, which hangs off Sally's shoulders, emphasises the tininess and seeming frailty of her frame.

The opening part of the narrative is widely understood as a commentary on women's filmmaking and an assertion of female vision, agency and subjectivity.[71] What is less frequently acknowledged, and what I want to bring to the fore here, are the *material* and *embodied* dimensions of the ways in which *The Tango Lesson* articulates a female or feminist 'point of view' (with all the directionality, intentionality and orientation this implies). This requires a rethinking, which I believe the film encourages, of subjectivity and of authorship not necessarily, or not necessarily only, as a particular discursive/enunciative position, voice or (visual) perspective – but also as lived, orientated corporeality.

An extreme close-up of Sally's pencil approaching the finely textured paper makes tangible the wavy grain of the wooden top of the pencil, the gritty coarseness of the graphite, the porous and flaky skin and short, blunt-cut nail of Sally's fingertip. It is precisely the materiality of the writing process that begins to counter the sense of abstraction characterising the space. When the pencil touches the paper, there is a notable pause, followed by a shot of Sally's envisioning of a scene from the film she has set out to write (we see the Red Model running across a patch of grass in a park). It is only then that the pencil moves, at first almost imperceptibly, slightly back towards Sally's body then forwards, hesitantly and with no real sense of direction, before the movement picks up speed and rhythm as the word '*rage*' forms on the paper to the uncomfortably screechy sound of graphite leaving its trace on the fibred surface. We also hear the word '*rage*' spoken by an eerily blurry non-diegetic voice on the soundtrack. This is followed by another shot of the same scene from the yet-to-be-written film, a visualisation of Sally's vision (the running Red Model is shot and collapses), after which we see a dissatisfied and increasingly frustrated Sally crumpling up the sheet of paper and throwing it away, before turning to the next blank sheet of paper to begin the process anew. The foregrounding of writing and its relation to the cinematic image grounds the opening of *The Tango Lesson*, and especially Sally's creation of *Rage*, in what del Rio calls an anachronistic 'representational model' – but it also begins to gesture towards a more corporeal, performative mode by scratching the surface (of representation) and drawing our attention to its textures.[72]

The opening sequence introduces, rather explicitly, questions around a female/feminist point of few, perspective and voice that have been central to feminist concerns around female subjectivity and agency. It also, however, highlights that creating a female or feminist voice or perspective is an endeavour that is far from straightforward. It thus foreshadows Sally's struggle to envisage and create an affirmative cinematic rendering of female subjectivity, agency and desire – one that does not, like *Rage*, remain ultimately tied to the 'male gaze' and cinema's phallocentric psychic underpinnings, even if it is in the shape of critique. Sally eventually turns away from representation and the gaze and towards the corporeality of performance and embodied perception – but this an arduous and convoluted process that is grounded in the body's phenomenological reorientation and the foregrounding of its lived materiality that tango enables.

What is also made graspable, from the outset, is the physically laborious process of writing as well as the complicated mediation between the writer's physical body, her mind (her ideas and her 'vision' of *Rage*) and the process of writing. Rather than asserting a sense of writing as a 'putting on paper' what the writer already has 'in her head', *The Tango Lesson* edges continually closer towards a sense of writing not as a straightforward 'expression' of thought, but as an embodied process, with specifically muscular and kinaesthetic dimensions, that is constitutive of bringing ideas into being. Writing/filmmaking becomes increasingly intertwined with tango throughout the film until they eventually 'become one'.

The phenomenological intertwining of dance, writing and thought provides an embodied articulation of the relationship between thought and movement that Maxine Sheets-Johnstone highlights in *The Primacy of Movement*. Challenging conventional understandings of the primacy of *perception* in phenomenology, she argues that *movement* is in fact constitutive of perception: perception results from movement. And the dancer (especially in the context of improvised dance) provides a 'bare bones example' of 'thinking in movement', a concept which requires the 'non-separation of thinking and doing'.[73] Importantly,

> [t]o say that the dancer is thinking in movement does not mean that the dancer is thinking *by means of* movement or that his/her thoughts are *being transcribed* into movement. To think is first of all to be caught up in a dynamic flow; thinking is itself, by its very nature, kinetic. It moves forward, backward, digressively, quickly, slowly, narrowly, suddenly, hesitantly, blindly, confusedly, penetratingly. What is distinctive about thinking in movement is not that the flow of thought is kinetic; but that the thought itself is. It is motional through and through; at once spatial, temporal, dynamic.[74]

It is precisely through the phenomenological rendering of the female writer's/dancer's/director's subjectivity in a way that unhinges (and queers, in Ahmed's sense) normative habits of movement and perception that *The Tango Lesson* takes shape as a graspably corporeal manifestation of dance and/in cinema – one with variously queer feminist resonances.

Sally's stare out of the window while writing/thinking is an early indication of the ways in which the film articulates a more general sense of 'vision' as 'thoroughly embodied, physical activity' that Ince begins to explore in her feminist phenomenological account.[75] Sally's gaze at Pablo in particular is framed, not as disembodied and objectifying, but as specifically haptic, tactile. When Sally first sees Pablo as he performs on stage in a Parisian theatre, as well as in a later scene in which she watches him dance in his kitchen, close-ups of her face highlight her engaged gaze. Notably, in both scenes Sally's hands are in the frame, cupping her cheeks as she rests her head, asserting the haptic, touching dimensions of her 'apprehension' of Pablo dancing. These are not instantiations of a simple reversal of gendered looking relations or of a return of the male gaze, but manifestations of a different kind of gaze, one that is grounded in the living, thinking, breathing, orientated body. Moreover, during the numerous and increasingly frequent close-ups of Sally's face/gaze, there are moments in which her eyes seem to glaze over as she averts her gaze slightly. They articulate a sense of Sally turning her gaze *inwards*, as it were, in order to see *beyond* the spatio-temporal confines of the objective space she inhabits and to widen her perceptual horizon, as she envisages Pablo in the film about tango that she decides to make after turning her back on *Rage*. The colourful optical visions of *Rage* are gradually replaced by an embodied, gestural 'vision' and mode of filmmaking.

For Ince, there is an early scene in *The Tango Lesson* that highlights this explicitly: when Sally location-scouts for *Rage* in a Parisian park, she 'runs around pacing out the dollies and levels that her camera will need to film the Red Model.'[76] Potter herself describes the making of the scene as follows:

> The scene was snatched as the sun went down at the end of the shooting day [...] We had more or less an hour to do about six set-ups, so we ran from location to location as the shadows got longer. My job as a performer was to look – really look – at the locations in the strange (but to me, natural) way that a director looks at a place: seeing it as it is, and simultaneously, superimposed, seeing it as it could be onscreen. When I saw the rushes I realised, with a shock, that one rarely sees a woman looking out like that on screen. Normally she is dragging the look towards her, as an invitation.[77]

What is perhaps underplayed in this account is the ways in which the ability to imagine and 'see' the film is linked to *being in, moving through* and *experiencing* the physical space in which the scene is supposed to take place. In this sense, *The Tango Lesson* articulates not only a reconfiguration of women's relation to looking and agency by privileging Sally's 'sharp, acquisitive' and desiring gaze that drives the story, but of the ways in which looking and agency are linked to bodily movement and spatiality.[78] Sally envisages scenes from the film and takes photographs with a small camera as she explores and traverses the space, walking down the steps towards the park, running across the grass while ducking to imitate the position of the camera during a low-angle tracking shot, crouching to catch a glimpse through the solid railing of an old stone bridge, before tracing the rough, cold surface of the railing with her hands. The scene foregrounds quite specifically how the creation of (visual) images occurs through a process that is intensely tactile, kinaesthetic and muscular, and thus challenges disembodied understandings not only of vision but of subjectivity and of cinema. This is but one early indication of the ways in which *The Tango Lesson* more generally privileges not only an embodied female gaze, but a particular mode of embodiment that resonates rather profoundly with queer feminist phenomenological concerns around gender.

Dance lessons: spatiality, movement, writing

Sally receives her first tango lesson from Pablo at the beginning of the First Lesson, following the film's prologue (Sally's frustrated attempt to write; initial glimpses of *Rage*; Sally's first encounter with Pablo following his performance at the Parisian theatre; Sally's location scouting). The lesson takes place in Pablo's Parisian apartment and functions to make strange and unfamiliar Sally's habitual modes of embodiment. Walking backwards and even simply walking forwards, on a flat surface, in an upright position, become something that Sally, who confidently moved across the open spaces of the park in the scouting scene just prior, 'can't do' – 'can't do' in the sense of Ahmed's assertion that a feeling of 'I can't' is linked to the bodily experience of 'restriction, uncertainty and blockage,' to 'becoming an object [that] no longer acts or extends' itself, and to the phenomenological experience of losing one's body.[79] Space no longer 'means', and is no longer experienced as, an opportunity for acting and moving as Sally's mode of embodiment comes to resemble the kind 'inhibited intentionality' that Young identifies as normatively 'feminine'.[80] The scene highlights that paying close and self-conscious attention to routine bodily movements is disorientating and puts us off balance. Sally continues to stare downwards, at her own feet, in an apparent attempt to (visually) control her own movement, but this increases her self-consciousness and she stumbles, incapable of putting one foot in front of the other. When Pablo than asks Sally simply to stand and to 'find her centre', she sways and almost falls over backwards. The sense of disorientation and lack of grounding embodied by Sally are augmented by the unfamiliar and chaotically cluttered space that is Pablo's apartment. Body and space do not fit, they are not aligned, making action impossible.[81]

The key resonances of the scene emerge from the foregrounding not only of the gendered dimensions of tango but of the specifically corporeal dimension of those modes of movement and comportment that are so habitual and effortless that they tend not to be experienced *as* bodily. Importantly, it is Sally's palpably corporeal presence within this space that contrasts heavily with the fetishised and abstracted presence of the female characters in her visions of *Rage*. The lack of music and the creaking floorboards that respond to Sally's every move serve as a continual reminder of the body's weight and relation to the ground. They give substance to the disappearance of Sally's relatively confident intentional relation to the surrounding space and the bodies and objects within it. In his discussion of the dancer's '*space of the body*', Jose Gil writes that 'the dancer evolves in a particular space, different from objective space. The dancer does not move *in* space; rather, the dancer secretes, creates space with his [sic] movement.'[82] This means that the dancer, like the gymnast or acrobat, 'prolongs the space that surrounds his [sic] skin' so that 'a new space emerges' in which 'interior and exterior are one and the same.'[83]

Gil's conceptualisation of the 'space of the body' is useful here as it makes central the reciprocal phenomenological relations between body and space. When viewed in the light of queer (and) feminist critiques and the gendered modes of embodiment foregrounded early on in *The Tango Lesson*, however, its universalising (masculine) assumptions become apparent. Gil conceives of the space of the body as a space for action, one in which the body moves without inhibition, without facing obstacles. 'In the space of the body, it is the body that creates its own referents to which all exterior directions must submit themselves.'[84] What surfaces during Sally's first lesson, however, is a different kind of 'space of the body', one that is shaped by the particularities of specifically gendered *pressures*.

Comfortably and unselfconsciously inhabiting the space of the body means that the body is capable of intentional, purposeful action; it means that the body is orientated – and to become orientated is to assert the space of the body. Ahmed reminds us that '[i]f orientation is about making the strange familiar through the extension of bodies into space, then disorientation occurs when that extension fails.'[85] Sally's disorientation occurs precisely because she fails to extend the space in Pablo's apartment, a space that is clearly marked and shaped by his presence and occupation. The visceral and tactile register of the sequence makes graspable the kinaesthesis of a failed extension of space, as well as of the ways in which '[s]paces "impress" on the body, involving the mark of unfamiliar impressions, which in turn reshape the body.'[86] The kinaesthetic and muscular trajectory of *The Tango Lesson* takes Sally through a journey of embodied reorientation through which different objects and bodies appear within her bodily horizon – and we are invited to encounter, and make contact, with the shifting modes of embodiment that take shape through and around Sally.

After the first lesson, Sally returns to her apartment in London to write. She sharpens a pencil in preparation and proceeds to sit in the same spot assuming the same rigid posture – but this time, she writes more fluently. The disorientation and lack of balance experienced during the first lesson seem to find their way into her script. The scene she writes, articulated yet again through her colourful visualisation of *Rage*, shows the Yellow Model losing her balance, slipping and tumbling down the set of concrete steps in the park and to her death. When Sally is stuck (in her writing) – when she is lost, and does not know which way to turn – she gets up and starts walking around the table in a clockwise direction before turning around and walking towards the window, where she stops and stares into the distance. This is followed by a cut to another scene from *Rage* (this time the Blue Model and the Red Model preparing for a photo shoot on a small boat on a lake in the park). The relations between the writer's vision and bodily movement are further developed and 'worked out' in this scene, articulating a notion of embodied 'vision' – 'vision' both in the sense of looking/seeing and in the sense of imagining the future, in this case the future of a film. The writer's subjectivity is thus more fully 'fleshed out', given both spatial and temporal substance. Writing becomes an increasingly dynamic activity, and when Sally is stuck/lost once more in a later scene (following her visualisation of the Blue Model's murder), she stands up and, rather gingerly, begins to walk forwards, then backwards, several times, repeating the very basic dance steps from her first lesson with Pablo, linking the dance even more directly with her creative activity as a writer/filmmaker. Sally's dance movements can thus be read, and felt, as an explicit attempt to widen her bodily and perceptual horizon and to bring new ideas/thoughts 'into view'.

Sally then steps out of her comfort zone (her writing room) and visits a dance hall in London (the Second Lesson), where she has a brief and awkward dance encounter with a heavyset older man. The experience seems to nonetheless inspire her as she returns to her apartment to write. This sequence is significant because we see the writing table from a different perspective for the very first time. It is the same table, in the same spot, yet our changed point of view, means that we experience it differently. What was previously in the background, behind the camera, is now in front: another small desk covered with books and writing utensils, a stool, a wastebasket, an electricity cable. Dancing is linked quite literally to a sense of reorientation here, to a turning around that brings different objects into view. Sally continues to face the same direction, but Sally's shifting 'perspective' and the widening of her 'horizon' manifest

Figure 3.2 Dancing Reorientations (*The Tango Lesson*)

themselves in graspably sensuous terms. The change in vantage point also functions to remind us of how quickly a particular perspective – in this case the frequently occurring, slightly high-angled long-shot of Sally at her writing table positioned in front of the window – can become so familiar as to appear universal and go unnoticed as a *particular* orientation towards the world. The shift efficiently dramatises how, depending on our 'zero point of orientation,' different worlds come into view. Crucially, it is dancing that instigates the widening of Sally's perceptual and experiential horizon: 'Extending into space also extends what is "just about" familiar or what is "just about" within reach.'[87] We might therefore think of both dance and cinema as orientation devices that, in their own distinctive ways, can bring certain things 'into view' and into the realms of the familiar – and it is precisely the reorientating capacities of dance and/in cinema that *The Tango Lesson's* phenomenological trajectory makes graspable.

Sally's vision of *Rage* – that tends to be brought into view via Sally's gaze – has a complex temporality that is intricately entangled with the multifaceted spatiality already touched upon. We often see her looking, but we do not know what she is looking 'at'. The object of Sally's vision (what she is facing, what is 'in front' of her and within her horizon; what her gaze is intended and directed towards) is the film she is occupied with and intends to bring into being. Sally's 'vision' is thus marked by a conventional spatiality, even when its object is not (primordially) 'present' within the physical space of the diegetic world. The normative orientation of vision, like movement, is ahead, *straight* ahead even, and towards what is 'in front'. It is directed towards the field of potential action that takes shape depending on which way we 'face'.[88] The temporality of 'vision' – of 'looking forward' or 'looking ahead' – is therefore future-orientated and connotes a range of positive values, linked as it is to trajectories of development, progress and (re)production (in Western, heteronormative, neoliberal contexts).

However, there is a sense in which Sally's vision of/in *Rage* faces the 'wrong' direction. *Rage* is looking back to an outdated feminist film theory, one concerned with psychoanalytic conceptions of desire, fetishism, voyeurism and castration anxiety.[89] The film-within-the-film figures 'as a stage of anachronistic abstraction that must be overcome in the interests of feminism's becoming' – and *The Tango Lesson* itself, as I have noted, articulates a transformation, or reorientation, from the backwards anger and frustrations of *Rage* to the embodied, sensuous coming into being of itself. In what follows, I build on del Rio's reading of the film as 'tak[ing] feminism's process of becoming as the organizing principle of its narrative structure and self-affective performativity,' while also moving the argument in a slightly different, specifically phenomenological direction.[90] I bring to the front the increasingly sticky entanglements of bodies, space and time – especially in terms of how they materialise and are given substance in and through dance – in order to make graspable how *The Tango Lesson* takes shape as, and gives shape to, a phenomenological reorientation with queer feminist resonances.

Going round in circles and opening up new ground

When the final model in *Rage* is shot, Sally is stuck once more. Her angry feminist vision does not have anywhere to go. She gets up again and begins to walk around in the room, pacing back and forth next to the table, both hands stuffed into her trouser pockets. She engages in the kind of 'going around in circles' that Sobchack suggests is linked to 'being lost' and to 'not going anywhere.'[91] It is a movement that is *pointless*: it does not have a point, both in the sense of not producing a valuable outcome and in the sense of not having a goal or aim, a point in the distance/future that it is directed towards. Its spatiality and temporality are redundant. For Sobchack, the 'shape' of this type of 'being lost' is 'round' – just like Sally's writing table.[92] (We also might note here Ahmed's reference to Deleuze and Guattari's evocation of the *round* table as a '*non*philosophical' table, one that people gather around, for roundtable discussions, rather than one that philosophy is written upon).[93] When we 'go around in circles' we are disorientated because, even though we might know where we are, we do not know where we are going. We are moving, yet stuck.

Sally breaks this vicious circularity when she changes direction and begins to walk *backwards*. From staring into the distance, her gaze returns to her own body, her own feet, as she begins to integrate basic tango steps into her movement. Her walking, almost imperceptibly, 'turns into' dance and thus acquires a 'point'. Dancing is, again, linked to a sense of reorientation, quite literally in this case, through a shift from the normative directionality of forward, albeit circular, movement, to a backwards movement in which the direction of movement is not aligned with the directionality of the body and the way it faces. Sally steps backwards (spatially) in order to move forward (theoretically, cinematically and politically). Breaking with normative habits opens up a new perspective on what is taken as familiar. For Ahmed, a queer phenomenology 'might be one that faces the back, which looks "behind" phenomenology' and the 'things' it is occupied with – for instance, tables. The writing table functions as an 'orientation device' in phenomenological writing – just as it initially functions as an orientation device for Sally's writing – and 'might reveal something about the "orientation" of phenomenology' – just as it might reveal something about the orientation of feminism and/in cinema.[94]

Ahmed's consideration of the significance of the writing table as the 'what' that phenomenology is written upon resonates with Sally's preoccupation with and tending towards her writing table.

> Even if it is not surprising that the object on which writing happens appears in writing, we might also point to how such writing turns its back on the table [...] Despite how the table matters it often disappears from view, as an object 'from' which to think and toward which we direct our attention.

This is why part of Ahmed's queer phenomenological project is concerned with 'bring[ing] the table to "the front" of the writing [...] By bringing what its "behind" to the front, we might queer phenomenology by creating a new angle.'[95]

In *The Tango Lesson*, the table comes to the front. In fact, it is there from the very beginning, when our point of entry into the film is via the gestures of the (domestic) labour that keep the table clear (Sally wiping the table). Rather than facilitating writing, however, the table gets in the way precisely because it comes to the fore, most poignantly when Sally becomes pre*occupied* with a mark on the table surface. The obsessive habit of cleaning/clearing the table is a failed attempt to create a neutral, clean slate, a *tabula rasa* from which to write and to forge a productive alignment between writer and table by relegating it to the background. Sally faces the table but the compulsive straightening of the paper, the pencil and the body means the alignment appears forced, calculated and fake. Her initially self-consciously rigid and self-referential comportment means that her intention to write does not sit comfortably with her bodily intentionality, characterised as it is by the alienating subject-object tension Young identifies as typical of feminine modes of embodiment.[96] There is a misalignment between Sally, the writing table and her writing tools – as well as between her 'progressive' feminist intentions and her 'backwards' theoretical orientations.

The foregrounding of what should be in the background (the table, the paper) constitutes a disruptive distortion of normative perceptual habits, of what is, or should be, familiar. Certain things are, and need to remain, in the background in order for focused, intentional action to take place. As Ahmed notes:

> The figure 'figures' insofar as the background both is and is not in view. We single out this object only by pushing other objects to the edges or 'fringes' of vision [...] inhabiting the familiar makes 'things' into backgrounds for action: they are there, but they are there in such away that I don't see them.[97]

Ahmed also writes that 'some things are relegated to the background in order to sustain a certain direction; in other words, in order to keep attention on what is faced. Perception involves such acts of relegation that are forgotten in the very preoccupation with what it is that is faced.'[98] Sally faces the table, paper and pencil in order to write, but her tools refuse to be relegated to the background and therefore attract her, and our, attention. The various close-ups of pencil and paper make graspable their patterned and textured materiality, pointing to the 'histories of their arrival.'[99] Crucially, Ahmed links the materiality of writing, and of the writer, and its disappearance within phenomenological writing to phenomenology's *gendered* orientation:

> The disappearance of familiar objects [the table, the paper], might make more than the object disappear. The writer who

does the work of philosophy might disappear, if we are to erase the sign of 'where' it is that he works. Feminist philosophers have shown us how the masculinity of philosophy is evidenced in the disappearance of the subject under the sign of the universal (Bordo 1987; Irigaray 1974; Braidotti 1991). The masculinity might also be evident in the *disappearance of the materiality of objects*, in the bracketing of the materials of out which, as well as upon which, philosophy writes itself, as a way of apprehending the world.[100]

In *The Tango Lesson*, the reappearance of the materials 'out of' which and 'upon' which writing takes place is crucial to the film's assertion of Sally's embodied subjectivity and vision. These materials include paper, pencil and the writing table – but they also, and perhaps most centrally, include the materiality of the body that makes writing, thinking and envisioning possible. It is through dance that the meaning-making capacities of the body are most tangibly tied to the writing and filmmaking process, before they gradually replace/incorporate it.

The most poignant example of how dance brings the background to the fore, in all its materiality, is when the reorientation and shift in perception that accompany Sally's shift from walking to dancing in the previously described sequence, lead Sally to notice an almost imperceptible crack in the wooden floor next to the table. The crack comes into view and its appearance leads to the dismantling and disintegration of the ground upon which Sally has been writing and dancing. It leads to a questioning not only of the tools (table, paper, pencil) on which philosophy (and cinema) is written, but of the ground on which these tools gather. When a builder (Heathcote Williams) appears and noisily removes one of the floorboards, the murky, dusty and grubby interiority of the ground – that which was previously out of sight, even as it constituted the ground that grounded Sally – comes to the front. The builder's rough and careless presence and handling of tools, the loud cracking sounds of metal splicing the wood, and the thumping sounds of the wooden plank thrown against the leg of the table and then bouncing off the floor, make Sally flinch. The bareness of the room means that the cracking, splicing and thumping sounds echo loudly and have a startling effect (on Sally), imbuing the unravelling of the ground with a palpably visceral dimension.

We might say that, phenomenologically, this scene, and the disintegration of Sally's home/world that it instigates, takes shape as a cinematic rendering of Ahmed's sense of disorientation:

> Moments of disorientation are vital. They are bodily experiences that throw the world up, or throw the body from its ground. Disorientation as a bodily feeling can be unsettling, and it can shatter one's sense of confidence in the ground or one's belief that the ground on which we reside can support the actions that make a life feel livable. Such a feeling of shattering, or being shattered, might persist and become a crisis. Or the feeling itself might pass as the ground returns or as we return to the ground. The body might be reoriented if the hand that reaches out finds something to steady an action.[101]

It might be tempting here to suggest that Sally's hand reaches out and finds in Pablo's a steadying presence that leads her onto new, safe and solid ground. However, it is tango itself, as a sensuously corporeal practice, that provides Sally with the means of reorienting herself – but this is not in any way a straightforward process and involves 'hard work'.[102]

The shattering of old ground opens up new ground (for perception and thought) because the damage to the floor means that Sally needs to leave her apartment in order for repairs to be carried out – so she travels to Buenos Aires to dance. She only returns to her apartment once more to write after this, when the Hollywood producers want to see a script for *Rage*. In this later scene, we see Sally sitting on a small island of safe ground, a patch of floorboards that provides just enough space for her table and stool. The remainder of the apartment is a skeleton as the floor has been stripped back, the wooden supporting beams providing the only safe ground to walk on. The apartment is a mess, a chaotically cluttered space, with floorboards strewn across the beams, leaning against the walls and the exposed dirt covering the interior surfaces with a layer of dust. It bears no resemblance whatsoever to the minimalist and ordered space it once was. The skeletal, bare-bones state of the writing room is highlighted most poignantly through a shot from outside and through the grid of the stained glass window that breaks up the muddled space even further. The framing gives the image a textured feel and highlights the tangibility and materiality of the space.

Nonetheless, the chaos (including the clutter on the writing table) seems to disappear into the background of Sally's perceptual field. Her intentional and purposeful occupation with the paper and pencil provides a palpable sense of how dance has begun to reorientate Sally's relations to filmmaking. Sally is purposefully engaged with the pencil and paper, and with *Rage*, as she writes fluently and without the previous hesitation. The sequence ends with Sally's final vision of rage (the Red Model is shot) and the violent impact of the shot (the Red Model collapsing) coinciding with part of the ceiling collapsing onto Sally's table. The disintegration of this previously familiar space, and the perceptual and kinaesthetic habits it has provided the ground for, continues – and this is the last time in the film we see Sally in her London apartment. It is also the last time we see her write. She abandons *Rage* and turns her attention to another film, 'something more personal… maybe something about tango.' The Third Lesson ends with Sally's turning away from London, *Rage* and the abstracted body of psychoanalytic feminist film theory.

It takes two to tango: 'working out' gender relations

After the collapse of the ceiling, *Rage* and the outdated, abstracted and disembodied feminist film theory it arguably stands for disappear from view and the corporeal relations between filmmaking and dance are more directly incorporated into *The Tango Lesson* itself. It becomes a film about its own becoming and about its turning away from backwards feminist concerns (about film) that cannot be represented in any straightforward manner. Especially in the final segment of the film that takes place in Buenos Aires (Lessons Ten, Eleven and Twelve), the feminist struggles that are initially played out in relation to the making of *Rage* are fleshed out even more directly. The materiality and meaning-making capacities of the body are made graspable, without the filmmaker's 'vision' being rendered explicitly *visible*. *The Tango Lesson* itself begins to take shape as the incarnation of Sally's/Potter's embodied vision, which emerges and is increasingly inseparable from the ways in which dancing shapes and reorientates the body.

However, this eventually seemingly seamless entanglement of tango and cinema does not materialise until the gender relations intrinsic to tango are worked out and worked though in the middle section (Lessons Four to Nine), which takes place in Paris, the 'city of love'. This is also the section that contains the most explicit references to the musical, especially with regard to the working out of binary oppositions (and the narrative conflicts they create) in the musical numbers. In Paris, the dance sequences are intertwined with Sally's and Pablo's developing romance. Neither character is 'at home' in Paris, so, arguably, they encounter each other on neutral ground. However, as cinema and filmmaking disappear into the background and tango becomes the central narrative concern, it is Pablo, the tanguero who wants to be in a film, who takes the lead, while Sally, the filmmaker who wants to learn how to dance tango, follows. This relationship is reversed in the final part of the film, when filmmaking comes to the fore yet again, albeit in more intricately embodied terms than in *The Tango Lesson*'s opening.

There are some rather clichéd uses of dance in this middle section. It draws on well-worn associations of dance with heterosexual romance and the ways in which desire, jealously, rivalry, competition and compatibility are articulated and worked out through dance performances. The gendered dimensions of tango in particular are played upon and are the source for fairly conventional portrayals of romance and heterosexual (in)compatibility as well as conflict. When Sally and Pablo move smoothly, unselfconsciously and in spontaneous harmony (especially in musical-esque sequences), this functions to develop their relationship, which is posited to be about romance as much as it is about professional, artistic, ethical and spiritual compatibility. Similarly, Pablo's sensual dancing with his former partner, as well as Sally's repeated, ostensibly enjoyable dance encounters with a particular dance partner in the Buenos Aires dance hall, precipitate moments of jealously, conflict and tension that variously extend into the narrative.

That said, the dance sequences embody a range of different narrative functions, aesthetic/formal styles and affective registers, and range from social dance and staged dance performances to utopian musical numbers. Variously they take place with diegetic music, non-diegetic music, or with no music at all. The extent to which the physicality of the dancing body is foregrounded therefore varies. For instance, the utopian register of the musical numbers that exhibit abundance, energy, intensity and excitement while glossing over (bodily) labour distances the spectator from the corporeality and effort of dance[103] – although these numbers are not 'impossible' in *The Tango Lesson* and characterised by the kind of 'realistic plot motivation' that distinguishes the dance film from the musical.[104]

The most utopian musical-esque numbers include Sally's and Pablo's dancing along the mist-laden banks of the Seine by night to a joyously playful extra-diegetic score, with big, fluffy snowflakes beginning to fall at the end. The sequence, reminiscent of *An American in Paris* (Gene Kelly, US, 1951), articulates their blossoming romance – Pablo 'bursts into dance', a short solo performance, immediately after announcing that he has separated from his previous (dance and romantic) partner. He then notes that he 'always wanted to be in films' before continuing to dance, this time with Sally, along the misty Seine, with light romantically reflecting off the dark, shimmering surface of the river. The utopian number is thus framed by a self-reflexive reference to Verón's presence as, essentially, himself, in the film, and thus to (the making of) *The Tango Lesson* itself. This is indicative of a more general pattern that ties dance numbers both to romance and to a self-conscious reflexivity about (dance in) cinema. For instance, it is when Sally announces that she is going to abandon *Rage* for a film about tango that Pablo spontaneously turns his cooking preparations into a performance, using various kitchen utensils as props. Similarly, when Sally and Pablo rekindle their connection after the fallout following the staged performance, their arrival in Argentina (Lesson Ten) is marked by a joyous dance in the pouring rain in the cobbled streets of Buenos Aires – a clear nod to *Singin' in the Rain* (Stanley Donen, US, 1952).

The central and most viscerally affecting tensions between Sally and Pablo surface in relation to the only staged performance in the film (with the exception of Pablo's performance in the opening part where Sally first 'lays eyes' on him) as well as the rehearsals leading up to it (Lesson Nine). This also functions as the most ostensible critique of heteronormative gender relations and their heightened manifestations in tango. The bone of contention, for Pablo, is Sally's inability to follow (him), and the dancers' incompatibility is articulated in specifically kinaesthetic and muscular terms. The majority of the social dance scenes (before, after and in between the rehearsals) are characterised by expansive, smooth and circular camera movements that invite kinaesthetic empathy with the harmonious movement of the dancers, while returning to Sally's face to link the kinaesthetic register specifically to her sensuous and enjoyable kinaesthetic experience. Sally dances unselfconsciously, immersed in her own movement, without experiencing the subject-object tensions characteristic of conventionally feminine modes of embodiment. Even in the crowded hall, with her dance partners' and other bodies in close proximity, Sally inhabits the space of the body comfortably; she extends space with purposeful intention. The male-female couple moves 'as one', an embodied articulation of the blossoming romance.

In the Fourth Lesson, for instance, there is an almost seamless transition (via a tracking shot) from the couple's sensuous dancing in the private and intimate space of Pablo's apartment to their public display of intimate sensuality in a Parisian tango salon. The dance is posited as spontaneously unfolding in the world of the film in this sequence, but manifests itself as a spectacularly staged (for the cinematic spectator) performance that conveys a graspably sensuous and riveting intensity. The sequence is marked by an oscillation between static long-shots that frame the dancers and their movement within the stunningly decorated space of the salon in tableau-like fashion, and close-ups and medium shots of their faces in close proximity, their gazes intertwined, and of their legs and feet entangled in a sensuously energetic flurry of movement. It is this dance sequence in particular that marks the beginning of Sally's and Pablo's romantic relationship – and it is immediately followed by the magically utopian dance along the Seine described above.

In the rehearsal scenes for the staged performance, on the other hand, unaccompanied by music with only the sounds of shoes on the wooden floor and the ruffling of fabric echoing in the bare room, movement is posited, for the first time since Sally's first lesson with Pablo, as inhibitingly self-conscious. The editing – jarring, including jump cuts; without rhythm, not in sync with the dancer's movements – provides a tangible articulation of the dancers' incompatibility. They clash, both physically and figuratively, because of Sally's inability to fulfil the gendered expectation of her dancing role: to follow, and not to lead. Pablo talks throughout, commenting on and criticising Sally's composure and her inability to 'let go',

Queer Encounters with Feminist Politics

to 'stop thinking', to exhibit 'less tension', to 'do less', and to stop 'blocking', 'leaning', 'doing too much' and using 'too much force'. He interrupts dance movements in order to repeat them, often several times, breaking down the coherent whole of the choreography into small, disjointed parts. He appears to drag Sally around, almost violently throwing her in the air.

Figure 3.3 Gendered Tension (*The Tango Lesson*)

Sally's body becomes an object and appears to be experienced as such. The framing aligns the spectator with Sally's kinaesthetic experience of being out of sync and not in control of her body, rather than with Pablo's frustrations. Sally's face (like her body) is tense and exhibits startled expressions when Pablo pushes and pulls her around in ways she fails to anticipate and thus experiences as jarring and abrupt, despite her best 'intentions'. She embodies a temporality that is both 'too early' (when she tries to anticipate movements that do not align with Pablo's intentions) and 'too late' (when she fails to follow). In the second rehearsal scene in particular, Sally's strong but delicate physicality is also most explicitly exposed. It gives shape to the viscerally corporeal dimension of Sally's being both 'out of time' and 'out of place'.[105]

When Sally and Pablo walk from their dressing room to the stage just before the actual performance, the sense of being unable to follow, of being (almost) left behind, is conveyed with muscular and kinaesthetic intensity.

As Pablo rushes through the labyrinth of narrow hallways and staircases, Sally can barely keep up – and neither can the camera. Its shaky, unsteady movements appear to always be a 'step behind', conveying a sense of what it feels like, in a phenomenological sense, to 'barely hang on', conjuring the muscular implications of what Barker calls the cinematic 'chase'.[106] During the performance itself, the tension between the dancers is palpable, their movements rigid and overly controlled. Close-ups of Pablo's angry, and Sally's tense and worried, faces augment the tension, while the bright back-lighting (through the framing of the majority of the performance from the back of the stage) illuminates the distance between the dancers' bodies in spectacular fashion.

It is thus only in those dance sequences that are explicitly posited as choreographed *in* the film (the seemingly improvised performances are of course scripted as well) that the heteronormatively gendered underpinnings of tango are explicitly challenged. This critique is eventually replaced by a more affirmative stance as Sally's embodiment of a reorientated and grounded, yet relational, subjectivity, takes shape in, and shapes, the final section of the film, where dancing, filmmaking and Sally's vision are most intricately intertwined. This is most tangibly articulated in relation to the spontaneous and improvised dancing towards the end of the film that involves Sally, Pablo and two additional male tangueros in various constellations and formations that Davis might refer to as 'queer tango'.[107]

Queer tango: embodied performances of dance, feminism and cinema

Erin Manning's exploration of 'relational movement' in tango provides a useful framework for making graspable the affective implications of these later dance sequences and the kinaesthetic and muscular points of contact they provide. It undermines common-sense assumptions about the leading/active–following/passive binary of tango and its gendered implications:

> We walk. I am leading, but that doesn't mean I am deciding. Leading is more like initiating and opening, entering the gap, and then waiting to follow her response. How she follows, with what intensity she creates the space, will influence how our bodies move together. I am not moving her, nor is she simply

responding to me: we are beginning to move relationally, creating an interval that we move together. The more we connect to this becoming-movement, the more palpable the interval becomes. We begin to feel the relation.[108]

The description resonates profoundly with the ways in which the kinaesthetic and muscular implications of the 'feeling of the relation' become palpable in *The Tango Lesson*. 'Relational movement means moving the relation [and not] the person,' the latter being what Pablo attempts to do during the rehearsals and staged performance.[109] Manning's account of what happens when we attempt to move the body is an uncannily apt description of these sequences: 'When we begin by moving her body, what we feel is resistance. The movement becomes a series of steps that we fall into, always a little too early or a little too late, our balance in disequilibrium, pulling and pushing.'[110] Relational movement, on the other hand, of the kind displayed during spontaneous and improvised dancing in *The Tango Lesson*:

> pushes and pulls in a different way, in a togetherness [...] that moves through a single intensive equilibrium that is always more than stable: meta-stable. This doesn't mean that we never lose balance. It means that balance can no longer be lost or gained because what is at stake is not a tangent but a curve. There is no stable axis around which we can move. We curve together, creating a folding interval out of which our moving bodies take form.[111]

The sweeping, encircling camera movements and the close-ups of entangled yet swiftly moving legs and feet during the social dance sequences in particular engage the spectator in the rationality of movement, while Sally's pleasurably kinaesthetic sensings of the movement relation remain our 'zero point of orientation, the point from which the world unfolds,' especially as we continue to return to her face, gaze and embodied 'vision'.[112]

The 'embrace', which tends to confine the female dancer to 'a small space', becomes the site of a reciprocal 'kinaesthetic connection'.[113] It provides what Davis calls a 'liminal space', one that is 'outside everyday life' and that 'can feel extremely uncomfortable or perfectly *at home*'[114] – and

The Tango Lesson's corporeal trajectory allows us to encounter, and accompany, the gripping move from jarring, tension and disconnect to mutuality and alignment; from feeling 'out of place' to feeling 'at home'.

There are a few moments in this final segment in which *The Tango Lesson* exhibits an overt and perhaps excessive self-consciousness about its own becoming. For instance, in a conversation about Sally's new film Pablo asks how many 'dance numbers' he will have in the film, to which Sally responds that there will be a story too. This is followed by Pablo's concern about his acting skills and whether he would need to take acting lessons, especially for his voice since there will be not only dancing but dialogue (keeping in mind that Pablo Verón, the actor who plays Pablo, is a dancer by trade rather than an actor). The conversation thus draws attention both to the doubly performative nature of dancing on film as well as the different skills involved in each type of performance, further blurring the distinctions between the characters (Sally and Pablo) and actors/artists/performers (Potter and Verón).

The conversation then takes a more serious turn when Pablo accuses Sally of not having taught him anything, whereas he has taught her how to dance tango. Sally then asks Pablo to imagine a scene involving a specific dialogue that has, in fact, taken place between Sally and Pablo earlier in the film. Pablo replies that maybe he does not want to be involved in this kind of scene, which prompts Sally to say that maybe she does not want him in her film anyway:

> because of course I haven't been doing anything this last year, I haven't been watching you, preparing you, creating a role for you in my head; I haven't been loving you as a director and as a woman. No, I have done almost nothing, except follow… but it doesn't suit me to follow, you see, it suits me to lead. And you can't deal with that!

In addition to challenging the conventionally gendered patterns of leading and following, the monologue verbalises the sense of filmmaking as intimately embodied, which is also fleshed out in the final part of the film. There is a further conversation between Sally and Pablo that takes place in an abandoned hair salon and asserts the sense of filmmaking as a corporeal endeavour. Sally and Pablo both face one of the big mirrors in the salon – they look at each other via the mirror – when Pablo asks: 'Are you looking at me? What do you see, Sally?' Sally responds: 'I see you on the screen.' For Pablo, this is disconcerting: 'Then you are not here with me. You have become a camera.' The dialogue gestures towards the phenomenological *likeness* of camera, film and filmmaker and the similar expressive and perceptual habits they embody – while simultaneously asserting the proximal-yet-distant relations the filmmaking process creates and that surface via *The Tango Lesson*'s complex and convoluted spatio-temporal resonances throughout.

The entanglement of dance and film(making), is most explicitly 'voiced' in these moments, but it is also most explicitly incorporated into the textures of the film in this final segment (Lessons Ten, Eleven and Twelve). While, on the whole, this affective, corporeal shift takes place incrementally throughout the film, there is a short scene at the beginning of Lesson Ten that constitutes a kind of textural marker: the underwater scene at the fountain that follow's Sally's and Pablo's reconciliation after the fallout from the staged performance. The encounter has various religious/mystical connotations, as Sally and Pablo first appear to baptise each other with water from the fountain, before Sally lowers her head into the water. This precipitates a dreamlike underwater shot, seemingly from Sally's perspective, of a clothed Pablo swimming towards the camera, with the hazy liquidity of the water shimmering in a blue-ish red light. While the move to colour might take us back to Sally's earlier imaginations of *Rage*, her 'vision' takes on a specifically haptic/tactile quality here: the textured materiality of the water touches, and connects, eyes and bodies and adds a palpable sense of substance to the (cinematic) space. Mayer also notes the 'heartbeat pulsing on the score', which augments an overall sense of interiority; of an embodied, sensuous 'vision'; of expression/perception as carnal.[115] In this sense, the moment constitutes a 'point of no re-turn' as it marks the coming into being of Sally's film about tango.

Sally is not yet sure exactly what kind of film she wants to make, but she is 'in the middle of working it out' – and this 'working out' takes place directly through dance from here on. For instance, in a scene involving Sally, Pablo and two other male dancers in a small dance studio, the dancers improvise and experiment with new steps and movement combinations. They hesitate, pause, speed up, repeat, slow down, discuss. Sally first participates and then steps back to watch the men. Again, the camera lingers on her gaze as it shifts from a look that engages and is clearly focused on the dancers (who we see from Sally's perspective), to one that is orientated both towards interiority and towards the future. This shift is indicated by a slight turn of Sally's head as her eyes glaze over. Her gaze is not directed towards anything that exists in the objective physical space that she occupies together with the male dancers. Instead, the shift in her gaze signals a shift in Sally's bodily, perceptual horizon and the possibilities that are now 'within reach'. Sally's reorientation, as she 'turns towards' and 'faces' her new film, is signalled not only by a tangible shift in what her gaze is directed and intended towards, but also by the fade-out of the diegetic sounds (the men dancing) and fade-in of a soothing yet eerie score that resembles the soundscape that accompanies Sally's explicit visualisations of *Rage* in the opening segment.

The same score also reappears at the beginning of the final dance sequence, the most spectacular and kinetically riveting performance in the film. However, Sally's gaze does not wander this time, but directly engages Pablo and the two male dancers, before she gets up and participates in the dance, which is posited, in a musical-esque manner, as entirely improvised. Sally incorporates herself directly into her own film, becoming part of her own embodied vision. *The Tango Lesson* gives shape to its own becoming in this sequence as the bodies of the dancer, the dance, the actor, the film and the filmmaker are most intimately intertwined and, arguably, 'become one'. This is possible because Potter, like Sally, 'relinquishes a representational for a performative method, thus augmenting her own capacity to act.'[116]

It is particularly notable that the affirmative entanglement of dance, cinema and feminism in this performance (as well as other dance sequences towards the end of the film) 'opens up' the unit of the male-female couple. As del Rio notes, 'Potter displays an ability to transform the dual-partnered structure of the dance and its reliance on a hierarchical gender dynamics into a multiple-partnered dance that rewrites binary relations between male and female as a playful dynamics of uncontainable difference.'[117] Importantly, Sally's dancing with three male partners in this sequence, in which her body is, at times, transferred between the men, 'does not register as an act of homosocial exchange. Instead, her own body

Queer Encounters with Feminist Politics

becomes the active force that lends the performance its sense of plurality and playfulness' – a playfulness that is *grounded* in the corporeality of the dancers and the film.[118] What the performance brings into being is a sense of 'queer tango' if we consider it, following Davis, 'as a rapidly emerging dance culture and as transgressive feminist ideal [that] not only "denaturalises gender, but "de-genders" tango.'[119] The queering of tango might involve non-gender-specific clothing (which Sally sports on various occasions throughout the film) or women's refusal to wait to be asked to dance and/or to follow. Tango is queered most 'radically', however, 'when the gendered binary between leader and follow is disbanded altogether.'[120] As the four dancing bodies move across and through the grand, abandoned space, the boundaries between leading and following are clearly blurred. What 'appears' instead is a graspable sense of the kinetic energy and intentionality of the 'body of the dance,' grounded as it is in Sally's/Potter's mode of embodiment.

The Tango Lesson thus manages to put the female body at the centre – not the to-be-looked-at body, but a phenomenological body, one that embodies subjectivity, interiority and a complex and multi-layered spatiality and temporality. It also constitutes a corporeal space in which feminism and cinema encounter each other. Tango, cinema and feminism mutually reorientate each other in and through the various bodies and

Figure 3.4 Queer Tango (*The Tango Lesson*)

modes of embodiment that amalgamate in the performative incarnation of a queerly corporeal feminism that is *The Tango Lesson*. And the film's sensuously affective register brings us into touching distance of the variously gripping encounters that take shape throughout.

Out of Your Skin, Out of Your Mind: Unnervingly Visceral Encounters with the Dancing Body in *Black Swan*

While *The Tango Lesson* counters the (cinematic) objectification of the female body and gives corporeal substance to the unity of body and mind, *Black Swan* tears that unity apart. *Black Swan* is much more kinaesthetically energetic and dazzling than *The Tango Lesson*. It is also more viscerally intriguing, captivating and, arguably, disturbing as we are asked to '*innerly accompany*' the dancer, Nina, and her disturbed and disturbing (by the standards of normative perceptual habits) relations to the world, in an uncomfortably visceral proximity.[121] The sensory register of *Black Swan* is both exhilaratingly kinetic and unnervingly tactile, a combination that draws us seductively – violently even – into the dancer's disintegrating world. Nina's body is at the core of both the film's dazzlingly kinetic and muscular energy and of its visceral and eerily repulsive tactile register.

While Sally dismantles the gender hierarchies that underpin normative incarnations of tango in *The Tango Lesson*, Nina crumbles under the heteropatriarchal pressures that weigh on the female body in the ballet context. Feminist critics have highlighted in some detail, and from a range of different theoretical perspectives, the ways in which patriarchal gender relations and hierarchies are reconstituted in ballet.[122] While both male and female bodies are 'on display' and exposed to the spectators' gaze during staged performances, the different kinds of movements executed by male and female dancers, and the different bodily shapes, physiques and capabilities required to do so, tend to reinforce heteronormative (active-passive, subject-object) binaries. These relations also extend beyond the stage where the more general bodily demands and economies of looking within the ballet context foster an alienated subjectivity in the female dancer that hinges on the paradoxical denial of the trained, labouring body's physicality. The weightless and ephemeral female body idealised in ballet encourages a perspective *on*, rather than *from*, the body.[123] *Black Swan*, as we will see, offers a visceral reversal of that tendency.

The graspable articulation of the dancing protagonist's troubled and slowly disintegrating subjectivity is prone to get 'under our skin'. It gives substance to the normally 'invisible' forces and pressures that shape female bodies, in ballet and beyond. However, *Black Swan* tends not to be read, and certainly not uniformly, as a 'feminist' or even as a 'woman's' film and it evoked a sharp divide in opinion about its gender politics upon release.[124] On the one hand, the film was sharply criticised for reproducing patriarchal, phallocentric discourses, a Western male imaginary as well as a clichéd pandering to a panoptical male connoisseur and the 'necrophiliac desire at the heart of the male imaginary.'[125] Of course, the spectacular staging of female death also makes an appearance in *The Tango Lesson*, in the form of *Rage*, the film that Sally turns her back on. *Black Swan*, on the other hand, turns *towards* death as Nina dies/commits suicide in the climactic final moment of the film, which is also the final moment of the climactic stage performance of *Swan Lake*. This leads Amber Jacobs, for instance, to assert that '*Black Swan* proceeds as if feminist film theory never happened,' (by reproducing 'the tyranny of the male gaze' criticised by Mulvey over 40 years ago) and thus allowing itself 'to absurdly, hyperbolically romanticize the patriarchal construction of femininity as a mere reflection.' For Jacobs, the film is characterised by a 'reactionary gender politics' because of the 'masturbatory' male perspective that the film privileges and from which the film was made.[126]

This line of argument is indicative of critiques of *Black Swan*'s gender politics more generally, focussed, as they are, on the construction of a (voyeuristic/exploitative/masturbatory) male gaze, the depiction of femininity as reflection/image/surface, as well as the destructively competitive relations between the female characters.[127] Importantly, these critiques are situated within a broadly ocularcentric critical frame, focussed first and foremost on looking relations and the film's pandering to a male gaze – although Jacobs' reference to *Black Swan* as a 'manmade "woman's film"' also suggest that *Black Swan* is somehow not only *about* but *for* women.[128] Notably, however, these gender-focussed debates tend to lack an acknowledgement of *Black Swan*'s intensely tactile and visceral register and the ways in which this might undermine understandings of subjectivity as grounded in disembodied, specular and symbolic relations (and the gender norms intrinsic to these relations, in cinema and beyond).

Most of these critiques seem to be grounded in reading the film at face value and in terms of a straightforward representational mode. However, *Black Swan's* tone and generic register are not so easily pinned down – and this is, in part, where some of the vast differences in popular and critical reception come from. Adrienne McLean, for instance, recounts her experience of hysterical laughter when seeing the film – while also acknowledging that *Black Swan* was probably not intended to be funny and that she might have laughed *at* rather than *with* the film 'for what might be construed as the wrong reasons'.[129] For McLean, *Black Swan* is 'risible, hilarious, parodic without apparently meaning to be.'[130] She reads the film in relation to 'camp' and 'kitsch', as a film that is 'so bad it's good' – without being aware of it – because the film takes itself too seriously, while getting the 'realities' of ballet blatantly wrong. McLean notes that it was her extensive knowledge of ballet, as well as of ballet in film, that kept her from taking the film as seriously as it takes itself.[131]

While McLean's account is an exception within the larger context of readings and critiques that mostly take the film 'seriously' – albeit for very different reasons and with very different understandings of what it is that *Black Swan* is serious *about* – it gestures towards the different spectatorial stances the film invites and the different affective registers circulating within and around the film. *Black Swan* is variously talked about as a dance film, backstage musical, psychological thriller, horror, body horror, erotic thriller, melodrama and as a 'contemporary version of what used to be called the "women's picture" [; ...] a revisionist version of a "disreputable" female-oriented genre film.'[132] *Black Swan* resonates with, and is compared to, films as varied as *Centre Stage* (Nicholas Hytner, US, 2000) and *The Red Shoes* (Michael Powell and Emeric Pressburger, UK, 1948) (foregrounding its alignment with the cinematic history of ballet); *All About Eve* (Josef L. Mankiewicz, US, 1950), *Repulsion* (Roman Polanski, UK, 1965), *Rosemary's Baby* (Roman Polanski US, 1968) and *Carrie* (Brian De Palma, US, 1976) (situating it within a larger cinematic trajectory of female rivalry, doubling and mental breakdown as well as body horror); as well as *The Wrestler* (Darren Aronofsky, US, 2008) (positing the film as part of Aronofsky's oeuvre that is increasingly concerned with the body, pain, ageing and celebrity). Aronofsky himself identifies Fyodor Dostoyevsky's novel *The Double* (1846) as a source of inspiration, as well as, more obviously, Pyotr Tchaikovsky's ballet *Swan Lake* (1877). Themes, tropes and motives around ballet, femininity, narcissism, over-identification, hysteria, madness, doubling, horror, disgust, ageing, stardom and physicality come together in, through and around *Black Swan* – and it is, I want to argue, the film's intensely and affectively visceral register, grounded as it is in Nina's/ Portman's corporeality, that provides the 'textural glue' that makes it all 'stick'.

Steven Shaviro suggests that *Black Swan* is perhaps most usefully read as an incarnation of Linda Williams' body genres, 'films that are aesthetically disreputable, precisely because they overtly work to incite physical responses in the viewers': 'sexual arousal, chills of fear, and bouts of weeping.' Williams's body genres include pornography, horror and melodrama – and, for Shaviro, '*Black Swan* is actually all three of these. The film moves from an initial creepiness to a culminating full-blown body horror; but along the way it titillates us with the phantasmatic, faux-lesbian scene of Natalie Portman's [note the reference to the actor rather than the character!] full-blown orgasm.'[133] Shaviro also identifies the faux-lesbian soft-core scene as a pivotal moment in the film as it 'marks both a breakthrough (an overcoming of sexual repression) and also a breakdown (as Portman's character finally learns that she can only fulfil her quest for aesthetic perfection at the price of her own existential self-destruction).' This is why this particular moment 'provides a bridge between horror (the revulsion of bodily metamorphosis, linked with the white swan – black swan duality of the *Swan Lake* ballet) and melodrama (the tears of unfulfillment, tied to a utopian negation of life as it is, in which every success is also a failure).'[134]

However, while body genres tend be marked by an aura of disreputability and 'bad taste', the ballet context and Portman's presence in particular, as well as the technical sophistication of the cinematography and digital effects (which are key to *Black Swan*'s visceral register), allow Aronofsky to package the film as a 'highbrow thriller' that retains a sense of 'horror and exploitation' as well as 'artistic seriousness'.[135] For Shaviro, there is a clear sense that Aronofsky 'knows what he is doing' in drawing on, and integrating, horror and melodrama in particular. He is 'using horror to update the old Hollywood melodrama [...] He is making new equivalents for the parts of melodrama that might otherwise now seem antiquated, and therefore (to some viewers) campy.'[136] This arguably results in *Black Swan* being a contemporary and reputable version of the 'women's picture', which, for Shaviro, aligns *Black Swan* with some of Todd Haynes's (queer) reworkings of classical Hollywood melodrama.

While I am slightly uncomfortable with assertions around *Black Swan* as a reputable and serious work of art that hinge, albeit implicitly, on understandings of the film as a product of a clever (white) male auteur and on a sense of seriousness and taste that is very explicitly gendered (male) and classed (middle-class), I am drawn to Shaviro's reading of the film because it gestures towards its variously entangled generic and affective registers. It reconciles the seemingly contradictory notions that the film is 'emotionally and wrenchingly intense, in a completely unironic way', while also being over-the-top and excessive, 'entirely lurid and hysterical.' For Shaviro, some of the negative critical reactions to *Black Swan* are indicative of a cultural elitism according to which 'nothing can be taken seriously unless it is, well, "serious".'[137] What Shaviro points to here is that it is precisely the film's emotional tonality and its visceral, psychophysical intensity that are 'real' and 'serious' – no matter how excessively lurid and hysterical the representational framework in which this intensity is embedded.

Critiques, like McLean's, of *Black Swan*'s 'abundant factual errors in depicting a dance company' and its 'complete lack of respect for its subject matter' that make the film 'pompous and shallow' (and therefore, for some viewers, funny) seem stuck in the realm of literalness – and the same goes, I want to argue, for critiques of *Black Swan*'s gender politics that focus on characterisation and the male gaze.[138] For Shaviro, there is no point in such critiques because 'psychophysical intensity is the *point*' of the film – and not representational realism – which is why 'thematic concerns [around ballet in particular] are deliberately flattened and simplified' so they do not interfere with the film's visceral and affective implications.[139]

I want to argue that ballet, and the ballet body, do *matter* in *Black Swan* – even if not in terms of the accuracy of their depiction – but in terms of how they provide the ground on which the film's visceral, tactile and muscular register, that hinges on the female ballet dancer's self-referential physicality and the impossible bodily demands of the ballet context, takes shape. The multi-layered processes of mirroring and doubling in *Black Swan* (that tend to be at the heart of feminist critiques of the film) do not only manifest themselves as a spectral play with images, surfaces and reflections, but take shape *in* and *as* the film's body. Doubling and the (horrifying) blurring of boundaries associated with it manifest themselves not only in relation to narrative or characters, but via *Black Swan's* tactile, muscular and kinaesthetic register that infiltrates the corporeal fabric of the film. What I want to trace in what follows, therefore, is *Black Swan's* visceral trajectory from multi-layered binaries and double-binds towards the simultaneous disintegration and amalgamation of binaries, boundaries and bodies.

Mirrors, reflections, doubles

Black Swan takes shape as a convoluted entanglement of relations of doubling, mirroring, binaries, boundaries and double-binds that are first set up and then increasingly blurred. In the first instance, *Black Swan* is a film about *Swan Lake*, Tchaikovsky's famous ballet – cinema as ballet's double and vice versa – that is essentially the story of a double: Odette, the White Swan, and her evil rival/twin, Odile, the Black Swan, who seduces Odette's lover, the Prince. Company director Thomas Leroy (Vincent Cassel) recounts the story of *Swan Lake* for his dancers, and, of course, for us, in the first ballet sequence (that turns out to be an internal audition for *Swan Lake*):

> We all know the story. Virginal girl, pure and sweet, trapped in the body of a swan. She desires freedom but only true love can break the spell. Her wish is nearly granted in the form of a prince, but before he can declare his love her lustful twin, the black swan, tricks and seduces him. Devastated, the white swan leaps off a cliff, killing herself, and, in death, finds freedom.

The story of *Swan Lake*, the ballet *in* the film is, in typical dance film/backstage musical fashion, also the story *of* the film. The framing narrative doubles the ballet set piece. Nina is the White Swan/good girl and Lily the Black Swan/bad girl who functions as Nina's rival – professionally (for the lead role in *Swan Lake*) and romantically/sexually (for Thomas). Nina kills herself in the final moments of the film which are also the final moments of the ballet – *Black Swan* and *Swan Lake* 'become one' – as the boundaries between set piece and framing narrative are increasingly blurred and eventually merge.

Dancing the dual role of the Swan Queen – the White Swan/Odette and her double/twin the Black Swan/Odile – is considered to be an extremely difficult task that requires the embodiment of a set of binary opposites (virginal-seductive, fragile-strong, weightless-sensual). Thomas chooses Nina to play the dual role and while he is convinced she can dance the White Swan, he considers the Black Swan to be 'more of a challenge'. Nina is not fuckable enough. She is (f)rigid, too controlled and unable to 'let go'. When she fails to respond to Thomas's advances after he invites her back to his apartment following the company's opening gala he gives her a 'homework' assignment: 'go home, touch yourself, live a little.' One of the central questions of *Black Swan* is therefore not only whether Nina can dance the Black Swan, but also whether she can become the sexually alluring 'bad girl' within the framing narrative – and this means that the boundaries between the character (in the film) and her role (in the ballet) become increasingly blurred.

The rivalry between the White Swan and the Black Swan in the ballet is played out in the surrounding narrative as well. Lily functions as Nina's double, as the incarnation of her darker and (sexually) repressed side. Nina is concerned that Lily wants to replace her, as the prima ballerina and as the object of Thomas's affection – in the same way that Nina herself is replacing Beth, the retiring star dancer and Thomas's ex-lover. There is a motif here of doubling and replacing that essentially makes the female characters interchangeable, and this is heightened by the characters' very similar appearances – dark hair, delicate features, slim build.

Katherine Fusco's discussion of the casting choices for *Black Swan* gestures towards the ways in which the motif of doubling (and replacing) also resonates with the wider context of Hollywood cinema, and women's place within it. For Fusco, the extratextual discourses of Portman's celebrity do not just inform her role in *Black Swan* – they are, in fact, *necessary* to how her character functions within the diegesis.[140] Part of Nina's transformation in *Black Swan* concerns the ways in which she comes to embody the dual role in *Swan Lake*. She does not just *play/dance* the White and Black Swan but *becomes* her role. Her skin metamorphoses and she grows feathers (an example of the film's technical mastery) and she dies a 'perfect' (i.e., 'real') death at end of the film/ballet. 'Nina is consumed by her role, so much so that the metaphorical loss of the star's identity into her role becomes *written on the body*' – and the loss of identity is made graspable through the visceral disintegration of Nina's bodily boundaries.[141]

The extratextual discourses highlighting Portman's physical transformation and taxing ballet training mean that the star-role relationship articulated *in* the film also resonate with Portman's role as the star *of* the film. Fusco points out that 'Portman makes clear that in her preparations for the role she worked and thought as a dancer, that she lived the part during filming. By encouraging audiences to think about her body and her daily habits, Portman encourages them to identify her as a *dancer*, thus decreasing the gap between the actress and her performance.'[142] The corporeal conflation of actor, character, dancer and dancing role creates a sense of 'embodied realism, as opposed to acting.'[143] Portman's/Nina's emaciated frame, with bones, especially her ribs, protruding through her translucent white skin, which also reveals the contours and movements of individual muscle strands, add to the film's unnervingly visceral register. It is precisely this notion of decreasing gaps and blurred boundaries between doubling relations that have graspably corporeal dimensions and that hinge centrally on Portman's/Nina's body that I (like the film itself) will return to throughout.

For Fusco, Portman's 'good girl' image and accounts of her dedication to ballet and her role mean that '*Black Swan* is as much a film about whether Portman can be a bad girl as it is a story about whether Nina can be the bad swan.'[144] There is a sense in which this corporeal layering is acknowledged within the film itself when Thomas shouts at Nina during one of the rehearsals: 'Seduce us – not just the prince, but the court, the audience, the entire world.' The parallels between Mila Kunis and her character Lily (as well as between Winona Ryder and Beth) are played on in similar terms, and there are clear resonances here, which are crucially tied to gendered notions of the body and embodiment, with Portman, the Hollywood star, being threatened by the rising starlet that is Kunis, while dreading the seemingly unavoidable fate of the ageing (by Hollywood standards) Ryder, whose star is clearly fading.[145]

An integral part of the various resonances and increasingly intimate entanglements between star, role and character, inter- and extra-textu(r)ally, is the blurring of boundaries between representation/reflection/mirror/image and performance that shapes *Black Swan*'s corporeal trajectories of transformation and transgression. There are some notable parallels here between *The Tango Lesson* and *Black Swan* in terms of the corporeal entanglement of dance and cinema – although in *Black Swan* the move from a representational to a performative register is tied to the dancer's body (and its disintegration) in a much more viscerally affecting manner. For one, 'Nina is not satisfied with simply representing the Swan Queen, or appearing to be or pretending to be. Instead, she must go beyond appearance and embrace being.' For Steen Christiansen, Nina's transformation is therefore also a transgression 'of fiction into life.'[146]

While *The Tango Lesson* questions the representational model through its move away from the film/representation (*Rage*) within the film, *Black Swan* turns its back on the *mirror*. Not only does Nina break the mirror in her dressing room during her fight with Lily just before the performance of *Swan Lake* (she violently throws Lily against the mirror and then stabs her with one of the shards), *Black Swan* more generally 'smashes the mirror of representation.'[147] For a film that is, at least initially, structured like a 'house

Figure 3.5 Nina Sayers/Natalie Portman (*Black Swan*)

of mirrors', situated as it is in 'the world of ballet that is set up as a world of reflection,' this equates to an ontological crisis – a crisis that parallels the increasingly unstable ontological status of Nina's world.[148] The blurring of boundaries between representation/reflection and performance takes place not only in relation to the bodies *in* and *around* the film, but also involves the body *of* the film that is increasingly shaped by digital special effects, which, crucially, manifest themselves primarily *on the surface* of the skin. Nina's skin – the boundary between inside and outside, the site of her tactile and sensuous encounter with the world – is animated and comes alive; it metamorphoses; it disintegrates and becomes porous, leaky. It is the tactile sensations of her skin that Nina is increasingly unable to trust – does her finger bleed? Has she ripped the skin off her finger? Is she growing feathers? Has she stabbed herself? – just as she cannot trust her reflection in the mirror. There are numerous moments in the film where Nina's mirror image takes on a life of its own, its movements and gestures not aligned with Nina's; body and image are out of sync. Crucially, the mirror/screen is aligned, *phenomenologically*, with skin (Nina's and ours) – can we trust it/them? – and therefore the relations of looking, reflection, surface and image are articulated not as specular but as profoundly *tactile* – as well as increasingly unreliable.

For Christiansen, it is the (digital) morph that provides 'the bridge between mirror and performance,' highlighted most poignantly in the final, public staging of *Swan Lake*, in which Nina 'physically morphs into the unreal being of swan-woman hybrid.'[149] But the morphing move also makes various other appearances in the film, especially in the shape of animated, moving, crawling skin – including primarily Nina's hands, back, arms and neck, but also Beth's open leg wound and Lily's tattooed back during the (imagined?) oral sex scene with Nina. The morph also surfaces in various moments of 'face-changing', when we see Nina's face appear on other characters (the random woman that Nina passes on the street; Beth, when she stabs herself in the face with a nail file during Nina's visit in the hospital; Lily, both during the sex scene and during the fight the leads to the smashing of the mirror; and one of the identical-looking white swans of The Court who puts Nina off-balance in the final performance). However, it is in relation to Nina's metamorphosis into a/the black swan in the climactic performance – which is also the Swan Queen's, Nina's and Portman's most spectacular performance and the most spectacular staging of the film itself as a performance (of technical mastery) – that the various binaries, boundaries and relations of doubling collapse. This includes 'the mirror-boundary between screen and spectator,' as we are pulled in by the film's dazzlingly kinetic energy and are ever more closely aligned with Nina's grippingly visceral phenomenal world.[150] Nina/Portman dances the dual role of White Swan and Black Swan masterfully and manages to embody an 'impossible' set of binary contradictions. Thomas is enthralled by the performance/Nina and so is her previously disinterested dance partner, David (Benjamin Millepied), while Nina's ambiguously overprotective yet jealous mother Erica (Barbara Hershey) is moved to tears.[151] Nina embodies, and 'lives', the role of Odile/the Black Swan by growing black feathers, morphing into an assertively seductive swan and kissing Thomas passionately backstage. She also 'lives' the role of Odette/the White Swan: the tears of tragic desperation

Figures 3.6 and 3.7 Mirror/Skin (*Black Swan*)

in the First Act are real, following her embarrassing fall (after seeing her face on one of the other dancers). And, of course, Nina bleeds to death in her fluffy white dress when Odette commits the film's/ballet's climactic suicide.

Christiansen's account of the transgressive implications of *Black Swan's* move towards digital effects and morphing (that are also foregrounded in the DVD commentary and extras) is particularly useful as it gestures towards the role of the *cinematic* body. It also functions as a reminder, however, that the sensing lived-body, that provides the *ground* both for the shattering of the mirror and for the surfacing of digital effects, risks disappearing within the context of a Deleuzian-inspired reading of the film's affective implications. Christiansen notes that in those moments in which the film:

> transitions to digital effects [it] morphs the image beyond its representational means, [...] beyond what we as spectators know is possible [...] The morph then, is the opposite of the mirror in *Black Swan*, the morph is the logic which resists and rejects the mirror logic set up by classical cinema and instead brings with a new kind of literalism.[152]

I want to argue that it is precisely a muscular, kinaesthetic and viscerally affective literalism that takes shape in *Black Swan* through and around the (female ballet) body's corporeality. The significance of this body is acknowledged in passing, when Christiansen notes that 'it is no accident that the morphing which takes place is centred on the body as the stable body has generally been the basis for a continuous sense of self.'[153] I want to push this line of argument further here by bringing the sensing, lived-body 'back in' in order to not 'lose sight' of the variously corporeal entanglements that take shape in, around and through *Black Swan*.

If '[m]orphing insists that we must accept as perceptually realistic that which is referentially unreal,' then we must not take for granted the body that makes perception possible in the first place.[154] In this sense, my attempt to grasp *Black Swan* aligns perhaps most closely with Tarja Laine's searching for a 'corporeal way of thinking about the film.' She reads *Black Swan* as a 'psychotic-corporeal experience of self-destructive psychosis,' conveyed through a 'painful corporeal aesthetics' that provokes in the spectator an '"embodied reflection" of [their] own materiality.'[155] It is precisely the distinction between 'having a body' and 'being a body' that the film dramatises, makes graspable and invites us to reflect upon. For Laine, the visceral articulations of pain are key to this as they prompt us 'to consider one's body not merely as an object one possesses, but essentially as a "subject that feels its own objectivity."'[156]

Body/image: 'perceived' and 'ideal' dancing bodies

Black Swan's mise-en-scène is littered with mirrors and reflective surfaces, including various moments in which Nina is caught in a *mise-en-abyme* of multiple reflections of herself. The mirror plays an important generic role in the dance film more generally and tends to function as a means of highlighting, visually, the distanced relation of the female dancer to her body (image). The mirror is linked to a 'constant referral to another as judge,' which evokes in the dancers 'a recognition of the ephemeral quality of empowerment in their physicality.'[157] It is through this emphasis on surface and reflection that we tend to be implicated in a complicated network of disembodied looking relations. The mirror functions as a distancing device, highlighting the dancer's alienation from the body that is perceived/experienced visually, from a distance, as object, as image. In *Black Swan*, however, it functions to blur the boundaries between the body and image and draw us into a relation of haunting, carnal proximity.

Susan Leigh Foster usefully identifies the different kinds of bodies – 'perceived', 'ideal', 'demonstrative' – that appear within the dance context. The perceived body 'derives primarily from sensory information that is visual, aural, haptic, olfactory, and perhaps most important kinaesthetic,' whereas the ideal body specifies 'size, shape, and proportions of its parts as well as expertise at executing specific movements.'[158] The demonstrative body mediates between the perceived and ideal: it 'didactically emphasises or even exaggerates actions' and 'isolates moments in a movement sequence or parts of the body in order to present an analysis of the ideal.'[159] This can occur through the dancer's own image in the mirror or through the bodies of teachers and other (better) dancers.

I have identified the tensions between these bodies as a central generic characteristic of the dance film elsewhere.[160] For instance, the frequent behind-the-scenes emphasis on blisters, bloody toes and injury in training/rehearsal sequences, the dancing characters' look in the mirror as well as references to eating disorders in films such as *Centre Stage*, *The Company* or *Save the Last Dance* (Thomas Carter, US, 2001), can be read as attempts to represent, *visually*, the perceived body and the dancer's striving for the ideal through an incorporation of the demonstrative body. The tensions between the perceived body and the 'impossible' ideal, mapped as they are onto other binary conflicts, tend to be spectacularly resolved in the climactic dance numbers in which the perceived body 'disappears', as it were, and becomes the ideal.[161] While the striving for the ideal, and for 'perfection', is a core concern in *Black Swan* (including clichéd depictions of Nina's eating disorder; her intense, self-destructive training regime; her obsession with control and perfection), it is the perceived, and the *perceiving*, body of the dancer that is the viscerally tactile, muscular and kinaesthetic 'zero point of orientation,' and *dis*orientation, of the film.[162]

Nina's striving for the embodiment of an impossibly weightless and ephemeral ideal is linked to the disintegration of her body and mind that result from her obsessive self-referentiality. But the female dancer's self-destruction is not simply represented and displayed for us. Instead, we are asked to 'accompany' the dancer and share her 'distorted' sensory relation to the world, as she sees, hears, and feels things that are not actually 'there'. We are provided with reassurances of the ontological status of the 'real' world in and of the film (which is distinguished from Nina's phenomenological world and what happens 'there'), but they occur less frequently as the film progresses. There are increasingly longer episodes in which events and experiences are represented *as if* 'really' happening – Nina's stabbing/killing of Lily, for instance, as well as their sexual encounter – before clarification is provided: Nina did, in fact, stab herself, while her sexual encounter with Lily turns out to have been what Lily calls 'some sort of lezzie wet dream' (or does it?).

That said, even when the ontological grounding of the diegetic world is more or less reassuringly re-established, the visceral intensity of Nina's phenomenal world is likely to leave a more lasting 'impression'. In a reversal of wider generic tendencies, the perceived/perceiving body prevails and, in a sense, *replaces* the ideal. This is perhaps most explicitly encapsulated in the closing lines of the film, in which a severely injured Nina (blood gushing from the self-inflicted stabbing wound in her stomach) lies on the stage at the end of *Swan Lake*, which concludes with the White Swan committing suicide: 'I *felt* it [...] it was perfect.' For Nina, it was perfect because her performance lost its 'pretend' character – she did not 'fake it'.

The intensely kinetic, yet unnervingly and hauntingly unanchored, proprioceptive register of *Black Swan* is established in the opening scene, a dance sequence resembling the prologue of the Bolshoi version of *Swan Lake* and which, as it turns out, takes place in Nina's dream.[163] It is the same dance that Nina performs with Thomas in a later rehearsal (discussed below). Nina dances the part of Odette/the White Swan in a glowingly white, translucent and seemingly weightless frilly dress, and is pursued by a menacingly dark creature (Rothbart). The dancers begin to circle each other and the camera appears to join in the increasingly frantic push and pull between the dancers' bodies as it circles the circling bodies and becomes what Fischer might call a 'kinetic third partner'.[164]

The scene is imbued with a thrilling sense of kinetic energy, a flurry of circular movement that seems unanchored and ungrounded, unbound by conventional rules of gravity, due to the lack of spatial markers that make it impossible to ground the movement relations between the dancers, and between the dancers and the camera. The blinding rays of light emanating from an unidentifiable light source (that might or might not be fixed to a particular point in space) add to the disorientatingly kinetic dynamism of the scene. The 'echoed mechanical rattle mixed with distorted laughter' on the soundtrack intensifies the creepily uncanny tone and also foreshadows more generally the 'tactile significance of sound' – especially in relation to the breathy and animalistic sounds that accompany Nina's 'hallucinatory' experiences as they 'acquire more tactile qualities' throughout.[165] The eerily energetic register established here, enabled primarily by the mobility of Super 16mm handheld cameras, foreshadows the tone and feel of the remaining dances sequences that grow in intensity and culminate in the dazzlingly gripping whirlwind that is the climactic final performance.

The final moments of the dream sequence emphasise the pasty, seemingly bloodless and translucently white skin of Nina's face and shoulders, while the bright spotlight from above foregrounds the sharp edges and contours of her jawline and tightly muscled and tensed back and arms. Her increasingly animalistic ferocity, unleashed by the figure of Rothbart, is underlined when Nina escapes his pursuit. She emerges from the threatening embrace wearing a much shorter and strapless dress with white feathers fluttering around in the air, a reminder of the violent and sexually charged nature of the transformation. The opening sequence thus encapsulates the trajectory of embodied, kinaesthetic and visceral transformation that characterises the film as a whole.

Our entry into the diegetic world of the film, following the opening prologue, is marked both by the foregrounding of Nina's corporeality *and* by an almost immediate unsettling of our perceptual habits and expectations. Once awake, Nina sits up in bed and loosens her neck by moving her head from side to side to the grinding sounds of realigning upper vertebrae. She then moves her feet to the loudly cracking sounds of metatarsals being put back into place. Nina's/Portman's physicality is given further substance when she performs stretches on the living room floor, with various mirrors exposing her emaciated frame from different angles as multiple 'versions' of her body appear within the frame. The mirrors function, in a fairly clichéd manner, to highlight the alienating (self-)surveillance that haunts the female dancer.

What is also foregrounded, however, is the more general significance of mirrors and other reflective surfaces to *Black Swan*'s unsettlingly ungrounded sensory register. The difference between the material presence of the body and its specular image is played with at various points, for instance when the close framing of Nina rubbing her feet and loosening her ankles is revealed as a reflection in the mirror as the camera moves back, re-establishing the distinction between body and image. While this is a fairly conventional framing pattern in the dance film, its employment in the context of *Black Swan*'s visceral, muscular and kinaesthetic register ties the mirror and the body's reflection/image directly to questions about the phenomenological presence and ontology of the body. It thus also conjures a certain self-consciousness, on part of the spectator, about how we encounter the on-screen body and the tactile, visceral and kinaesthetic resonances it might provide. Does it make a difference whether we encounter a body or its reflection (on screen)? But also: how do we know which is which? Can we trust our senses to 'detect' the difference? And, perhaps most importantly, does it matter?

Black Swan's visceral and kinaesthetic register is tied to Nina's corporeality – but not in any straightforward manner. The phenomenological world of the film moves from a grounding in its diegetic universe to a grounding in Nina's perceptual horizon, which is increasingly removed from the materiality of the diegetic world. As her body disintegrates, Nina's interiority is increasingly less bounded, blurring the distinction between exteriority and interiority, surface and substance, subject and object. The most viscerally intense, and disturbing, moments later on in the film align the spectator with what turn out to be Nina's hallucinatory experiences (or do they?). These are frequently moments that bring us into an unsettling and uncomfortably close relation of proximity to Nina's violently disintegrating, rupturing and transforming body: her fingernails appear bloody; she first rips a strip of skin off finger and later cuts her hand with a pair of scissors; her toes are suddenly webbed, swan-like; her skin becomes animated 'gooseflesh' and small black feathers begin to grow, one of which is framed in extreme close-up as Nina pulls it out from underneath her skin; her legs break violently as if smashed by some invisible, uncontrollable force; and, of course, she morphs into a swan-like creature in the final performance. It is the questionable ontological status of these occurrences that renders the spectator's alignment with Nina's tactile, muscular and kinaesthetic mode of existence far from straightforward – yet intensely and grippingly visceral.

The visceral tensions and resonances between the various manifestations of the dancer's body and its reflections/re-incarnations (that appear in the mirror as well as through the various relations of doubling) crucially shape *Black Swan*'s corporeal trajectory. They invoke an unsettling uncertainty about which of the spaces and bodies are 'real' and about what is merely perceived 'as if' real. *Black Swan* thus questions the ontology of experience itself and challenges the aforementioned distinction between primordial experiences ('whose content is present, bodily given') and non-primordial experiences ('that do not have their object bodily present before them') – a distinction that is central to a phenomenological conception of empathy *and* to understandings of *filmic* empathy.[166] Nina's experience blurs this distinction: she experiences *as* real – and *not*, crucially, 'as if' real – that which is not 'there'. The content of her experience is both 'bodily present' (she feels pain) and not present, not primordially given, not 'there' (her legs are not broken; skin still covers her finger). If, as D'Aloia argues, 'the act of empathising consists in primordially experiencing something that is non-primordially given,' then *Black Swan's* unstable ontological register also blurs the boundaries that tend to keep the spectator at a 'safe distance', drawing us in in a way that gets us 'too close for comfort.'[167] Perhaps this gestures towards the ways in which even experiences 'that do not have their object bodily present before them,' like empathetic experiences or the *cinematic* experience, might be experienced not only *as if* real, but *as* real, if only momentarily, especially if we consider the real in relation to notions of *perceptual* realism and its affective resonances.

Weighty pressures: bodily disintegration and visceral disembodiments

Nina crumbles under the pressures of the ballet world and this is perhaps most poignantly articulated via Nina's disturbingly dysfunctional relationship with her mother, the former dancer who had to give up her career when she fell pregnant with Nina. Erica embodies the cliché of the overbearing, overambitious ballet parent who wants to re-live her (unfulfilled) dream of ballet stardom through her daughter – yet, she also clearly does not want to be outdone. The mother-daughter relationship/rivalry in *Black Swan* is thus 'shot through by a deadly ambivalence' and manifests itself as the kind of 'double bind' that is 'at the basis of schizophrenia: two contradictory demands ("do better than I did", "don't outdo me") are made simultaneously.'[168] This constellation adds to the various binaries and doubling relations that shape the film and provide the grounds for *Black Swan's* visceral rendering of an 'obscene over-proximity' that also, crucially, shapes the spectatorial engagements the film invites, demands even.[169] Erica's disturbingly close and intrusively tactile relationship to her daughter is articulated in graspably visceral terms and adds to the affective charge that gathers on the surface of Nina's increasingly porous skin. Erica frequently touches Nina's skin, her face, her hair; she tucks her into bed and even undresses her. She demands to see the scratch wounds on Nina's back (that seem 'real' within the diegetic world of the film, at least initially) and clips Nina's fingernails to prevent her from scratching, hurting her (piercing her skin) in the process.

In what Fisher describes as an 'excruciatingly awkward and disturbing scene', we see Nina masturbating in her bedroom (following Thomas's 'homework' instructions).[170] Towards the end of the lengthy scene, just as Nina turns over, seemingly at the brink of orgasm, she catches a glimpse of her mother, asleep in the armchair next to her bed. The disturbingly disorientating nature of Nina's discovery is articulated through a startled/startling jump cut (from medium close-up to medium shot of Erica on the chair) that follows an extreme close-up of Nina's face. After being drawn into Nina's pleasurable experience (through close-ups and the dramatically sensuous music that slowly increases in volume) the unexpected cut to Erica, accompanied as it is by a joltingly abrupt change in score, jerks us back, a muscular and viscerally affective reminder of our complicity in the invasion of Nina's bodily space.

In another less sexually charged but equally invasive scene, Erica presents Nina with a massive cake to celebrate her new role as the Swan Queen. A sense of repulsive, nauseating over-proximity is made tangible when Erica forces Nina to lick the revoltingly bright pink icing off her finger, with the frequent depictions of Nina's anorexic/bulimic behaviours elsewhere in the film heightening the disturbingly affective charge of the scene. The specifically gendered pressures that 'gather around', shape and impress upon the female ballet body are linked specifically to the skin as boundary, surface and as a key site for our expressive-perceptive relations to the word. Crucially, it is precisely this sense of over-proximity that also characterises *our* relationship with Nina, positioned, as we are 'as though breathing down her neck rather than seeing through her eyes.'[171] We are deprived of 'any comforting "objective" distance' or 'proper perspective'.[172] For Laine the camera constitutes a 'haunting, paranoid presence' as we are always just behind Nina, looking over her shoulder, breathing down her neck.[173]

The sense of a threateningly invasive over-proximity also surfaces in Nina's relationship with Thomas. I would argue that Thomas's character does *not* function, first and foremost, as the bearer of the male gaze or as a surveilling patriarchal presence in *Black Swan*. Such a reading ignores the tactile dimensions of the 'pressure' he exerts on his dancers, and Nina in particular. When he first appears at the audition he selects certain dancers by tapping their shoulder – his touch determines the dancers' professional fate. There are also numerous shots in which Nina's and Thomas's faces appear in extreme close-up in the same frame – in 'breath-taking' proximity, as it were – during the casting rehearsal and when Nina watches Lily dance, for instance, but most notably perhaps in the two scenes in which Thomas kisses Nina. The first kiss, in Thomas's office, is clearly unwanted by Nina. The invasion of bodily boundaries takes her by surprise and she reacts by biting his lip in a decidedly physical, tactile repudiation – just as she eventually crushes Erica's hands with the bedroom door when she invades the privacy of Nina's bedroom one too many times. Heteropatriarchal pressures (including those that manifest themselves in the destructive relations *between* women), and attempts to resist these pressures, take shape in the haptic realm of touch and bodily contact.

The second kiss between Thomas and Nina takes place in a rehearsal scene in which Thomas dances with Nina in a dubious attempt to help her 'perfect' the role of the Black Swan. Thomas dances the role of the Prince seduced by the Black Swan in the ballet. However, it is Thomas who seduces Nina in this scene. The complex entanglement of the framing narrative with the story of the ballet enables the uncomfortably enticing bodily encounter. The camera stays close to the dancers' bodies and faces, tracing and mirroring Thomas's hands, often in close-up, as they move across Nina's body, her waist, legs and breasts. He tells Nina to 'feel [his] touch' and 'respond to it'. The dance choreography conveys Nina's ambivalent fascination, a mixture of fear, hesitation and desire, in muscular terms, as she, playfully, frees herself from Thomas's grip but then allows herself to be pulled back into the tight space of the embrace. The scene culminates in Thomas asking Nina to open her mouth, multiple times and with a breathy urgency, before kissing her. Nina reciprocates what is, by now, overtly sexual contact and Thomas begins to touch Nina's crotch, his hand again in close-up. The resistance against the transgression of bodily boundaries appears to be gone and the seductively sensual score increases in volume. We are reminded, in a jolting manner reminiscent of the masturbation scene, both of our complicity in the highly problematic sexual encounter and of the vulnerability that comes with this kind of 'opening up' (by Nina as well as the spectator) when the extra-diegetic music stops abruptly as Thomas pulls back – again, just as Nina seems about to come. Thomas's seduction is not 'real' – he is 'faking it' to teach Nina a lesson – but her heavy breathing is a visceral reminder of the 'realness' of the encounter. The ontology of experience and affect as conveyed in and through the film is further destabilised here and the contradictory resonances and disorientating push-and-pull of the spectatorial encounter further foregrounded.

These uncannily ambivalent, yet overtly tactile, muscular relations also surface in Nina's encounters with her various doubles, including Beth, Lily as well as Nina's specular/reflective doubles. When they first meet in the dance studio, for instance, Lily puts Nina off-balance when she enters the rehearsal space during Nina's auditioning for the Swan Queen. Lily has a graspably, and proprioceptively, disorientating and dizzying effect. The mobile camera sways, shakes and stumbles, loses its sense of orientation in space, and, like Nina, struggles to find its feet and regain a sense of balance. Lily then brushes up against Nina as she leaves the studio, in another disorientating invasion of the 'space of the body.'[174] And there is also, of course, Nina's sexual encounter with Lily that occurs later in the film as well as Nina's stabbing of Lily. The threatening pressure embodied by the rivalling double is experienced and resisted in the realms of tactility and musculature.

We might also note here the viscerally shocking scene at the hospital of Beth repeatedly stabbing her cheeks with a nail file, while shouting, again and again, that she is 'not perfect' but 'nothing', which remains ambivalent with regard to its ontological status. A face-change, from Beth's to Nina's, occurs midway through the stabbing just as Nina tries to wrestle the nail file from Beth, who bites Nina's arm in return. When Nina runs towards the elevator to flee the scene she notices the bloody nail file in her equally bloody hands; whether and how the stabbing occurred remains unclear. Was the entire event one of Nina's hallucinations? Did Beth stab herself and did Nina experience the stabbing as a kind of self-mutilation because of her newfound empathy with Beth? Or did Nina attack Beth as an incarnation of her ageing, undesirable double? The deadly combination of female rivalry (Beth threw herself in front of a car when she was replaced by Nina; and Nina's visit in the hospital is an attempt to reach out to Beth because Nina herself fears being replaced by Lily) and self-doubt/feelings of inadequacy (not being 'perfect', being 'nothing') is played out at the surface of the body in excruciatingly visceral terms.

Kinaesthetic thrills: how dance might sweep you off your feet

The unnerving and at times terrifying corporeal intensity of *Black Swan* is heightened by the seductively exhilarating kinetic energy of the dance sequences that we get a 'taste' of in the opening prologue and which reach their crescendo in the final performance. The wide-ranging and seemingly unanchored camera movements that continuously break the 180-degree rule, often with mesmerisingly energetic 360-degree sweeps, create a spectacular sense of kinetic dynamism. The camera dances with and around Nina (whether she dances alone or as part of a couple/group). It is precisely the kinetic *relations* between Nina's movements and the camera's that convey a thrillingly muscular and kinaesthetic sense of freedom. What is therefore ultimately seductive in and about *Black Swan* is not Portman's/Nina's/the Black Swan's sexual allure, but the sense of a spellbindingly uncontained spatiality that we cannot help but be drawn towards.

The claustrophobically paranoid proximity and destructive self-referentiality that is conveyed elsewhere contrasts with the exhilarating kinaesthetic thrill enabled by the muscular dynamics of the dance sequences – and this contrast, I want to argue, heightens the affective charge of each of these binary modes of spatiality (inward/outward, inhibited/assertive, self-referential/directional). This is yet another contradiction that is played out on and through the female dancing body that remains our 'zero point of orientation' and *dis*orientation.[175] Crucially, the use of Super 16mm allows for the camera to stay close to the dancer's body while remaining highly mobile. During the dance sequences (the rehearsals in the studio and later on the stage, as well as the staged climactic performance), Nina's head, neck and shoulders, and sometimes her arms, dominate the frame as the camera fluidly moves around her, often in a 360-degree circular motion, changing direction, engaging in a kinetic push-and-pull, moving in close to her skin, breathing down her neck, gathering momentum and gaining some distance before sweeping back in. There are occasional close-ups of Nina's feet as well as long-shots establishing a sense of Nina's movement in (objective) space – including a few shots from the auditorium in front of the stage during the dress rehearsal and the final performance. However, the overall affective attitude that shapes the dance sequences is one of immersion and kinaesthetic involvement. Yet again, we are denied any kind of '"objective" distance' or 'proper perspective'[176] – we see the texture of Nina's/Portman's skin, movement of muscle strands, bones protruding through the skin and the thin clothing – only this time the proximity to the body does not 'feel' claustrophobically enclosing and intrusive, but thrillingly mobile and energetic.

It is precisely when the kinetic dynamism is at its most exhilarating (in the final performance) that the various binaries, boundaries and relations of mirroring and doubling dissolve and amalgamate in an ambiguously dystopian climax: the White Swan and Nina die a 'perfect' death. The tears and blood are real, not fake. Of course, the ontological status of the diegetic 'reality' of *Black Swan* has been entirely unhinged by this point so we do not know for sure what really happens 'in the end'. I want to suggest that 'what happens' (in narrative terms) is not the 'point' of the film in any case. If *Black Swan* leaves a 'lasting impression' on the viewer it is because of its visceral resonances and the excruciating unravelling of the female dancer's embodied sense of self that is brought within uncomfortably touching distance and that gets under our skin.

Overall, the encounter with *Black Swan* is ambiguous because of the multiple bodies, modes of embodiment and textural layers that come together in and around the film. *Black Swan* is not a 'feminist' film and it might not explicitly engage with feminist (film theoretical) concerns. However, the female body that appears and takes shape in the film, as well as the (cinematic) modes of embodiment it gives shape to, carry variously troubling resonances. While it is not inscribed with a conventional sense of (narrative) agency, it 'carries' the film. The film's body is the dancing body's double, mirroring its movements, gestures, stances, attitudes and tendencies. There is, of course, no guarantee that the troubled and troubling female body that appears in *Black Swan* also makes a certain kind of gender trouble 'appear' – but it 'clear[s] a space on the ground' for a corporeal reshaping of gender norms and relations to surface through the multi-layered and multi-textural entanglement of bodies that takes shape in and around *Black Swan*[177] – and a queer feminist film phenomenology helps us to unpack this.

Ahmed notes:

> what bodies 'tend to do' are effects of histories rather than originary. We could say that history 'happens' in the very repetition of gestures, which is what gives bodies their tendencies. We might note here that the labor of such repetition disappears through labor: if we work hard at something, then it seems 'effortless'. This paradox – with effort it becomes effortless – is precisely what makes history disappear in the moment of its enactment. The repetition of the work is what makes the work disappear.[178]

The work, labour and history of bodies do *appear* in and around *Black Swan* (as well as *The Tango Lesson*). This includes the bodies of characters, of actors, of the film – and, arguably, the spectator. As Laine points out, the film directs our 'sensual awareness' to both the richness and fragility of material existence and thus provokes an 'embodied reflection' of our own precarious materiality.[179] It is precisely here, in the mutually affective encounters of embodied histories that *Black Swan* enables, that an affirmative unhinging of binary gender norms might surface.

What encountering *The Tango Lesson* and *Black Swan* in this manner makes graspable, then, are the possibilities for a muscular, kinaesthetic reshaping of gender and gender relations that the coming-together of the social, generic, representational and performative contexts of dance and cinema provide – not necessarily, but potentially. *The Tango Lesson* performs its turn *away* from representation and *towards* embodiment more overtly and with a degree of self-reflexivity, while the turning towards sensuousness and affect is more intricately woven into *Black Swan*'s muscular, kinaesthetic fabric. The foregrounding of the female dancers' corporeality, together with the particular sensory registers of both films, gives shape to modes of embodiment, perception and affect that open up possibilities for the kind of spectatorial contact that is shaped by, and in turn shapes, the bodily horizons, habits and tendencies surrounding the films. A queer feminist film phenomenology, of the kind I propose here, enables us to grasp the convoluted corporeal trajectories that allow for cinematic incarnations of gender trouble to appear: the kind of spatio-temporally and perceptually twisted trouble that we might be touched and moved by in our encounter with *The Tango Lesson* and *Black Swan* – if we allow ourselves to be drawn in.

4

Queering the Sports Film: Failure and Gender (Tres)Passing in *2 Seconds* and *Offside*

Turning away from dance and towards a different kind of public physical display with a long history of cinematic 'appearances', this chapter explores the productive resonances, alignments and points of contact between cinema, gender and sport – from a broadly phenomenological perspective and via textural encounters with *2 Seconds* and *Offside*.

Despite the longstanding and reciprocal relationship between sport and cinema, the sports film has only recently received more sustained critical attention (including work by Aaron Baker, Séan Crosson, Leger Grindon and Dan Streible).[1] Notably, it is primarily in the context of film historical and cultural studies approaches to cinema (which are concerned with identity and identity politics), as well as in relation to question of genre, that the sports film has come under critical scrutiny.

While it is beyond the scope of this book to fully engage with the complexities of genre and (the usefulness of) categorisation, it is important to acknowledge that broad sets of sports film conventions have been identified.[2] In his extensive work on the boxing film, for instance, Grindon notes that the genre is structured around a 'series of dramatic conflicts that represent widespread social problems.' These include:

> (1) the conflict between body and soul or material versus spiritual values; (2) the critique of the success ethic expressed as

the conflict between individual competition fostered by market forces versus human cooperation and self-sacrifice; (3) a conflict between the opportunity success offers the boxer for integration into mainstream society versus loyalty to the marginalised community from which he [sic] arose; and (4) a masculinity crisis, traditionally associated with romance, arising from the conflict between the manly ethos of the ring and a woman's influence. Finally, a male emotional problem can arise from two related conflicts: when anger at injustice clashes with powerlessness to eliminate oppression, or when stoic discipline in the face of life's cruelties conflicts with sensitivity towards others.³

Notably, these are all, essentially, *gendered* conflicts. They evolve around the problems of a 'masculinity in crisis' and are played out through, on and around the spectacularly displayed male body. Grindon's work is indicative of critical work in this area more generally, which tends to be underpinned by variously explicit acknowledgements of the inherently masculine nature of the genre – and these are tied to assumptions about sport itself as a fundamentally male-centred activity and institution.

Female protagonists, whose numbers have increased significantly in frequency since the late 1990s, are variously problematic in this rigidly gendered representational space. The athletic heroine challenges the foundations of the sports film in a way that is tellingly reminiscent of the troubling entrance of female protagonist in the action cinema in the 1980s.⁴ I have begun to explore the ways in which female athleticism causes all kinds of gender and genre trouble in the sports film elsewhere, by considering its incompatibility with generic conventions.⁵ The (symbolic, metaphorical and narrative) significance of sport in film hinges on its implicit associations with men and masculinity and the ways in which sporting masculinities are tied to specific notions of (hetero)sexuality, class and nation in particular. When embodied by, or tied to, a female protagonist, sport and athleticism lose their generic functions.

Gender, genre and other kinds of trouble tend to be variously contained in the female sports film. *Million Dollar Baby* (Clint Eastwood, US, 2004), given its generic shift from boxing film to melodrama and a narrative twist that renders the female boxing body paralysed and invisible, is a particularly poignant example. *Million Dollar Baby* also highlights how the athletic female body's troubling implications are more pronounced, and more violently contained, if athletic physicality is to be believably and 'authentically' embodied by female characters on screen – when exertion does not appear 'as patently fake'.[6]

It is worth noting here that sport, athleticism and physical performances make relatively frequent appearances in lesbian/queer cinema – and not only in relation to the clichéd lesbian associations of female-only spaces like the locker-room – affirming Desmond's suggestion that athletic competence continues to be 'tinged with the suspicion of lesbianism'.[7] We might think of Lisa Aschan's *Apflickorna* (*She Monkeys*, Sweden, 2011), where vaulting provides the context for a queer female adolescent coming-of-age story;[8] the coming-out/lesbian romance narrative of *The Gymnast* (Ned Farr, US, 2006) that takes place in and through gymnastics and acrobatics;[9] the role that swimming, diving and gymnastics play in facilitating the lesbian (under)tones of the relationships between a group of girls at an elite boarding school and their teacher (Eva Green) in *Cracks* (Jordan Scott, UK, 2009);[10] the acrobatic circus performances in Patricia Rozema's *When Night is Falling* (Canada, 1995); and of course, albeit reluctantly, we might think of *Personal Best* (Robert Towne, US, 1985). In these films (with the exception of *Personal Best*), sport and athletic activity facilitate the articulation of queerly lesbian contact, desire and eroticism. They enable not (only) a 'lesbian visual economy' that is easily re-appropriated by a straight male gaze, but a corporeal and sensuous register that invites more fully embodied spectatorial engagements by rendering lesbianism and queer female desire tangible, graspable.[11] Athletic embodiments and performances also play a central role in *Water Lilies*, *Tomboy* and *Girlhood*, Sciamma's female adolescent coming-of-age trilogy. *Tomboy* and *Girlhood* are the focus of Chapter 5, where I argue that the foregrounding of queer modes of embodiment, movement and spatiality are key to the 'queerness' of Sciamma's queer feminist cinema.

I also want to briefly point to the significance of sport as one of the few social and media contexts that continue to provide a certain public lesbian and queer female visibility, both implicitly and explicitly. The 'common-sense' associations of female athleticism with tomboyism, gender transgression and lesbianism mean that lesbianism tends to 'appear' through and around the female athlete. Much of the humour in *Bend it Like Beckham* (Gurinder Chadha, UK, 2002) and *But I'm a Cheerleader* (Jamie Babbit, US, 2001), for instance, emerges from the films' self-conscious and comical engagements with the lesbian connotations of girls' and women's sport. Of course, in the real-world context of competitive sport, coming out as lesbian can, and often does, still have damaging implications, especially in terms of finance and sponsorship, but there is a significant, and growing, number of 'out' female athletes, often with considerable public/media profiles, and I would argue that the sports context plays an increasingly central role with regard to (sometimes affirmative) queer female visibility.

There is also a more general sense that LGBTI activism and culture are entering an 'athletic phase' as many of the battles around diversity, inclusion, visibility, access and human rights are fought out, broadly, in the realm of sport, both locally and globally, with mega sporting events like the Olympics providing an important platform for global LGBTI activism, for instance.[12] The current revival of roller derby as an athletic activity, institution and social context that continues to push the boundaries around trans, genderqueer and non-binary inclusion in sport and beyond is another example of the growing entanglement between queer activism and sport.[13]

Towards a Queer Feminist Sports/Film Phenomenology

In keeping with the overarching aims of this book, I want to move, not necessarily beyond, but perhaps around, existing debates on sport and film (including those concerned with gender), and explore how the intersections between sport and cinema provide a space in which conventional and straightforward notions of temporality and spatiality, and the ways in which they tend to be tied to particular identity formations, can be, and are, challenged. A phenomenology of sport and the sporting body as developed by feminist and queer critics such as Iris Marion Young, Judith Butler and Jacqueline Allen-Collinson, accounts for the corporeal and affective dimensions of sport and athleticism.[14] A (queer feminist) phenomenology of *sport* resonates, in some ways profoundly, with (queer feminist) *film* phenomenological concerns and I want to explore these resonances through an engagement with two very different, and in a sense atypical, sports films in *2 Seconds* and *Offside*. Both films play with, and disrupt, the conventions that normally structure our (spectatorial) encounters with sport, and their disorientating tendencies are tied to the female protagonists who provide the grounds for variously twisted modes of spatiality and temporality to surface in and through the films.

2 Seconds is an independent Canadian production, variously described as a sports comedy/drama/romance. The film opens with Laurence, called Laurie (Charlotte Laurier), a professional downhill mountain-bike racer, losing a championship race and then her job – she is too old and just not good enough anymore. Not only does *2 Seconds* begin with what would conventionally feature as the climactic final sporting competition, the protagonist also loses the race, a defeat without any redeeming features whatsoever, and things go downhill (in all senses) from there. However, despite Laurie's sporting career coming to an end as the film opens, *2 Seconds* is very much a film *about* cycling. It is the embedding of cycling in a non-competitive, non-sporting context, and in relation to an initially unemployed, single, ageing protagonist, that enables the film to evoke a sense of queerness that hinges, at least in part, on its unravelling of what Freeman calls 'chrononormativity' or 'homogenous empty time' and Halberstam refers to as 'straight time'.[15] In a chapter aptly entitled 'Bad timing', Freeman explores how the disruption of straight(forward) time allows for the emergence of variously queer temporalities that can, and do, constitute points of resistance to normatively conventional temporal orders, organised as they are around generationality, genealogies of descent, (re)production and the mundane workings of everyday (public and domestic) life. Laurie's continuous 'queer failure' to incorporate the rhythms and directionality of normative temporal registers disrupts assumptions of the givenness of 'straight time'.[16]

Jafar Panahi's *Offside* offers a very different, although equally twisted, encounter with sport, that hinges primarily on the disruption of a normative spatial order, although notions of immediacy and bad timing play an important affective, visceral role as well.[17] Disorientation, spatial and otherwise, is articulated in and through *Offside* via its focus on a group of young women in Tehran who disguise themselves as men in order to attend a World Cup qualification football match – women are forbidden access to sports stadia in Iran. They fail in their attempts at 'gender (tres) passing', however: they are arrested by army officers and forced to spend the entirety of the game in a holding pen outside the stadium walls.[18] Despite their physical proximity to the sporting action, the women are denied conventional spectatorial access. They never get to see any of the match – and neither do we (with the exception of two very brief glimpses). *Offside* disrupts and reorientates taken-for-granted ways of accessing and engaging with sport. It is through its disorientatingly twisted sensory regime, intimately tied as it is to the sidelined positionality of its crossdressing protagonists, who are utterly 'out of place', that *Offside* challenges, in tangibly corporeal terms, the ways in which notions of gender, sexuality, nation and the global normally intersect in and around the (mediated) spectacle of sport.

In his exploration of 'Time and timelessness in sport film', David Rowe writes that discussions around the mediation of sport have tended to focus on television as our primary means of accessing sport and of 'witnessing sports events in real time.'[19] Much is made of the commercial and cultural significance of the 'liveness' of television. Immediacy and the unpredictability of the unfolding drama are crucial to the spectator appeal of both live sporting events and televised sports coverage – and this is something that cinema is typically unable to provide. Together with the frequent lack of 'believable' athletic performances, this is why, according to some critics, sports *films* often just 'don't work.'[20]

At the same time, sport is said to be 'essentially cinematic' because it is 'inherently and densely consequential and visual.'[21] Rowe usefully highlights that the fictional sports film is not necessarily the poor relation of televised sport, or indeed of actual sporting events, but that the encounter of sport and cinema *can* open up different possibilities. Cinema can do certain things with and to sport that television cannot.

> Sport film, freed from the demands of the 'live' sporting moment, has the freedom to *play with time and space* in different ways. Sweeping across spaces and epochs, reversing

chronologies and juxtaposing places in a manner that defies the demands of individual physical presence at singular sports events anchored to the stadium site.[22]

Pushing the discussion around cinema's potentially productive entanglement with sport even further in the direction of the argument I want to develop here, Rowe also notes that 'the thread that runs through what can be defined as a bona fide sport film is not just, teleologically, a filmic treatment of sport.' Sports films might also 'register the inherent, contradictory dimensions of the institution of sport itself, and the often *profound phenomenological ambivalence* of those who engage with it.'[23] While Rowe's analysis remains safely within the fairly normative terrain of men's sport and masculinity, it also gestures towards conceptual avenues to explore the question of 'phenomenological ambivalence', and how exactly it might undermine normative modes of temporality and spatiality by how it registers on screen, in order to push further into the queer feminist realms of gender and sexuality.

It is no surprise, perhaps, that Rowe's analysis focuses primarily on *Zidane, un portrait du 21e siècle* (*Zidane: A 21st Century Portrait*, Douglas Gordon and Philippe Parreno, France, 2006), a film that raises very explicit questions about time and temporality and that has been the focus of considerable critical attention.[24] For Rowe, *Zidane* engages directly with 'film time' (i.e., the experience of different temporalities that cinema makes possible) *as well as* with the particular temporalities of sport, that is 'sport time'.[25] The notion of 'sport time' captures the sense that sport is 'a cultural form that is always preoccupied with temporality' – it is 'a prison of measured time' – in terms of 'the temporal rhythms' of participation and spectatorship, labour and consumption.[26] It is the resonances and productive entanglements of 'film time' and 'sport time' that *Zidane* manages to foreground, and make strange, so effectively and affectively. The film achieves this by taking a 'a real time sport event and [deconstructing] it, purporting in some ways to render what its principal subject is experiencing, but rationing its perspective and playing with the audience's perceptions of play'.[27]

Beugnet proposes a similar argument in her groundbreaking book *Cinema and Sensation*, where she points to Jean-Max Colard's claim that

Zidane dislocates the conventions of sport spectatorship: 'it is not the players who revolve around the ball [...] it is, on the contrary, the galaxy of the stadium and its spectacular machinery that revolve around one single player.'[28] Importantly, it is the centrality of the 'expansive physical and sensory experience' offered by *Zidane* that is key to the 'affective power' both of the 'drama of the match' and of the 'drama of film's material[ity].'[29] For Beugnet, the spectatorial experience offered by *Zidane* – 'for those spectators who allow themselves to be drawn in' – is one of 'wonderful, ravishing sensory overload, a perception-expanding event where the outer field, though never *seen*, is always felt, sensed and recomposed through the changes of intensity that affect the audio-visual field.'[30]

Both *Offside* and *2 Seconds* achieve similar kinds of transformations – albeit in a less slick and technologically motivated, but much more gritty, tangible and phenomenologically grounded, manner.[31] They do not necessarily offer a 'perception-expanding event,' but one that reorientates our senses and perceptual habits. Nonetheless, the emphasis, in Beugnet's work in particular, on the sensory and affective implications of *Zidane*, and their entanglements with the corporeal dimension of both cinema and sport, opens up a range of conceptual and analytical possibilities. I want to pursue these further by exploring the resonances between phenomenology based accounts of cinema (as outlined in Chapter 2) and the relatively recent emergence of what we might call a queer feminist sports phenomenology.

Inspired by Young's phenomenological incursion into debates around sport, gender and embodiment in 'Throwing like a girl', Jacquelyn Allen-Collinson has made vital contributions to a feminist phenomenology of the sporting body in recent years.[32] Her writing is part of a broader move towards a carnal sociology of sport, which has emerged primarily in response to the abstract, theoretical versions of the sporting body that continue to circulate, curiously, within debates around sport and gender. Asserting the inextricable entanglements of movement, perception and intentionality, John Hockey and Allen-Collinson link the 'habituated bodily action' that social life generally demands, but that is heightened in the sports context, to the incorporation of pre-reflective perceptual, sensory habits.[33] There are echoes her with Merleau-Ponty's idea of the 'corporeal schema': 'an incorporated bodily know-how and practical sense; a *perspectival grasp* upon the world from "the point of view of the body."[34] In other words, the athlete's 'immersion in habitual training practices' shapes her sensory register and modes of movement, spatiality and intentionality.[35]

In his account of 'the dramaturgy of action and involvement in the sports film,' Murray Pomerance notes that the sports film, more so than televised sports coverage, offers unique opportunities to convey precisely a sense of the participant's experience and perception: through the kinds of positionings and movements of the camera – in touching distance of the athletic body and/or sporting equipment; moving amongst athletes providing point of view shots – that would get in the way in the context of 'real' sporting events. The sports film additionally enables the linking of individualised athletic activity to the larger socio-cultural context in which it is embedded. Pomerance identifies a formal pattern, a 'threefold layering of significance' in actions scenes in the sports film – panoramas, action shots and character portraits – that tend to be 'incorporated together into a grammatically meaningful and "authentic" cinematic rendition of sport activity'.[36]

'Panoramas', typically in the form of long-shots, locate the sporting action geographically and socially, and 'emphasize the sport activity as a social enterprise, involving economic organization, roles, power alignments, gender displays, and moral outcomes'.[37] Action shots, on the other hand, provide 'details of individualized sport performance and diegetic composition', 'tell us precisely what is going on and with precisely what implication in terms of the logical flow of sequence', and provide us with a sense of 'the alignment, structure, intent, resource base, and strategy of athletic act itself'.[38] In other words, when combined, panorama and action shots ensure the temporal and spatial coherence of the sporting action *and* link individualised experience/agency to a broader socio-geographical context. The character portrait then asserts the ways in which an athletic act 'is carried out within the envelope of a character' and his/her 'personality'.[39] It provides a rational framework of possible cause-and-effect relations that both reinforce an overall sense of normative coherence – and thus the grounds for spectatorial identification. This is because we encounter sporting protagonists in the context of the fictional sports film first and foremost *as characters* (and not as athletes).[40]

In what follows, I want to challenge the fairly clear-cut boundaries and distinctions between individual experience and the social as well as between character and athlete proposed by Pomerance – with the tools provided by a queer feminist sports/film phenomenology and with the help of *2 Seconds* and *Offside*. A queer feminist sports/film phenomenology highlights the social embeddedness and situatedness of embodiment, intentionality, spatiality and action. It accounts for the ways in which social pressures and tendencies both shape and are shaped by the bodies that occupy and extend spaces in particular ways – and the ways in which these processes are magnified and potentially subverted within the sports context *and* within cinema. The gendered dimensions of embodiment – that is, the ways in which social structures and gender norms come to be incorporated at the level of the body – and the role of the sports context in both reinforcing *and* challenging binary notions of gender are asserted in Judith Butler's 'Athletic genders', regrettably not very widely known. A queer feminist sports/film phenomenology also accounts for the entanglement of bodily movement, feeling and affect and, importantly, it challenges assumptions of the givenness of time and space. It therefore enables us to grasp the queerly defiant tendencies and orientations of *2 Seconds* and *Offside* and the ways in which they subvert the conventions and expectations that normally structure our engagement with both cinema and sport.

A Waste of Time? Bad Timing and Queer Failure in *2 Seconds*

The common narrative structure in films featuring sport-based stories involves winning and success – either in relation to sporting victory, or, and this is a much more pervasive pattern, in terms of 'winning the respect of others' and/or gaining self-respect.[41] Not so in *2 Seconds*. Laurie, the female cycling protagonist, loses: her race, her job, her identity as a professional athlete, her home, her youthful looks, others' respect and self-respect, hope, optimism and a sense of purpose. While the narrative journeys of sporting protagonists tend to evolve around the 'suturing of identity and respect', asserting an 'ideology of competitive individualism,'[42] the story of Laurie takes shape around a narrative trajectory of failure. In doing so, it 'dismantles the logics of success and failure with which we currently live' in a way that echoes Halberstam's assertions, in *The Queer Art of Failure*, that we need to find an alternative 'to cynical resignation on the one hand and naïve optimism on the other.'[43]

Laurie's failures are affirmative without succumbing to a naïve, cruel optimism.[44] Her failures are also 'queer', not necessarily because of her bisexuality, which plays a marginal role in narrative terms, but because they function to situate Laurie outside a framework of success that, 'in a heteronormative, capitalist society equates too easily to specific forms of reproductive maturity combined with wealth accumulation.'[45] This success narrative with its future-orientated temporal trajectory, organised as it is around development and progress, is also tied both to the kind of heteronormative temporality that Freeman refers to as 'chrononormativity'[46] and to the normatively straightforward orientations that Ahmed argues ensure that we stay 'in line' – and 'follow' rather than 'cross the line' – of conventional genealogy.[47] In other words, success and, by extension, happiness, means moving one's life in the 'right' direction at the 'right' time.[48]

The queer (and) feminist critics mentioned here variously highlight the normally taken-for-granted spatial, temporal and affective dimensions of success, winning, progress and happiness – all elements of the 'ideology of competitive individualism' that underpins the sports film and that is so intrinsically intertwined with the foundations of what bell hooks has called the 'white supremacist capitalist patriarchy.'[49] Crucially, the unearthing of the temporal, spatial and sensory registers of normative ideological and affective structures tends to take place, within critical discourse, in relation to those events, objects and practices that unhinge or queer or twist the otherwise invisible, unfelt norm. This is precisely what *2 Seconds* (and, as we will see, *Offside*) manages to achieve. It is through the disorientating modes of spatiality and temporality that shape the film, and that are embodied and given shape by its non-conforming sporting protagonist, that *2 Seconds* makes strange the larger heteropatriarchal grounding of sport, cinema as well as the sports film.

Racing against time

Questions of time and temporality, linked as they are to specific modes of spatiality and perception, are foregrounded in *2 Seconds* from the outset. I want to discuss the opening segment in some detail as it clears the ground upon which the film's affective and spatio-temporal trajectory begins to take shape. *2 Seconds* opens with panoramic shots of a vast mountain range and the icy, sloping surface of a glacier. Various constructions are visible in the margins at the bottom of the frame – a long wooden fence, a cable car station and a building with various antennas, satellite dishes and a post with a rhythmical blinking red light. The final shot of the opening credit sequence shows the blinking light in front of the partially snow-covered mountain range as the audio recording becomes audible on the soundtrack, in sync with the rhythm of the light: '5, 4, 3, 2, 1, 0… we have ignition.' The countdown signals our entry into the diegetic word, which is, at least initially, the world of competitive sporting action. We then see two racers flying down a gritty, winding path and past the camera with breathtaking speed; dust and gravel whirl up around the spinning wheels, conveying a sense of the corporeal risk and danger of their pursuit. Our initial encounter with the film, and with sport (in the film), is thus tied to the importance of (objective, measurable) time and of (good) timing, as well as to the grippingly visceral materiality of cycling.

We are then introduced to the protagonist, Laurie, when we join her and three other female downhill racers, all clad in their racing outfits, in the claustrophobically enclosed space of a cable car – they are on their way to the top of the mountain where their race, the 'pro women's final', is about to get underway. The three women (who are American, with the bilingual Canadian Laurie the odd one out) compare their scars and proudly recount the stories of how and when their previous athletic pursuits have left lasting 'impressions' on their bodies. Butler's assertion that, 'when we think of the athlete's body, we are drawn to […] a body whose contours bear the marks of a certain achievement,' resonates with the kind of athletic body introduced in this scene.[50] So does Ahmed's suggestion that 'past histories […] surface as impressions on the skin' and shape our bodies' 'affective forms of (re)orientation.'[51] The close-up of a pinkish-white, short but slightly bulging scar on the calf of one of the women, and then of a long, thin scar that runs along the sternum of the woman (sitting opposite Laurie) who also sports a number of facial piercings, chains and a choker, foreground how the women's histories of athletic engagement in a 'dangerous' (i.e., masculine) sport surface on their bodies.

What appears, then, in our initial encounter with the characters is a sense of (corporeal) gender trouble. This hinges, at least in part, on the 'challenges to the norm that effectively unsettle the rigidity of gendered expectations and broaden the scope of acceptable gender performance' that women's sport enables.[52] If, as Butler notes, 'certain ideal feminine morphologies come into crisis' through the 'laboured crafting of the athletic body,' it is precisely this crisis that the foregrounding of wounds and scars gestures towards.[53] The likening of scars to 'jewellery' in the women's conversation also plays disruptively with the heteropatriarchal norms around the decoration and ornamentation of the female body, which 'should betray no signs of wear, experience, age.'[54]

Laurie's age (the body's incarnation of time) and her physical deterioration are highlighted, in fairly humorous fashion, when one of the women notices a grey hair on Laurie's head. Her body betrays her as it betrays unwanted signs of ageing. Laurie checks her appearance in the shiny surface of her racing helmet, which is curved and uneven and thus provides a spatially distorted, twisted reflection – similar to the reflection in the convex surface of the wheel of a truck that she uses in a later scene to observe herself cutting off the scandalous grey hair with a pair of shears. It is this kind of slanted, oblique and disorientating reflection of the world that according to Merleau-Ponty produces a 'general effect [that] is "queer"' – and Ahmed uses this as a starting point to develop her phenomenological account of the spatial dimensions of queerness as a twisted orientation, as a mode of gender and sexual embodiment that is 'bent and crooked' and that does not extend (into) the 'straight' world comfortably.[55] She notes that 'queer moments do happen' in phenomenology and that they function to highlight 'how subjects "straighten" any queer effects' because of our tendency to want to 'see straight' and be orientated in space.[56]

Space, from a phenomenological point of view, is not objective and determined by measurable coordinates, but is 'shaped by the purposefulness of the body' and thus constitutes a 'system of possible action.'[57] This is why, normally, 'the body "straightens" its view in order to extend into space' purposefully and intentionally. Queer moments must be overcome, therefore, 'because they block bodily action.'[58] We might say that *2 Seconds* begins with a series of rather queer moments that are intimately tied to Laurie and her situatedness in the athletic sphere and that reach their twisted crescendo in the downhill race that follows the ride in the cable car. The start of the racing sequence in particular gives concrete, tangible shape to the sense of a bent and twisted orientation blocking bodily action.

In downhill racing, athletes do not compete so much against each other as against the clock/time. The racers start individually, at timed intervals. They are not surrounded by other bikers; they race on their own. As Laurie waits for her turn behind the starting area – a small wooden platform with a metal gate that opens at the end of each racer's countdown, marked as a series of electronic beeps – we are provided with a lengthy close-up of the big stopwatch that is positioned to the side of the platform. The racers are thus surrounded by both aural and visual assertions of objective, measured time – their fiercest opponent. The relentlessness of time, and of time passing, is made tangible through the extreme close-up of the clock face that takes up the entire screen, with the bright yellow second-hand moving persistently across the black background to the sound of the countdown. Time is given a specifically spatial dimension here and is explicitly linked to movement. What is conveyed and arguably heightened, cinematically, are the enveloping sensory pressures of time that weigh on the racers, and that might, on occasion, weigh them down.

Rowe observes that, 'it is at the point when time is at its most crucial – the turning point of a sport contest – that film convention requires time to *stand still*.'[59] This is precisely what happens when it is Laurie's turn on the starting platform. A medium shot shows Laurie on her bike in front of the gate. Her full-face racing helmet and protective glasses create a tightly enclosed space around her head and her heavy, tense breathing, accompanied by an unnervingly monotone sync score, becomes audible as other diegetic sounds are more or less drowned out. We are positioned inside the helmet and the audiovisual framing conveys a textural sense of the felt experience within this intimately – claustrophobically, even – enveloping space. Laurie's ever more resonant breathing echoes within this space that keeps sound at close proximity, highlighting both its tactile quality and also the blurring of boundaries between inside and outside that is linked to the sense of hearing, especially as far as sounds emanating *from* the body are concerned. Laurie's athletic body is not visible, wrapped up as it is in racing boots, a padded suit and full-face helmet. Yet, the densely textured soundscape provides us with a tangible intimation of the phenomenological experience of the racer.

In their attempt to 'grasp the phenomenology of sporting bodies', Hockey and Allen-Collinson usefully highlight the importance of 'the aural and respiration' to the sporting experience, noting that sportspeople 'become acutely aware of, and attuned to, their breathing' and that 'these respiratory patterns provide constant and almost instantaneous feedback on bodily states'.[60] Smooth, coordinated, controlled breathing is linked to successful performances, to 'feelings of "flow"' and to 'the experience of optimal fulfilment and engagement in an activity, of being "in the zone", where *time just flies*'.[61] On the other hand, 'tense or erratic breathing is often the enemy of effective bodily control and coordination and thus sporting performance'.[62] Breathing patterns are thus linked not only to 'information' about bodily states and thus potential sporting success, but to 'rhythm and timing' and to the kind of 'distorted' *experience* of time that athletic activity can provide and that can be highly rewarding and pleasurable, leading to 'happiness, even euphoria'.[63]

It is important, therefore, that the gradual sensory shift from outside to inside in the moments immediately preceding the race is also accompanied by a slowing down of cinematic time, interweaving a sense of the corporeality of the sporting body with the making graspable of time and temporality. The medium shot of Laurie waiting in tense and anxious anticipation of the countdown alternates with an over-the-shoulder shot of the clock: Laurie is looking at the seconds ticking away. The sound of the second-hand also echoes loudly on the soundtrack, reasserting the materiality of movement and time as well as Laurie's increasingly distorted sensory experience and 'sense' of time. The slowing down and dragging on of time *in* the film and *for* Laurie, is made visible and audible here. The subsequent extreme close-up of Laurie's face, which shows her slowed-down, slurred blinking eyes framed by her racing glasses, accompanied by the echoing sounds of her laboured, drawn-out breathing, further increases a sense of corporeal proximity.

The shot of Laurie's face is interspersed with two increasingly more proximate extreme close-ups of the pointy end of the second-hand on the clock. The movement of the second-hand, increasingly laboured and at notably prolonged intervals, offers a visual and aural breaking down of time – the explicit visual and aural markers of a second's 'duration' are out of sync with the normative rhythms of objective, measured time. The tiny reverberations of the second-hand following each move become more and more perceptible and, together with the weighty, clunky sounds of each move, also assert the material implications, and substance, of movement and time. Time becomes 'sticky' here and takes on a palpably distorted 'consistency'.

In itself, this slowing down of time is a relatively common occurrence in the sports film. As Rowe notes, at 'critical sport film moments, *time is arrested* as contingencies unfold, and irrevocable outcomes transpire both on the scoreboard and in individual and collective lives.'[64] What is unusual about *2 Seconds* is the grounding of temporality in the sensuous corporeality of the (queer female) protagonist and the utterly anti-climactic implications of this moment that ends, rather startlingly, on a whimper. As the seconds-hand hits the zero mark indicating the start of the race – in extreme close-up and extreme slow motion – the standing still or arresting of time is most closely approximated cinematically. What is conveyed is a sense of what Butler might call 'the suspended moment, the body *out of time*.'[65]

While spectators tend to be seamlessly sutured into the climactic suspension of time in the sports film, *2 Seconds* instead confronts the spectator with a jarring, and arguably comical, return to the normatively objective spatio-temporal dimensions of the diegetic world. The final (suspended, distorted) movement of the clock is followed by an abrupt cut to the metal gate swinging open *in real* (diegetic) *time*. We are, almost violently, pulled out of Laurie's phenomenal world and thrown (back) into the sensory world of the diegesis that seems thin and empty following the densely textured and intimately proximate sensory envelopment of the preceding moments. We hear the metallic sounds of the gate springing open, but then the soundscape becomes eerily and disorientatingly quiet, with only the barely perceptible sounds of the wind providing a sense of the wide-open space on the mountaintop. A few spectators surround the starting platform, as do a handful of journalists with their cameras pointed at Laurie, ready to take a picture of the athlete in action. However, Laurie does not move. She is clearly still 'in the zone'[66] and 'out of time'.[67] While time stands still for Laurie, time moves on mercilessly in the word she occupies. Laurie thus appears not so much only 'out of time' but also 'out of place' in the context of the sporting world in which every second 'counts'. She remains motionless and simply stares straight ahead into the distance for what seems like an eternity to the small diegetic audience – who remain silent but exchange baffled looks and shrug – and also, arguably, to the spectator of the film who has, up until this point, been aligned with Laurie's distorted sense of time and sensitised to her corporeal experience.

When Laurie's breathing becomes audible again on the soundtrack it acts as a sign that she rejoins the normative phenomenal world; she takes a deep breath and finally takes off on her downhill ride. The action sequence makes tangible the physical impact of the race on the bike and the biker as well as the kinaesthetic thrill that comes with blistering speed. Long and extreme long-shots situate Laurie within the spectacularly rugged mountain landscape and alternate with more proximal shots that convey the gritty materiality of the whirlwind ride across the uneven gravel-covered ground. The camera, when providing us with shots over the handlebars that approximate the first-person point of 'view' of the racer, and particularly when attached to the bottom of the bicycle frame, shakes violently, conveying a sense of the weight of the bike and the biker, the pull of gravity, and the rattling reverberations resulting from the continuous, crunching, dusty collision of wheel and gravel. Combined with the equally juddering frontal close-ups of Laurie's face that highlight the droplets of condensed sweat gathering on the inside of her racing glasses, this results in an overall framing of the sporting action that asserts the 'felt' implications of such a breathtakingly exhilarating bumpy ride.

The sequence conveys a sense of an athletic body in sync with itself, its technological extensions (the bike) and the environment. The rumbling, reverberating, layered soundscape, comprised of the noises emanating from the bike's/Laurie's movement across the ground and through the air, while conveying a sense of the potentially dangerous implications of the kinetic energy embodied in and by the film, adds an overall sense of textural coherence to the sequence, making tangible the interconnected textures of bodies, objects and space. It provides a palpable sense that Laurie's is a body that confidently and assertively extends and moves through space, that is in control, and that embodies the kind of believably athletic mode of being-in-the-world that lends a sense of athletic authenticity. While the use of long and extreme long-shots in sporting sequences usually functions as a 'panorama', the situating of Laurie within the unmarked and largely untouched mountain landscape operates rather differently. Rather than embedding the athlete in a specific socio-cultural context, the racing sequence removes Laurie from the confines of socio-cultural pressures and its gritty smoothness asserts instead the pleasures of athletic activity and movement for the sake of athletic activity and movement.

The sequence also further asserts the *dissonances* between (the pleasures of) the phenomenological sporting body and the normatively spatio-temporal structures and pressures already gestured towards in the disorientatingly twisted moments leading up to the racing sequence. When Laurie crosses the finish line her echoed breathing becomes audible again, as does the voice of the announcer over the PA system. Laurie is palpably out of breath after the physically demanding race, but while her breathing is heavy, it is also smooth and controlled and makes tangible the affective pleasures associated with (certain kinds of) corporeal exertion. As Hockey and Allen-Collinson note, 'respiratory patterns' are 'co-related with emotion or feeling states.'[68] When Laurie leans on the handlebars to catch her breath, water trickles off the pedals and frame of her bike, with dripping sounds highlighting its liquid texture. Here, the filmic body gestures towards the symbiotic relation between biker and bike (the water appears to be sweat seeping out of Laurie's helmet, but the bike also seems to sweat) while also stressing the athletic body's corporeal, felt dimensions.

However, the following cut to a medium close-up of Laurie taking off her helmet foregrounds, and makes graspable the affective tensions between Laurie's mode of embodiment on the one hand, and (hetero)normative expectations and pressures on the other. There is a notable jarring between the aural and temporal layers that are co-present in this shot. Laurie removes her helmet in slow motion and begins to shake her head from side to side. In what appears to be a self-consciously subversive reference to the ways in which the (sexualised) female racer tends to be represented in popular culture, Laurie's hair does not elegantly brush across her face. Instead her tousled chin-length dark hair is soaked with sweat, as is her face, and strands of messy hair stick to Laurie's clammy skin while droplets of sweat spray from her head – all in slow motion. Laurie's eyes are closed and her deep and heavy yet controlled and resoundingly self-assured breathing, slowed-down and in sync with her slow-motion movements, is foregrounded on the soundtrack, as are guttural sounds and moans that seemingly imply both exertion and pleasure (in a way that also has sexual connotations). Together with Laurie's facial expression – she slowly cracks a gratified, content smile – these elements convey a sense of the 'happiness, even euphoria', that comes with the sensory experience of the rhythmic, coordinated and smooth 'shape or flow of sporting action.'[69]

The shot also contains another temporal and aural (and thus spatial) layer, however. When Laurie's slowed-down breathing reappears on the soundtrack, the announcer's voice and some of the diegetic environmental sounds remain audible in the sonic background – and they continue at 'normal' speed. The mode of temporality grounded in, and tied to, Laurie – the athlete revelling in a state of pleasurable, sweaty post-race exhaustion – co-exists with, but is simultaneously removed from, the normative, objective temporal order of the 'real' world of the film. The spatial dimensions of sound also mean that two different modes of spatiality brush up against each other rather awkwardly in this scene.

The content of the announcer's speech also further cements the jarring dissonances between the phenomenology of the sporting experience and the larger social-cultural pressures within which athletic activity takes shape and acquires meaning. Laurie's resounding breathing is accompanied by the announcer commenting on what a 'huge disappointment' this race has turned out to be for Laurie: '4:03:26, that's about two seconds away from first place; now, a full two seconds away from first place may as well be measured in light-years in this competition.' What is made explicitly tangible here is the contrast between the affective, embodied implications of sporting activity and its value when objectively measured by accepted standards of (sporting) success. Laurie seems oblivious as to her 'failure' and appears, at least momentarily, to fail productively and to engage in the kind of dismantling of the normative logics of winning/losing and success/failure advocated by Halberstam in *The Queer Art of Failure*.[70]

When Laurie gets fired, her boss reminds her: 'You waited, you lost at least two seconds [...] If you'd gone on the signal, you'd be on the podium right now.' What is asserted here is the arbitrariness of objectively measured time and success. Laurie's failure is not down to her being a slow racer – but to 'bad timing'.[71] The embeddedness of Laurie within the productively disjointed spatio-temporal logics of the film in this opening segment allows her to emerge as a queer figure, that is a figure with the potential to disrupt the spatio-temporal underpinnings of (hetero)normatively teleological incarnations of intentionality, productivity and progress.

Queer-ing time, or: On (not) 'having a life'

Laurie's boss tries to put a positive spin on her forced retirement by framing it as an opportunity for her to finally 'get a life'. Laurie is not just out of sync with the normative temporal logics of the sporting context, but of 'life' in general. 'I don't need a life, this is my life,' is her response. The life that Laurie does not need or want is the kind of life her boss suggests she should 'get'. And the life that Laurie has, and is about to lose – that of an adult professional female athlete ('this') – does not, apparently, live up to the accepted, and naturalised, standards of what it means to 'have a life'.[72]

To 'have a life', Freeman writes, means to be synchronised with the 'larger temporal schemae [of] a chronobiological society' that are maintained by 'narratives of movement and change,' which include 'teleological schemes of events or strategies for living such as marriage, accumulation of health and wealth for the future, reproduction, childrearing, and death and its attendant rituals.' Pursuing these sequences 'of socioeconomically "productive" moments is what it means to have a life at all.'[73] By these chrono-heteronormative standards, Laurie clearly does not 'have a life at all' as the unfolding narrative conveys. Freeman also asserts that 'having a life entails the ability to narrate it [...] in a novelistic framework: as event-centred, goal-oriented, intentional, and culminating in epiphanies or major transformations. The logic of time-as-productive thereby becomes one of serial cause-and-effect: the past seems useless unless it predicts and becomes material for a future.'[74] Of course, the normative logics of the 'having a life' trope also resonate with the narrative conventions of mainstream cinema.[75]

The sense that Laurie does not 'have a life' – or rather that hers is a queer (non-heteronormative and non-productive) life – is intimately tied to her mode of embodiment throughout the film. As I have shown, the opening segment variously foregrounds Laurie's not-fitting-in in specifically temporal terms, particularly in relation to belatedness, bad timing and being 'out of time'. It also highlights, and takes advantage of, the sports context as a space in which processes of (gendered) embodiment are magnified as the body in motion takes centre stage. While the remainder of the film is removed from the (institutionalised) sports context, it is in relation to athleticism and (non-productive) athletic activity that a queerly disruptive sense of non-chrononormativity is articulated. It is specifically through the interweaving of the twisted and disorientating temporalities of sport and cinema that queerness takes shape in *2 Seconds*.

Freeman asserts the significance of time and its various incarnations for the affirmation and perpetuation of heteronormativity, noting that 'institutionally and culturally enforced rhythms, or timings, shape flesh into legible, acceptable embodiment' and that 'naked flesh is bound into socially meaningful embodiment through temporal regulation.'[76] Laurie's appearance – her muscular physique, very short hair (following the loss of her job), no make-up, mostly sporty and/or tight fitting outfits that expose her muscular arms and legs and her obsession with bikes and biking – draws on the figure of the tomboy, which, in relation to adult women, always already connotes a sense of belatedness: flesh not-yet-shaped into acceptable (feminine) embodiment. Tomboyism, in a Western context, tends to be tolerable as a pre-adult phase that is eventually overcome when an acceptable embodiment of femininity is achieved. This narrative trope of 'achievement' is one that is fairly commonly employed in relation to mainstream depictions of the tomboy. It makes the figure of the tomboy visible and simultaneously curtails its troubling potential by disrupting common-sense associations between tomboyism, female masculinity and lesbianism.[77] When embodied by adult women tomboyism connotes both belatedness and failure. The figure of the tomboy also makes the figure of the lesbian 'appear' in certain contexts, however – and the sticky entanglements of female athleticism and lesbianism mean that the sports context provides particular fruitful ground for queer female figurations to surface.

Laurie's queerly distorted relation to time is foregrounded throughout and I have begun to explore how a twisted and twisting temporality begins to surface through and around the protagonist. Before tracing how this mode of spatio-temporal embodiment takes shape in the remainder of the film, I want to note Freeman's assertion that, while cinema tends to be part of the wider institutional forces that contribute to the performative reconstitution of chrononormative patterns, it is also uniquely positioned to disrupt these patterns. On the one hand, film 'creates a historically specific *shared temporality*, setting limits on how long the spectator can dwell on any one object or experience any one story, and thus socializing (or, we might say, binding) the gaze.'[78] On the other, disruptions of the normative temporalities in and of film can 'become productively queer ways to "desocialize" the gaze and intervene in the historical condition of seeing itself' – and certain disruptive aesthetics might have not just 'desocializing but resocializing' implications.[79] I want to go beyond a consideration of look and the gaze (in cinema) – here and elsewhere in the book – and explore the ways in which sensory registers and embodied modes of perception more generally might be de- and re-socialised in and through film. Freeman begins to think through the potentially 'queer politics of cinematic style' and I want to build on her work by foregrounding the possibilities of certain cinematic forms 'dislodg[ing] referentiality' at the level of temporality, spatiality and sensuousness.[80]

2 Seconds's tracing of Laurie's post-sport 'life', or lack thereof, takes place entirely in the urban context. A high-angle establishing shot, showing a vast, urban cityscape, facilitates the transition from the rugged natural landscape of the racing track to the built environment of the city – and, by extension, the industrious and frenzied temporal rhythms that structure city life. The temporal logics and pressures of the sporting context might manifest themselves slightly differently than those of the wider socio-economic context (in the film), but they function in very similar ways: they

Figure 4.1 Laurie (*2 Seconds*)

reinforce a sense of time as structured, productive and teleological. If we 'have a life', we learn to incorporate these normative temporal logics to the extent that 'institutional forces come to seem like somatic facts.'[81] This is also why normative forms of temporal experience that are structured by 'seemingly ordinary bodily tempos and routines' come to appear as 'natural to those whom they privilege.'[82] In other words, naturalised understandings of the 'value and meaning of time' are always already underpinned 'by historically specific regimes of asymmetrical power' – separating those who 'have a life' from those who do not.[83]

When we first see Laurie following the loss of her job, she looks different. Her chin-length, bobbed hair has all but disappeared and been replaced by an extremely short cut that foregrounds the angular and plain features of Laurie's face, and that is also, as her brother notes, 'seriously aerodynamic'. The tight-fitting clothing draws attention to the surface of her muscular, compact and fairly masculine bodily shape. After encountering Laurie's nerdy, single, scientist brother, with whom she has moved in 'just for now', we are introduced to her mother, who has Alzheimer's and lives in a nursing home. Both are peculiar figures with variously odd relations to time. The scientist brother, obsessed with objectivity, control, numbers and rational thought, seems removed from the messy realm of lived, felt experience. He is planning his 'life', wants to move it forward, in the right direction, which is why he is now 'seriously looking for a girlfriend.' He might not have a 'life', but he absolutely wants to get one. Laurie's mother, on the other hand, seems to have had a life – but she does not remember. She has lost her memory and her 'past' – and therefore also a sense of the present. Time, as passing and productive, does not exist for her.

When Laurie visits her mother she is sitting in a wheelchair by the window, staring into the distance and moving back and forth in the wheelchair, slowly but persistently. She is moving to pass the time and to feel (the passing of) time, but she is not going anywhere. She moves without direction and a without a sense of productive purpose or intent. It is movement for the sake of movement that seems soothing and that seems to provide her with a sense of grounding in the here and now. When Laurie sees her in this state, she comments that it 'must be the wheels', gesturing towards the sensory, affective pleasures that certain kinds of movement provide. At first, Laurie's mother does not recognise her daughter. However, when Laurie sits down on a rocking bench and starts to move back and forth, in sync with her mother's movement in the wheelchair, her mother joins her on the bench and appears to suddenly remember her daughter, asking Laurie how she is and when she came back to the city. Laurie's mother's regaining of a sense of the past, and thus the present, is specifically linked to movement and rhythm – the kind of movement that does not take us anywhere and might well be considered 'pointless' and a 'waste of time' within a chrononormative frame. The scene also points to the significance of a *shared* sense of rhythm and time and its role in generating a sense of connection and belonging. As Freeman notes with reference to Pierre Bourdieu's notion of *habitus*, 'cultural competence and belonging itself are matters of timing.'[84] The particular corporeal and affective implications of different kinds of (queer, twisted) movements and temporalities that are given shape through Laurie's encounter with her mother resonate with, and further assert, Laurie's alignment with a mode of embodiment that does not fit (hetero)normative spatio-temporal logics and patterns.

They also provide a tangibly affective link to the often aimless movement that Laurie engages in throughout the film and that functions to assert a particularly non-chrononormative, queer sense of time. Following the visit with her mother, Laurie goes for a bike ride. The lead-up to the cycling scene constitutes a self-conscious play with the variously sticky entanglements of the bike, the biker, movement and time. In preparation for the ride, Laurie reassembles her bike. It is the one thing she has brought with her, the one remaining material connection to her former 'life'. An overhead shot shows us Laurie as she stands in front of a pile of individual, disassembled parts of her bike in her brother's living room – her life is in pieces. The camera begins to spin (in a clockwise direction) at increasingly faster speed as Laurie manually begins to put her bike, and her 'life', back together. When the camera comes to a standstill again, the bike is assembled – although one important piece, the 11-tooth sprocket, is missing. The manipulation of cinematic *movement* is linked, overtly and self-consciously, to the manipulation of cinematic *time*. The preparation sequence also includes a close-up of the ticking clock on the living room wall (which resembles the clock on the starting platform in the opening sequence), with a very slow, gradual dissolve superimposing an image of the spinning bicycle wheel onto the clock face.

The bike ride itself has no aim or purpose. We see Laurie cycling uphill, on a wide, paved road leading out of the city, only for her to turn around at the top and begin to cycle down again. When she reaches the top, she is visibly and audibly out of breath and her sweaty face conveys the intermingling of exhaustion and pleasure that we have already seen in the opening sequence – only this time, there are no time pressures. Laurie begins her cycle before dawn, in the dark, and catches a glimpse of the sunrise at the top of the mountain. She is clearly not in sync with the normative and acceptable temporal rhythms and patterns of 'life'. This is why Laurie's movements are, while physically demanding and exhausting, unrestrained and unbound by normative tendencies and pressures.

Ahmed usefully points to the different meanings and phenomenological dimensions:

> of the word 'pressure': the social pressure to follow a certain course, to live a certain kind of life, and even to reproduce that

life can feel like a physical 'press' on the surface of the body, which creates its own impressions. We are pressed into lines [straightforward ones, which we should follow], just as lines are the accumulation of such moments of pressure, or what I call 'stress points'.[85]

Social pressures to 'have a life', or at least to try and 'get' one, can be felt at the surface of the body – and these pressures are felt most acutely when our mode of embodiment is *not* aligned with, and *not* in line with, normative habits, tendencies, orientations, directions and intentions. In *2 Seconds*, the foregrounding of the surface and materiality of the athletic female body as well as the sensuous dimensions of time and space give shape to and thus convey a graspable sense of these pressures (that are not so easily made 'visible' in straightforward representational terms). It is specifically in relation to athletic activity – which enables a foregrounding of the spatio-temporal, felt dimensions of (queer female) embodiment – that normative pressures are both given a tangible presence in the film and, at the same time, resisted and made strange. A sense of queerness is therefore not necessarily tied to a specific (character) identity but surfaces via the multi-layered textural and sensory register of the film.

Affective encounters across time, or: How 'cycling can make you drunk'

The improvised plastic sprocket that Laurie has used to fix her bike breaks off when she picks up speed on the downhill cycle and this leads to her first encounter with Lorenzo (Dino Tavarone), the grumpy, old former professional cyclist with Italian origins who now owns a tiny bicycle shop in an old factory building at the end of a dead-end street. Laurie enters the shop to buy a new sprocket and this is the beginning of a series of wonderfully humorous and poignantly affective encounters. In Lorenzo, Laurie finds an unlikely queer ally – he is a figure equally 'out of time'. Stepping into his shop is like stepping 'back in time'. Lorenzo refuses to be rushed; he needs time (and 'peace and quiet') to work on and repair bikes. Like Laurie he is not in sync with normative temporal patterns and expectations. When customers enter his shop, he leaves them waiting. He refuses to engage in small talk with them, a waste of time that he would rather spend (at) tending to his bikes. He also never laces a wheel during the day: 'too much noise, too many people – wheels like intimacy.' When Lorenzo tells Laurie about his experience as a young cyclist, he also puts into words the distorted and disorientating experience of time that comes with cycling and that is made tangible in relation to Laurie's character at various points in the film: 'I don't know if you know, but cycling can make you drunk. You lose all sense of time. The speed becomes a drug […] you are not aware of anything [and] just keep pedalling.' What centrally connects the characters, therefore, is a shared sense of a twisted and not straightforward embodiment of time (linked to athletic activity).

Lorenzo repairs bikes manually, granting them exceptional tenderness, attention and care, which contrasts with the utter lack of attention and care he offers his customers. His intimately tactile relationship to the materiality and surface of bicycles, and the individual parts that make them up, is foregrounded through frequent close-ups of his calloused hands touching and moving across the metallic surfaces of wheels, sprockets and frames. The evocation of sensuality in relation to bikes and biking aligns Lorenzo's mode of being-in-the-world with Laurie's, as she is repeatedly shown fixing her bike in her brother's living room. They are allies even if they do not 'see eye to eye' in some of their encounters, which are initially framed as a clashing of *generations* (i.e., those separated by progressive, linear time). Lorenzo sees himself as part of a disappearing generation of 'real cyclists' who do not shy away from hard work and 'enjoy the pain' that comes with cycling; and he sees Laurie has part of today's generation of 'kids' who are 'spoiled' because they rely on technology and 'don't like pain enough.' However, through their various encounters in Lorenzo's shop, they gradually develop a mutual recognition of their similarly queer situatedness in relation to time and space that begins to take shape as an intimately close connection. It is a decidedly 'queer' relationship, grounded in a shared sense of lack of (spatio-temporal) fit and of being 'out of time' that is variously tied to their similarly visceral, tactile and muscular relations to cycling. Their similar names – Laurence/Laurie, Lorenzo – also suggest a sense of affective doubling/mirroring across gender, age, culture and time.

The lasting impressions that cycling leaves on the body are asserted primarily through Laurie. Her muscular, athletic physicality is the (visible) result of the habituated bodily action of cycling. Her sweaty face and heavy breathing assert the lived corporeality of the cyclist, as do close-ups of Laurie bandaging her bloodied ankles. The impressions that biking leaves on the biker are perhaps most humorously and viscerally affectively articulated in a scene in which Laurie takes off her cycling shorts and sits down in large bowl filled with ice cubes and cold water in order to soothe her bruised bottom. While Lorenzo does not cycle anymore – he is too old – his body continues to bear the marks of a lifetime of cycling. He notes that the seat of his treasured old bike that he keeps in his shop, and that nobody is allowed to touch, 'is still engraved' on him.

Towards the end of the film, Laurie and Lorenzo engage in a wonderfully competitive exchange about who has suffered the most from cycling and who enjoys pain more (recalling the female racers' bragging about their scars in the opening sequence of the film): Lorenzo cannot sit down anymore because of his back pain. Laurie's ankles hurt and she has broken her collarbone three times, as well as her tibia. Lorenzo has an artificial knee. Laurie has a pinched sciatic nerve. Lorenzo has lost all feelings in his hands from clutching the handlebars. Laurie gets pimples on her forehead from sweating, which Lorenzo says is 'aesthetic' and does not count. When they agree that aesthetic suffering does count after all, Lorenzo pulls down his trousers and reveals a cycling tan that seems imprinted on his skin even though he has not 'worn shorts in 30 years'. Lorenzo also has black fingernails from working with gears and chains. They additionally share experiences of not being able to 'perform' sexually because prolonged cycling can make you numb 'down there'. It is a shared sense of the pleasurable pain and suffering that come with cycling and the cumulative sedimentation of the embodied experience of cycling, intertwined as it is with a twisted embodiment of time, that connects the characters. It is cycling, therefore, that opens up possibilities for resistance to chrononormative pressures.

The development of Laurie's wonderfully queer connection with Lorenzo, the primary relationship in the film, parallels Laurie's (not) finding her feet in her new job as a bike courier – and it is only in the very final moments of the film that these different worlds collide. Laurie and Lorenzo share a sense of (the value and meaning of) time and timing within the world of Lorenzo's shop, which seems removed from the

Queering the Sports Film

Figure 4.2 Life as a Bike Courier (*2 Seconds*)

outside world in space and time and which 'extends their shape.'[86] This contrasts markedly with the outside world that provides the setting for the narrative strand that evolves around Laurie's work. Her new occupation means that cycling remains central to the film, even if it no longer takes place as a sport. However, the similarities with and parallels to the sports context are variously alluded to – and this is one of the ways in which *2 Seconds* plays, subversively I would argue, with the conventions of the sports film.

Laurie joins a group of seasoned, and mostly male, bike couriers. She is the new member of a team in which she needs to prove herself: her cycling skills are initially questioned, partially because she is a 'girlie'. When the other couriers realise the extent of Laurie's cycling abilities, some of them feel threatened and attempt to undermine her – a trope frequently employed to articulate team dynamics in the sports film. The point of cycling is no longer winning races, medals and championships, but it is extremely competitive nonetheless. The couriers race against the villainous inner-city taxi drivers, against each other, and most importantly, against time. Time seems even more rigorous and regimented as the couriers are under enormous pressure to complete deliveries on time. Questions of time, temporality, timing and timeliness continually resurface throughout this segment, in particular through the manipulations of time – slowing down, speeding up – during cycling sequences, with the sonic reverberations of Laurie's breathing tying the cinematic rendering of time to the corporeality of the cyclist. By removing cycling from the context of competitive sport and embedding it in a less 'playful' and more overtly socio-economic context, *2 Seconds* links the particular modes of embodiment cultivated in and through athletic activity, and their potentially queer implications, to the larger spatio-temporal and affective structures that shape our world and the bodies that occupy it (and are occupied within it).

Unsurprisingly, Laurie struggles to incorporate the rigidly temporal rhythms and patters that normally structure the daily 'life' of a courier. Laurie is under pressure to be on time and therefore, rather often, running late. While the other couriers cut corners whenever they can to 'save time' and to make the most productive use of their time, Laurie takes on deliveries to distant locations so she can cycle for longer. The first time she is out on a delivery she cycles past the destination: 'I guess I forgot I have to stop somewhere'. When the other couriers ask her why she does not join them for lunch anymore, she responds: 'I'm never downtown at noon. Downtown you stop all the time. I want to ride.' The queer temporality embodied by Laurie is perhaps most poignantly articulated in a scene in which we see Laurie receiving a radio call from her boss as she cycles over a bridge. When he asks her where she is, Laurie looks up and around her, seemingly confused and disorientated. She does not know where she is and has to get her bearings and reorientate herself in space and time before she can provide information about her location. When she tells her boss that she 'forgot to stop', he reminds her, angrily, that she is 'not paid to ride'. The scene gestures towards the feelings of being 'in the zone' that engagement in the repetitive, rhythmic movements of athletic activities such as running and cycling can provide and that can make us lose all sense of objectively constituted time and space.[87]

Queer modes of embodiment and temporality are more explicitly intertwined with a sense of queer *desire* in the final part of *2 Seconds*, following Laurie's and Lorenzo's fairly comical verbal exchange about injury and suffering. The conversation takes a more serious turn when Lorenzo recounts his most 'painful' cycling experience. Lorenzo's story is articulated through a series of flashbacks that are explicitly framed as Laurie's *visualising* of Lorenzo's experience, with Lorenzo's monologue functioning as a voiceover. A young, dashing Lorenzo (played by Jonathan Bolduc) leaves Italy for the first time to participate in a race in the US. He is ahead of the pack and the likely winner when his wheel gets caught in a hole on an empty, rural country road. That is when he sees a young woman, 'the prettiest girl in the world,' who stands at the side of the road. Lorenzo's account of the brief encounter recalls his earlier description of losing a sense of time through cycling: 'I forget where I am, I don't even know if I'm breathing. It's like time was standing still. It was love at first sight. I don't know how long I've stood there. My mind goes blank, I forget everything.' With the exception of the reference to love at first sight, this is also a very apt description of Laurie's experience of losing two fatal seconds in the race depicted in the opening segment.

Lorenzo is violently pulled back into the here and now of the race by a coach who orders him to get back on his bike. Lorenzo wins, but, as he notes, 'winning is relative.' The encounter with the young woman is life-changing for Lorenzo, even though, or perhaps because, he never sees her again. Cycling is suddenly 'not the same' and Lorenzo fails to see the point of 'riding for hours and hours, going nowhere.' He loses his desire to get on his bike, the only kind of desire he has ever known, and does not care anymore if he wins or loses. His only goal, from that moment on 'was to find that girl... and make time stand still again.' Lorenzo's desire is an impossible one, its directionality and temporality queer and 'backwards'. He acknowledges that he 'had a chance and made the wrong decision' by getting back on the bike, and that 'after... after it's too late.' Lorenzo, like Laurie, embodies a sense of belatedness. He also, like Laurie, does not have what normally counts as a 'life'. He hangs onto the past and is orientated towards it. His appearance in his shop, which is filled with objects from his cycling past (his bike, newspaper clippings and photographs of his cycling success), is as a figure from a different time – and his longing for the past, and the girl he met 'there', while underpinned by his heterosexuality, is profoundly queer and certainly not straightforward.

The framing of the exchange – Lorenzo's narration, close-ups of his face in the here-and-now of the film, alternating with visual 'flashbacks' that are explicitly marked as products of Laurie's imagination – also continues to weave an increasingly more complex layering of temporal relations around the characters, in which cycling and desire are intimately intertwined. It is also from this multifaceted opening-up of spatio-temporal possibilities that more explicit articulations of Laurie's (sexual) desire emerge. As she embarks on her next courier delivery following the exchange, she continues to re-visualise parts of Lorenzo's story, especially those involving the mysterious young woman. She imagines herself in Lorenzo's shoes, engaging in the exchange of looks of 'love at first sight' with the woman. Incidentally, it is because of her preoccupation with the young woman, which brings a dreamy smile on her face, that Laurie loses track of time and place for a second time. The close framing of Laurie on the bike also obscures the viewer's sense of where she is. When she receives a radio call from her boss she lifts her head as the camera pulls back – and she realises, and we with her, that she has somehow ended up on a country road (similar to the one in Lorenzo's story). Again, a disorientating sense of time is both grounded in the phenomenology of the cyclist and, in this case explicitly, linked with queer desire. The directionality of this desire (for a woman) is both backward (towards the woman in Lorenzo's past) and forward (as Laurie encounters the woman at the end of the film). The figure of the woman, whose visual appearance (in the film) is, at least initially, the product of Laurie's imagination and who embodies a range of complex temporalities, also provides an additional, queerly twisted yet tangible connection between Laurie and Lorenzo.

In the perhaps most poignantly comical twist of the film, the young woman, billed as La Bella and played by Suzanne Clément, also appears as a 'real' character in the 'real' diegetic world of the film. Laurie encounters her when she fails, yet again, to complete a delivery on time. La Bella is a photographer and, incidentally, works at a racing course and is responsible for the photo finish: she produces photographs that break down movement and time into minute detail to enable more precise, scientific evidence of who wins a race (a fairly obvious reference to Eadweard Muybridge's stop-motion photography of Leland Stanford's trotter, which is considered to be one of the most significant precursors of cinema).[88] They meet when

Laurie drops off a (late) delivery in the darkroom in the stadium and time slows down briefly when Laurie first sees La Bella. La Bella sets a timer to keep track of the developing negatives and the seconds tick away in the background as the women look at each other in a queerly twisted rendition of 'love at first sight'.

This uncanny encounter that further scrambles the temporal coordinates of the film precedes the final sequence, a bike race that the couriers have organised amongst themselves, for fun rather than with seriously competitive aims. Laurie and La Bella are there too, but just to watch, because Laurie lost her bike in the accident that ultimately led to her (belated) encounter with La Bella. The queerly utopian feel of this final and supposedly climactic racing sequence is linked to Lorenzo, who suddenly appears out of nowhere and gives Laurie his treasured bike and racing top so she can participate in the race. Laurie kisses La Bella before getting on her bike, leaving behind only Lorenzo and La Bella, who takes a picture of Laurie cycling away. Lorenzo eventually takes a proper look at La Bella and, startled, seems to recognise her, presumably as the young woman from his past.

The various temporal layers that shape the film come together in this final sequence in a queerly twisted refusal to succumb to the pressures of heteronormative temporalities and desire. *2 Seconds* ends with a still of Laurie mid-race and with a broad grin on her face. We do not get to see the end of the race and who wins, because this is not the 'point' of cycling in the film. It is, instead, the affirmative reshaping of spatio-temporal relations, the various encounters and points of contact they open up, and the possibility of a different kind of 'life' they gesture towards, which surface as the lasting resonances the film leaves behind.

On Being *Offside*: Lines and (Tres)passing

Panahi's *Offside* might appear as more overtly queer than *2 Seconds* – at least for the Western audience that constitutes the primary audience for the film, which was banned in Iran. *Offside* does not so much have a protagonist as an ensemble of central characters, six young women who remain nameless and are billed as First Girl (Sima Mobarak-Shahi), Smoking Girl (Shayesteh Irani), Soccer Girl (Ayda Sadeqi), Girl with Tchador (Golnaz

Framani), Girl Disguised as Soldier (Mahnaz Zabihi) and Young Girl (Nazanin Sediq-zadeh). The women are disguised as men for the purposes of gaining entry into Teheran's Azadi stadium to watch a football match. At first 'glance', then, *Offside* evolves around a group of cross-dressing characters who foreground potentially potent, and potently queer, questions around (in)visibility, passing and the performative dimensions of gender.

All the characters fail to pass *in* the film – they are caught and forced to spend the entirety of the game in a makeshift holding pen outside the stadium walls, guarded by military officers. However, the believability of their failure to pass plays out much more ambiguously in relation to spectatorial engagements *with* the film. The gender disguise is made 'visible' in relation to First Girl and Young Girl, for instance – it is the disguise itself that 'appears' (we can 'see' that they are girls dressed as boys). However, Smoking Girl, in particular – the most forward, cheeky and vocal character – embodies her gender disguise so convincingly, that it is, I would argue, difficult to 'see' how and why she did not pass within the diegetic world of the film. Her troublingly ambiguous appearance thus invokes a self-reflective mode of spectatorship. We are encouraged to reflect upon *what it is* that appears when she appears on screen, or rather, what *would* appear if we did not know about the disguise and that she was 'really' a

Figure 4.3 Smoking Girl (*Offside*)

woman. More broadly, questions around *how* sex, gender and sexuality appear in different contexts therefore underpin the engagement with 'gender (tres)passing', or what Roshanak Kheshti calls a 'transgender move', in and through *Offside*.[89] The film encourages a mode of spectatorial self-reflexivity that is intimately tied to questions around what the body does or can (not) reveal/make visible that are also evoked by *Tomboy* (as discussed in Chapter 5).

Cross-dressing, or the gender disguise trope, in what Chris Straayer has called the 'temporary transvestite film', is fairly well-established in Western mainstream cinema. While promising to trouble a binary gender order, it tends to serve conservatively heteronormative purposes in films such as *Some Like it Hot* (Billy Wilder, US, 1959), *Mrs Doubtfire* (Chris Columbus, US, 1993), *Victor/Victoria* (Blake Edwards, UK/US, 1982) and *Tootsie* (Sydney Pollack, US, 1982).[90] Straayer identifies a set of generic characteristics that encapsulate the temporary transvestite film's heteronormative underpinnings. They include:

> the narrative necessity of the disguise; adoption by a character of the opposite's sex's specifically gender-coded costume (and often its accessories, makeup, gestures, behaviors, and attitudes); the simultaneous believability of this disguise to the film's characters and its unbelievability to the film's audience; visual, behavioural, and narrative cues to the character's 'real' sex; the transvestite character's sensitization to the plight and pleasures of the opposite sex; reference to biological sex difference and the 'necessary' cultural separation of the sexes; a progression towards slapstick comedy and increased physicality; heterosexual desire thwarted by the character's disguise; accusations of homosexuality regarding the disguised character; romantic encounters that are mistakenly interpreted as homosexual or heterosexual; an 'unmasking' of the transvestite; and, finally, heterosexual coupling.[91]

These patterns, and the use of comedy in particular, both create and control queer possibilities, and they also both challenge and ultimately reaffirm normatively binary gender codes. Within the Western mainstream representational context, the gender disguise trope tends to take place in relation to male characters disguised as women (often for comedic effect), rather than female characters disguised as men. Femininity, and feminine excess, is something that is easily put on and taken off, whereas masculinity is much less easily performed; it is what remains when feminine excess is stripped away. Depictions of male characters' frequently failed attempts at performing femininity (i.e., that which does not come 'naturally' to them) are at the heart of the humour of gender disguise comedies. Women's attempts at passing as men – as, for instance, in *Albert Nobbs* (Rodrigo Garcia, UK, 2011) – are much less funny. They constitute much more serious, and potentially troubling, transgressions of gender norms – and these depictions also tend not to follow the gender disguise/temporary transvestite trope outlined by Straayer.

These patterns emerge specifically in relation to, and are enabled by, the gendered representational conventions of Western mainstream cinema that are broadly structured around the visual display of a spectacular femininity and the objectification and sexualisation of the female body for the purposes of securing the stability and coherence of male subjectivity. The female body and gender/looking relations are incorporated rather differently in Iranian cinema, especially the New Iranian Cinema, and the ways in which it is embedded in the boarder socio-cultural and political context of post-revolutionary Iran – a point I return to in more detail shortly.

It is worth noting here that the gender disguise trope has made a relatively recent, occasional appearance in the (Western) sports film context. *Juwanna Man* (Jesse Vaughan, US, 2002), for instance, features a male sporting protagonist, Jamal Jeffries (Miguel A. Núñez Jr.) who 'poses' as a woman, Juwanna Man, in order to play on a professional women's basketball team. One of the ways in which we are constantly reminded of the disguised character's 'real' sex is in relation to his superior athletic abilities. He fails at 'playing like a girl'. The gender-segregated nature of the sports context, as well as normative equations of athleticism and maleness/masculinity, provide a particularly suitable context for the humorous and spectacularly heteronormative reassertion of binary gender norms. *She's the Man* (Andy Fickman, US, 2006) constitutes a notable exception in this context – and one worth mentioning in relation to *Offside*. *She's the Man* features a female protagonist, Viola (Amanda Bynes), who appears in male disguise. Viola pretends to be her twin brother, Sebastian (James Kirk), in order to play football/soccer, as the girls' team at her high school has been cut. While *She's the Man* does, following Straayer's generic patterns, eventually re-establish reassuringly heteronormative binary gender norms, the film also offers a critical commentary on the gender segregated nature of sport and girls'/women's marginalisation in this context – and, importantly, it is *not* Viola's/Sebastian's inferior athletic skills that lead to the eventual dismantling of the disguise.

On the surface, *Offside* appears broadly aligned with the temporary transvestite trope, with the exception, perhaps, of explicit references to sexual desire that might be queerly (mis)read and of a narrative culminating in heterosexual coupling (all of which are central to *She's the Man*, for instance). That said, the 'gender (tres)passing' trope signifies in a much more complex and ambiguously queer manner in *Offside*, especially when taking the Iranian historical and socio-political context, and the particular (cinematic) manifestations of gender and sexuality it enables and reinforces, into account. As Kheshti notes, the white, Western-centric assumptions and post-structuralist tenets underpinning queer theory, and associated notions of gender and sexual 'subversion', including trans, cannot adequately grasp the particular incarnations of gender and (hetero)sexual norms that are re-made within the Iranian context.[92] These tensions are particularly pronounced, and visible, in relation to cinema and its (potentially) trans- and intercultural dimensions. Similar contradictions also arise in relation to sport, and women's presence within that context, as I discuss below.

Offside emerges from the broader context of the New Iranian Cinema that developed in response to, and is significantly shaped by, the post-revolutionary political and cultural situation in Iran. It is characterised by a broadly neo-realist aesthetic, including the use of non-professional actors and practices of filming on location. Panahi recruited non-professional actors for *Offside* and most of the filming took place in Tehran's Azadi Stadium on 8 June 2005, during the World Cup qualifying match (Iran vs. Bahrain) that provides the backdrop to the film. Since Panahi was unable to obtain official permission to shoot inside the stadium, the filmmaking process resonates, and is intimately intertwined, with the film's content as well as its formal and affective implications. Panahi and his crew had to smuggle small, handheld cameras into the stadium.

Figure 4.4 First Girl, (tres)passing (*Offside*)

The filming had to take place as unobtrusively and invisibly as possible, resulting in an even more tangibly neo-realist documentary mode and in a heightening of the 'aesthetics of veiling' that is more generally characteristic of the New Iranian Cinema.[93] For instance, the disorientating camera movements, disjointed editing and close framing of First Girl as she walks towards the stadium, the camera at shoulder height, always just behind or beside her, convey the sense of risk, vulnerability and the fear of being 'found out' experienced by the character. They also make acutely graspable the material dimensions of risk and (tres)passing (gender and otherwise). Like the female characters, Panahi, his crew and his camera are not supposed to be where they are – they are *offside* (on the wrong side of the fence that surrounds the stadium) and too 'forward'. Sites, moments and processes of '(tres)passing' thus manifest themselves in a multifaceted, multi-layered and multi-textural manner in and through *Offside* – and not just in relation to questions of gender and sexuality. The depictions of cross-dressing and gender disguise, and their potentially queer implications, need to be considered in terms of how they are situated, and how they resonate, within the larger network of signifying relations that revolve around questions of (in)visibility, appearance, passing and veiling.

Robert Stam links the transgressive, illegal, implications of being 'offside' to the transgression of other 'lines' in a way that resonates productively with Ahmed's account of the straightforward spatio-temporal structures that ensure that we stay 'in line', and that we 'follow the line', rather than cross it.[94]

> The meanings of the title – *Offside* – come to ripple outward from the initial literal denotations of transgressing an invisible yet consequential virtual soccer line to evoke the symbolic transgression of other lines, both visible and invisible, lines between law and desire, between etiquette and its disruption, between inside and outside, between men and women, and between documentary and fiction. Challenging one line – for example in relation to gender – subtly impacts all the other lines.[95]

An acknowledgement of the literal and symbolic transgression of various 'lines' is useful as it highlights the intersections of different divides – and it is this crossing of lines that makes *Offside* an example of what Stam calls 'offside cinema'.[96] However, in order to grasp more fully the troubling resonances of the film, we should also account for the sensuous, visceral and spatio-temporal dimension of the transgressing, reshaping, twisting and blurring of visible and invisible lines that underpin the more 'obvious', and more easily discernible, patterns of (tres)passing in the film. It is in relation to this corporeal, sensuous realm that *Offside* reorientates normative perceptual habits and tendencies.

The complex interweaving of the materiality of the filmmaking process, form and content surfaces particularly poignantly in relation to *Offside*'s ending. The sense of tension and urgency that saturates the final scenes, which take place primarily inside a small van that takes the young women away from the stadium and to the Vice Squad headquarters during the closing moments of the game, is imbued with a graspably realist dimension. The scenes were shot during, and thus embody, the film crew's frantic escape from the stadium after they were 'found out' by security personnel. 'Panahi, like the women in the film, also had to do an "end run" around the authorities' – about which more later.[97]

Offside's broadly neo-realist tendencies also include the narrative's unfolding in real time, which contrasts starkly with the temporal dislocations and disorientations of *2 Seconds*. *Offside*'s running time is approximately 90 minutes, the duration of a football match – and there is even a half-time toilet break. Together with the use of non-professional actors, who get to choose their own gender-disguise strategies and appearances, and location shooting, the narrative's unfolding in real time makes for a film that, as Panahi notes, transgresses the boundaries between documentary and fiction:

> The film is constructed like a documentary in which I have inserted fictional characters. Are we in a documentary, or is this fiction? I wanted the action to reflect this ambiguity. We tried to preserve a unity of time, so with each second that passes, I want the audience to feel that they are watching a real event unfold. The places are real, the event is real, and so are the characters and the extras.[98]

Offside, then, also engages in a certain generic (tres)passing in a way that 'self-reflexively highlights the machinations of cinema.'[99] It thus raises important questions about how the 'reality' (of cinema and of gender) appears on screen, and about how veiling, passing, disguise and (in)visibility manifest themselves, and are given visibility, both on and off-screen.

It is also worth noting here that Panahi was prepared for all eventualities and had an alternative ending in mind, accounting for the possibility of an Iranian loss and a lack of public celebrations. This preparedness to 'go with the flow' of events as they unfold feeds into the graspable sense of immediacy and unpredictability that permeates the film. Together with the unfolding of events in real time *in* the film, it also, importantly, foregrounds *Offside*'s affinity with the live coverage of sporting events. It is, in part, this affinity, and the expectations around sports spectatorship associated with liveness, that allow for the denial of conventional spectatorial access to the footballing action in *Offside* to carry additional affective, disorientating weight. More generally, the intermingling of generic elements of live sports coverage, the sports documentary and the fictional sports film heightens the subversively troubling implications of the complete disregard for even the most basic expectations around 'the sports gaze' that depends on 'identification, nearness, and participation.'[100]

The Iranian context: cinema, football and the 'nation'

Kheshti explains that 'the New Iranian cinema of the 1990s has emerged as a premier institution for the construction of notions of Iranianness and national belonging and is a privileged site for the contestation of Hollywood's hegemony and the repressive tactics of the Islamic Republic of Iran.'[101] It is, in other words, a cinema that emerged in response to both local/national and global pressures. *Offside* engages centrally with the marginalisation and oppression of women in Iran, and within the sports context. At the same time, the film avoids playing into 'Western stereotypes about women and sport under Islam' and decentres 'assumptions and biases that inhere around discourses of the non-Western woman in sport.'[102] *Offside* also works partially within, while profoundly subverting, the norms and regulations of the censorship code imposed by the Ministry of Cultural and Islamic Guidance, especially with regard to the modesty rules around codes of dress, gaze and behaviour that have profoundly shaped 'the portrayal and treatment of women' in Iranian cinema.[103]

Hamid Naficy notes that from the mid-1980s:

> an aesthetics and grammar of vision and veiling based on gender segregation developed, which governed the character's dress (long, loose-fitting), behaviour and acting (dignified, no body contact between men and women), and gaze (averted look, no direct gaze) [...] In addition, women were often filmed in long shot and in inactive roles so as to prevent the contours of their bodies from showing. Both men and women were desexualised and cinematic texts became androgynous.[104]

These conventions mean that sex, gender and sexuality 'appear' differently on screen – or, we might say, sex, gender and sexuality appear on different grounds. Perhaps paradoxically, the aesthetic and narrative tropes that developed, at least in part, in response to censorship also open up a range of queer possibilities. They are, as Kheshti argues, 'partly responsible for the formation of what has come to be a ubiquitous figure in the New Iranian cinema: the "cross-dressing" or "passing" figure.'[105] Khesthi identifies what she calls a 'transgender move', a 'temporary space of political and agential potential' that evolves around the cross-dressing or passing figure.[106] Kheshti takes care not to suggest a simplistic, causal link between these formations and argues instead that the 'ever-present tropes of passing and cross-dressing in Iranian cinema' constitute an 'originary site of representation' that 'has opened up sites of cultural and discursive possibility.'[107]

While the cross-dressing/passing protagonist might have been 'originally conceived as a vehicle for the representation of "unveiled" female agency [...] it figures additionally as a queer trope.' Kheshti's account of this (tres)passing figure is thus highly relevant here:

> I read the transgendered narrative trope of the cross-dressing figure in Iranian cinema as one with the potential for polyvalent meanings of resistance and transgression that get read differently through various routes of intra and transnational circulation. I read trans and queer presences within the aesthetics of resistance in the New Iranian cinema that simultaneously resists the post-revolutionary nation-state and various Euro-American imperial forces (for example, Hollywood). I aim to map the instances where queer and transgender spaces enable moments of subjective transcendence [...] These are not openings that will *necessarily* be occupied by queer or transgender subjects; instead, these openings are available, even momentarily, as *spaces of queer and transgender ontology* that [...] have also come to be manifested in social life thanks in part to the spaces established within these filmic sites.[108]

The complex implications, asserted here by Kheshti, of how films such as *Offside* circulate and signify – locally, nationally, transnationally – and of the role they play in contemporary negotiations around Iranianness and Iranian identity are worth foregrounding here. They gesture towards the very similar roles played by cinema and sport (especially football) in offering spaces for the negotiation of Iranianness and belonging in a context that is marked by the intersections of the local, the global, gender, sexuality and nation.

Both sport and cinema are situated at the intersection of, and blur the boundaries between, the public and the private in a way that furthers the exclusion, marginalisation and invisibility of women. For instance, in Iran women are allowed to watch the public spectacle of sport, but only in front of the television and within the confines of the home. As Kim Toffoletti notes, sports fandom and spectatorship constitute practices of social identification and belonging, especially in the context of international sporting events that mobilise public assertions of 'the nation' and offer a space for 'the formation of collective identities and communities.'[109] Women's exclusion from the sporting sphere is therefore profoundly linked to the ways in which particular gender relations and figurations underpin understandings of the nation and the ways in which they are asserted and negotiated in the public realm.

With regard to cinema, especially its contribution to discourses around national identity and the nation, women's position is similarly precarious. Modesty rules demand the veiling of female characters because cinema is a public spectacle, meaning the female body is exposed to the looks of men who are not close relatives – even when female characters are depicted in domestic spaces where they would normally be unveiled. This makes it difficult to portray women 'realistically' within domestic spaces. More generally, the requirements around veiling and modesty turn the 'acceptable' representation of women into a rather complicated and difficult endeavour. It limits the extent to which women can be 'present' within cinema. In the Iranian context, therefore, the troubling and transgressive implications of *Offside* (which led to the film's ban in Iran) hinge primarily on the presence of *unveiled* female characters, rather than, as it might in the Western context, on their cross-dressing and disguise.[110]

It is worth noting here that this is not an attempt to tie the significance and meaning of the film to specific and seemingly self-contained signifying and reception contexts. Rather, the aim is to gesture towards the various sense-making regimes that 'gather around' the film and that help to contextualise the cinematic presence of the unveiled, cross-dressing Iranian female football fan as well as the various resonances that emerge from the intermingling of cinema and sport and women's appearances within that context. In this sense, I follow Kheshti's assertion that gender (tres) passing, or the 'transgender move', 'figures as a temporary space of political and agential potential that many spectators – domestic, diasporic, foreign – seek in the post-1990s New Iranian cinema.'[111] It is particularly appealing that Kheshti gestures towards an account of the troubling implications of the (tres)passing trope that foregrounds movement, space and spatiality. The (tres)passing trope does not necessarily manifest itself in the representation of a 'transgender subjectivity'. Instead, it 'figures as a *move* – one of many moves performed by characters that embody various forms of liminality (gendered, ethnic, agential, and economic).' Characters do not necessarily take on a trans identity, but they might occupy '*the space* of transgender potential in order to move through or survive a circumstance that s/he presumably could not otherwise' – such as watching a football game in a stadium as a woman.[112]

Queering sports/film spectatorship: reshaping perceptual expectations and habits

It is via the female characters' positioning within, and negotiation of, the spaces of sport *and* cinema (and their variously local, national and inter-/trans-national dimensions), that a temporary space of troublingly queer potential is carved out in and through *Offside*. It is worth noting here that Smoking Girl draws an explicit comparison between cinema and sport – in a perhaps self-conscious reference to the visceral encounter between sport and cinema embodied by *Offside* – when she demands an explanation from one of the soldiers about why exactly there are prohibitions around the physical proximity between unrelated men and women. 'Why can't women go in there [the stadium] and sit with men? […] Why can they in movie theatres?' The soldier's contradictory as well as unconvinced and unconvincing replies highlight the arbitrary nature of the rules he has been charged with implementing. He is repeatedly outwitted and pushed into a (rhetorical) corner by Smoking Girl and fails in his attempts to explain and rationalise why women are not allowed to sit with men in the stadium (or the cinema), ultimately resorting to various versions of 'they just can't', shouted at ever increasing volume and with rising exasperation.

This exchange is part of a lengthier conversation in which Smoking Girl (an unveiled female character) and the soldier (a male character who is unrelated to Smoking Girl, played by an actor who is unrelated to the actor playing Smoking Girl) are framed intimately close together by a

Queering the Sports Film

Figure 4.5 Soldier and Smoking Girl in Touching Distance (*Offside*)

two-shot. They sit on the ground outside the stadium, more or less back to back, with parts of their bodies touching. The soldier sits outside the holding pen, leaning against the widely spaced metal bars of the portable barriers, while Smoking Girl leans against the bars from the inside. She is framed through the bars as the camera stays *onside*, that is, outside of the temporary prison. However, rather than reinforcing the barrier between the soldier and Smoking Girl, the framing foregrounds the arbitrary nature of boundaries as well as their porousness and permeability. Not only can we look through the barrier, it also does not prohibit, and in fact *enables*, physical proximity and contact between unrelated characters/actors. What is also highlighted in the scene is the seemingly arbitrary nature of where and when modesty rules apply: the proximity between the soldier and Smoking Girl seems fine (at least within the diegetic world of the film), while it is precisely this kind of proximity between unrelated men and women that is prohibited inside the stadium, which is just on the other side of the wall (and thus closed off from the women's and our gaze).

The conversation is also indicative of the interactions between the young women and the equally young soldiers more generally, and it is not only in relation to questions around gender segregation that 'the female dialecticians repeatedly demolish their male guardians' arguments.'[113] The women also clearly have superior knowledge about football, the Iranian players and team tactics. If 'authentic fandom' and (emotional) investment in sport are key sites for the assertion of national identity, patriotism and pride, then the experience of *Offside*'s young female protagonists – draped in Iranian flags and with the national colours (green, white and red) painted on their faces, yet excluded from the spectacularly public celebration of the nation – acts as a microcosm that gives tangible presence to the surrounding macrocosmic relations between the nation, the transnational and the global.[114]

Saeed Talajooy usefully describes *Offside*'s seemingly simple and fairly straightforward narrative in specifically spatial and kinetic terms when he writes that the film's:

> plot becomes a *centripetal force* for a multiplicity of *centrifugal elements* that *hover in circles* around it, a locus of negotiation for dispersed sounds and images that register humanity while provoking a meta-filmic tension between the immediate documentation of reality and the premeditated, concentrated, heightened, and formalized verisimilitude of fictional realism.[115]

The limited events and actions taking place within the confined spaces of the film – they are public spaces (the streets, the stadium, buses), but the generally tight framing of the characters conveys a sense of spatial and perceptual containment – reach out towards and make contact with what is *not* 'there', with what does not have a *visible* presence in the film, but which nonetheless 'appears'. This is one of the ways in which Panahi makes graspable the wider social and political concerns that cannot be explicitly represented in any straightforward way. As Talajooy notes, Panahi's 'critique is more reflected in his form which is designed to attract attention to what is not shown.'[116]

In *Offside* – reviewed variously as 'one of the finest football films ever made,' and a 'Farsi *Bend it Like Beckham*' – what is most notably *not* shown is football.[117] It is football that, in this case, remains veiled and hidden, that falls 'victim' to modesty rules and that needs to be conveyed and articulated in ways that skirt the restrictions around gender segregation and the gaze. By denying the spectator conventional (visual) access to the football action in a film that is *about* football, and by thwarting and frustrating spectatorial expectations around sport and the sports film, football becomes 'present', and 'appears', in *Offside* through its resounding absence. What is heightened through our positioning with the female characters and their perceptual horizons is 'the tendency of the camera to offer additional limits,' which as Talajooy suggests 'presents new forms of looking at life rather than representing life.'[118]

Within the larger context of accounts that tend to focus on *Offside*'s limited and limiting visual economy, I want to foreground the film's sensory regime and the reshaping of our perceptual habits and tendencies this enables. *Offside* might frustrate our sports scopophilia but our alignment with the female characters is not (only) frustrating; it also offers opportunities for more fully embodied engagements. We are encouraged to empathise and align ourselves with the twisted and disorientating modes of perception that the soldiers enforce on the characters and that the film, in turn, enforces on us. We are not so much invited to share the characters' (visual) point of view as the spatial and perceptual modalities that the film weaves around their sidelined collective.

Denied conventional spectatorial access, the women nonetheless 'follow' the game and the ups and downs of the unfolding drama, and they do so in an intensely and affectively corporeal manner. In *Offside*, the footballing action appears – to the young women and to the spectator – both through the densely textured sonic landscape and through the various embodied engagements with the game that are made graspable throughout. The thickly layered soundscape includes the referee's whistle, the chanting of the crowd from inside the stadium and the impromptu commentary provided by one of the guards who can see the game through the bars of a door in the stadium wall; it envelops the women and 'fills' the (onscreen) space that surrounds them. The lack of visual access heightens the implications of sound and its spatial and tactile dimensions as it resonates and reverberates in, around and between bodies. While the stadium wall constitutes a barrier for visual access, the noises emanating from inside the stadium appear to lap over and around it, seeping through its (invisible) cracks. The sonic manifestations of the footballing action foreground the visceral connections and points of contact sport enables and thereby twist and dis-/reorientate our normative sensory habits, tied as they are to the primacy of the straightforward, linear gaze.

The embodied component of the young women's investment in the game is perhaps made most explicit when they mimic the physically animated spectatorial engagements of those guards who do have visual access to the game and offer, albeit inadequate and factually incorrect, commentary. We are implicated in the corporeal relay of visceral, affective tension and response. In one particularly poignant scene, the increasing volume of noise from inside the stadium indicates the beginning of the second half and pulls two of the guards away from the holding pen to the barred opening in the stadium wall that is just a few feet away. We see the women in mid-shot, their bodies pressed against and their hands tightly gripping the barrier, with their faces grimacing in anticipation and tension, and their eyes glued to the soldiers watching the game. The soldiers' bodies, in turn, are pressed tightly against the bars covering the opening to the stadium as if wanting to get closer to the action (just as the young women do). They grip the vertical bars as they fidget and squirm and move their weight from one foot to the other in a corporeal embodied response to the tension on the field.

The focus on the women's faces and upper bodies – their tensed facial expressions and postures as they hold on tightly both to the barrier and to each other – is intercut with medium long-shots that show the soldiers from behind, meaning their bodies block our view of the game. We do, however, see glimpses of the spectators in the stadium whose embodied reactions to the action are mimicked by the soldiers, who, presumably, do not have a clear view of the game either. In other words, engagement with the game in and through *Offside* is facilitated through a textured layering of bodies, movements, gestures and sounds that offers a sense of contact, proximity and (bodily, sensuous) intimacy that conventional visual access is unable to provide.

When Iran score the crucial goal that eventually takes them through to the 2006 World Cup, the noise in the stadium erupts. A medium long-shot of the soldiers shows us first the spectators in the stadium (in the background) and then the solders themselves jumping up and down, throwing their arms into the air, screaming and hugging each other, before a cut to the women in the holding pen doing exactly the same. The celebrations

Queering the Sports Film

Figures 4.6. and 4.7 Embodied Engagements (*Offside*)

of the nation's 'success' are intimately tactile, with both the women and the soldiers hugging and kissing each other – albeit with physical contact taking place in a strictly gender-segregated manner as the women remain inside the holding pen, a space the soldiers never enter. The women, bearing the symbols of 'the nation' (flags, face paint), begin to dance and chant football songs, making the soldiers' celebrations seem uninspired and unenthusiastic in comparison. The sequence is indicative of how *Offside*'s non-normative sensory regime – intimately tied as it is to the sidelined positionality of its cross-dressing female characters, who are utterly 'out of place' – conveys the ways in which discourses of gender and nation intersect in and around the (mediated) spectacle of sport in tangibly corporeal terms.

Offside situates the spectator with the women and forces us to share their agonisingly limited (in terms of conventional spectatorial expectations around sports *and* the sports film) access to the sporting spectacle. We only catch two *very* brief glimpses of the football pitch. It appears in the background when one of the guards chases an escaped female intruder (Soccer Girl) through the stadium, and this serves only to highlight, and perhaps remind us of, the resounding absence of visible football action elsewhere. What this achieves, however, is a foregrounding of (our) engagement with football as an affectively spatial, textural and muscular encounter. The significance of football spectatorship/fandom as a corporeal, visceral experience is also gestured towards elsewhere in *Offside*, for instance, through the old, blind and physically impaired man on the bus in the opening segment, who undertakes what is, for him, a difficult trip to the stadium. When one of the younger men notes that he 'could have watched the game at home,' he replies that 'the stadium is something else. You shout, you sing, you go with the flow.' Similarly, when the soldiers tell the imprisoned women that, if they are so interested in the game, they 'could have stayed at home and watched it on TV' – which arguably would have provided much more rewarding visual access to the game – they reply that they want to 'watch the game up close.' The purely visual dimension of sports spectatorship is clearly marginalised in these exchanges, as it is by the film itself.

At one point the women also 'act out' the game in the holding pen, in an enactment of bodily mimicry of the action on the pitch. When the temporarily missing prisoner (Soccer Girl) returns after having seen some of the football action during her escape, she wants to convey a sense of 'what happened'. She moves the prisoners around in the pen and tells them what positions to take up and which player they 'are' (based on similarities in hair style, height, footballing skills), further foregrounding the embodied, directional and orientated dimensions of sports spectatorship and fandom. Similarly, when the women are transported to the Vice Squad headquarters in a police van towards the end of the film/game,

Queering the Sports Film

Figure 4.8 Embodied Engagements (*Offside*)

their only access to the dramatic final moments of the match is via the radio commentary that is unclear and cuts out numerous times. Notably, their engagement with the game via the radio commentary is characterised by a tangibly visceral tension. The women's comportment and gestures recall their (at)tending to the soldier's commentary at the stadium. They hold on to each other, grasp each other's arms and fidget nervously. A medium long-shot (from the front of the van) shows us the tightknit collective in the enclosed space in the back of the vehicle as they 'face' the radio and stare at it, hanging on to the commentator's every word. During the final minutes, they push past each other and move closer to the radio (and the camera). The commentator notes the 'electric atmosphere' in the stadium, which is given shape, and made palpable, through the women's affectively intense muscular engagement. Although the situation creates multiple removes from the footballing action, the affectively corporeal relay taking place within it conveys the sense of an intimately close, touching and moving encounter.

It is this phenomenological reshaping of perceptual horizons, with which we are invited to empathise (in fact, we do not really have a choice), that makes *Offside*'s multifaceted working through of gender, (dis)appearance, (tres)passing, community and nation graspable. It allows the film to gesture beyond the confines of the tightly enclosed and seemingly restricted spaces in the diegesis and give a resounding, palpable presence to that which is 'not shown':[119] the inter- and trans-national contexts of football and cinema; the local/global implications of feminist and queer politics; as well as normative structures of embodiment and perception.

Offside's ending captures the celebrations that erupted on the streets of Tehran after the final whistle of the game, with the Iranian team's win securing qualification for the 2006 World Cup in Germany. Traffic comes to a standstill as the crowds take over the streets, with the captured women as well the police officers joining in the celebration. In the final (shaky, handheld) shot of *Offside*, we follow First Girl, who is still 'in disguise', as she disappears into the crowd holding a sparkler in each hand – First Girl is also, therefore, the 'Final Girl'.[120] It is a profoundly ambiguous moment, marked by the palpable intermingling of celebration and mourning. Her failed attempt at (tres)passing – she is a first-timer while some of the other characters are more experienced – is motivated not only by a desire to see the game. She also wants to honour and mourn her friend who died during another match, the World Cup qualifier against Japan that took place in Azadi Stadium on 25 March 2005, when the police opened fire on the crowds who demonstrated against the Islamic Republic and sang 'Ey Iran' – a song used by opposition groups who do not recognise the national anthem of the Islamic Republic.[121] This song also appears on the soundtrack in the final moments of *Offside*, with the crowd dancing along on the streets. It is not entirely clear if the sound is non-diegetic or if it emerges from somewhere in the public square.

This ambivalence – the blurring of representational boundaries – adds to the ambiguously utopian, carnivalesque atmosphere of the celebration sequence that Stam describes in his Bakhtinian reading of the film. 'After the victory, the women, in violation of patriarchal gender etiquette, join in the open-air celebrations in the streets. As a provisional, ephemeral, laughing communitas, they actively participate in the carnivalesque takeover of the public sphere.'[122] The women, who are still in drag, are no longer excluded but merge with, and are incorporated into, the 'body of the nation.' However, it is the lingering sense of mourning, that is embodied by and 'gathers around' First Girl in particular, as well as the tangibly provisional and ephemeral nature of the joyful coming together of 'the nation', that resonate most profoundly as the women's eventual participation is deeply qualified. What leaves a more profound and lasting impression, however – if we open ourselves up to a sensuous cinematic encounter – is the unhinging of normative modes of embodiment and perception, and their variously twisted resonances, that takes shape around the characters.

Overall, then, the queer feminist phenomenological encounters with *2 Seconds* and *Offside* in this chapter provide a graspable sense of the affirmatively troubling spaces of possibilities that the entanglement of sport and cinema can open up. Sport, in its many live and mediated manifestations, tends to assert normative modes of embodiment (of gender, sexuality, race/ethnicity, class, nation and their multiple intersections), with variously local and global reach, through the kinds of bodies that cohere in and around sport. The affective foregrounding of those types of embodiment that do *not* fit this normative mould in *2 Seconds* and *Offside* functions to unhinge, and make strange, the taken-for-granted and normally unfelt modes of temporality, spatiality and perception that underpin normative incarnations of sport and/in cinema. It is through the non-straightforward and twisted habits, orientations and tendencies that both films give shape to that variously queer feminist spatio-temporal formations and figurations are put within spectatorial reach.

5

Céline Sciamma's 'Queer' Cinema: Affirming Gestures of Refusal in *Tomboy* and *Girlhood*

This chapter explores the usefulness of a queer feminist phenomenological approach to 'queer' cinema. With specific reference to Céline Sciamma's body of films, it offers a phenomenologically grounded answer to Davis's Deleuzian-inflected question, as discussed in Chapter 2: 'But what's a queer film?' I read *Tomboy* and *Girlhood* as particularly poignant incarnations of contemporary tensions in queer film (theory), especially around (in)visibility, identity (politics), performativity and representation. Both films engage centrally with questions of gender and sexuality while refraining from inscribing rigid gender and sexual identities onto their characters (and the same goes for *Naissance des pieuvres* (*Water Lilies*, 2007), the first part of Sciamma's female adolescent coming-of-age trilogy, which is not discussed here). The films speak to, and negotiate, the at times conflicting aims and preoccupations of queer film (theory) on the one hand and feminist film (theory) on the other. What the textural encounters in this chapter make graspable, is how those tensions and conflicts are embodied, and 'worked out', via the films' sensory, tactile, muscular and kinaesthetic registers – or what So Mayer might call the films' 'uncommonly sensual figurations.'[1] The films make strange what usually is, and makes, common 'sense' in relation to gender, sexuality, childhood and adolescence in cinema.

While the argument developed here is applicable to questions of queerness and/in cinema more generally, Sciamma's films serve as particularly fruitful case studies as they manage to avoid the drawbacks of a narrowly defined identity politics through a foregrounding of embodiment, corporeality and sensuousness. *Tomboy* and *Girlhood* do feature fairly explicit lesbian/queer/trans content. *Tomboy* is the story of Laure (Zoé Héran) who moves into a new neighbourhood with her family and passes as a boy amongst her new friends, calling herself Mikaël, while *Girlhood* sees its protagonist, Marieme/Vic (Karidja Touré), take on a range of differently gendered appearances and behaviours throughout the film, including specifically male-identified ones in the final segment.[2] However, my concern here (as in the rest of the book) is not with how male, female, trans, straight, bisexual or lesbian identities are represented or given visibility. At the same time, I do not want to lose sight of the situatedness of (gender and sexual) embodiment, which Davis's Deleuzian account risks doing in its attempt to track how 'queerness recedes from lived experience through character and/or narrative politics to an aesthetics and/or affect.'[3] Instead, I propose that a phenomenologically based and queerly orientated textural analysis allows us to make (un/common) sense of the films' queer feminist leanings and attitudes: of how they are orientated, of who or what they are directed towards, and of their resonances with bodily tendencies, gestures and modes of embodiment as they are shaped by and acquired within the textures of the social.[4]

Sciamma's coming-of-age trilogy has emerged within a mainstream media landscape characterised by the proliferation of lesbian, and more recently trans, visibility. As Michele Aaron notes, one of the legacies of the New Queer Cinema has been the more general queering of Western popular culture and the commercialisation and repackaging of queer for mainstream audiences.[5] What is problematic about this co-optation of 'queer' is that it loses its critical, oppositional and transgressive edge. Lesbian sexuality in particular is also often re-appropriated for a heterosexual male gaze in ways that raise important questions about viewing pleasures and about who mainstream films with gay, lesbian or trans content are 'for' and who they appeal to (and why) – *Black Swan* with its (hallucinatory) lesbian sex scene being a notable case in point. It also raises important, and complicated, questions about how queer/gay/lesbian/trans identities, and gender and sexuality more generally, can or should (not) be represented in cinema – and also about whether representations of queer gender and sexual identities are essential, or even necessary, in contemporary queer cinema. It thus links to fundamental questions around where and how we might identify what is, and can be, 'queer' about queer cinema, and about where we might 'locate' its queerness. *Tomboy* and *Girlhood* emerge very specifically from, and arguably in response to, this wider representational and critical landscape: the aftermath of the New Queer Cinema and queer (film) theory, and the resultant tensions around (in)visibility, identity (politics), representability, legibility, recognisability and intelligibility that continue to shape this context.

Both films refrain from representations of specific, stable and narrowly defined gay, lesbian or trans identities. Nonetheless, they are profoundly queer feminist films and the young female protagonists are central to this – but *not* because of the identity categories inscribed on them in conventional cinematic terms. Instead, the films' queer feminist implications and resonances hinge centrally on the modes of movement, comportment and spatiality as well as the sensuous, tactile and kinaesthetic ways of being-in-the-world that take shape around, and in relation to, their troubled and troubling protagonists.

The young female bodies are at the very core of the films – visually, narratively and sensuously – a risky move considering the 'over-determined physicalities' of adolescent girls (in (French) cinema) in particular.[6] Various physical activities are depicted in both films – football, swimming, running, fighting and dancing in *Tomboy*; and American football, dancing and fighting in *Girlhood* – and it is through these performances that the body's more general centrality is made most explicit. However, the female bodies are not 'on display', or staged to-be-looked-at, in conventionally gendered ways. They function as intensely corporeal, tactile and muscular articulations of the phenomenological ways of being-in and becoming familiar with and orientated in the world that take shape in and through the films. They constitute the ground on which gender and sexuality are 'worked out' and 'worked through' *cinematically* in *Tomboy* and *Girlhood*, based on the bodies' textural incorporations. The athletic sequences foreground what is perhaps more subtly woven through the textures of the films as a whole: the making tangible and graspable of queer feminist orientations in tactile and kinaesthetic terms.

As in previous chapters, I am deeply indebted to Ahmed's queer phenomenology, which offers an account of orientation that 'points to how spatial distinctions and awareness are implicated in how bodies get directed in specific ways. In other words, orientation for [Ahmed, as for] me is about how the bodily, the spatial and the social are entangled'.[7] *Tomboy* and *Girlhood* offer sensuous, visceral encounters with the various forms and shapes this entanglement might take – and the young characters' bodies are the very centre, 'the zero point', that the spatial and the social emanate from and that they are 'orientated around' in the filmic worlds they occupy.[8]

While Sciamma's cinema does not subscribe to, or articulate, a particular identity politics, a consideration of the queer feminist embodiments and orientations in and of her films provides the grounds for encountering *Tomboy* and *Girlhood* as sensuous incarnations of an embodied 'politics of refusal', of both gender/sexual and cinematic norms.

Trans, Lesbian or Queer? Passing, (Mis)Recognition and (Dis)Appearance in *Tomboy*

In her second feature, Sciamma moves from the adolescent world of *Water Lilies* into the realm of childhood and pre-pubescent bodies – that is, bodies whose visible markers of sexual difference are not yet developed. Within critical debate, *Tomboy* tends to be situated in relation to the wider cinematic and media contexts of trans representations.[9] With a few exceptions, such as *The Danish Girl* (Tom Hooper, UK/US, 2015), *Dallas Buyers Club* (Jean-Marc Vallée, US, 2013) and *Boys Don't Cry* (Kimberly Pierce, US, 1999),[10] mainstream representations of trans identities are rare, unless we use trans, as Keely Saunders does, as an umbrella term that also includes depictions of drag and cross-dressing, of which there exists a much more visible mainstream cinematic history and an associated set of generic conventions.[11] While the trans trope has tended to serve hetero- and cis-normative narrative purposes in mainstream representation – by functioning as a means of deception, manipulation, comedy or terror –

Tomboy is an example of more recent representations, which also include *Nånting måste gå sönder* (*Something Must Break*, Ester Martin Bergsmark, Sweden, 2014) and *52 Tuesdays* (Sophie Hyde, Australia, 2013), that are centrally, and largely affirmatively, *about* the trans experience.

Cinematic engagements with female-to-male (FTM) transition in particular are fairly atypical. Keely Saunders notes that, 'along with non-binary, questioning or fluid gender identities,' FTM characters and stories are 'commonly under-represented in the media compared with more familiar male to female trans-lives.'[12] *52 Tuesdays* and *Albert Nobbs*, which variously conjures cross-dressing, trans and lesbian tropes through the mesmerising performances of Glenn Close and Janet McTeer, constitute exceptions, as does *Boys Don't Cry*, which was groundbreaking in its non-rationalising and non-trivialising depiction of the trans experience.[13] It refrains from providing a rationale as to *why* Brandon Teena/Tina Brandon (Hillary Swank) wants to pass as, and *be*, a man, and instead, depicts the process and experience of living a trans life (in not entirely unproblematic terms) and its violent, deathly consequences. *Tomboy* is fairly unusual then in its preoccupation with the FTM trans experience as well as its focus on a pre-pubescent child – if, indeed, how use the trans label to identify what it is the film is 'about' and what it 'does'.

Darren Waldron reads *Tomboy* as part of contemporary public discourses in which 'the subject of gender nonconformity in children is a prominent concern.'[14] He also notes a 'preoccupation with boys' within those debates and the narrative and visual conventions through which they are articulated.[15] This preoccupation with boys, and with how they might 'do' femininity, mirrors the more general historical trajectory of trans visibility identified by Saunders as primarily confined to cross-dressing men. This is not too surprising, perhaps, considering the different ways in femininity/femaleness and masculinity/maleness are culturally constructed. Variously, femininity is conceived of as excess, as masquerade, as something to be put on (make-up, jewellery, shoes, clothes, hair, gestures, smiles), whereas masculinity is 'natural', a given. This is reflected in critical discourses more generally that tend to focus on the socio-cultural construction of women and femininity, while 'we hear much less about the "construction of men".'[16]

Waldron also notes that gender fluidity or gender nonconformity is more commonly accepted in girls than in boys, because departures from traditional femininity in girls, exemplified by the figure of the tomboy, are much more pervasive.[17] For Halberstam, this is no great surprise as cross-gender behaviour in girls is 'associated with a "natural" desire for the greater freedoms enjoyed by boys' – as long as sexual difference is not fundamentally challenged.[18] In fact, the tomboy trope – in relation not just to children/adolescents but female character of all ages – is relatively common in mainstream cinema, yet critically neglected. Lynne Stahl provides a rare – to my knowledge, unique – exploration of mainstream cinematic incarnations of the tomboy narrative and suggests that tomboyism functions primarily as a phase to be overcome on the way to acceptable and desirable womanhood. Tomboyism's troubling links with lesbianism (rather than transgenderism!) are thus both gestured towards *and* disavowed through the eventual reaffirmations of heteronormative narrative arcs and conventionality.[19]

While tomboy characters tend to be obsessively domesticated, feminised and/or paired off with male love interests, there are also those characters who emerge from the narrative as tomboys (such as in *Fried Green Tomatoes* (Jon Avnet, US, 1991), for instance). It is in relation to this sustained and uncontained tomboyism that associations with lesbianism are, though not explicitly visible, no longer 'plausibly unnoticeable'.[20] As Stahl points out, however, recalling earlier arguments by White and Whatling, even those films in which tomboyism is heteronormatively contained and tomboy characters end up on the straight and narrow, as it were, 'leave – and sometimes create – room for sustained deviant [spectatorial] possibilities in the same instant that they attempt to smother them.'[21]

What surfaces, perhaps inadvertently, from these discussions is the slippery, messy unruliness of gender and sexual categories (and the political stakes in those categories) that are variously overlapping *and* contradictory. The discourses and debates emerging from and cohering around *Tomboy* thus speak, rather poignantly, to the questions of visibility, representability, legibility, intelligibility and appearance (of sex, gender and sexuality) that the film itself raises and works through. *Tomboy* is variously identified as a trans, lesbian or queer film in popular discourses, while it tends to be read as a trans film within academic debates, with trans inconsistently defined as in-/excluding cross-dressing, drag, passing, gender nonconformity, gender fluidity, tomboyism, non-binarism, transgenderism and transsexuality. Waldron, for instance, situates *Tomboy* within the larger representational and discursive (media, medical and policy) context of 'gender nonconformity' and reads the film as being equally concerned with 'the experiences of a girl who passes as a boy as with those of "boyish" girls.'[22] Stahl, on the other hand, explicitly excludes *Tomboy* from her study of the tomboy narrative in cinema, because she reads it as an example of transgender representation. For Stahl, it thus does not fit a project that is interested 'in a specific narrative and cinematic history that sees tomboyism as inextricably bound up with femaleness and lesbianism, not transsexuality.'[23] Stahl usefully adds that 'the suppression of trans discourses within tomboy narratives could itself make a compelling study'.[24]

There is a slightly problematic slippage here, then, between cinematic representation and critical discourse that hinges on circular relations between meaning, identification and naming. What is tomboyism exactly? If we have identified 'a cinematic history that sees tomboyism as inextricably bound up with femaleness and lesbianism, not transsexuality', does this not perhaps mean that we have only defined certain gender-nonconforming behaviours and appearances in girls *as* 'tomboyish' *if* they are linked to lesbianism and/or eventually outgrown? And does this mean that the same gender-nonconforming behaviours and appearances, when linked to transgenderism or transsexuality – or even simply *not* linked to a (latent) lesbianism – are then not tomboyish, but… genderqueer?

I am playing devil's advocate here and am certainly not advocating a rigid definition of tomboy-qualifying characteristics. And while it is true that (cinematic) representations play an important part in the discursive construction of networks of meaning that link, for instance, 'tomboyism' with 'lesbianism', we also need to be cognisant of the constitutive, performative implications of naming and of the ways in which critical discourses are implicated in the perpetuation of normative structures of meaning. (We might ask similar questions about the seeming lack of filmic representations of trans men/boys: Does our reading of gender nonconformity in girls and women as tomboyism preclude the transgender trope from 'appearing'?) How the tomboy becomes 'visible' or 'legible', then, and how and under which circumstances the tomboy 'appears' – to adapt Villarejos's argument around 'lesbian appearance' once more – depends on the discursive and interpretive contexts from which we take our clues. Tomboyism has tentative, ambiguous and shifting ties to sex, gender and sexuality, but is crucially implicated in their legibility. It constitutes a kind of gender nonconformity with uneasy links to both lesbianism and transgenderism, via a semiotic chain that is characterised by unpredictable and often contradictory twists and turns.

If considered within the larger context of the tomboy trope, *Tomboy* seems fairly conventional, despite its refusal to reintegrate Laure into hetero-conventionality (Laure emerges from the narrative as a tomboy).[25] If considered within the larger context of trans representation, we might note that the film replays a rather conventional narrative of passing – 'dissimulation, discovery and confrontation'[26] – and a familiar arc of suspense: it is a question of *how*, not *whether*, Laure will be found out. *Tomboy* also breaks the representational, generic mould with its focus on transgenderism in a 'girl' (if what we 'see' is a trans rather than a tomboy narrative), although the film is centrally about, to adapt Tim Palmer's phrase, 'the world of boys,' about ways of being a boy and about boyhood masculinity.[27]

Tomboy posits an understanding of gender as somehow both 'authentic' and 'put on'. Laure unselfconsciously and seemingly 'naturally' engages in the performative reconstitution of masculinity when she is with her family, who equally unselfconsciously and uncritically read and address her as a 'girl' – a girl, it should be noted, who embodies gender very differently than her girly and effeminate younger sister, Jeanne (Malonn Lévana). However, this 'known' disconnect between sex and gender goes unremarked and, importantly, *unfelt* within the confines of the domestic space of the family home. As well as Jeanne, Laure's father (Matthieu Demy) and pregnant mother (Sophie Cattani), who remain nameless, are part of the initially warm and comforting domestic interior where Laure's gender-nonconformity, including her androgynous/boyish appearance, behaviours and tastes, are not only accepted but supported. Heteronormative societal pressures do not seem to encroach upon the familial realm, which constitutes a safe and familiar corporeal and affective space that not only accommodates but embraces Laure's queerly gendered mode of embodiment. It is within this context that Laure is most plausibly read as a 'tomboy', or as a 'boyish girl'. Importantly, however, Laure does not exhibit the kind of unhappiness, anger and rebelliousness (against gender norms) that characterise filmic articulations of the tomboy trope.[28] Laure does not rebel 'against' anything or anyone – she does not seem to *have* to. The domestic space of the home extends the shape of Laure's embodiment unconditionally, at least initially.

The family home is only part of the phenomenal world that Laure inhabits. Waldron notes the 'dialectical configuration of space between the domestic interior,' where Laure is known to be a (tom)boyish girl, and the 'communal exterior', the space outside the home, where Laure interacts with the other children in the neighbourhood her family has just moved into, and where her (tom)boyish demeanour leads her to be (mis) read as a boy.[29] It is when she goes along with the (mis)recognition and begins to pass as a boy that her (entirely unaltered) appearance and behaviours take on transgendered implications. This is crucial, as the variances in what her (tom)boyish demeanour *means* and how it is *read* – by Laure's family ('she is a girl'); by the other children in the film ('this is a boy'); and, in a rather different, shifting manner, by the spectator ('is this a (tom) boyish girl who passes as a boy?'; 'is this a 'really' a boy?'; 'is this a trans boy?') – is entirely dependent on the knowledge and experience that we bring to the encounter, exposing the conditionality of visibility, legibility and appearance.

Laure's first encounter in the new neighbourhood is with Lisa (Jeanne Disson). It is one of the film's most crucial moments because it constitutes the first instance of (mis)recoginition/passing – but also because it leaves a certain ambiguity around agency and intent. We do not quite know whether Lisa assumes Laure is a boy when she says, 'You're shy? [...] Won't you tell me your name?', or if she is playing it safe because she is not quite sure – but her cautiously flirtatious manner, which is very plausibly interpreted by Laure as a sign of being (mis)read, as well as the absence of a questioning response to Laure's answer – 'Mikaël, my name is Mikaël' – insinuate as much. The camera lingers on Laure's face after she names herself Mikaël and interpellates herself as a boy, rather than showing us Lisa's reaction directly. Instead, Lisa's acceptance of Laure as Mikaël is confirmed by a cut from the close-up of Laure/Mikaël as s/he holds Lisa's gaze to a scene of both children walking through the woods. Overall, then, this first encounter does not offer a clear sense, due to the ambiguous constellation of dialogue, body language and looks, about whether it is Lisa's (mis)recognition or Laure's 'deceit' that comes first. This ambivalence does not function to encourage the viewer to contemplate the temporality of the encounter, however. It serves instead to downplay the importance of rationality, sequence and cause-and-effect relations and heightens the affective charge of the encounter, which might be best understood as a playful and mutually affirming all-at-once.[30]

In this sense, *Tomboy* diverts from the mainstream conventions of the passing narrative, in that it is 'not preoccupied with "putting on a gender" because Laure's behaviour obtains a permanence and sense of authenticity.'[31] The film is not concerned with questions of intentional deceit, and associated notions of agency, in terms of how gender might be performed. It also, however, and as already gestured towards, stays away from constructing a sense of gender as somehow fixed or innate as it reveals 'the conditionality of all gendering,' both by 'highlighting the performative strategies undertaken by boys to comply with compulsory masculinity' and through Jeanne's overtly feminine appearance and behaviour that are equally depicted as a kind of 'authentic performance', as something she does rather than an innate tendency.[32] *Tomboy* carefully and sensitively negotiates these tensions (between essentialism and a postmodern relativism) without ever fully resolving them – a powerfully affirmative stance.

This is another aspect of the film that sets it apart from conventional, mainstream representational patterns where cross-dressing or passing tend to have specific narrative motivations or aims and tend to be framed as conscious, purposeful deceit. Laure's 'deceit' has no obvious purpose other than passing itself, similar to Brandon Teena's in *Boys Don't Cry*. Laure's 'deceit' is also, at least at first, not a conscious act, *un*like Brandon's mindful attempts to hide the parts of his physical body that might reveal his 'secret', with the process of transformation being explicitly depicted in a lengthy scene early on in *Boys Don't Cry*. When Laure 'appears' as a boy in the initial encounter with Lisa, Laure is not 'putting on an act'. Rather, it is a strictly binary sex/gender system, which is unable to accommodate Laure's mode of being-in-the-world, that leads Lisa to (mis)identify her as a boy in order to enable an interpersonal encounter with an intelligible (i.e., gendered) subject. A similar kind of (mis)identification or (mis)recognition might also be evoked in the viewer's first encounter with Laure in *Tomboy's* opening sequence (discussed in more detail below).

In a gesture of refusal (of cinematic conventions and societal expectations), the film disregards the 'why?' and 'when?' of Laure's gender-nonconformity and focuses instead on the 'how?'. This lack of a rational justification conjures a wonderfully refreshing opening-up of the film's sensuous, embodied and affective resonances. It also has potentially disconcerting or disorientating implications, however, as it prohibits a neat and reassuring categorisation of Laure's gender and sexual identity. Does Laure go along with the initial (mis)recognition because she is attracted to Lisa? Can the gender disguise therefore be read as Laure's attempt to act on her (forbidden) desire for Lisa? Is Laure therefore a 'lesbian'? Or is she really just a (tom)boyish girl, so used to being misrecognised as a boy, that it is just easier, and perhaps more fun, to play along with it? Or does Laure genuinely feel like a boy, and want to be a boy? And are gender nonconformity and passing therefore manifestations of a trans identity? These are just some of the possible ways in which the film might make sense to viewers – and film reviews, online discussion boards and more general public media discourses provide an indication that the film is, indeed, made sense of in all of these ways. Notably, the ascribing of a particular (lesbian or trans) identity to the protagonist can lead to fairly heated debates about why certain identity attributions are/not appropriate and which identity groups might therefore 'claim' the film and its character – an example of (paranoid) identity politics at work in ways that are not entirely productive.

Making 'sense' of (the) Tomboy

Halberstam notes that trans narratives tend to be 'dedicated to forcing the transgender subject to *make sense*' – to those who might not, and/or might want to, understand *why* deviance from gender norms takes place, thereby reinforcing the givenness and normativity of binary gender as that which does not need to be explained to make sense.[33] This kind of rationalising is precisely what *Tomboy* refuses to engage in. Rather than making sense of its protagonist by imposing a logical explanation, the film makes sensuous, tactile, muscular and kinaesthetic 'sense' of a particular way of being, and finding one's way, in the world.

The opening sequence introduces us to the protagonist and her world in a specifically tactile, muscular and kinaesthetic manner. It is *Tomboy*'s textural, sensory register that shapes our initial contact with the film and thus invites an embodied, haptic mode of spectatorial engagement. Importantly, the film's sensuous qualities are tied closely to its, at this point, unnamed and unidentified protagonist and her sensory engagement with the world. The opening sequence is crucial in its foundational interweaving of the film's textural register with its thematic concerns around sex/gender, visibility and passing, which enables a sidestepping of considerations of trans narratives and the 'transgender gaze'.

We first come into contact with (the) *Tomboy* (the character/figure/film) when the heavy, muffled, enveloping sound of wind, as if reverberating in one's own ears, materialises on the soundtrack, steadily increasing in volume before there is a cut from the black screen with opening credits to a close-up of the back of a child's head. The shot is slightly angled, so we are looking up, and all we see is a slender neck, short, shaggy hair, and the top of skinny, angular shoulders in a blue T-shirt. We are seemingly situated on some kind of vehicle, as we move forward, along with the character, through a tree-covered landscape. The bobbly texture of the washed-out T-shirt, the fine blonde hairs on the delicately textured skin, the wind finding its way through the already ruffled, messy hair and the sun rays gently sliding across the hair, skin and fabric are in focus, while the lush, green surroundings, with the sunlight breaking through the swaying leaves, move past us, envelop us even, in a sensuously blurry play of colour, movement and light. The sounds of the wind, which give the diegetic world a thickly textured feel before we see it, also take shape visually through the swaying movements of the branches and leaves and, perhaps more importantly, through the fluttering strands of hair. The densely reverberating soundscape, together with the finely textured materiality of hair, skin and fabric, provides a tangible sense of the character's sensory world: of whirling air brushing across the skin of the face; of fluttering strands of hair on the scalp; of wind insistently tugging at the fabric of the shirt.

The character we are introduced to here is Laure, the as-yet-unnamed protagonist. It is rather presumptuous to use a gendered pronoun, and to refer to Laure as 'she' at this point, as conventional, legible markers of gender and sexual difference are notably absent. If anything, we might say that what appears in this very first shot is a 'boy', or 'boyishness' – although more knowing audiences, which in this case might include the majority of spectators, given the film's name as well as extra filmic/promotional discourses, are likely to read this first appearance differently, about which further below.

The audiovisual framing of *Tomboy*'s opening moments provides a sense of proximity, not necessarily because we are visually close, or because we share the character's visual perspective, but because we are invited to share her phenomenal world in what is an intimately sensory encounter. The soundscape in particular, resembling the wind brushing past and reverberating in one's ears, crucially links sound, touch, proximity and contact. The only sounds we hear are the ones created with, or on, the body as the air makes contact with its surface and even enters its folds, resounding insides the ear cavity and not leaving any space for other, less proximal sounds to intermingle. It is the kind of sound experience that is by necessity tied to the individual and that cannot normally be shared. The wind reverberating in *my* ears can only be heard by *me*. The particular audiovisual framing described here therefore creates an impression of the 'space of the body' as tightly enclosed yet marked by a pleasurable sensory richness.[34] The body is cocooned by the densely textured, cushioned soundscape.

Tomboy's opening provides a graspable sense of how this sensorial envelopment might be experienced and felt. It provokes a spectatorial relation of tactile empathy to a character that does not yet make any 'sense' otherwise: no name, no narrative context, no face. This lengthy opening shot, which lasts for around 15 seconds, gives us time to take in the minute textural details and their sensory resonances, before there is a cut to a point-of-view shot of the trees, branches and leaves moving past and across the screen in a blurry haze of texture and movement, ruptured by the glistening sun rays rhythmically breaking through the leafy layers, blinding us momentarily. The disorientatingly contrasting texture (shadowy leaves – blindingly bright sunlight) is interwoven with the movement of fuzzy shapes and patterns (of leaves and branches) across the screen, which is too fast for our eyes to keep up, serving as an embodied reminder of the intrinsically tactile, kinaesthetic nature of perception. It evokes the kind of haptic gaze that intimately links vision and touch, and thus invites a spectatorial attitude of openness and vulnerability that enables the film to make contact.

When a hand, presumably Laure's, appears on the screen, in front of the blurry background, a sense of three-dimensional (optical) depth returns to the image, while the significance of contact and touch is also reinforced and given a specifically spatial dimension. The small, delicate hand, fingers slightly bent, is in focus in the centre of the screen, as the fine blonde hairs on the wrist and fingers catch the sunlight and become visible on the fair, freckled surface of the skin. The hand and fingers move slightly, responding to the pressure of the wind, engaging in a playful dance with the invisible force of the moving air, crucially linking surface, texture and hapticity with movement, spatiality and orientation. As the hand leaves the frame again, a gradual change in focus increases the blurriness of the leaves and branches in the background, until the screen is filled with a hazy, shifting pattern of fuzzy, overlapping, indistinct circles of green and light. This is followed by a cut to a frontal close-up of the character's face with the textured pattern of the previous shot mirrored by the oscillating movement of sunlight and shade across the skin of her face, the wind tugging at the strands of her short, messy hair. Importantly, her eyes are closed as she moves her head slightly, left and right, up and down, seemingly engrossed in the pleasurable sensation of the wind brushing against her skin, alternately giving in to and pushing against the dense yet malleable pressure of the air, in a playful and sensuously tactile and muscular to-and-fro. The scene conveys an impression of the warm, soothing sensation of sunrays touching the surface of the skin, intermingling with the crisp, clean coolness of the air, and of the muscular effort of resisting, responding to and moving against the pressure of the wind.

The densely textured and richly sensuous register of the film introduced here is intimately tied to Laure and her corporeal presence in the world, which begins to make sensuous, tactile, kinaesthetic, muscular and spatial 'sense' to us. We then see Laure open her eyes and briefly look around, visually taking in her surroundings, before a cut to a shot inside a car provides an initial sense of the spatio-temporal and narrative context: Laure is standing on the passenger seat, her upper body sticking out of the sunroof. This is followed by a cut that returns to a frontal close-up of Laure's face that is held for a few seconds, even when the sound of the wind, deeply entangled as it is with the sensuous texture of the phenomenal world unfolding in the opening sequence, is abruptly replaced by complete silence. The subsequent cut to a black title screen – with *'Tomboy'* first written in blue, then changing to red, before settling on a blue-red-blue-red-blue-red alternation, asserting the incipient blurring of gender boundaries and binaries – marks the end of the opening sequence.

The rich sensory texture of *Tomboy's* opening is intimately tied to Laure's 'unsettlingly androgynous' appearance.[35] Given the film's title, an awareness of the gender nonconformity associated with tomboyism and sensitivity towards a potentially not-quite-straightforward legibility of gender is likely to underpin our initial encounter with the film. Out of context, Laure might conceivably be identified as a boy – a possibility we are invited to contemplate when we first make contact with, and get close to, Laure in the opening scene – prefiguring Lisa's above-mentioned (mis)identification in a later sequence. The interweaving of an intimately sensuous encounter with Laure in/and the film, which makes 'perfect sense', as it were, with the simultaneous foreclosing of a straightforwardly intelligible gender identity evokes a contradictory tension in our spectatorial relation with Laure/the film.

While we get intimately close to the body, giving us (as I have shown) opportunities for identification and empathy with a particular sensory experience and way of being-in-the-world that hinges on Laure's corporeal presence, that body refuses to disclose what it is 'normally' presumed to be ultimately accountable for. The lengthy, lingering shots of the back of Laure's head, and especially of her face, draw us in as they foreground the intricately detailed textures of the body, its surface that makes contact with the world and its sensuous, muscular interiority that negotiates its spatial relations with the world. Yet, gender, that which arguably renders us intelligible as subjects, and which is read off the body *in the last instance*, remains elusive.

Tomboy's opening thus resonates with, and foreshadows, 'the complex relations in time and space between seeing and not seeing, appearing and

Céline Sciamma's 'Queer' Cinema

disappearing, knowing and not knowing' that gather around transgenderism and that, as Halberstam notes, are 'difficult to track.'[36] Halberstam identifies a range of different cinematic treatments of transgenderism 'that resolve these complex problems of temporality and visibility,' most notably the 'rewind'.

> [T]he transgender character is presented at first as 'properly' gendered, as passing in other words, and as properly located with a linear narrative; her exposure as transgender constitutes that film's narrative climax, and spells out both her decline and the unravelling of cinematic time. The viewer literally has to rewind the film after the character's exposure in order to reorganize the narrative logic in terms of the pass.[37]

Whenever a character has been read, and accepted, by the audience as male or female (although how exactly we might determine such a reading/acceptance is not entirely clear) and is subsequently exposed as a trans character, this 'causes the audience to reorient themselves in relation to the film's past in order to read the film's present and prepare themselves for the film's future. When we "see" the transgender character, then, we are actually seeing cinematic time's sleight of hand.'[38]

In *Tomboy*, the androgyny and gender ambiguity that surround Laure from the very beginning mean that cinematic time is unravelling *at the same time* as it is constituted. Laure is never '"properly" gendered' to begin with. There is a certain vagueness about *when* Laure first 'appears' as a boy or as a girl or as trans (to the spectator) – and it is this vagueness that further complicates, and heightens, Halberstam's assertion that:

> the transgender film confronts powerfully the way that transgenderism is constituted as a paradox made up in equal parts of visibility and temporality: whenever the transgender character is seen to be transgendered, then he/she is failing to pass and threatening to expose a rupture between the distinct temporal registers of past, present, and future.[39]

Beyond the 'rewind' (that evokes a reassuring spectatorial reorientation and retrospective sense-making), Halberstam identifies a potentially more useful and affirmative cinematic treatment of transgenderism: the constitution of a transgender gaze that allows us to 'look *with* the transgender character instead of *at* him.'[40] For Halberstam, *Boys Don't Cry* constitutes a 'quantum leap' in trans representations because it articulates 'the specific formal dimensions of a transgender gaze,' rather than locating transgenderism 'in between the male and female gaze and alongside unrelenting tragedy.'[41] However, even as groundbreaking a film as *Boys Don't Cry* does not manage a sustained commitment to a transgender look (Halberstam convincingly argues that the transgender look is replaced by a reassuring lesbian gaze that affirms the binary constitution of sex and gender), in part due to the inherently heteronormative underpinnings of narrative and visual structures, and their associated viewing pleasures, in (mainstream) cinema. *Tomboy's* strength lies in its undercutting of the significance of the gaze, and of the visual more generally, which is no easy feat given that 'gender assignments rely so heavily on the visual,' especially in the context of cinema.[42]

The casting of Héran, with her lanky and troublingly androgynous physique, mesmerisingly enigmatic face, and unselfconsciously tomboyish demeanour, is key to the ways in which *Tomboy's* explorations of gender nonconformity and passing are worked out. Héran's appearance imbues her performance with a sense of corporeal and affective authenticity and makes Laure's diegetic passing unnervingly believable. It underpins the sensuous resonances of the film and our embodied engagement with it, while at the same time conjuring a self-consciousness about the normalised assumptions implicit in our 'reading' of others when we encounter them. Laure's 'appearance' does not change throughout the film and she is not visually transformed in any way – even though she conjures different kinds of gender and sexual identities when she appears to different characters and in different spaces in the film. As spectators, we are unquestionably in on Laure's secret when her body is *visually* exposed in the bathroom scene that takes place relatively early on in the film (immediately following Laure's first encounter with Lisa and the other children in the neighbourhood). However, even given our privileged access to knowledge and the superior spectatorial positioning that arguably comes with it, *Tomboy* evokes a lingering, and periodically resurfacing, impetus for the spectator to engage in a self-reflexive questioning of our perceptual habits. Even towards the end of the film, we are encouraged to ask ourselves: How would we 'read' Laure if we encountered her out of context? This question remains, and remains unanswered, because issues around gender (identity), legibility and passing are worked out of primarily outwith the realm of the visual.

It is a kind of pleasurably puzzling elusiveness that drives our continued spectatorial turning and tending towards Laure: Are there any signs that give her 'real' gender away? Surely we would 'see' them, given how intimately close we are? We might follow Laure's journey in (sheepish) anticipation of a rupture, a glitch in her corporeal performance, that reassures us of our privileged position of spectatorial superiority and omniscience (we 'know' she is 'really' a girl; we have 'seen' evidence of this in the bathroom scene) – but this reassurance never materialises. Yes, *Tomboy* replays an arc of suspense typical of passing narratives, encouraging spectatorial anticipation of the moment in which Laure's secret is discovered – and Laure *is* 'found out' eventually, but not because she somehow fails to appear as a boy; there is no glitch. The children find out that Laure is 'really' a girl when the film's interior/domestic and exterior worlds collide, as Laure's mother becomes aware of and discloses Laure's passing to another parent. It is through the performative speech act of naming, through a *discursive* reshaping of Laure's positionality within the binary sex/gender system, that her appearance becomes troubling, 'disgusting' even, as one of the boys asserts, in the exterior world of the film.

The authenticity and permanency of Laure's queerly gendered mode of embodiment is articulated perhaps most poignantly when her mother forces her to wear a dress, and violently drags her, screaming, out of the apartment to make her apologise for lying to her friends about being a boy. The unshapely dress, which hangs on and clearly does not fit Laure's lanky angular frame, gives her the appearance of a boy in drag. It recalls an earlier, though more humorous, scene in which Lisa wants to play 'girls' with Laure and covers her face in make-up. There is a delightfully potent disconnect between Lisa's assertion that 'It suits you! You look great as a girl,' and the comically grotesque, brightly coloured lipstick, rouge and eye shadow on Laure's face that clash with her short, messy hair and boyish white tank top. During this scene, and while touching Laure's face, Lisa also announces that the group of friends is planning to go swimming the next day, drawing Laure's, and our, attention to the materiality of her (female) body. This adds yet another layer of complexity to a moment in which a jarring multitude of gendered meanings, resonances, signs, affects and connotations cohere in and around Laure's corporeal presence.

Testing the limits of the body

While *Tomboy* adheres to a range of generic, narrative and visual conventions that guide us on our journey through the film, it is its *physical* dynamic that most powerfully and affectively shapes our spectatorial engagement. Sciamma herself speaks of her film in these (embodied, visceral) terms, noting, for instance, that *Tomboy* is more 'choppy' than *Water Lilies*, because it 'follows the rhythms of childhood' and therefore works with a 'different energy'. More importantly, she sees the 'physical dynamic' of *Tomboy* 'not in the narrative which unfolds, but in the questioning of, "What body do I have?"' For her, 'the body is the limit of the film, and therefore it is also the object of the film.'[43]

The limits of the body, and thus the film, are most vigorously tested in those moments in which it is most explicitly on display. As in *Girlhood* (as we will see) it is in the context of athletic, physical activities that the limits of the body, its shape and its corporeal significance are most tangibly 'worked out'. In *Tomboy*, the muscular and kinaesthetic dimensions of Laure 'finding her feet' as a boy are articulated most graspably in relation to football (a particularly gendered physical activity) and swimming (where the material shape of the body is most visibly exposed).

There are two different football sequences, both relatively early on in the film, when Laure is still 'new' (to the neighbourhood and to her life as a boy) and tries to integrate herself into the existing group, which consist of a handful of boys and Lisa, the only girl. Lisa complains that the boys never let her play because she is 'useless'; football clearly is for boys, not for girls. In the first football scene, everyone is involved in the game, except for Lisa (because she is a girl) and Laure (because she is 'new' and a bit shy). Lisa wonders why Laure is not taking part in the game – because clearly, as a boy, she should be – and notes that Laure is 'not like the others'.

Watching the game from the sideline, Laure is fascinated by the physical performance. It is the excessive display of the boys' performative articulation of normative masculine, which a quintessentially masculine sport

Céline Sciamma's 'Queer' Cinema

Figure 5.1 Lisa and Laure/Mikaël Watching the Football Game (*Tomboy*)

such as football enables, encourages and even demands, that appeals to Laure. She smirks, approvingly, as the boys take off their shirts, give each other congratulatory high-fives after scoring and spit on the ground. The sequence ends with a rather comical looking constellation that highlights the chaotic dynamics of sex/gender/desire that emerge from the footballing encounter. The final three shots consist of a medium shot of one of the boys, staring back at Laure in an almost aggressive and confrontational manner, returning a gaze that he might experience as threateningly objectifying; a frontal close-up of Laure who, in turn, holds her gaze (at the boy), unwaveringly; and a close-up that shows Lisa in profile, looking (desiringly?) at Laure. Lisa and the boy direct, albeit very differently charged, gazes at Laure, marked by longing and aggression retrospectively, granting Laure a 'masculine' position in this network of looks and affirming her ability to pass as a boy.

There is also an important *embodied* dimension to this encounter, however. Despite Lisa's attempts to direct Laure's attention towards her, Laure *faces* the boys and their actions. Facing, for Ahmed, is a '"somatic mode of attention" that allows us to be touched by the proximity of others.'[44] Laure's proximity to the footballing action is articulated through the framing, which approximates her embodied engagement and positioning (rather than point of 'view'). At times, the camera increases our proximity to the muscular dynamics of the game, closing in on the boys' performative displays of masculinity (athletic skill, spitting, goal celebrations). The reaction shots of Laure betray her empathetic engagement with the corporeality of the performances (of football and masculinity): her upper body sways when she shifts her weight from one foot to the other; her hands and arms fidget restlessly; she tenses her upper body as she turns to face the action; the twitching muscles around her mouth and pursed lips reveal both an approving smirk and the gathering of saliva in response to the boys' spitting. For Waldron, *Tomboy* shows how 'Laure's embodied consciousness invests in the corporeal strategy of mimesis.'[45] This is *not*, importantly – or certainly not always/necessarily – a conscious or intentional strategy. Instead, what this sequence in particular gestures towards is a sense of muscular, kinaesthetic empathy that is enabled by Laure's corporeal orientations and habits, by who or what she is *facing* – and her bodily tendencies are, in turn, shaped by the encounter. What surfaces here is the mode of spectatorship the film itself makes possible – if we are inclined to *face* it in particular ways.

The muscular and tactile dimensions of Laure's (and the film's) corporeal journey manifest themselves more explicitly in a scene in the bathroom (shortly after the first and before the second football game). Laure is framed from behind, in a mid-shot that shows us both her back (from the waist up) and the front of her body as reflected in the mirror. On the surface, this scene of Laure gazing at her reflection in the mirror might seem to cry out for a psychoanalytic reading. However, the psychic dynamics of looking, recognition, identification and subjectivity, while gestured towards, are not what this moment *centrally* evokes. Laure's relation to her mirror image takes shape as a palpably haptic and muscular encounter. She first pulls up her grey tank top, revealing, and probingly touching, her skinny, flat stomach and chest. She then takes the top off altogether exploring the contours of her lean – emaciated, even – upper body with her hands, squeezing her biceps, tracing the shape of her collarbone, pushing back her shoulder, turning left, then right, so she can see her back, the twisting motion accentuating the outline of her ribs protruding through the skin. The camera moves closer, with a cut to an over-the-shoulder shot/medium close-up about halfway through the mirror scene, drawing us further into the encounter. We no longer look at Laure looking at herself in the mirror, but we look in the mirror with her.

Figure 5.2 Touching the Body/Image (*Tomboy*)

The scene constitutes a sensuous, tactile remoulding of conventional body-image relations. Laure only looks at her face and meets her own gaze, conjuring the kind of (mis)recognition linked to psychoanalytic conceptions of subject formation, in the very final moments of the scene. Up until then, Laure's eyes follow her hands as they trace the contours of her body, explicitly linking vision, movement and touch. She also takes her eyes off her mirror image at one point and looks directly down at her hands, probing the muscular texture of her arms. Laure's encounter in/with the mirror is not about searching for a coherent sense of self. 'Who am I?' is not the question explored here – Laure knows 'who' she is and the kind of affirmative (self)recognition afforded by the encounter with the mirror image is not what she is 'looking for'.

In the wake of being (mis)recognised as a boy by Lisa and the boys, and after witnessing, and being touched and moved by, the boy's performative display of normative masculinity during the first football scene, the mirror allows Laure to explore and test the limits of her body. Could she pass if she were to take off her shirt and expose her upper body? Laure is comfortable 'in her own skin' – but what are the links between her 'felt' embodiment and the affective resonances this body might evoke? What exactly 'appears' when Laure is present? These are questions we are invited to (at)tend to(wards). Laure's upper body, pre-pubescent as it is, does not yet bare the visible signs of sexual difference. Through the explicit linking of vision, movement, touch and (bodily) texture, the scene foregrounds the corporeal dimensions of appearance, (mis)recognition and identification – as they are explored in and by the film, but also as they shape our encounter with the film. How Laure is read does not depend on what her body looks like, but on how it appears, and on 'what' appears when her body is present – not in terms of fixed or innate biological facts, but with regard to the lived-body's tactile, muscular and kinaesthetic capabilities that shape, and are shaped by, differently gendered modes of embodiment.

It is in the final moments of the scene that Laure lifts her gaze (from the reflection of her body to the refection of her face), looks herself in the eye, as it were, smirks and spits in the sink, mirroring the boys' behaviour during the football game. Her smirking gaze conveys a self-congratulatory confidence in her ability to pass, which she puts to the test when joining in with the boys in the following football scene, which traces, in muscular, kinaesthetic and spatial terms, Laure's entry and subsequent immersion into the world of boys. The game is already in full flow when Laure arrives and she casts an isolated figure in the leafy suburban landscape. She is framed by an extreme long-shot, standing in front of a bluish-grey wall, watching the boys play, before eventually joining in. Her fidgety demeanour (she tenses her shoulders, tucks at her shirt, rubs her hands across the fabric covering her torso and pulls up her shorts) betrays a specifically tactile sense of nervous self-consciousness. Her capabilities for playing football and for 'play[ing] at being a boy' are about to be tested.[46]

Butler asserts the significance of 'the space of concerted collective action and improvisation' that team sports provide with regard to how gender norms and ideals continue to be reconstituted.[47] She proposes a phenomenological understanding of sport that usefully illuminates the embodied implications of the football sequences in *Tomboy*. When collective sporting action takes place, what emerges is:

> a situation in which bodies are being made, in which the tacit sculpting of bodies takes place dramatically and in concert [...] one of the consequences of playing together is that the physiology of the body is transformed through the process of that collective action. The bodies that begin the game are not the same bodies that end the game.[48]

It is by tracing the ways in which Laure is finding her feet and coming to feel 'at home' within the masculine world of boys/football in the remainder of the sequence that *Tomboy* reinforces the already established (tactile, muscular and kinaesthetic) entanglements between visibility, legibility and passing and gendered modes of embodiment. Butler emphasises the significance of bodily action in a *shared* corporeal space and notes the intercorporeal resonances and mutual shaping of bodies that take place within it. In sport, 'bodies engage in the rituals of self-production *only in relation to other bodies in motion*,' and we might claim that:

> bodies are decentered in relation to one another, that they find and pursue their centre outside themselves in a shared corporeal space, what Merleau-Ponty, the phenomenologist, called 'the flesh of the world.' This is a corporeal space that is not simply composed of the various bodies by which it is inhabited; it is rather, a *set of rules, norms, and relations by which a body assumes its bearings and its shape*; in turn, these norms are altered in the course of their inhabitation, those bodily rituals and incarnations by which such ideals and norms are given new life.[49]

It is *Tomboy's* conjuring of precisely these corporeal resonances that grounds its incarnations of gender (ambiguity) more firmly in the realm of lived experience and reasserts the continued privileging of an embodied spectatorial attitude.

When Laure first joins in, she is frequently framed on her own, with the boys appearing in the margins of the frame. The relatively static framing, along with Laure's continued self-conscious touching and tugging at her shirt, gives shape to a hesitant and inhibited intentionality. She is among the boys but has not yet adjusted to the game's rhythms and movements. Encouraged by a few successful footballing moves, which are accompanied by an increasingly mobile camera and more dynamic editing, Laure gradually sheds her inhibiting self-referentiality and her body begins to 'extend the shape' of the game's 'corporeal space' much more comfortably and confidently.[50]

Laure takes off her shirt, again touching her stomach, a specifically tactile affirmation of the self, and then looks around to assess whether her exposed upper body has affected a change in her 'appearance'. The camera follows Laure's initially timid steps – the footballing action taking place, again, outside the frame – and the close framing conveys a sense of the enclosing self-referentiality conjured by the 'pressure' of the binary sex/gender system that underpins the cultural logics of intelligibility. However, when Laure's survey of the group confirms a reassuring lack of reaction from the boys, she spits on the ground and engages in the action much more unselfconsciously. What the sequence traces here is what happens when the 'spectatorial point of view' of one's own body, that 'lets the body appear as a bounded kind of thing' is 'relinquished in favour of engaged bodily action.'[51] Laure's initial hesitation is linked to her inability to give up her perspective *on*, and take up a perspective *from*, the body. Crucially, her initial, inhibitingly alienated, perspective *on* the body is articulated as a specifically embodied and tactile perspective: Laure's touching, tracing and probing the surface and contours of her body add a textured, corporeal dimension to Butler's assertion that 'it appears that the spectatorial point of view works to defeat and break apart the sense of kinesthetic continuity that characterizes engaged bodily action, that sense of not knowing where the body ends and its instrument begins,' and that 'too much self-consciousness paralyzes action altogether.'[52]

The gradual shift in Laure's mode of embodiment is made graspable through her increasingly engaged participation in the game: there is no self-referential touching; her gaze and (bodily) attention are directed towards the ball and the footballing action (rather than her own body and others' apprehension of it); and her face betrays concentration and focus. The palpable shift in the modes of directionality, intentionality and spatiality embodied by Laure are emulated by the shift in framing and the more immediate and reciprocally engaged mode of spectatorship it evokes. The game evolves increasingly around Laure at the centre of the footballing action. While the handheld camera keeps Laure in the centre of the frame it also becomes progressively more mobile, moving among the players, closing in on Laure's grimacing face, flexed muscles and dribbling feet, with quicker cuts between shots and changing angles further adding to the sense of kinaesthetic freedom and energy. Laure's integration into the 'world of boys' and their masculine corporeal space is therefore not only shown to us. It is, first and foremost, articulated via a shift in the modes of

Céline Sciamma's 'Queer' Cinema

Figure 5.3 Laure/Mikaël in the 'World of Boys' (*Tomboy*)

movement and comportment embodied by Laure *and* the film. The filmic body engages in a mutually empathetic relation with Laure as it simultaneously adjusts to *and* moulds the shape of her embodied consciousness. If, as D'Aloia argues 'watching a film is an experience of a relationship between bodies in space,'[53] then the spectatorial attitude invited by this scene of Laure's emphatic 'occupation' in and of the boys' corporeal world is underpinned by a similarly responsive (tactile, muscular and kinaesthetic) empathy.[54]

Tomboy traces Laure's negotiation of the different ways in which her embodied existence takes shape and makes sense in the interior and exterior worlds of the film. Gradually, these worlds encroach upon each other and ultimately, and not surprisingly, they collide. This collision is instigated by the figure of the mother, who comes to stand, and not entirely unproblematically, for the larger social and institutional contexts in which Laure's queer embodiment is not a viable, and intelligible, option. There is a heart-wrenching moment in the scene cited above, as Laure's mother forces her to wear a dress and drags her into the exterior world of the film, dressed as a girl, in order to 'straighten things out' with her friends and their parents.

The mother explains to a distraught Laure, who does not want to face, and 'come out' to, Lisa in particular, that she does not mind Laure 'playing

Figure 5.4 Laure/Mikaël in 'Drag' (*Tomboy*)

the boy' and that it 'doesn't even make [her] sad,' but that they 'have no choice' but to come clean because of the impending start of the new school year. It is within the larger social/institutional context that Laure's non-conforming embodiment of gender is unintelligible and thus forecloses subjecthood. As Butler argues, 'the body that one lives is in many ways a body that becomes livable only through first being cast in a culturally intelligible way. In other words, the cultural framing of the body precedes and enables its lived experience.'[55] Laure acquires two different but equally viable kinds of intelligibility throughout the film – she is intelligible as a (tomboyish) 'girl' in the domestic space of the home and intelligible as a 'boy' in the exterior, yet bounded and sheltered, world of childhood. The spectator, however, who, like Laure, moves between these two different corporeal, affective spaces, is confronted with a continued oscillation of sense-making logics, which reinforces a palpably self-reflexive mode of embodied spectatorship.

It is when these worlds collide *in* the film that Laure's mode of being becomes unintelligible and therefore unlivable. It is at this point in the film – when Laure is 'exposed' by her mother and then confronted by the other children who demand to 'see' evidence of Laure's biological sex in a scene that carries haunting resonances with Brandon's exposure in *Boys Don't Cry* – that a generic ending that somehow falls back on the binary sex/gender system seems inevitable. As the narrative nears its ending, *Tomboy* poses the same questions that Laure, wearing the blue dress, is asked by her mother, just prior to being dragging to Lisa's apartment: 'Got an idea? 'Cos if you do, please say so, I can't think of any. Have you got a solution?' A solution, that is, other than assuming a clearly defined and legible subject position within the gender binary? Endearingly, the film refuses to provide any kind of clear-cut solution.

In the final scene, we see Laure, by herself, looking out onto the leafy suburban environment from the balcony of the family home. She spots Lisa, standing underneath a tree, gazing up, clearly looking for another encounter. Lisa's turning and tending towards Laure is significant for a number of reasons. The corporeal trajectory of Laure's variously troubling embodiment of gender is interwoven with her increasingly intimate friendship with Lisa. Lisa likes 'Mikaël' and their relationship acquires elements of a romance, including a few timid kisses. Lisa is therefore most directly affected by the revelation of Laure's secret. However, when Laure is cornered and backed up against a tree in the woods by the boys who insist on 'checking' 'if *she* is really a girl', Lisa replies 'Leave *him* alone'. Lisa here engages in the kind of affirmative recognition of Laure's queer identity that Brandon receives from Lana (Chloë Sevigny), his girlfriend, in *Boys Don't Cry*. In a similar, though perhaps more excruciatingly harrowing, scene, in which Lana is forced to check on the physical evidence of Brandon's sex, 'Lana refuses to look when Brandon unbuckles his pants, telling him, "Don't… I know you're a guy."'[56] The boys pressure Lisa to examine Laure, by forcing her to admit that, if Laure is really a girl, their kissing was 'disgusting'. Unlike Lana, Lisa does appear to look, although we cannot be quite sure. Only their upper bodies are in the frame when Laure and Lisa stand facing each other. They continue to look at each other as Lisa seems to unzip and/or pull down Laure's shorts and then briefly glance downwards, at Laure's crotch. We are unable to see what exactly Lisa does, and what exactly she sees.

As Halberstam notes, there are moments, gestures and glances throughout *Boys Don't Cry* that suggest that Lana is somehow aware that Brandon is different – and the same goes for Lisa who realises early on that her new friend is 'not like the others.' This dynamic, in addition to Lisa's return to Laure at the end of the film, imbues her character with queer resonances, which, like Lana's, tend to get lost as they pale in relation to the more explicit queerness of the protagonists. Nonetheless, it is Lisa's instigation of the film's climactic final encounter that enables the refreshingly affirmative opening-up of queer spaces of possibility – rather than the re-establishment of a binary order that narrative closure normally demands. Laure spots Lisa standing outside her apartment. When Laure joins her, they are framed in a two-shot, first coyly staring at the ground, before looking at each other, when Lisa asks 'What's your name?'. The final shot is a close-up of Laure who breathes in heavily before answering 'My name is Laure.' The shot of Laure's serious, thoughtful face is held for various seconds, as Laure's eyes dart around nervously, unsure as to where to look, before fixing her gaze on Lisa. A cut to a black screen signals the end of the film, just as the hint of a smile begins to appear on Laure's face.

Sciamma has commented on the significance of the final scene, noting that the 'end of the film is like the end of a lie – but it doesn't end on "I'm a girl"; it ends with the act of Laure saying her name.' She adds that 'the act of stating who you are asserts the possibility of not having to hide in order to be who you are.'[57] Sciamma considers this to be an act of liberation – and not a return to the norm. The final encounter between Lisa and Laure is one of mutual acknowledgment that queers both characters. It constitutes a subtly emphatic refusal of closure (in all its manifestations) and undercuts the primacy of vision in establishing intelligible and mutually affirmative intersubjective relations. Halberstam notes that *Boys Don't Cry*, creates:

> a position for the transgender subject that is fortified from the traditional operations of the gaze and conventional modes of gendering but also makes the transgender subject dependent on the recognition of a woman. In other words, Brandon can be Brandon because Lana is willing to see him as he sees himself [...] and she is willing to avert her gaze when his manhood is in question.[58]

By anchoring the working out of subjectivity and intelligibility in the realm of embodiment, rather than the disembodied gaze, *Tomboy* manages to sidestep the binary sex/gender system that even a 'transgender subject' like Brandon ultimately reaffirms. Through its making graspable of the phenomenological dimensions of what we might refer to as the non-binary, rather than trans, experience, *Tomboy* gestures towards the possibility of making meaningful contact with ambiguously gendered others. Through its tactile, muscular and kinaesthetic incarnations and negotiations of legibility and appearance, *Tomboy* constitutes a weighty unhinging of the binary sex/gender system that underpins normative configurations of transgenderism, gender nonconformity and passing – in cinema and beyond.

Queer Shape-Shifting: Embodied Trajectories of Transformation and Resistance in *Girlhood*

Girlhood is the final instalment of Sciamma's female coming-of-age trilogy. In many ways, *Girlhood* seems bigger, more serious and more grown-up than its predecessors: it moves from the realms of childhood and early adolescence to late adolescence and the transition to adulthood; it is shot in CinemaScope and is visually grander and more spectacular; and it also opens up the 'world of girls, girls alone' by situating its protagonist(s) in a more specific socio-historical and political context. [59] As So Mayer writes: '*Girlhood* goes where the others don't as Marieme/Vic leaves home and enters the adult world on the margins of white French society, full of risks and opportunities.'[60]

Tomboy, like *Water Lilies*, is in some way an 'atemporal' film, in that the young characters' world is fairly self-contained and removed from the wider real-world context, but *Girlhood* is very specifically set in 'the world of today.' Not only does the film feature specific fashion styles, versions of mobile phones and brands of sneakers, soft drinks, alcohol and sweets (entirely absent from *Tomboy*), *Girlhood* also evokes the specific social, cultural and political context of contemporary France through the characters' venturing into various kinds of public, crowded spaces (public transport, the mall, the big open plaza around La Grande Arche) that leads to a range of conflicts and tensions around the intersections of race, gender and class.

Like *Tomboy*, *Girlhood*'s appeal hinges, at least in part, on the mesmerising face of its young female protagonist, often framed in close-up, looking on, an indication of her sidelined positioning in the hetero-patriarchal, white world of contemporary France. Marieme's face is as mesmerising as it is unrevealing. It is determined yet inaccessible, her often closed, tensed mouth betraying only the lack of 'voice' available to those living at the margins. While the close-up tends to provide access to the inner life and emotions of characters, and thus encourage spectatorial identification, *Girlhood*, like *Tomboy*, privileges a spectatorial encounter with the muscular, kinaesthetic and spatial modes of being-in-the-world embodied by its young female protagonist(s) over more conventional cinematic articulations of subjectivity and agency via the gaze, face and voice and the opportunities for spectatorial identification they provide.

In part, Marieme's face is as spellbinding as it is stoically enigmatic because it is *not* a white face and *Girlhood* certainly plays on, and makes the most of, the 'representational anomaly' of black faces and black skin filling the cinema screen, often in close-up.[61] The all-black and predominantly female cast, and a narrative that situates its young black protagonist in the marginalised, violent and (cinematically) overdetermined space of the Parisian banlieue projects, have emerged as some of the key points of discussion around *Girlhood*. The film is often lauded for giving visibility to non-white *female* actors within the larger context of increasing numbers of mostly *male* actors from ethnic-minority backgrounds in France. Ginette Vincendeau ascribes this, in part, to 'the legacy of the *beur* [...] and *banlieue* cinema of the 1980s and 1990s,' which demonstrated 'the

Figure 5.5 Marieme (*Girlhood*)

viability and relevance of multicultural stories in both mainstream and auteur cinema.'[62]

Within critical debate, *Girlhood* tends to be situated in relation to the broader context of *banlieue* cinema. *Girlhood* is characterised by the generic interweaving of the coming-of-age trope with 'the grammar of the *banlieue* film from which [it] borrows many familiar aspects: concrete buildings, walkways and esplanades frame characters whose clothes and language label them as *banlieue* youth.'[63] Its release also coincided with the 20th anniversary of *La Haine* (1995), Mathieu Kassovitz's quintessential *banlieue* film that sparked an explosion of this type of largely social realist drama in France. *Girlhood* is often considered to be the latest highlight in the cycle of *banlieue* films and comparisons with *La Haine* were rife upon its release.[64]

Girlhood is not characterised by the gritty realism that is linked to the overtly political stance of the *banlieue* social drama, however. Instead, Sciamma adopts what Vincendeau calls 'an intensely aestheticising gaze' in her '"impressionistic" tale of youth.'[65] Sciamma admits that she is interested in 'the choreography of the girls' bodies, the energy of their performances (dancing, fighting), the light on their skin', and fascinated by 'bands of black girls in real life, their "energy and way of speaking."'[66] This aestheticising look at the racial 'other', fuelled by a self-acclaimed fascination with this otherness (which, importantly, has specifically corporeal and visceral undertones), has led to damning critiques of the film as a 'racist, exoticising fantasy of a privileged white filmmaker,' for 'perpetuating the image of black women as victims of oppression' and for 'demonising black men,' countering the praise it received for its making visible of ethnic minority identities and its depiction of 'girls valorising each other.'[67]

A phenomenological approach offers a nuanced alternative to the 'political-aesthetic split' that, as Vincendeau notes, characterises existing debates. In what follows, I trace *Girlhood's* embodied (muscular, kinaesthetic and spatial) trajectory and explore the queer feminist potential of its corporeal and affective resonances. This is, again, an attempt to avoid the drawbacks of a narrowly defined identity politics – which *Girlhood* itself refuses – while acknowledging the situatedness of experience. *Girlhood* accounts for Marieme's variously marginalised positionality through its unhinging of straightforwardly white and heteropatriarchal modes of embodiment and being-in-the-world, articulated as they are through the muscular, kinaesthetic and spatial dimensions of 'the choreography of the girls' bodies,' 'the energy of their performances' and their appropriation of space 'in a male-dominated [and white] world.'[68]

It is additionally worth noting that Sciamma herself attempts to deflect comparisons with *La Haine* and 'all this cinema about the Urban Western.'[69] Instead, she identifies the 'Janes' as her sources of inspiration – Jane Campion, Jane Austen and Calamity Jane – in order to assert that *Girlhood* is, first and foremost, 'a coming of age story about young women' that happens to be 'set in the suburbs with a black girl.'[70] In doing so, Sciamma attempts to (re)position herself and her film more specifically in relation to a larger trajectory of women's/feminist filmmaking, authorship and criticism – as well as, via the reference to *Calamity Jane* (David Butler, US, 1953), to cinema's variously queer history.[71]

Girlhood is not an obviously queer film – at least in terms of its subject matter. It is only in the final part of the narrative that LGBTI themes are explicitly engaged with. In this sense, it perhaps seems odd to see *Girlhood* featuring so prominently on the queer film festival circuit (despite its out lesbian director). It is *not* so strange, however, if we acknowledge that *Girlhood's* (feminist) queerness lies elsewhere: in its muscular habits and kinaesthetic tendencies; its corporeal resonances and textural entanglements; its embodied twists and turn; and its affective shape-shifting and palpable reorientations. These are woven into the film's textural fabric and shape its sensuous trajectory throughout, before surfacing more explicitly towards the end.

As with her other films, Sciamma refuses to tie her protagonist to a specific and fixed identity (is Marieme straight? bi? trans?), but acknowledges that she is somehow 'queer': 'There are several ways to be queer: [Marieme] is really trying out the different identities that society has set for her. She is not inventing them, she's trying them out.'[72] She goes from being a 'shy, quiet girl' to a 'more iconic, empowered girl, part of a group with this more feminine side,' but she can also be 'one of the boys.'[73] Notably, Marieme's embodiment of these various identities is shaped most significantly through her relations to other *female* characters. If her identity is anchored at all, it is in relation to the variously corporeal and affective resonances that reverberate around the female characters' embodied presence, including in particular her younger sister, the other members of the *bande* and Monica (Dielika Doulibaly), her flatmate, in the final segment of the film. As Sciamma notes, *Girlhood* is 'about how the great love stories and great sentimental journey for girls is among girls.'[74] *Girlhood*'s queerness, then, lies in its unhinging of normative modes of gendered embodiment as well as of the normative (lack of affirmative) relations between women that tend to be woven into the fabric of heteronormative patriarchal relations.

In addition to *La Haine*, *Girlhood* also evoked comparisons with Richard Linklater's *Boyhood* (US, 2014), released earlier in the same year, partly because of the coming-of-age subject matter, but mainly due to the films' matching titles. The comparison is in many ways farfetched, however. As Robbie Collins points out, while *Boyhood*, explores 'the passing of time' and 'the making of history,' *Girlhood* is 'set in, and celebrates, the immediate, impulsive here and now.'[75] Sciamma herself variously welcomes and refutes the comparison: the connection of *Bande de filles*' English title to Linklater's film was accidental, she asserts. Although she admits that the films engage in a useful dialogue around growing up and coming-of-age, *Boyhood* and *Girlhood* 'believe very different things in cinema.' While both films 'attempt to encapsulate a universal experience', *Boyhood* offers a conventionally normative account of the coming-of-age trope: 'What's universal in America [and more specifically in US cinema] about teenagehood is a middle-class white boy with average dreams. We pick a character at the margins and say what's universal is a 16-year-old black girl.'[76]

To claim universality for a story with an entirely black cast and a young black female protagonist is problematic, and not only because *Girlhood* was made by a (relatively) privileged white filmmaker. On the one hand, assertions that Marieme is not a *black* heroine, but a 'contemporary heroine', betray a seemingly progressive colour-blindness, and echo non-white filmmakers' and actors' resistance to 'being seen in terms of their ethnic origins for fear of being ghettoised.'[77] This understanding of *Girlhood* as not being *about* race is echoed in various reviews; for example, the claim that '*Girlhood* is not a film about the black experience so much as the trials of youth.'[78] On the other hand, Sciamma's appropriation of the racial 'other', and of the *banlieue*, to her 'auteurist vision' risks discounting the specificity of the experience and situation (in the phenomenological sense) of the racial 'other'.⁷⁹

What *Girlhood* manages to achieve, I want to argue, is a careful negotiation of a range of seemingly binary and mutually exclusive positions: universality vs. specificity; difference vs. otherness; racial stereotypes vs. affirmative/positive images. As with *Tomboy*, Sciamma draws on generic and representational clichés (of *banlieue* cinema; of urban-set films featuring disaffected black youth; of the coming-of-age genre; of the female adolescent in French cinema) while at the same time remoulding these clichés and refusing to follow their straightforwardly white and heteropatriarchal 'lines'. Eric Kohn gestures towards this contradictory ambiguity, noting that '*Girlhood* deals with race by implication,' while 'its main line of inquiry is universal (which, ironically, makes it something of anomaly among movies exclusively focused on minorities).'⁸⁰ Similarly, Barbara Speed suggests that while *Girlhood* 'says things about race, class, and French society, [...] these are always firmly grounded in Marieme and her story.' This is because we never 'leave Marieme's headspace', which arguably 'stops you drawing out the film to make it answer to a much broader sociopolitical narrative.'⁸¹ In other words, what emerges here, and as I explore further in what follows, is a sense that *Girlhood* engages with questions of race, gender, sexuality and wider socio-political issues not via conventional representational strategies, but through muscular, kinaesthetic and spatial incarnations of the ways in which oppressively racialised and gendered social structures are embodied and felt and, importantly, resisted and refused. It is not necessarily that we never 'leave Marieme's headspace' (although we are firmly positioned 'with' Marieme throughout the film), but that we are offered a visceral encounter with the affectively corporeal trajectory of her shapeshifting journey.

Girlhood conveys this journey in five parts – in addition to the American football opening sequence – that are clearly separated by black screens. The first part introduces us to a shy, quiet and reserved Marieme and her restrictive home life, which consists of taking on a mothering role for her two younger sisters; dealing with a bullying, violent older brother while her mother is mostly absent and at work; her lack of educational prospects (she is told she has to leave school because of her grades); and her first encounter with Lady (Assa Sylla), Fily (Mariétou Touré) and Adiatou (Lindsay Karamoh), the *bande de filles*. Part two shows Marieme growing more confident in the company of the three other girls, as the plain clothes and braids of childhood of the first part are replaced by wavy open hair, tight jeans and a black leather jacket that match the style of the other members of the *bande*. Part two also includes the much-talked-about scene of the four girls dancing to Rihanna's 'Diamonds', as well as the first of two fight sequences, in which Lady, the leader of the *bande*, is defeated by a girl from another gang.

In part three, Marieme asserts herself and her frustrations and desires even more confidently as she dares to pursue a 'forbidden' relationship and sexual intimacy with a boy, Ismaël (Idrissa Diabaté), who is a close friend of Marieme's thuggish brother. She also challenges and defeats the leader of the other gang in a brutal street fight. Part four sees Marieme leave home and her friends; in an attempt to refuse the dead-end life set out for her she agrees to work as a drug dealer for gangster Abou (Djibril Gueye). In the fifth and final part, Marieme undergoes the most dramatic physical transformation, as we see her selling drugs wearing a short blonde wig, heavy make-up, a tight-fitting short red dress and high heels, while she takes on an overtly masculine appearance outside her drug-dealing activities: she wears short braids, plain baggy clothes and even binds her breasts in order to conceal her feminine bodily shape. Marieme also shares an apartment with Monica, a more conventionally feminine character, and the two women 'appear' as a couple at various points, especially in the domestic context of the kitchen and, most poignantly, when they slow dance together at Abou's party towards the very end of the film.

The changes in Marieme's appearance are clearly linked to her transformative journey and are indicative of *Girlhood's* more general non-essentialising stance. As Sciamma notes, her aim was to show how 'identities are worn like costumes' and she likens *Girlhood* to the 'superhero genre' in that Marieme's transformations are tied to the realisation of 'what power the "costume" gives her.'[82] However, *Girlhood* goes beyond the surface layer of the costume that can easily be put on and taken off and locates its protagonist's variously transformative journey in the realm of embodiment, spatiality and sensuousness – and the muscular and kinaesthetic register is asserted from the onset.

Feeling social 'pressures', or: On (not) having a 'voice'

Girlhood opens with a highly aestheticised slow-motion sequence of an American football match. The scene is fairly decontextualised and its ties to the narrative and diegetic world of *Girlhood* are tenuous. It does not really make (rational) sense and echoes, at least in part, the fantastic, ahistorical and utopian register of the musical 'number'.[83] Two teams, fully dressed in American football regalia, emerge from the tunnel as the energetically hypnotic score increases in volume; together with the slow-motion framing of moving bodies, the sonic swell adds to the sense of decontextualised abstraction. Both teams seem to take the game seriously – there are crunching tackles, hostile stares and helmet against helmet standoffs. Yet there is no referee, and there are no coaches or spectators of any kind in the empty stands that are surrounded by the impenetrable black darkness of the night sky. Both teams also wear the same team name on the back of their jerseys and engage in a joint celebration at the end of the game, leaving all sense of rivalry and confrontation behind. There are no references to American football in the remainder of the film and, while the scene is linked to our introduction to *Girlhood's* diegetic world 'proper' (we see the players, including Marieme, returning to the *banlieue* projects following the game), the football sequence itself appears removed in time and space and takes on a utopian register.

There is a certain ambiguity around the players' gender as they emerge from the tunnel and run towards and past the camera in the blurry opening shot. Their heads are covered by helmets, their faces obscured by protective grilles and their bodily shapes concealed by thickly padded outfits – but we get occasional glimpses of ponytails sticking out of helmets, and of eye make-up. What is centrally conveyed in this sequence is a sense of uninhibited kinetic energy and corporeal, muscular contact that is shaped by the players' movements and by the energetically rhythmic sync score that gradually intensifies throughout. The sequence is shot entirely in slow motion as the camera puts us in touch with the players' assertively dynamic physicalities and traces the collective contours of taut bodies brimming with energy. Questions of gender, and gendered embodiment, are thus woven into the affective fabric of *Girlhood* from the (utopian)

Figure 5.6 Celebrating Female Physicality (*Girlhood*)

onset. The sequence plays with the masculine associations of American football (including the strong, powerful, energetic and assertive modes of movement and comportment characteristic of those playing the sport) and creates an affectively visceral juxtaposition between the quintessentially masculine modes of embodiment that take shape in the scene and the visible indicators of (and common-sense assumptions about) femininity that are present, albeit ambiguously, throughout.

The opening sequence stands in stark contrast to the general invisibility, in cinema and beyond, of strong, powerful and unrestrained female bodies of various shapes and sizes 'revelling in the joy of their own strength' – especially without being exposed to an intrusive (male) gaze.[84] We are offered an encounter with the collective and exuberant kinetic energy and corporeal dynamism of bodies that extend an ambiguously abstract space which appears unmarked by the restrictive textures of the social. It is a self-enclosed space that is removed from the diegetic world of the film to which we are subsequently introduced. The opening sequence thus not only introduces us to the muscular, kinaesthetic and spatial register, tied as it is to the uninhibited and confident female physicalities. It also provides a contrast to, and thus foregrounds, the imprisoning pressures of the heteropatriarchal white world that the girls normally inhabit and that they return to following the opening sporting action.

Sound, noise and voice also play an important role in *Girlhood*'s opening incarnation of the muscular and spatial dimensions of the girls' corporeal presence. When they take off their helmets and begin their post-game celebrations, their voices, initially audible as unintelligible chatter, are the first diegetic sounds that appear on the soundtrack alongside the non-diegetic score. They gradually transform into the rhythmic roars of celebratory chants, almost overpowering the music. The opening sequence ends with a long-shot of the teams in the centre of the floodlit field, with the depthless, impenetrable night sky taking up the majority of the frame, before the floodlights turn off and the entire screen turns to black. The film's title, '*Bande de filles*', appears on the screen and only the girls' echoing chants remain present on the soundtrack. Their voices provide a sound bridge into *Girlhood*'s diegetic world as they turn into sonorous yet indecipherable chatter that continues to increase in volume as the silhouettes of the girls walking towards the camera become progressively more distinguishable from the black void from which they emerge. The thickly textured and reverberating entanglement of animated and cheerful voices gives the group a corporeal presence, even when individual bodies and faces cannot be clearly demarcated.

The girls move through the darkness as a lively, hustling and bustling unit, the energy and dynamism of their collective corporeal presence intimately entangled with the enchantingly chaotic vitality of their resounding sonic presence. But as the girls enter the projects, with a low-angle shot emphasising the high-rise apartment blocks towering over the group, the volume (perceived loudness, intensity) of the densely textured, layered sounds enveloping the girls diminishes, along with the volume (size) of the group, as the girls peel off one by one or in small groups to return to their respective homes, as well as the volume (spatiality) of individual bodies, as the girls' assertively confident comportment is replaced by slouched postures, tensed shoulders, hands stuffed in pockets, bowed heads and downcast eyes. The dark shadows of anonymous male figures, cast against the dimly lit walls of the high-rises, line the walkway and assert the sombre and intimidating atmosphere, as their muffled conversations and menacing shouts replace the girls' joyous chatter. Marieme is identified as *Girlhood*'s protagonist as we experience the disintegration of the group and the isolating journey through the palpably hostile environment with her. Marieme emerges from the group and there is a gradual shift in spectatorial alignment in our initial encounter, from the corporeal collective to the figure of Marieme.

Céline Sciamma's 'Queer' Cinema

The opening offers a palpable contrast between an energetic, assertive and expansive physicality on the one hand and an inhibited, self-referential and contained mode of comportment on the other, foregrounding the corporeal resonances of social *pressures*. This juxtaposition resonates with Ahmed's queer phenomenological account, already evoked in relation to *2 Seconds*, where she notes that social 'pressure' to lead a certain kind of life might be experienced as a 'physical "press" on the surface of the body' and that, over time, bodies tend to 'take the shape' of these pressures.[85] What Ahmed articulates here, and what *Girlhood*'s opening begins to make graspable, are the ways in which 'persons live out their positioning in social structures along with the opportunities and constraints they produce.'[86] The lived-body and its cinematic incarnations are shaped by, and give shape to, these structures – and *Girlhood*'s sensory opening register offers an embodied encounter with their 'pressing' resonances. The film's overall trajectory coheres around the muscular, kinaesthetic and spatial juxtaposition that shapes our entrance into the film and traces Marieme's refusal to give in to the heteronormatively patriarchal norms that 'pressure' her to follow the course of the life set out for her. The gendered (rather than racialised) dimensions of these pressures and of Marieme's 'positioning in social structure' are foregrounded throughout, which is why the film might resonate not so much as being 'about' race and more profoundly as being 'about' gender.

Girlhood's opening also gestures towards the precarious implications of a phenomenological, affective register within larger social and representational contexts in which language and representation are dominant modes of expression and signification. It highlights the juxtaposition not only between different modes of physicality, but also between vocality/noise and voice/speech. The girls' chatter and laughter gives them an aural presence, but also links to their physical, spatial incarnations: these are sounds that are produced by and emanate from, while also gesturing back towards, the body. However, while we can *hear* the girls, and while their voices reverberate beyond the screen, they do not have 'a voice'. Their patter is largely incomprehensible and we are unable to make out exactly *what it is* they say. Overall, their raucous presence in this scene, which also foreshadows the noisy confrontation between the *bande* and another (black) girl gang in a metro station, risks reinforcing stereotypical associations of black femininity with a kind of animalistic, irrational, out-of-control and excessive corporeality. That said, the tone, rhythm and energy of their patter as they walk through the darkness as a group, still resonating with the dynamic energy of the American football sequence, also provide us with a palpable sense of positivity, energy, elation and confidence. Both in the opening sequence and throughout, especially during moments of corporeal collectivity and infectious laughter (about which more later), *Girlhood* opens up different registers of meaning – what Bolton, following Irigaray, calls a 'feminine syntax' or a 'gestural code of women's bodies.'[87]

It is this intertwining of embodiment and spatiality with sound, noise and voice that is key to Marieme's working out of her place in the world *as well as* to the film's working out of a mode of articulation that makes Marieme's corporeally affective transformations graspable. *Girlhood* is a much more 'vocal' film than *Tomboy*. There is more dialogue and there are numerous moments in which Marieme attempts to 'voice' her frustrations with the life set out for her (including her conversation with the guidance councillor who tells her that she cannot stay at school; her confrontation with her mother's boss who offers her a dead-end job as a cleaner; and in the hotel scene in which she says goodbye to the other three members of the *bande* before moving on to become part of Abou's drug cartel). Overall, however, dialogue is of secondary importance with regard to *Girlhood's* articulation of Marieme's working out her options in a world that is not 'for' her and that does not 'extend [her] shape.'[88] As Kohn suggest, 'the themes in play unfold in physical terms.'[89]

Various different kinds of bodily performances take place throughout the film and it is during these moments that the sense of corporeal resistance, refusal and assertion is conveyed most palpably and offers the most profoundly affective resonances. In particular, these moments include the American football match, the *bande's* dancing to Rihanna's 'Diamonds' in a hotel room, another dance sequence in the public space around La Grande Arche and two brutal street fights. Those moments are crucial because they convey a sense of Marieme's and the girls' assertive and unconstrained physicalities, engendering a powerfully visceral contrast with the constrained and pressured modes of embodiment that take shape outside of those moments. As Harris points out, 'to see these same bodies stilled elsewhere in the film by violence and taboo is thus all the more agonising.'[90]

As foreshadowed by the American football scene, affirmative assertions of corporeal collectivity take place when the girls manage to find, and 'occupy' (in Ahmed's sense), spaces that are removed from the otherwise overbearing pressures of the social[91] – spaces, in other words, in which they are amongst themselves and manage to create, at least temporarily, a 'world of girls, girls alone.'[92] Dori Thomas points to *Girlhood's* articulation of a notable difference:

> between who these girls are when they are together and who they are when they are surrounded by those who hold them back or would seek to control them. Throughout the film, the girls are constantly changing their behavior and their appearances to suit their surroundings – they do so, because that's how they survive.[93]

While Marieme's shape-shifting is, in part, about survival, it is also clearly an embodied manifestation of resistance and refusal and an unapologetic assertion of corporeal presence. These assertions are most palpable when the girls are together, when they *do* things together, when they 'connect', when they 'turn towards' each other and when the affective and corporeal resonances between them surface and, at times, erupt in gripping manifestations of profoundly queer phenomenological orientations.

Laughter and 'Diamonds': affecting assertions of collective corporeal presence

These corporeal tropes come together, and are conveyed most affectively, in the first hotel room scene, which also includes the girls' rendition of Rihanna's 'Diamonds'. Sciamma notes that 'there is no safe space for girls' in Marieme's world.[94] Renting a hotel room (with stolen money) is an attempt to create a (temporary) space that allows for abandon and intimacy. The room takes on a utopian quality, evoking the decontextualised feel of the American football match – although the pressures and confines of the outside world are much more proximate and occasionally rupture the confines of the utopian spaces (for instance, through phone calls from Marieme's brother). Hotel rooms are ambiguous sites in that they constitute a complex intersection of the public and the private – they are both and neither. In *Girlhood*, they function as an alternative to the various restrictions, restraints and pressures the girls encounter in the private (their homes) *and* the public realm (school, the metro, the mall, the plaza and the city more generally).

Homes, in particular, are ambivalent spaces in all of Sciamma's films, but *Girlhood* foregrounds the heteropatriarchal pressures of the home most explicitly. To a certain extent, the conventionally gendered implications of the public – private divide are turned on their head. As Sciamma describes, in '[t]he neighborhood outside and even at home, the men make the rules and there is an authority the girls have to live by. But when they go to a public space like in the city, it's kind of a stage where they get to perform.'[95] These public 'performances', in which the girls unapologetically assert their physical, sonic presence include their confident, sassy and loud strutting through the mall; the shouting match with another girl gang on a metro station platform; the dance moves they practice to the music played from their mobile phones on the metro; and the street fights. The girls variously re-appropriate and occupy public spaces that are not 'meant' for them in these moments, through behaviours, appearances and modes of taking up space that disrupt the normatively white, straight, patriarchal expectations and tendencies that normally shape these spaces and the bodies that occupy them. In one particularly touching scene, the girls stage a dance-off in a public plaza in the city, following the stunningly shot set-piece that traces the girls' smiling faces as they stand in front of La Grand Arche at the beginning of the fourth segment of the film. There are number of lengthy close-ups that linger on the dancers' gyrating hips and crotches. The framing does not appear intrusive, however, as the joyous and elated performances are contained within the protective bubble of the girls' collective corporeal presence.

The *bande's* get-together in the hotel room earlier (in the second segment of the film) constitutes a key moment in *Girlhood's* gradual incarnation of the powerfully affective resonances of female solidarity, mutuality and intimacy. It is also a corporeal, sensuous manifestation of Marieme's integration into the group, as she turns from shy and reserved onlooker to the visceral, muscular, kinaesthetic centre of the group – *and of the film*. In the preceding confrontation with another girl gang in the metro station, for instance, Marieme stays in the background, observing and taking in the aggressive posturing and shouting with a tensely closed mouth and slight frown. As the girls enter the hotel room, Lady, Adiatou and Fily sit down on the bed. Marieme throws herself on top of the entangled bodies with some force; she wants to be 'in the middle'. A less-than-impressed Lady pushes Marieme off her legs and a pillow fight ensures as the girls begin to laugh, at Lady (for being angry) and at Adiatou who gets up to perform a hysterically comical rendition of a pop song before throwing herself back onto the pile of bodies. The girls now laugh uncontrollably, *at* and *with* each other, as high-pitched shrieks alternate with raucous snorts and deep, guttural, resounding howls. They are in stitches, doubled-over, holding their bellies, unable to speak, seemingly taken over by an irresistible force that has their bodies firmly in its grip. Their laughter is overwhelmingly infectious, the kind that is difficult to fake. The scene conveys a palpable sense of corporeal authenticity, as the young actors themselves seem genuinely entangled in the joyous and pleasurable affective resonances that emanate from and reverberate around their bodily intimacy – it is difficult not to laugh along with them, or at least crack the hint of a smile.

Simon Critchley notes that laughter is affective because it is 'a corporal response [...] a muscular phenomenon, consisting of spasmodic contraction and relaxation of the facial muscles with corresponding movements in the diaphragm' – it is precisely the physicality of laughter that is infectious.[96] Bolton very usefully distinguishes between different kinds of women's laughter, not all of which have subversive implications. In cinema, where 'many stories are not about women's lived bodies, [laughter] is usually an indication of their reactivity, rather than activity' and conventionally functions to indicate a type: giggler, hag, bitch, challenge. In films that are also *about* women's lived bodies, such as *Girlhood*, women's *collective* laughter in particular might evoke 'a phenomenological encounter, through which we are able to join them in a place [that is otherwise] inexpressible.'[97] The cinematic incarnation of this kind of hearty, rebellious infectious female laughter:

> reaches out and has an effect on the audience that dialogue does not provide. It is a phenomenological communication of their lived bodies in all their desperation, isolation, alienation, or

joyful rejection [...] conveying the lived bodies of women [and] thus enabling viewers to join them in laughter as a *place* where women's voices can be heard.[98]

The moments of laughter in *Girlhood* conjure this kind of affectively embodied engagement and make palpable the confidence, unselfconsciousness and abandon that add a sense of corporeal substance to the girls' collective presence. The moments assert Bolton's suggestion that 'women laughing together can be a form of rebellion – a laugh of solidarity, of denial of patriarchal power.' It can convey a sense of '*refusal* to go along with the societal structures which are being imposed on [women], uniting them in a kind of socio-political sisterliness.'[99] Crucially, women's laughter is often juxtaposed with speech – especially when female characters do not have a 'voice' in the conventional sense. What a broadly phenomenological (Irigarayan) approach enables is a consideration of women's laughter not only as a 'place for women's discourse' but as part of a 'gestural code of women's bodies' that bypasses, as it were, conventionally dominant systems of signification, including language and speech.[100] Laughter, like the various other embodied forms of articulation and assertion that shape *Girlhood's* corporeal trajectory, gains significance when the language that is available is inadequate to the task of conveying experiences, connections, frustrations and desires. The making graspable of the physicality of (collective) laughter in *Girlhood* therefore opens up spaces for spectatorial encounters that make corporeal, sensuous 'sense' of the girls' world and experiences.

Figure 5.7 Laughter and 'Diamonds' (*Girlhood*)

The hotel room turns into an even more explicitly abstract and utopian space when a close-up of Lady blowing smoke from a shisha pipe into the camera cuts to a close-up of Lady's downcast face and bare shoulders bathed in shimmering, blue light. Lady lip-syncs to the non-diegetic music, as Rihanna's 'Diamonds' appears on the soundtrack and drowns out any diegetic noise. Lady lifts her head to stare straight into the camera, acknowledging its presence and seemingly performing directly 'for' us. As the camera tracks back, Adiatou joins Lady in the frame and both characters now lip-sync, singing with/at each other, and begin to dance together, hands intertwined. The close, mobile framing conveys a sense of bodily intimacy and mutuality as the girls respond to each others' slow and rhythmic movements, with the blue light giving the scene a dream-like feel. As with the American football match, the performance takes place in an affective sphere that is removed from the reality of the diegesis and any sense of the characters performing *for* an audience, other than each other, disappears. Instead, they clearly revel in the joy of the connections, resonances and kinetic energies generated by their joint presence and their 'tending toward' each other.[101]

Fily then enters the frame and joins the dancers, before we see Marieme still sitting on the bed, watching the dancers, her upper body swaying to the rhythm of the song in almost imperceptibly small movements. The camera slowly closes in on Marieme's face, emphasising her gaze that distances her from the performance and the girls' collective elation and energy, while the rhythmic swaying of her body also conveys the emergence of a physical connection. We are drawn towards Marieme as the camera brings us closer and closer, just as Marieme is drawn to the girls' collective corporeal energy. As Sciamma notes, the scene is 'really about how friendship is choreography and the birth of a friendship between the characters but also *between the audience and the character*.'[102] When Marieme joins the others, all four dancers are briefly framed together, in mid-shot, with Marieme dancing in the centre of the frame. The camera then reverts to the closer framing of the characters from the shoulders up, moving amongst the dancers, adding to the sense of kinaesthetic and muscular energy, while also conveying the joyous elation in their faces, always returning to Marieme, who becomes the corporeal and affective centre that the dancers, *and the film*, circulate around.

Towards the end of the song, which is, unusually for the cinematic context, played in its entirety, the girls' voices, singing along, become audible on the soundtrack as the diegetic world begins to encroach upon the utopian space of the performance. The 'number' ends with the girls hugging each other, out of breath and laughing and we then see all four characters sleeping on the hotel bed, before Marieme returns home to her abusive older brother the next morning. Again, the contrast between the affective resonances of the girls' collective laughing/dancing and the isolated figure of Marieme walking timidly through the bleak landscape of tower blocks, quietly entering her home, is palpable. It serves to underscore the significance of embodied experience and the ways in which heteropatriarchal social pressures are lived.

A final (queer) twist

As the narrative progresses, Marieme asserts herself more and more forcefully. This is made viscerally explicitly in the street fight sequence in which a determined and ruthless Marieme defeats her opponent, with the close framing and mobile camera conveying the corporeal intensity and brutality of the fight. It is, however, in the final segment that gender and sexual norms are most profoundly unhinged as Marieme's continually twisting and turning corporeal journey undergoes an unexpected change in direction. Marieme decides to leave behind everything she knows. She refuses to follow the 'line', and the 'life', set out for her.[103] Marieme takes on two contrasting kinds of appearances and identities in this final segment, one of which is explicitly posited as a performance (of gender) with a specific purpose: she dons a short blonde wig, high heels, a tight red dress and make-up when she sells drugs to Abou's clients – and sheds this costume as soon as she has fulfilled her task.

Her new everyday appearance also constitutes a fairly dramatic shift. Marieme takes on a manly appearance and becomes 'one of the guys' of Abou's drug cartel. We might read her adaption of a masculine mode of embodiment as a refusal to be confined by the multiply marginalised social positionality associated with feminine modes of embodiment and womanly appearance, and, in the same vein, as a way of protecting herself from abuse, sexual harassment and other forms of gendered violence –

although the exact reasons for the radical change in appearance and mode of embodiment are never clarified. Marieme even binds her breasts, which is revealed when she meets with her boyfriend Ismaël. He is visibly taken aback when he discovers the bandages as he slips his hand underneath her shirt. He wants to know 'why?', but is never given an answer. As in *Tomboy*, Sciamma stays away from *why* in order to focus on *how* her characters live their gender.

This part of the narrative thus combines Marieme's taking on of a male appearance (which is sometimes read as an indication of her trans identity) with her continuing relationship with Ismaël (although this storyline takes up relatively little screen time) as well as with her ambiguous and increasingly intimate relation with the conventionally feminine Monica. It is this twisted and contradictory intermingling of gender and sexuality within the film that evokes a sense of queerness most explicitly. Perhaps surprisingly, it is the final segment that has drawn relatively little attention in critical reviews.

It opens with Marieme walking up the red-carpeted stairs to a stylish apartment to deliver drugs at a party – a white, upper-class space that is otherwise completely invisible in *Girlhood*. She is explicitly, and perhaps excessively, sexualised, for the first time in the film, as her walk up the stairs is aestheticised by the slow-motion framing and the slow and rhythmic sync score that conveys a sense of (sexual) tension, suspense and danger/risk. A low-angle shot closes in on her high heels, ankles and shimmering calves, before moving up her legs, revealing a short, sleeveless red dress and a blonde wig. After delivering the drugs, she returns to the backseat of the car waiting for her in the street and immediately sheds her costume (wig and dress).

We then see her with her new *bande*: two young men, both fellow drug dealers, and Monica. Marieme sits between the men on the couch, wearing short braids and plain, unshapely clothes, her 'manspreading' posture resembling theirs, as they eat pizza and watch a football match on TV. Monica sits curled up at the side of the couch, taking up very little space, and is clearly not interested in the football match. Marieme sports a serious, angry almost, facial expression throughout, as she talks with the guys, one of whom makes unwanted sexual advances towards Monica. Just as Marieme was integrated into the *bande de filles* by adjusting to the rhythm and corporeal dynamic of the group, she is now incorporated into the gang of boys.

We then see Marieme and Monica walking back to their apartment at night. Marieme carries Monica the final part of the way because her feet hurt from walking in high heels. Their laughter and physical proximity recalls the tactile and muscular intimacy amongst the members of the *bande de filles* that Marieme has left behind. This moment also sets up a significant contrast, which structures the final segment, between Marieme's stoic, reserved, cold and aggressive comportment when she is amongst the boys and her relaxed, open and caring tendencies when she is with Monica. As one of the guys, Marieme becomes a part of, and helps perpetuate, the violent pressures exerted on young women (like her) by the heteropatriarchal world she lives in and that she has previously experienced herself. This shift in behaviour and attitude can certainly be read as a refusal to occupy the position of the female 'victim', but it also adds to the more general sense of Marieme as an ambiguous heroine, one who does not invite any kind of straightforwardly comfortable identification. *Girlhood's* foregrounding of an embodied, muscular and kinaesthetic mode of spectatorship mitigates these tensions and posits Marieme's latest and perhaps most extreme shape-shifting as part of *Girlhood's* overall corporeal trajectory.

It is through Marieme's continued, and explicitly sexual, relationship with Ismaël and the simultaneously emerging, far more tactile and embodied, relation to Monica, that *Girlhood* challenges gender and sexual

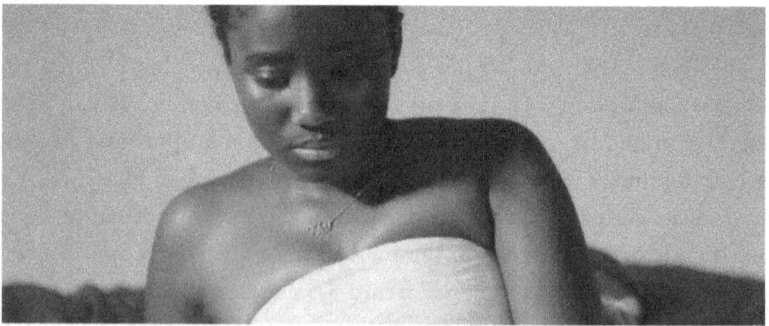

Figure 5.8 Twisting Binary Gender (*Girlhood*)

Céline Sciamma's 'Queer' Cinema

binaries most profoundly. This is encapsulated in the sequence surrounding Ismaël's discovery of Marieme's breast binding. When Ismaël leaves Marieme's room, slamming the door on his way out because he cannot make sense of Marieme's appearance, the camera moves down from her serious, thoughtful face to her bare shoulders, gold necklace and bound torso, with the slight swelling of her breasts bulging over the bandage, and her visibly heavy breathing betraying her inner turmoil. The image encapsulates a multitude of contradictory meanings around gender and sexuality and is then juxtaposed with an equally complex and contradictory scenario: Monica applies makeup to Marieme's eyes and lips, softly smiling as she does so, then tenderly moving blonde strands of hair from the wig out of Marieme's face with her fingers before gazing into Marieme's eyes.

Following the subsequent drug delivery, Marieme joins Monica at one of Abou's rooftop parties. Her appearance is ambiguously gendered as she has taken off the blonde wig, but not the big sparkly earrings, and replaced the short red dress with her baggy clothes, while her face is still covered in make-up. Monica asks Marieme to dance and they engage in an intimate slow dance, arms around each other's shoulders and waist and looking into each other's eyes in an obviously romantic and sexually charged encounter. They are violently interrupted by Abou who pulls Marieme towards him, attempting first to dance with her and then to kiss her. Marieme's physical refusal of Abou's advances (she shoves him away and then slaps him in the face) marks the end of her drug-selling career.

In the end, Marieme turns away from everything: the *bande*, Abou and his gang (including Monica), Ismaël (she tells him she does not want to be 'a good girl' and marry him) and her family. She returns to her family home once more in the final scene of the film and rings the doorbell, but changes her mind at the last minute. The closing shot sees Marieme, with her short braids, make-up, earrings and unshapely, boyish clothes, walk away from the door of the apartment block and the camera, and towards the railing at the edge of the building from where she can oversee the surrounding area. In an interview, Sciamma notes the significance of Marieme's appearance in this scene: 'In the last shot of the film, Marieme wears the braids of childhood, the makeup of a diva, and the clothing of a boy. She's possibly everything or none of those.'[104] We see Marieme, now crying, from behind and then in profile (when she turns around), as the camera begins to track towards and then past her until she disappears from the right side of the frame. The camera stops moving when only the out-of-focus surroundings (leafy trees, other tower blocks in the distance) are visible in the frame as *Girlhood*'s signature sync score grows louder on the soundtrack. Marieme then walks back into the frame, her face in profile and close-up, briefly hesitating as she reaches the centre of the screen, breathing in deeply and swallowing, before continuing her move across.

Sciamma says the following about the film's ending and her protagonist's identity:

> I don't have this secret story I'm not telling: I'm finishing my movie where I know it should be finished. It's really about leaving her on the side and going to that blurry horizon and you expect the credits to roll because it's like ten seconds. But she's getting back in the frame and you're going to have to put up with her in the frame. It's not that open, it's really saying something. It's the most political shot I ever did in my life.[105]

The final moments of the film are an assertion of Marieme's corporeal presence, of the muscular, breathing physicality, of her kinetic energy and directionality, and her refusal to be stilled and confined, by the heteropatriarchal world she inhabits – and, perhaps most importantly, by the cinematic frame.

Overall, what this queer feminist phenomenological encounter with *Tomboy* and *Girlhood* makes graspable, I hope, is a sense of the films' corporeally affective qualities. It also fleshes out, and gives concrete shape to, the kind of critical tending towards cinema that asserts the centrality of sensuousness and corporeality to the queerness of certain kinds of (queer) films: those that hinge on, and foreground, the materiality of embodiment and performance. The focus on the embodied resonances evoked by the textural entanglement of the bodies in, of and around *Tomboy* and *Girlhood* provides a model for how we might account for cinematic queerness in relation to the spatial and kinaesthetic implications of non-conforming incarnations of gender and sexuality. This project's focus on muscularity, spatiality, movement, temporality and perception has begun to provide a queer feminist phenomenological answer to the questions that Davina Quinlivan raises in her exploration of 'how "queer" cinema might feel': How can we foreground and put to critical use the concordances of embodied film theory and queer spectatorship? And how might we explore the sense of queer cinema as haptic experience *as well as* the queer implications of haptic enquiry.[106] We might say that what has taken shape here, throughout this book, is a reorientation, not just of film criticism (by (at)tending to the sensuous dimensions of cinema) but of *phenomenological* film criticism (by (at)tending to the variously twisted dimensions of embodiment). And this reorientation allows us to grasp the queer feminist cinematic tendencies that variously surface in and through (certain kinds of) queer feminist film.

Conclusion

Collectivities, the Familiar and (Un)Common Sense

So, what happens when film phenomenology encounters queer/feminist phenomenology? What kind of queer feminist film phenomenology takes shape – and what does it allow us to *do*? What emerges from the various encounters in this book, I hope, is an affirmative opening-up of possibilities for thinking, and feeling, the relations between gender, the body and cinema differently.

A queer feminist film phenomenology makes graspable cinema's potentially wide-reaching embodied resonances, especially in relation to those kinds of films and generic contexts that foreground embodiment through performances and activities that are saturated with specific socio-cultural meanings around issues as varied as success, the national, the global, stardom, age, politics, desire, tomboyism, romance and fandom. It is through the embodied and affective networks from which *The Tango Lesson*, *Black Swan*, *2 Seconds*, *Offside*, *Tomboy* and *Girlhood* emerge and which the films might, in turn, infiltrate, that they reshape (hetero)normative and binary figurations of gender and sexuality, in different ways and to varying extents.

This does *not* mean that *The Tango Lesson*, *Black Swan*, *Two Seconds*, *Offside*, *Tomboy* and *Girlhood* make 'sense' to viewers in the ways suggested here *only* or *necessarily*. It is a spectatorial opening-up to, and orientation towards, the sensuous, muscular and kinaesthetic dimensions of the cinematic encounter that allows us to be moved and touched by the films' queer feminist resonances. Opening oneself up to this mode of viewership – of haptic, rather than optic, visuality – is 'to some extent a voluntary act.'[1] For Marks, it 'implies making oneself vulnerable to the image,' allowing for spectatorial distance, tied as it is to visual mastery, to diminish, and submitting to a viewer-image relation of proximity and mutuality, in which 'the viewer is more likely to lose herself in the image, to lose her *sense of proportion*.'[2] Of course, this mode of viewing, which is never solely haptic, but in which embodied engagements and encounters are foregrounded relative to more traditional spectatorial positionings, can be pleasurable: it might resonate with non-visual, embodied knowledges and other experiences that we *recognise* (corporeally rather than intellectually), but that are not necessarily representable in conventional cinematic terms. An embeddedness in and familiarity with the corporeal contexts that the films emerge from (dance, sport, queer culture) might make this kind of spectatorial orientation 'easier' – because we might more readily recognise *what is already familiar*. But cinematic modes of embodiment might also, in turn, *shape* what appears within our bodily horizons and the textures of the social by infiltrating the realms of familiarity and (un)common 'sense' – if we let them.

Ahmed's phenomenological account of the familiar and familiarity highlights the spatial and affective dimensions of what our bodies already know:

> Familiarity is what is, as it were, given, and which in being given 'gives' the body the capacity to be orientated in this way or that. The question of orientation becomes, then, a question not only about how we 'find our way' but how we come to 'feel at home' […] Familiarity is shaped by the 'feel' of space or by how spaces 'impress' upon bodies. This familiarity is not, then, 'in' the world as that which is already given. The familiar is an effect of inhabitance; we are not simply in the familiar, but rather the familiar is shaped by actions that reach out towards objects that are already within reach.[3]

This sense of the familiar is closely linked to the phenomenology of orientation – and processes of familiarisation and orientation are foregrounded in and through bodily performance: becoming, and being, orientated is about 'making the strange familiar through the extension of bodies into space,' while 'disorientation occurs when that extension fails.'[4] They are also, therefore, linked to embodied understandings of (un)common 'sense' – and thus provide a framework for conceptualising how or why certain films evoke bodily and affective resonances; how or why they might touch or move us in particular ways; and how we might (come to) recognise certain cinematic embodiments and affective figurations *as familiar*.

This mode of viewing, one that makes us vulnerable in our opening-up to the image, also carries a 'violent potential', however, which is 'always there' when we give up a sense of safe distance.[5] As the various cinematic encounters in this book make graspable, embodied and haptic engagements might be characterised by relations of smoothness, synchronicity, alignment and mutuality – or they might involve relations of tension, disjointedness, jarring, abrasion and intrusion. These relations are not necessarily predetermined *by* the film, but are dependent on the affinity between the modes of embodiment in, of and around the film. It is important to re-emphasise the *reciprocal* nature of the viewer-film relations proposed here. Not only might films embody and resonate with *already-formed* socially situated modes of embodiment, spatiality and movement – and as such with viewers who might recognise these *as familiar* and to whom they make (un)common sense. Cinema might also play a role in *shaping* (intelligible) ways of being-in-the-world by offering encounters with modes that are not (yet) familiar and that do not yet make (un)common sense.[6]

It is in this sense that *The Tango Lesson*, *Black Swan*, *2 Seconds*, *Offside*, *Tomboy* and *Girlhood* carry 'minor' resonances. The films function not only as *expressions* of variously troubled and troubling modes of embodiment. They also 'forge the means for another consciousness and another *sensibility*,'[7] and manifest themselves as the sensuous, affective and graspable '*projection* of a community'– one with queer feminist orientations and tendencies.[8] Or to put this slightly differently, we might conceive of *The Tango Lesson*, *Black Swan*, *2 Seconds*, *Offside*, *Tomboy* and *Girlhood* as part of a 'queer feminist vernacular,' to adapt Farmer's phrase, that takes shape, and makes (un)common sense, through cinema's embeddedness within broader socio-cultural constellations of embodiment and affect.[9]

Conclusion

We might think here of the ways in which the (hetero)normative abstraction, self-referentiality, disembodiedness and objectification of the female body is unsettled in the films encountered in this book – even though, or perhaps because, this body is put on display. It is uncompromisingly and unflinchingly situated at the films' (visual, narrative, affective, corporeal and sensuous) centre. Yet it is a kind of body that seems irrecuperable to the white, straight male gaze and psychic structures that conventionally contain it. It remains teasingly just out of heteropatriarchy's reach. What emerges are modes of embodiment that are intensely, and troublingly, tactile, muscular and kinaesthetic, and that unhinge normative incarnations of spatiality, temporality and perception. Through offering corporeal and affective encounters with the ways of being-in-the-world that take shape through these modes, the films push – with variously forceful, subtle, troubling and seductive attitudes – their specifically situated, yet non-deterministic, sense-ibilities of gender into the realms of (un)common sense.

This includes the specifically grounded and kinaesthetic sense of female subjectivity, interiority, agency and creativity the takes corporeal shape in and through *The Tango Lesson*; the viscerally gripping and disorientating sense of heteropatriarchal pressures (on the female body) that *Black Swan* puts us in touch with; the sense of queerness as marked by and experienced though a variously twisted, backwards and sideways temporality that becomes graspable in and through *2 Seconds*; the tangibly situated and embodied mode of perception that gives shape to the lived experience of marginality in *Offside*, a film that also conjures an opening-up of our bodily horizons with regard to the different ways in which gender and sexuality might 'appear' on screen and beyond; the affirmatively non-binary embodiment of gender that *Tomboy* refuses to dissolve into reassuring gender and sexual binaries; and, finally, the tenaciously brave assertion of girls' (and women's) corporeal, affective journeys as most significantly grounded in decidedly sensuous, tactile and visceral female collectivities.

It is in this sense that the films might reach out to, touch, pull in or seduce certain kinds of spectators and created a communal sense of a shared sense-sibility – whether in relation to dance, (women's) sport or queer/feminist (sub)cultures; other spaces, activities and performances that challenge the norms of appropriately gendered embodiment; or queer/feminist activist contexts. It is a certain affinity (whether real or imagined, existing or longed for) to the gendered modes of embodiment made graspable cinematically that enables the affective entanglement of spectatorial ways of being-in-the-world with the corporealities that take shape in and though the films. With regard to the body of films encountered in this book, these modes of embodiment cohere around the felt experience of marginality, spatio-temporal containment and female bodies that do not 'fit' – *as well as*, crucially, around corporeal resistance, refusal and resilience; around the reshaping and reorientating of not only bodies but worlds.

Overall then, what the queer feminist film phenomenology that takes shape in this book, reparatively orientated as it is, allows for, is an exploration of the convoluted questions around gender and sexuality in cinema that keeps the body close to hand and within reach – but without yielding to the essentialising tendencies of a narrowly defined identity politics. This is what an affirmative entanglement of 'feminist' and 'queer' can *do*, in cinema and beyond.

Notes

Citational networks and transmissions are important indicators of how the queer/feminist body of work that underpins this book has taken shape over time. I acknowledge these interconnections by citing not only original sources, but also the works that have brought these sources into my conceptual, political, affective horizon and have thus provided me with a sense of the often complex, twisting, turning and crooked trajectories of relevant ideas and debates.

Introduction: Starting Points, Directions, Tendencies

1. Sara Ahmed, *Queer Phenomenology: Orientations, Objects, Others* (London: Duke University Press, 2006), pp. 160, 147.
2. See Amy Villarejo, *Lesbian Rule: Cultural Criticism and the Value of Desire* (London: Duke University Press, 2003), pp. 1–25, on the question of lesbian visibility and 'appearance'.
3. Vivian Sobchack, *The Address of the Eye: A Phenomenology of Film Experience* (Princeton: Princeton University Press, 1992); Sobchack, *Carnal Thoughts: Embodiment and Moving Image Culture* (Berkeley: University of California Press, 2004); Laura U. Marks, *The Skin of the Film: Intercultural Cinema, Embodiment and the Senses* (London: Duke University Press, 2000).
4. Jennifer Barker, *The Tactile Eye: Touch and the Cinematic Experience* (Berkeley: University of California Press, 2009); Lucy Donaldson, *Texture in Film* (Basingstoke: Palgrave Macmillan, 2014); Ian Garwood, *The Sense of Film Narration* (Edinburgh: Edinburgh University Press, 2013); Tarja Laine, *Feeling Cinema: Emotional Dynamics in Film Studies* (London: Bloomsbury, 2011).
5. Ahmed, *Queer Phenomenology*; Judith/Jack Halberstam, *In a Queer Time and Place: Transgender Bodies and Subcultural Lives* (New York: New York University Press, 2005); Halberstam, *The Queer Art of Failure* (London: Duke University Press, 2011); Ann Cvetkovich, *An Archive of Feeling: Trauma, Sexuality and Lesbian Public Cultures* (London: Duke University Press, 2003); Elizabeth Freeman, *Time Binds: Queer Temporalities, Queer Histories* (London: Duke University Press, 2010).

6. Robyn Wiegman, 'The times we're in: queer feminist criticism and the reparative "turn"', *Feminist Theory* 15/1 (2014), p. 6.
7. See Barker, *The Tactile Eye*, pp. 23–6, on 'textural analysis'.
8. Sobchack, *Carnal Thoughts*, p. 6.
9. Rosi Braidotti, *Metamorphoses: Towards a Materialist Theory of Becoming* (Malden: Blackwell/Polity Press, 2002), p. 7; quoted in Sobchack, *Carnal Thoughts*, p. 6, my emphasis.
10. Sedgwick, 'Paranoid reading and reparative reading; or, you're so vain, you probably think this introduction is about you', in E. K. Sedgwick (ed.), *Novel Gazing: Queer Readings in Fiction* (Durham: Duke University Press, 1997).
11. Eve Kosofsky Sedgwick, *Touching Feeling: Affect, Pedagogy, Performativity* (Durham and London: Duke University Press, 2003), p. 8.
12. On the various 'false dichotomies' that underpin such an opposition, and the ways in which an 'outdated' paranoid mode is often equated with an 'outdated' feminist criticism, while 'queer' tends to be aligned with a more 'enlightened' reparative mode, see Jackie Stacey, 'Wishing away ambivalence', *Feminist Theory* 15/1 (2014), pp. 39–49.
13. Sedgwick, 'Paranoid reading and reparative reading', p. 8, emphasis in original.
14. Wiegman, 'The times we're in', p. 16, my emphasis.
15. Marks, *The Skin of the Film*.
16. Brett Farmer, 'Loves of Siam: contemporary Thai cinema and vernacular queerness', in P. A. Jackson (ed.), *Queer Bankok: Twenty-First-Century Markets, Media, and Rights* (Aberdeen and Hong Kong: Hong Kong University Press, 2011), p. 85.
17. Ibid.
18. Ahmed, *Queer Phenomenology*, p. 8.
19. John Hockey and Jacquelyn Allen-Collinson, 'Grasping the phenomenology of sporting bodies', *International Review for the Sociology of Sport* 42/2 (2007), p. 117.
20. Freeman, *Time Binds*, p. xxii; Halberstam, *In a Queer Time and Place*, pp. 1; 4–5.
21. Roshanak Khesthi, 'Cross-dressing and gender (tres)passing: the transgender movie as a site of agentic potential in the New Iranian Cinema', *Hypatia: A Journal of Feminist Philosophy* 24/3 (2009), p. 158.
22. Following Ahmed's queer phenomenological account, I use the word 'twist' in place of 'queer' throughout to highlight the spatial dimensions of gender and sexuality. Ahmed notes the 'etymology of the word "queer", which comes from the Indo-European word "twist". Queer is, after all, a spatial term, which the gets translated into a sexual term, a term for a twisted sexuality that does not follow a "straight line", a sexuality that is bent and crooked' (*Queer Phenomenology*, p. 67).

23. Lucy Bolton, 'Giggling girls and crackling crones: the phenomenology of women's laughter', Keynote, *Film-Philosophy* Conference, Liverpool John Moores University (6–7 July 2011).
24. Many thanks to Jenny Chamarette for highlighting this overall trajectory.

Chapter 1: Gender and the Body in Feminist and Queer Film Criticism

1. See Ahmed, *Queer Phenomenology*, pp. 67; 83; 107 for a critique of the heteronormative assumptions underpinning ideas about progress as happing along 'straightforward' lines and about the straight lines (vertical and horizontal, as in the family tree) that structure genealogies of descent.
2. Freeman, *Time Binds*, p. 70, my emphasis.
3. Meryl Altman, 'Teaching 70s feminism' (July 2001). Available at: https://userpages.umbc.edu/~korenman/wmst/70waves1.html (accessed 2 April 2017); quoted in Freeman, *Time Binds*, p. 59.
4. Ibid., p. 62.
5. Ibid., pp. xv; xxii.
6. Ibid., p. 62.
7. For a discussion of 'facing' as a 'somatic mode of attention', see Ahmed, *Queer Phenomenology*, p. 200, referencing Thomas Csordas, *Body/Meaning/Healing* (New York: Palgrae Macmillan, 2002), pp. 241–6.
8. See Marjorie Rosen, *Popcorn Venus: Women, Movies and the American Dream* (New York: Coward, McCann & Geoghega, 1973); Molly Haskell, *From Reverence to Rape: The Treatment of Women in the Movies* (Chicago: University of Chicago Press, 1974).
9. Laura Mulvey, 'Visual pleasure and narrative cinema', *Screen* 16/3 (1975), pp. 6–18.
10. Bolton, *Film and Female Consciousness: Irigaray, Cinema and Thinking Women* (Basingstoke: Palgrave Macmillan, 2011), p. 10.
11. Mary Ann Doane, 'Remembering women: psychical and historical constructions in film theory', in E. Ann Kaplan (ed.), *Psychoanalysis and Cinema* (London: Routledge, 1990), p. 48; quoted in Bolton, *Film and Female Consciousness*, p. 10.
12. Bolton, *Film and Female Consciousness*, p. 12.
13. Doane, 'Remembering women', p. 47; quoted in Bolton, *Film and Female Consciousness*, p. 12.
14. Linda Williams 'Body genres: gender, genre, excess', *Film Quarterly* 44/4 (1991), pp. 2–13; Stacey, *Star Gazing: Hollywood Cinema and Female Spectatorship* (London: Routledge, 1994); Barbara Creed, *The Monstrous-Feminine: Film, Feminism, Psychoanalysis* (London: Routledge: 1993); Carol J. Clover, *Men,*

Women and Chainsaws: Gender in Modern Horror Film (Princeton: Princeton University Press, 1992).
15. Elena del Rio, 'Rethinking feminist film theory: counter-narcissistic performance in Sally Potter's *Thriller*', *Quarterly Review of Film and Video* 21/1 (2004), p. 11.
16. Ibid.
17. Ibid.
18. Ibid.
19. Ibid., p. 12, my emphasis.
20. Alison Butler, *Women's Cinema: The Contested Screen* (London: Wallflower, 2002), pp. 6–24.
21. Teresa de Lauretis, *Alice Doesn't: Feminism, Semiotics, Cinema* (Bloomington: Indiana University Press, 1984), pp. 8–9, my emphases; quoted in Butler, *Women's Cinema*, p. 14.
22. Butler, *Women's Cinema*, p.15, emphasis in original.
23. For an overview of the intersecting pressures shaping identity, see Kimberlé Crenshaw, *On Intersectionality: The Essential Writings of Kimberlé Crenshaw* (New York: Perseus, 2012).
24. Butler, *Women's Cinema*, p. 18, my emphasis.
25. Bolton, *Film and Female Consciousness*.
26. Sedgwick, 'Paranoid reading and reparative reading; or, You're so vain, you probably think this introduction is about you', in E. K. Sedgwick (ed.), *Novel Gazing: Queer Readings in Fiction* (Durham: Duke University Press, 1997), p. 8, emphasis in original; quoted in Freeman, *Time Binds*, p. xiii.
27. Freeman, *Time Binds*, p. xiii.
28. See Catherine Grant, 'Secret agents: feminist theories of women's film authorship', *Feminist Theory* 2/1 (2001), pp. 113–30.
29. Claire Johnston, *Notes on Women's Cinema* (London: Society for Education in Film and Television, 1973), front cover; quoted in Grant, 'Secret agents', p. 115.
30. Kaja Silverman, *The Acoustic Mirror: The Female Voice in Psychoanalysis and Cinema* (Bloomington: Indiana University Press, 1988); quoted in Grant, 'Secret agents', p. 115.
31. Grant, 'Secret agents', p. 119.
32. Ahmed, *Queer Phenomenology*, pp. 13, 29, 80.
33. Gilles Deleuze and Félix Guattari, *Kafka: Towards a Minor Literature*, trans. Dana Polan (Minneapolis: University of Minnesota Press, 1986), p. 16; quoted in Patricia White, 'Lesbian minor cinema', *Screen* 49/4 (2008), p. 410.
34. Nick Davis, *The Desiring-Image: Gilles Deleuze and Contemporary Queer Cinema* (New York: Oxford University Press, 2013), p. 5.
35. Ibid., emphases in original.
36. Meaghan Morris, *Too Soon Too Late: History in Popular Culture* (Bloomington: Indiana University Press, 1998) p. xvii, emphasis in original; quoted in Butler, *Women's Cinema*, p. 20.

37. Butler, *Women's Cinema*, p. 21.
38. Davis, *The Desiring-Image*, p. 5.
39. Butler, *Women's Cinema*, p. 21, emphases in original.
40. Deleuze and Guattari, *Kafka*, p. 17; quoted in White, 'Lesbian minor cinema', p. 412.
41. Judith Butler, *Gender Trouble: Feminism and the Subversion of Identity* (New York: Routledge, 1990).
42. Barbara Mennel, *Queer Cinema: Schoolgirls, Vampires and Gay Cowboys* (London: Wallflower, 2012); Clare Whatling, *Screen Dreams: Fantasising Lesbians in Film* (Manchester: Manchester University Press, 1997); Patricia White, *unInvited: Classical Hollywood Cinema and Lesbian Representability* (Bloomington: Indiana University Press, 1999).
43. White, *unInvited*, p. 8; quoted in Mennel, *Queer Cinema*, p. 4.
44. Richard Dyer, 'It's being so camp as keeps us going', in *The Culture of Queers* (London: Routledge, 1977/2005); Andy Medhurst, 'Camp', in A. Medhurst and S. R. Munt (eds), *Lesbian and Gay Studies: A Critical Introduction* (London: Cassell, 1997).
45. White, *unInvited*.
46. Whatling, *Screen Dreams*, p. 54.
47. Anne Friedberg, 'Identification and the star: a refusal of difference', *Star Signs: Papers from a Weekend Workshop* (London: BFI, 1982), p. 53; quoted in Whatling, *Screen Dreams*, p. 54, my emphasis.
48. Ahmed, *Queer Phenomenology*, p. 102.
49. Ibid., p. 104, emphasis in original.
50. Ibid., p. 103, emphasis in original.
51. Annamarie Jagose, *Queer Theory: An Introduction* (New York: New Work University Press, 1997), p. 71, my emphasis.
52. Finn Mackay, *Radical Feminism: Feminist Activism in Movement* (Basingstoke: Palgrave Macmillan, 2015) usefully lays out some of the key points of contention.
53. Jagose, 'Queer theory', *Australian Humanities Review* 4 (1996), Available at http://www.australianhumanitiesreview.org/archive/Issue-Dec-1996/jagose.html (accessed 2 April 2017), para. 6.
54. David Phillips, 'What's so queer here? Photography at the Gay and Lesbian Mardi Gras', *Eyeline* 26 (Summer 1994), pp. 16–19; quoted in Jagose, 'Queer theory', para. 6.
55. Jagose, 'Queer theory', para. 6.
56. Ibid., para. 4.
57. Ibid., para. 13.
58. Ibid., para. 3.
59. Ahmed, *Queer Phenomenology*, p. 56.
60. Ibid., p. 15, emphasis in original.

61. B. Ruby Rich, 'New queer cinema', *Sight and Sound* 2/5 (1992), pp. 30–4; Rich, 'Queer and present danger', *Sight and Sound* 10/3 (2000), pp. 22–5.
62. Films mentioned by Rich include Todd Haynes's *Poison* (US, 1991), Isaac Julien's *Young Soul Rebels* (UK, 1991), Derek Jarman's *Edward II* (UK, 1991), Tom Kalin's *Swoon* (US, 1992), and Gregg Araki's *The Living End* (US, 1992).
63. Michele Aaron, 'New queer cinema: An introduction', in M. Aaron (ed.), *New Queer Cinema: A Critical Reader* (New Brunswick: Rutgers University Press, 2004), p. 3.
64. Rich, 'New queer cinema', pp. 30–1.
65. Mennel, *Queer Cinema*, p. 4, my emphasis.
66. Rich, 'New queer cinema'; Anneke Smelik, 'Art cinema and murderous lesbians' in M. Aaron (ed.), *New Queer Cinema*; Anat Pick, 'New queer cinema and lesbian films', in M. Aaron (ed.), *New Queer Cinema*.
67. White, 'Lesbian minor cinema', p. 410.
68. Pick, 'Lesbian films', p. 105.
69. Ibid., pp. 105–6.
70. White, 'Lesbian minor cinema', p. 411.
71. Ibid., p. 410.
72. Ibid., p. 411.
73. Ibid.
74. Ibid. pp. 413–14.
75. Ibid., p. 414, my emphasis.
76. Deleuze and Guattari, *Kafka*, p. 18, my emphasis; White, 'Lesbian minor cinema', p. 412.
77. White, 'Lesbian minor cinema', p. 411.
78. Pick, 'Lesbian films', p. 115, my emphasis.
79. Villarejo, *Lesbian Rule*, pp. 22, 4, my emphasis.
80. Ibid., p. 7.
81. Ibid., p. 3.
82. Ibid., my emphasis.
83. Ibid.
84. Ibid., p. 11, my emphasis.
85. See So Mayer, 'Uncommon sensuality: New queer feminist film theory', in L. Mulvey and A. Backman Rogers (eds), *Feminisms: Diversity, Difference and Multiplicity in Contemporary Film Cultures* (Amsterdam: Amsterdam University Press, 2015) for of discussion of uncommon sensuality and/in queer feminist film.
86. N. Davis, *The Desiring-Image*, p. 3.
87. Rich, 'Queer and present danger'.
88. N. Davis, *The Desiring-Image*, p. 5, my emphases.
89. Ibid., p. 5.
90. Ibid.

91. Ibid.
92. Ibid., emphasis in original.
93. Ibid., p. 26.
94. A. Butler, *Women's Cinema*; White, 'Lesbian minor cinema'.
95. N. Davis, *The Desiring-Image*, p. 10.
96. Ibid., p. 24.

Chapter 2: Film and Embodiment: Queer-ing Film Phenomenology

1. Elena del Rio, *Deleuze and the Cinemas of Performance: Powers of Affection* (Edinburgh: Edinburgh University Press, 2012), p. 1.
2. Thomas Elsaesser and Malte Hagener, *Film Theory: An Introduction Through the Senses* (New York and London: Routledge, 2010).
3. del Rio, *Powers of Affection*, p. 2.
4. Ibid.
5. Ibid.
6. Ibid.
7. Ahmed, *Queer Phenomenology*, p. 2.
8. del Rio, 'Film', in H. R. Sepp and L. Embree (eds), *Handbook of Phenomenological Aesthetics* (London and New York: Springer, 2010), p. 111, my emphasis.
9. Sobchack, *Carnal Thoughts*, p. 2.
10. Ibid., emphases in original.
11. Sobchack, *The Address of the Eye*, p. xiv.
12. Ibid., p. xiii.
13. del Rio, *Powers of Affection*.
14. Sobchack, *The Address of the Eye*, p. xviii.
15. Ibid., p. xv, my emphases.
16. Ibid., emphases in original.
17. Ibid., p. xiv.
18. Ibid., p. xv.
19. Ibid.
20. Ibid., p. 161, my emphasis.
21. Ibid., my emphases.
22. Ibid., p. 157, my emphasis.
23. Ibid., p. 161.
24. Barker, *The Tactile Eye*; Adriano D'Aloia, 'Upside-down cinema', *Cinema: Journal of Philosophy and the Moving Image* 3 (2012), pp. 155–82; D'Aloia, 'Cinematic empathy: spectator involvement in the film experience', in D. Reynolds and M. Reason (eds), *Kinesthetic Empathy in Creative and Cultural Practices* (Bristol and Chicago: Intellect, 2012); Vittorio Gallese and Michele

Guerra, 'Embodying movies: embodied simulation and film studies, *Cinema: Journal of Philosophy and the Moving Image* 3 (2012), pp. 183-210.
25. Barker, *The Tactile Eye*, p. 3, my emphases.
26. Ibid.
27. Ibid., pp. 93-106.
28. Ibid., p. 94.
29. Ibid., p. 96-7.
30. D'Aloia, 'Upside-down cinema', p. 155.
31. Ibid., p. 157.
32. Ibid., p. 155.
33. Ibid., pp. 155-6, emphases in original.
34. Ibid., p. 164, emphases in original.
35. Ibid., p. 165, emphasis in original.
36. Ibid.
37. Barker, *The Tactile Eye*, pp. 106-19.
38. Ibid., p. 107.
39. Ibid., p. 81, my emphases.
40. Ibid., p. 81.
41. Ibid., pp. 81-2, my emphasis.
42. Sobchack, *The Address of the Eye*, p. 5, emphasis in original.
43. D'Aloia, 'Cinematic empathy', p. 95.
44. Ibid., p. 96.
45. Béla Balázs, *Béla Balázs' Early Film Theory: Visible Man and the Spirit of Film*, trans. Rodney Livingston (New York: Berghahn, 1924/2010); Jean Epstein, 'Bonjour Cinema and other writings', trans. Tom Milne, *Afterimage* 10 (1921/1981), pp. 8-39.
46. Béla Balázs, *Béla Balázs' Early Film Theory*, p. 64, emphasis in original; quoted in D'Aloia, 'Cinematic empathy', p. 96.
47. D'Aloia, 'Cinematic empathy', pp. 96-7.
48. Dee Reynolds, 'Mirroring movements: empathy and social interactions', p. 31.
49. Reynolds, 'Kinesthetic engagement: Embodied responses and intersubjectivity', in D. Reynolds and M. Reason (eds), *Kinesthetic Empathy in Creative and Cultural Practices* (Bristol and Chicago: Intellect, 2012), p. 87.
50. Ahmed, *Queer Phenomenology*, p. 182.
51. Edith Stein, *On the Problem of Empathy*, trans. Waltraut Stein (Washington: ICS Publications, 1917/1989), p. 61; quoted in Ahmed, *Queer Phenomenology*, p. 182.
52. D'Aloia, 'Cinematic empathy', p. 94.
53. Stein, *On the Problem of Empathy*; quoted in D'Aloia, 'Cinematic empathy', p. 94.
54. D'Aloia, 'Cinematic empathy', p. 94, first emphasis mine.
55. Ibid., p. 94.
56. Ibid., pp. 94-5, emphasis in original.

57. Ibid., pp. 95, emphases in original.
58. Ibid., pp. 95; 98, emphases in original.
59. Ibid., p. 95.
60. Ibid.
61. Ibid., p. 98, my emphasis.
62. Ibid., p. 102.
63. Ibid., p.103.
64. Ibid., pp. 103–4, my emphases except final emphasis in original.
65. Ibid., p. 95, emphasis in original.
66. Sobchack, *Carnal Thoughts*, p. 5.
67. Garwood, *The Sense of Film Narration*; Donaldson, *Texture in Film*.
68. Donaldson, *Texture in Film*, p. 6.
69. D'Aloia, 'Cinematic empathy', p. 98, emphases in original.
70. Albert Michotte, 'The emotional involvement of the spectator in the action represented in a film: toward a theory', in G Thinès, A. Costall and G. Butterworth (eds), *Michotte's Experimental Phenomenology of Perception* (Hillsdale: Lawrence Erlbaum, 1953/1991), p. 209; quoted in D'Aloia, 'Cinematic empathy', p. 98.
71. Ahmed, *Queer Phenomenology*, pp. 129–33.
72. Sobchack, *Carnal Thoughts*, p. 6; Sobchack, *The Address of the Eye*, pp. 143–63.
73. Sobchack, *The Address of the Eye*, p. 143.
74. Ibid.
75. Ibid., pp. 143–4.
76. Ibid., p. 144.
77. Ibid.
78. Sobchack, *The Address of the Eye*, p.159, quoting Richard Zaner, *The Problem of Embodiment: Some Contributions to a Phenomenology of the Body* (The Hague: Martinus Nijhoff, 1971), pp. 249–51.
79. Sobchack, *The Address of the Eye*, p. 159.
80. Ibid., p. 144.
81. Ibid.
82. Ibid., my emphases.
83. Sara Heinämaa and Lanei Rodemeyer, 'Introduction', *Continental Philosophy Review* 43/1 (2010), p. 1.
84. Ibid., p. 10, my emphasis.
85. Ibid., p. 2.
86. Ibid.
87. Johanna Oksala, 'A phenomenology of gender', *Continental Philosophy Review* 39/3 (2006), pp. 229, 231.
88. Ibid., p. 231.
89. Ibid.
90. Heinämaa and Rodemeyer, 'Introduction', p. 4.

91. Oksala, 'A phenomenology of gender', p. 231.
92. Iris Marion Young, 'Throwing like a girl: a phenomenology of feminine body comportment, motility and spatiality', *Human Studies* 3/2 (1980), pp. 137–56.
93. Oksala, 'A phenomenology of gender', p. 232.
94. Ibid.
95. Ibid.
96. Ibid., p. 242, emphasis in original.
97. Ibid.
98. Ibid., p. 234, my emphasis.
99. Ibid.
100. Ibid., my emphasis.
101. Ibid., my emphasis.
102. Ibid., p. 235
103. Ibid., emphasis in original.
104. Ibid., p. 236.
105. Ibid., p. 236–7.
106. Ibid., p. 237.
107. Ibid.
108. Ibid.
109. Ibid., p. 238.
110. Alia Al-Saji, 'Bodies and sensings: on the uses of Husserlian phenomenology for feminist theory', *Continental Philosophy Review* 43/1 (2010), p. 15.
111. Ibid.
112. Ibid., my emphasis.
113. Ibid., pp. 15–16.
114. Heinämaa and Rodemeyer, 'Introduction', p. 5, my emphasis.
115. Al-Saji, 'Bodies and sensings', p. 16.
116. Ibid.
117. Oksala, 'A phenomenology of gender', p. 238.
118. Ibid., p. 239.
119. Ibid., p. 240.
120. Ibid., p. 241.
121. Ibid., p. 240.
122. Ibid., p. 239, emphasis in original.
123. Sobchack, *Carnal Thoughts*, p. 6.
124. Oksala, 'A phenomenology of gender', p. 242, emphasis in original.
125. Sobchack, *Carnal Thoughts*, p. 7.
126. Ibid., p. 6.
127. Braidotti, *Metamorphoses*, p. 7; quoted in Sobchack, *Carnal Thoughts*, p. 6.
128. Sobchack, *Carnal Thoughts*, p. 5, emphases in original.
129. Ibid., p. 6.
130. Al-Saji, 'Bodies and sensings', p. 15.

131. Sobchack, *Carnal Thoughts*, p. 5.
132. Sobchack, *The Address of the Eye*; Sobchack, *Carnal Thoughts*; Marks, *The Skin of the Film*; Barker, *The Tactile Eye*; Bolton, *Film and Female Consciousness*; Martine Beugnet, *Cinema and Sensation* (Edinburgh: Edinburgh University Press, 2007); Jenny Chamarette, *Phenomenology and the Future of Film: Rethinking Subjectivity Beyond French Cinema* (Basingstoke: Palgrave Macmillan); Kate Ince 'Bringing bodies back in: for a phenomenological and psychoanalytical film criticism of embodied cultural identity', *Film-Philosophy* 15/1 (2011).
133. Dyer, 'White', in *The Matter of Images: Essays on Representation* (London and New York: Routledge, 1993), p. 143.
134. Ahmed, *Queer Phenomenology*, pp. 6–7.
135. Dyer, *White* (London and New York: Routledge, 1997), p. 2.
136. Ibid.
137. Oksala, 'A phenomenology of gender', pp. 238–9, emphasis in original.
138. del Rio, *Powers of Affection*, p. 144.

Chapter 3: Queer Encounters with Feminist Politics: Dancing Bodies in *The Tango Lesson* and *Black Swan*

1. Jane C. Desmond, 'Making the invisible visible: staging sexualities through dance', in J. C. Desmond (ed.), *Dancing Desires: Choreographing Sexualities On and Off the Stage* (Madison: University of Wisconsin Press, 2001), p. 7.
2. José Gil, 'Paradoxical body', in A. Lepecki and J. Joy (eds), *Planes of Compositions: Dance, Theory and the Global* (London and New York: Seagull Books, 2009), p. 89.
3. Bonnie Meekums, 'Kinesthetic empathy and movement metaphor in dance movement psychotherapy', in D. Reynolds and M. Reason (eds), *Kinesthetic Empathy in Creative and Cultural Practices* (Bristol and Chicago: Intellect, 2012), p. 54.
4. For a brief account of the female dancer in early cinema (i.e., Loïe Fuller) as well as of subsequent entanglements of female dancers/artists with film (i.e., Maya Deren, Yvonne Reiner), see Lucy Fischer, '"Dancing through the minefield": passion, pedagogy, politics and production in *The Tango Lesson*', *Cinema Journal* 43/3 (2004), pp. 46–7.
5. Katharina Lindner, 'Spectacular (dis-)embodiments: the female dancer on film', *Scope: An Online Journal of Film and Television Studies* 20 (2011), pp. 1–18; Adrienne L. McLean, *Dying Swans and Madmen: Ballet, the Body and Narrative Cinema* (New Jersey: Rutgers University Press, 2008).
6. Reynolds' notion of the dance's body/body of the dance is explained in more detail below ('Kinesthetic empathy', p. 123).

7. Mulvey, 'Visual pleasure and narrative cinema'; Ann Daly, 'Classical ballet: a discourse of difference', in J. C. Desmond (ed.), *Meaning in Motion: New Cultural Studies of Dance* (London: Duke University Press, 1997).
8. Susan Hayward, *Cinema Studies: The Key Concepts* (London and New York: Routledge, 2000), p. 1.
9. Desmond, 'Making the invisible visible', p. 20.
10. Amelia Jones, 'Kinesthetic empathy in philosophical and art history: thoughts on how and what art means', in D. Reynolds and M. Reason (eds), *Kinesthetic Empathy in Creative and Cultural Practices* (Bristol and Chicago: Intellect, 2012), p. 14, my emphasis.
11. See Reynolds and Reason (eds), *Kinesthetic Empathy in Creative and Cultural Practices* (Bristol and Chicago: Intellect, 2012).
12. Reynolds, 'Kinesthetic empathy', p. 123.
13. D'Aloia, 'Upside-down cinema', p. 155.
14. Susanne Langer, *Feeling and Form: A Philosophy of Art Developed from 'Philosophy in a New Key'* (London: Routledge and Keegan Paul, 1953), p. 175, emphasis in original; quoted in Reynolds, 'Kinesthetic empathy', p. 123.
15. Reynolds, 'Kinesthetic empathy', p. 123.
16. Ibid., p. 124, emphases in original.
17. Desmond, 'Making the invisible visible', p. 13, emphases in original.
18. del Rio, *Powers of Affection*, p. 114.
19. Desmond, 'Making the invisible visible', p. 3.
20. Ibid., my emphasis.
21. Ibid.
22. See Villarejo, *Lesbian Rule*, pp. 1–25, on the relationship between of lesbian visibility and 'appearance'.
23. Desmond, 'Making the invisible visible', pp. 4; 7.
24. Ibid., p. 5.
25. Rick Altman, *The American Film Musical* (Bloomington: Indiana University Press, 1987); Dyer, 'Entertainment and utopia', in R. Dyer (ed.), *Only Entertainment* (London: Routledge, 1992); Rubin, 'Busby Berkeley and the backstage musical', in S. Cohan (ed.), *Hollywood Musicals: The Film Reader* (New York: Routledge, 1993/2002); Lindner, 'Spectacular (dis-)embodiments'.
26. Desmond, 'Making the invisible visible', p. 5.
27. Ibid., pp. 5–6.
28. Ibid., p. 6.
29. Ann Cvetkovich, 'White boots and combat boots: my life as a lesbian go-go dancer', in J. C. Desmond (ed.), *Dancing Desires: Choreographing Sexualities On and Off the Stage* (Madison: University of Wisconsin Press, 2001), pp. 315–48.
30. Elspeth Probyn, *Outside Belongings* (London and New York: Routledge, 1996), p. 14; quoted in Jonathan Bollen, 'Queer kinesthesia: performativity on the

dance floor', in J. C. Desmond (ed.), *Dancing Desires: Choreographing Sexualities On and Off the Stage* (Madison: University of Wisconsin Press, 2001), p. 285.
31. Bollen, 'Queer kinesthesia', p. 309.
32. Ibid., p. 309, my emphasis.
33. Ibid., pp. 309, 301.
34. Ibid., p. 309.
35. Ibid., p. 301.
36. Ibid., p. 309–10, my emphasis.
37. Ahmed, *Queer Phenomenology*.
38. Sobchack, *The Address of the Eye*, p. 3.
39. Bollen, 'Queer kinesthesia', p. 310.
40. Biddy Martin, 'Extraordinary homosexuals and the fear of being ordinary', *Differences* 6 (1994), p. 101; quoted in Bollen, 'Queer kinesthesia', p. 310.
41. Martin, 'Sexualities without genders and other queer utopias' *Diacritics* 24 (1994), p. 104, my emphasis; quoted in Bollen, 'Queer kinesthesia', p. 310.
42. Bollen, 'Queer kinesthesia', p. 310.
43. Erin Manning, 'The elasticity of the almost', in A. Lepecki and J. Joy (eds), *Planes of Compositions: Dance, Theory and the Global* (London and New York: Seagull Books, 2009), p. 108, my emphases.
44. Jones, 'Kinesthetic empathy in philosophical and art history', p. 14.
45. Desmond, 'Making the invisible visible', p. 13.
46. Ibid., p. 25.
47. Jennifer DeVere Brody, 'Opening sequences', in J. C. Desmond (ed.), *Dancing Desires: Choreographing Sexualities On and Off the Stage* (Madison: University of Wisconsin Press, 2001), p. 395, emphasis in original.
48. Susan Potter, 'Mobilising lesbian desire: the sexual kinaesthetics of Dorothy Arzner's *The Wild Party*', *Screen* 52/4 (2011), pp. 452, 442.
49. Ibid., p. 449.
50. del Rio, *Powers of Affection*; Mayer, *The Cinema of Sally Potter: A Politics of Love* (London: Wallflower Press, 2009); Ince, 'Feminist phenomenology and the films of Sally Potter', in J. Boulé and U. Tidd (eds), *Existentialism and Contemporary Cinema: A Beauvoirian Perspective* (Oxford and New York: Berghahn, 2012).
51. Kathy Davis, 'Should a feminist dance tango? Some reflections on the experience and politics of passion', *Feminist Theory* 16/1 (2015), p. 3.
52. Ibid.
53. del Rio, *Powers of Affection*, p. 143.
54. K. Davis, 'Should a feminist dance tango', p. 5.
55. Ibid., p. 8.
56. Ibid., p. 11.
57. Loïc Wacquant, 'Carnal connections: on embodiment, apprenticeship, and membership', *Qualitative Sociology* 28/4 (2005), p. 466, my emphasis; quoted in Davis, 'Should a feminist dance tango', p. 12.

58. K. Davis, 'Should a feminist dance tango', p. 12.
59. Fischer, '"Dancing through the minefield"', p. 54.
60. Del Rio notes that '*Rage* unmistakably points to all the major premises of feminist film theory: the figure of the crippled director as a literal embodiment of male castration anxiety and projection of lack onto woman; the voyeuristic and fetishistic effects of the male gaze on women's bodies and the association of the female body with narcissistic exhibitionism and spectacle' (*Powers of Affection*, p. 131).
61. Ibid., pp. 131–2.
62. Ibid., p. 130.
63. London, Paris and Buenos Aires are important locations concerning the history of tango – Buenos Aires as its 'birthplace' and London and Paris as 'two European capitals with strong historic ties to tango' (Fischer, '"Dancing through the minefield"', p. 50).
64. K. Davis, 'Should a feminist dance tango', p. 8, my emphases.
65. Ibid.
66. Ahmed, *Queer Phenomenology*, pp. 30–6.
67. Ibid., p. 29.
68. Ibid., p. 20.
69. Ibid., p. 62.
70. Ibid., p. 51.
71. See del Rio, *Powers of Affection*; Ince 'Feminist phenomenology'.
72. del Rio, *Powers of Affection*, p. 132.
73. Maxine Sheets-Johnstone, *The Primacy of Movement* (Amsterdam and Philadelphia: John Benjamins, 2011), pp. 420–1.
74. Ibid., p. 421, emphases in original.
75. Ince, 'Feminist phenomenology', p. 169.
76. Ibid., p. 169.
77. Sally Potter, 'Bruises and blisters', *Sight and Sound* 7/11, LFF supplement (1997), p. 4; quoted in Ince, 'Feminist phenomenology', p. 169.
78. Ibid., p. 169.
79. Ahmed, *Queer Phenomenology*, p. 139.
80. Young, 'Throwing like a girl'.
81. Ahmed, *Queer Phenomenology*, p. 51.
82. Gil, 'Paradoxical body', p. 85, emphases in original.
83. Ibid., pp. 85, 87.
84. Ibid., p. 88.
85. Ahmed, *Queer Phenomenology*, p. 11.
86. Ibid., p. 9.
87. Ibid., p. 8.
88. Ibid., p. 65.
89. del Rio, *Powers of Affection*, pp. 131–2.

90. Ibid., p. 131.
91. Sobchack, *Carnal Thoughts*, pp. 13–35.
92. Ibid., p. 24.
93. Ahmed, *Queer Phenomenology*, p. 182, citing Deleuze and Guattari, *What is Philosophy*, trans. Hugh Tomlinson (New York: Columbia University Press, 1994), p. 28, my emphasis.
94. Ibid., p. 3.
95. Ibid., p. 4.
96. Young, 'Throwing like a girl'.
97. Ahmed, *Queer Phenomenology*, p. 37.
98. Ibid., p. 31.
99. Ibid., p. 63.
100. Ibid., p. 34, my emphasis. There are some obvious links to be made between Ahmed's critique of the disappearance of materiality (of objects and bodies) in phenomenology and the arguments around the disappearance of the cinematic apparatus as a necessity for its ideological functioning.
101. Ibid., p. 157.
102. Ibid., p. 62.
103. Dyer, 'Entertainment and utopia'.
104. Steven Cohan, 'Introduction: musicals of the studio era', in S. Cohan (ed.), *Hollywood Musicals: The Film Reader* (New York: Routledge, 2002), p. 2.
105. Ahmed, *Queer Phenomenology*, p. 13.
106. Barker, *The Tactile Eye*, pp. 106–19.
107. K. Davis, 'Should a feminist dance tango', p. 9.
108. Manning, 'The elasticity of the almost', p. 108.
109. Ibid., p. 108.
110. Ibid., p. 109.
111. Ibid.
112. Ahmed, *Queer Phenomenology*, p. 8.
113. K. Davis, 'Should a feminist dance tango', p. 8.
114. Ibid., p. 12, my emphasis.
115. Mayer, *The Cinema of Sally Potter*, p. 132.
116. del Rio, *Powers of Affection*, p. 132.
117. Ibid., p. 142.
118. Ibid.
119. K. Davis, 'Should a feminist dance tango', p. 9.
120. Ibid., p. 9.
121. D'Aloia, 'Cinematic empathy', p. 95, emphasis in original.
122. Jan Brace-Govan, 'Looking at bodywork: women and three physical activities', *Journal of Sport and Social Issues* 26/4 (2002), pp. 403–20; Daly, 'Classical ballet'.

123. Judith Butler, 'Athletic genders: hyperbolic instance and/or the overcoming of sexual binarism', *Stanford Humanities Review* 6/2 (1998). Available at http://web.stanford.edu/group/SHR/6-2/html/butler.html (accessed 2 April 2017).
124. Mark Fisher and Amber Jacobs, 'Debating *Black Swan*: Gender and horror', *Film Quarterly* 65/1 (2011), pp. 58–62.
125. Ibid., p. 59.
126. Ibid., p. 60.
127. Gabrielle O'Brien, 'Mirror, mirror: fractured female identity in *Black Swan*', *Screen Education* 75 (2014), pp. 102–7; Katie L. Gibson and Melanie Wolske, 'Disciplining sex in Hollywood: a critical comparison of *Blue Valentine* and *Black Swan*', *Women and Language* 34/2 (2011), pp. 79–96.
128. Fisher and Jacobs, 'Debating *Black Swan*', p. 62.
129. Adrienne L. McLean, 'If only they had meant to make a comedy: laughing at *Black Swan*', in M. Pomerance (ed.), *The Last Laugh: Strange Humors of Cinema* (Detroit: Wayne State University Press, 2013), p. 143.
130. Ibid., p. 146.
131. McLean, *Dying Swans and Madmen*.
132. Steven Shaviro, '*Black Swan*' (5 January 2011). Available at http://www.shaviro.com/Blog/?p=975 (accessed 2 April 2017), para. 10.
133. Ibid., para. 6.
134. Ibid.
135. Katherine Fusco, 'The actress experience: cruel knowing and the death of the picture personality in *Black Swan* and *The Girlfriend Experience*', *Camera Obscura* 82/1 (2013), pp. 13; 20.
136. Shaviro, '*Black Swan*', para. 5.
137. Ibid.
138. McLean, 'Laughing at *Black Swan*', p. 156.
139. Shaviro, '*Black Swan*', para. 5, emphasis in original.
140. Fusco, 'The actress experience', p. 4.
141. Ibid., p. 10, my emphasis.
142. Ibid., p. 13, my emphasis.
143. Ibid., p. 19.
144. Ibid., p. 24.
145. We might note here that it is precisely the themes of doubling, replacing and ageing that have been central to queerly appropriative readings of the lesbian resonances between the female performers/stars, Eve Harrington (Anne Baxter) and Margo Channing (Bette Davis), in *All About Eve* (Joseph L. Mankiewcz, US, 1950) – see White, *unInvited*, pp. 202–12.
146. Steen Christiansen, 'Body refractions: Darren Aronofsky's *Black Swan*', *Academic Quarter* 3 (2011), pp. 306–7.

147. Ibid., p. 307.
148. Ibid., pp. 309–10.
149. Ibid., p. 307.
150. Ibid., p. 313.
151. In context of the relations of doubling and the blurring of various binaries and boundaries discussed here (reality/representation/reflection/mirror/image; intra-/inter-/extra-textu(r)ality; being/becoming), it is also worth noting that Millepied choreographed the film and subsequently married Portman. Thanks to So Mayer for drawing my attention to this.
152. Ibid.
153. Ibid., p. 314.
154. Ibid., pp. 313–14.
155. Tarja Laine, *Bodies in Pain: Emotion and the Cinema of Darren Aronofsky* (Oxford and New York: Berghahn, 2015), pp. 130, 136.
156. Laine, *Bodies in Pain*, p. 132, quoting Sobchack, *Carnal Thoughts*, p. 178.
157. Brace-Govan, 'Looking at bodywork', p. 411.
158. Susan Leigh Foster, 'Dancing bodies', in J. C. Desmond (ed.), *Meaning in Motion: New Cultural Studies of Dance* (Durham: Duke University Press, 1997), p. 237.
159. Ibid., p. 238.
160. Lindner, 'Spectacular (dis-)embodiments'.
161. For a more detailed exploration of these larger generic patterns, see Lindner, 'Spectacular (dis-)embodiments'.
162. Ahmed, *Queer Phenomenology*, p. 8.
163. Laine, *Bodies in Pain*, p. 131.
164. Fischer, '"Dancing through the minefield"', p. 47.
165. Laine, *Bodies in Pain*, p. 131.
166. D'Aloia, 'Cinematic empathy', p. 94.
167. Ibid.
168. Fisher and Jacobs, 'Debating *Black Swan*', p. 58.
169. Ibid., p. 59.
170. Ibid.
171. Fusco, 'The actress experience', p. 22.
172. Fisher and Jacobs, 'Debating *Black Swan*', p. 58.
173. Laine, *Bodies in* Pain, p. 166.
174. Gil, 'Paradoxical body', p. 97.
175. Ahmed, *Queer Phenomenology*, p. 8.
176. Fisher and Jacobs, 'Debating *Black Swan*', p. 58.
177. Ahmed, *Queer Phenomenology*, p. 160.
178. Ibid., p. 56.
179. Laine, *Bodies in Pain*, p. 130.

Chapter 4: Queering the Sports Film: Failure and Gender (Tres)Passing in *2 Seconds* and *Offside*

1. Aaron Baker, *Contesting Identities: Sports in American Film* (Chicago: University of Illinois Press, 2006); Séan Crosson, *Sport and Film* (London: Routledge, 2013); Leger Grindon, *Knockout: The Boxer and Boxing in American Cinema* (Jackson: University Press of Mississippi, 2010); Dan Streible, *Fight Pictures: A History of Boxing and Early Cinema* (Berkeley: University of California Press, 2008).
2. See for instance Glen Jones, 'In praise of an "invisible genre"? An ambivalent look at the fictional sports feature film', *Sport in Society: Cultures, Commerce, Media, Politics* 11/2–3 (2008), p. 122.
3. Grindon, *Knockout*, pp. 6–7.
4. Yvonne Tasker, *Spectacular Bodies: Gender, Genre and the Action Cinema* (London and New York: Routledge, 1993).
5. Lindner, 'Corporeality and embodiment in the female boxing film', *Alphaville: Journal of Film & Screen Media* 7 (2014). Available at http://www.alphavillejournal.com/Issue7/HTML/ArticleLindner.html (accessed 2 April 2017); Lindner, 'Gender trouble in female sports films', in J. Hargreaves and E. Anderson (eds), *Routledge Handbook of Sport, Gender & Sexuality* (London and New York: Routledge, 2014).
6. Murray Pomerance, 'The dramaturgy of action and involvement in the sports film', *Quarterly Review of Film and Video* 23 (2006), p. 313.
7. Desmond, 'Making the invisible visible', p. 19.
8. See Lindner, 'Queering texture: tactility, spatiality and kinaesthetic empathy in *She Monkeys*', *Camera Obscura*, 32/3 (2017).
9. See Lindner, '"In touch" with the female body: cinema, sport and lesbian representability', in K. Ross (ed.), *The Handbook of Gender, Sex and Media* (Oxford: Wiley-Blackwell, 2011).
10. See Lindner, 'Questions of embodied difference: film and queer phenomenology', *NECSUS European Journal of Media Studies* 1/2 (2012), pp. 199–217.
11. White, *unInvited*, p. 174.
12. We might think of the LGBTI rights protests surrounding the 2014 Winter Olympics in Russia as an example.
13. For an example of how the entanglement between sport and queer activism has begun to make an appearance in cinema, see So Mayer's discussion of *In The Turn* (Erica Tremblay, US, 2014) in So Mayer, *Political Animals: The New Feminist Cinema* (London and New York: I.B. Tauris, 2016), pp. 140; 202–3.
14. J. Butler, 'Athletic genders'; Hockey and Allen-Collinson, 'Grasping the phenomenology of sporting bodies'; Young, 'Throwing like a girl'.
15. Freeman, *Time Binds*, p. xxii. Halberstam, *In a Queer Time and Place*, pp. 1; 4–5.

16. Halberstam, *The Queer Art of Failure*.
17. Ahmed, *Queer Phenomenology*, p. 67.
18. Kheshti, 'Cross-dressing and gender (tres)passing', p. 158.
19. David, Rowe, 'Time and timelessness in the sports film', *Sport in Society: Cultures, Commerce, Media, Politics* 11/2–3 (2008), p. 149.
20. Pomerance, 'The dramaturgy of action and involvement in the sports film'; Jones, 'In praise of an "invisible genre"?'
21. Pomerance, 'The dramaturgy of action and involvement in the sports film', p. 311.
22. Rowe, 'Time and timelessness in the sports film', p. 148, my emphasis.
23. Ibid., my emphasis.
24. See for instance Beugnet, *Cinema and Sensation*, pp. 170–5.
25. Rowe, 'Time and timelessness in the sports film', p. 148.
26. Ibid., p. 148; referencing Jean-Marie Brohm, *Sport: A Prison of Measured Time* (London: Pluto Press, 1978).
27. Ibid., pp. 152–3.
28. Jean-Max Colard, '*Zidane, A Portrait du XXIème siècle* de Douglas Gordon et Philippe Parreno', *Les Inrockuptibles* 547 (2006), p. 54; quoted in Beugnet, *Cinema and Sensation*, p. 172.
29. Beugnet, *Cinema and Sensation*, p. 172.
30. Ibid., emphasis in original.
31. *Zidane* was made using 17 synchronised cameras and a combination of high-definition digital video and 35mm film.
32. Jacquelyn Allen-Collinson, 'Running embodiment, power and vulnerability: notes towards a feminist phenomenology of female running', in E. Kennedy and P. Markula (eds), *Women and Exercise: The Body, Health and Consumerism* (London and New York: Routledge, 2010). Jacquelyn Allen-Collinson and Helen Owton, 'Intense embodiment: senses of heat in women's running and boxing', *Body and Society* 21/2 (2015), pp. 245–68. Hockey and Allen-Collinson, 'Grasping the phenomenology of sporting bodies'.
33. Hockey and Allen-Collinson, 'Grasping the phenomenology of sporting bodies', p. 117.
34. Ibid., my emphasis, quoting Nick Crossley, *The Social Body: Habit, Identity and Desire* (London: Sage, 2001), p. 123.
35. Ibid.
36. Pomerance, 'The dramaturgy of action and involvement in the sports film', pp. 317–18.
37. Ibid., p. 319.
38. Ibid., pp. 319–23.
39. Ibid., p. 322.

40. Ibid.
41. Garry Whannel, 'Winning and losing respect: narratives of identity in sports films', *Sport in Society: Cultures, Commerce, Media, Politics* 11/2–3 (2008), p. 195. These patterns are linked to the grounding of the sports film within the larger context of a 'depoliticised' (diegetic) world (p. 196).
42. Ibid., pp. 195–6.
43. Halberstam, *The Queer Art of Failure*, pp. 1–2.
44. Lauren Berlant, *Cruel Optimism*, (Durham and London: Duke University Press, 2011).
45. Halberstam, *The Queer Art of Failure*, p. 2.
46. Freeman, *Time Binds*, p. xxii.
47. Ahmed, *Queer Phenomenology*, pp. 15–16.
48. Sara Ahmed, *The Promise of Happiness* (Durham and London: Duke University Press, 2010).
49. bell hooks, *We Real Cool: Black Men and Masculinity* (New York and London: Routledge, 2004), p. xi.
50. Butler, 'Athletic genders', para. 1.
51. Ahmed, *Queer Phenomenology*, p. 2.
52. Butler, 'Athletic genders', para. 16.
53. Ibid., para. 21.
54. Sandra Lee Bartky, 'Foucault, femininity and the modernization of patriarchal power', in I. Diamond and L. Quinby (eds), *Feminism and Foucault: Reflections on Resistance* (Boston: Northeastern University Press, 1988), p. 68.
55. Ahmed, *Queer Phenomenology*, p. 65–7.
56. Ibid., p. 66.
57. Ibid., 65–6.
58. Ibid., p. 66.
59. Rowe, 'Time and timelessness in the sports film', p. 149, my emphasis.
60. Hockey and Allen-Collinson, 'Grasping the phenomenology of sporting bodies', pp. 6, 120.
61. Ibid., p. 119, my emphasis.
62. Ibid., p. 120.
63. Ibid., p. 119.
64. Rowe, 'Time and timelessness in the sports film', p. 149, my emphasis.
65. J. Butler, 'Athletic genders', para. 4, my emphasis.
66. Hockey and Allen-Collinson, 'Grasping the phenomenology of sporting bodies', p. 119.
67. J. Butler, 'Athletic genders', para. 4,
68. Hockey and Allen-Collinson, 'Grasping the phenomenology of sporting bodies', p. 120.
69. Ibid., p. 119.

70. Halberstam, *The Queer Art of Failure*, pp. 54–5.
71. Freeman, *Time Binds*, p. 21.
72. Ibid., pp. 4–5.
73. Ibid.
74. Ibid., p. 5.
75. David Bordwell and Kristin Thompson, *Film Art: An Introduction* (New York: McGraw-Hill, 2010).
76. Freeman, *Time Binds*, pp. 3–4.
77. Lynne Stahl, *Unhappy Medium: Filmic Tomboy Narrative and Queer Feminist Spectatorship*, PhD Dissertation, Cornell University (2015).
78. Freeman, *Time Binds*, p. xviii, my emphasis.
79. Ibid.
80. Ibid., p. xix.
81. Ibid., p. 3.
82. Ibid.
83. Ibid.
84. Ibid., p. 4.
85. Ahmed, *Queer Phenomenology*, p. 17.
86. Ibid., p. 20.
87. Hockey and Allen-Collinson, 'Grasping the phenomenology of sporting bodies', p. 119.
88. Rebecca Solnit, *River of Shadows: Eadweard Muybridge and the Technological Wild West* (New York: Viking, 2003).
89. Khesthi, 'Cross-dressing and gender (tres)passing', p. 158.
90. Chris Straayer, *Deviant Eyes, Deviant Bodies: Sexual Re-orientation in Film and Video* (New York: Columbia University Press, 1996), p. 42.
91. Ibid., pp. 43–4.
92. Khesthi, 'Cross-dressing and gender (tres)passing', p. 160.
93. Hamid Naficy, 'Veiled vision/powerful presences: women in post-revolutionary Iranian cinema', in M. Afkhami and E. Friedl (eds), *In the Eye of the Storm: Women in Post-Revolutionary Iran* (London and New York: I.B.Tauris, 1994).
94. Ahmed, *Queer Phenomenology*, pp. 15–16.
95. Robert Stam, 'Carnival, radical humor, and media politics', in R. Martin (ed.), *The Routledge Companion to Art and Politics* (New York and London: Routledge, 2015), p. 270.
96. Ibid., p. 269.
97. Ibid.
98. Jafar Panahi and Maryam Maruf, 'Offside rules: an interview with Jafar Panahi'. *Open Democracy* (6 June 2006). Available at https://www.opendemocracy.net/arts-Film/offside_3620.jsp (accessed 2 April 2017), para. 16.

99. Sarah Niazi, 'Urban imagination and the cinema of Jafar Panahi', *Wide Screen* 1/2 (2010) Available at http://widescreenjournal.org/index.php/journal/article/view/33/45 (accessed 2 April 2017), para. 6.
100. Ava Rose and James Friedman, 'Television sports as mas(s)culine cult of distraction', in A. Baker and T. Boyd (eds), *Out of Bounds: Sports, Media, and the Politics of Identity* (Bloomington: Indiana University Press, 1997), p. 4.
101. Khesthi, 'Cross-dressing and gender (tres)passing', p. 160.
102. Kim Toffoletti, 'Iranian women's sports fandom: gender, resistance, and identity in the football movie *Offside*', *Journal of Sport and Social Issues* 38/1 (2014), pp. 75–6.
103. Hamid Naficy, 'Islamizing film culture in Iran: a post-Khatami update', in R. Tapper (ed.), *The New Iranian Cinema: Politics, Representation and Identity* (London and New York: I.B.Tauris, 2002), p. 46.
104. Naficy, 'Veiled vision/powerful presences', pp. 132–3.
105. Khesthi, 'Cross-dressing and gender (tres)passing', p. 158.
106. Ibid., p. 158.
107. Ibid., p. 161.
108. Ibid., p. 161, my emphases.
109. Toffoletti, 'Iranian women's sports fandom', pp. 77–8.
110. Terri Ginsberg and Chris Lippard, *Historical Dictionary of Middle Eastern Cinema* (Toronto and Plymouth: The Scarecrow Press, 2010), pp. 322–3.
111. Khesthi, 'Cross-dressing and gender (tres)passing', p. 162.
112. Ibid., p. 161, my emphases.
113. Stam, 'Carnival, radical humor, and media politics', p. 270.
114. Toffoletti, 'Iranian women's sports fandom'.
115. Saeed Talajooy, 'Directors', in P. Jahed (ed.), *Directory of World Cinema: Iran* (Chicago: Intellect, 2012), p. 37, my emphases.
116. Ibid., p. 38.
117. David Parkinson, '*Offside* review' (10 April 2006). Available at http://www.empireonline.com/movies/offside/review/ (accessed 2 April 2017); Jonathan Romney, '*Offside*', *Screen Daily* (17 February 2006). Available at http://www.screendaily.com/offside-sweden-2006/4026227.article (accessed 2 April 2017).
118. Talajooy, 'Directors', p. 38.
119. Ibid.
120. For a discussion of the cinematic figure/trope of the 'Final Girl' see Clover, *Men, Women, and Chain Saws*.
121. Julian Graffy, 'A nation of two halves', *Sight & Sound* 16/6 (June 2006). Available online http://old.bfi.org.uk/sightandsound/review/3260 (accessed 2 April 2017).
122. Stam, 'Carnival, radical humor, and media politics', p. 270.

Chapter 5: Céline Sciamma's 'Queer' Cinema: Affirming Gestures of Refusal in *Tomboy* and *Girlhood*

1. Mayer, 'Uncommon sensuality', p. 96; referencing Kara Keeling, *The Witch's Flight: The Cinematic, the Black Femme and the Image of Common Sense* (Durham and London: Duke University Press, 2008).
2. 'Marieme' becomes 'Vic' (for victory/*victoire*) when she joins the girl gang/ *bande de filles* and is given a gold necklace with her new name on it. She is referred to as Vic by the members of the *bande*, but is known as Marieme in the other contexts and spaces of the film. For reasons of clarity, I refer to the character as Marieme throughout.
3. Ibid., p. 88.
4. Ahmed, *Queer Phenomenology*, pp. 7; 130.
5. Aaron, 'The new queer spectator', in M. Aaron (ed.), *New Queer Cinema: A Critical Reader* (New Brunswick: Rutgers University Press, 2004).
6. Tim Palmer, *Brutal Intimacy: Analyzing Contemporary French Cinema* (Middletown: Wesleyan University Press, 2011), p. 34.
7. Ahmed, *Queer Phenomenology*, p. 181.
8. Ibid., p. 8.
9. See Keeley Saunders, 'Gender-defined spaces, places and tropes: contemporary transgender representation in *Tomboy* and *Romeos*', *Journal of European Popular Culture* 5/2 (2014), pp. 181–93.
10. We might note here the considerable critical acclaim, including Oscar nominations, received by straight and cis actors playing trans characters.
11. Saunders, 'Gender-defined spaces, places and tropes'.
12. Ibid., p. 185.
13. Halberstam, *In a Queer Time and Place*, pp. 54–5.
14. Darren Waldron, 'Embodying gender nonconformity in "girls": Céline Sciamma's *Tomboy*', *L'Esprit Créateur* 53/1 (2013), p. 61.
15. Ibid., p. 62.
16. Marjorie Garber, *Vested Interests: Cross-Dressing and Cultural Anxiety* (London: Penguin, 1993), pp. 101–2; quoted in Saunders, 'Gender-defined spaces, places and tropes', p. 185.
17. Waldron, 'Embodying gender nonconformity in "girls"', p. 62.
18. Halberstam, *Female Masculinity* (London: Durham and London, 1998), p. 185.
19. Stahl, *Unhappy Medium*.
20. Ibid., p. 29.
21. Ibid., p. 10.
22. Ibid., p. 60.
23. Ibid., p. 19.

24. Ibid.
25. Ibid., p. 24.
26. Waldron, 'Embodying gender nonconformity in "girls"', p. 63.
27. Palmer, *Brutal Intimacy*, p. 35
28. Stahl, *Unhappy Medium*, p. 24.
29. Waldron, 'Embodying gender nonconformity in "girls"', p. 68.
30. I refer to the protagonist as 'Laure' and 'she' (rather than he, s/he, he/she, they), for purposes of avoiding an obscure and confusing writing style – although this might more accurately reflect the lack of clarity around sex/gender, visibility and legibility that continue to surface throughout the film. In using a feminine pronoun I follow Waldron's not entirely unproblematic suggestion that this is a sensible move as it mirrors 'how Sciamma refers to Laure in interviews' and, more importantly, because it avoids 'collapsing transgender subjectivities within an account of gender nonconformity' (Waldron, 'Embodying gender nonconformity in "girls"', p. 72). My referring to Laure as she/her is also a reflection of what 'appears', as it were, in my own encounter with the film.
31. Waldron, 'Embodying gender nonconformity in "girls"', p. 60.
32. Ibid.
33. Halberstam, *In a Queer Time and Place*, p. 54, my emphasis; quoted in Saunders, 'Gender-defined spaces, places and tropes', p. 183.
34. Gil, 'Paradoxical body', p. 97.
35. Céline Sciamma, *Tomboy* DVD interview (2011).
36. Halberstam, *In a Queer Time and Place*, p. 78.
37. Ibid.
38. Ibid.
39. Ibid.
40. Ibid., emphases in original.
41. Ibid., p. 91.
42. Ibid., p. 104.
43. Sciamma, *Tomboy* DVD interview.
44. Ahmed, *Queer Phenomenology*, p. 200; referencing Thomas Csordas, *Body/Meaning/Healing* (New York: Palgrae Macmillan, 2002), pp. 241–6.
45. Waldron, 'Embodying gender nonconformity in "girls"', p. 66.
46. Sciamma, *Tomboy* DVD interview.
47. Butler, 'Athletic genders', para. 6.
48. Ibid.
49. Ibid., my emphases.
50. Ahmed, *Queer Phenomenology*, p. 20.
51. Butler, 'Athletic genders', para. 8.
52. Ibid.
53. D'Aloia, 'Upside-down cinema', p. 155.

54. Ahmed, *Queer Phenomenology*, p. 62.
55. Butler, 'Athletic genders', para. 12.
56. Halberstam, *In a Queer Time and Place*, p. 87.
57. Sciamma, *Tomboy* DVD interview
58. Ibid., p. 89.
59. Palmer, *Brutal Intimacy*, p. 35.
60. Mayer, '"She's getting back in the frame": interview with Céline Sciamma', *The F Word: Contemporary UK Feminism* (5 May 2015). Available at http://www.thefword.org.uk/2015/05/celine_sciamma_interview/ (accessed 2 April 2017).
61. Dori Thomas, 'A review of Céline Sciamma's *Girlhood*: an honest and emotionally powerful take on the coming-of-age genre', *Side B Magazine* (5 June 2015). Available at http://sidebmagazine.tumblr.com/post/120774164350/a-review-of-c%C3%A9line-sciammas-girlhood-an-honest (accessed 2 April 2017).
62. Ginette Vincendeau, 'Minority report', *Sight & Sound* 25/6 (2015), p. 24.
63. Ibid., p. 27.
64. Sue Harris, 'Film of the week: *Girlhood*' (14 Dec 2015). Available at http://www.bfi.org.uk/news-opinion/sight-sound-magazine/reviews-recommendations/film-week-girlhood (accessed 2 April 2017).
65. Vincendeau, 'Minority report', p. 27.
66. Ibid., quoting Sciamma.
67. Ibid.
68. Ibid.
69. Sciamma, quoted in Mayer, '"She's getting back in the frame"'.
70. Ibid.
71. Barbara Creed, 'Lesbian bodies: tribades, tomboys and tarts', in J. Price and M. Shildrick (eds), *Feminist Theory and the Body: A Reader* (New York: Routledge, 1999).
72. Sciamma, quoted in Mayer, '"She's getting back in the frame"'.
73. Ibid.
74. Ibid.
75. Robbie Collins, '*Girlhood* review: "A coming-of-age classic"', *The Telegraph* (13 May 2015). Available at http://www.telegraph.co.uk/film/girlhood/review/ (accessed 2 April 2017).
76. Sciamma, quoted in James Mottram, 'Céline Sciamma interview: step aside *Boyhood*, it's *Girlhood* time', *Independent* (24 April 2015). Available at http://www.independent.co.uk/arts-entertainment/films/features/cline-sciamma-interview-step-aside-boyhood-its-girlhood-time-10199093.html (accessed 2 April 2017).
77. Vincendeau, 'Minority report', p. 24.
78. Mottram, 'Céline Sciamma interview'.
79. Vincendeau, 'Minority report', p. 27.

80. Eric Kohn, 'Cannes review: Céline Sciamma's *Girlhood* is one of the best coming of age movies in years', *Indiewire* (15 May 2014). Available at http://www.indiewire.com/article/cannes-review-celine-sciammas-girlhood-is-one-of-the-best-coming-of-age-movies-in-years (accessed 2 April 2017).
81. Barbara Speed, '*Girlhood* avoids easy answer in its portrayal of growing up in the Paris suburbs', *New Statesman* (12 May 2015). Available at http://www.newstatesman.com/culture/2015/05/girlhood-avoids-easy-answers-its-portrayal-growing-paris-suburbs (accessed 2 April 2017).
82. Alison Nastasi, '*Girlhood* director Céline Sciamma on reclaiming childhood, casting her girl gang, and how her film mirrors *Boyhood*', *Flavorwire* (30 January 2015). Available at http://flavorwire.com/502100/girlhood-director-celine-sciamma-on-reclaiming-childhood-casting-her-girl-gang-and-how-her-film-mirrors-boyhood (accessed 2 April 2017).
83. Dyer, 'Entertainment and utopia'.
84. Harris, 'Film of the week: *Girlhood*'.
85. Ahmed, *Queer Phenomenology*, pp. 17; 160.
86. Bolton, 'Giggling girls and crackling crones'.
87. Ibid.
88. Ahmed, *Queer Phenomenology*, p. 147.
89. Kohn, 'Cannes review'.
90. Harris, 'Film of the week: *Girlhood*'.
91. Ahmed, *Queer Phenomenology*, p. 62.
92. Palmer, *Brutal Intimacy*, p. 35.
93. Thomas, 'A review of Céline Sciamma's *Girlhood*'.
94. Sciamma, quoted in ReBecca Theodore-Vachon, 'Interview: black women's lives matter in *Girlhood*', *RogerEbert.com* (7 February 2015). Available at http://www.rogerebert.com/interviews/interview-black-womens-lives-matter-in-girlhood (accessed 2 April 2017).
95. Ibid.
96. Simon Critchley, 'Humour as practically enacted theory, or why critics should tell more jokes', in R. Westwood and C. Rhodes (eds), *Humour, Work and Organization* (London and New York: Routledge, 2007), p. 22.
97. Bolton, 'Giggling girls and crackling crones'.
98. Ibid., my emphasis.
99. Ibid., my emphasis.
100. Ibid.
101. Ahmed, *Queer Phenomenology*, p. 129.
102. Sciamma, quoted in Jordan Rossi, 'The interview: Céline Sciamma – *Girlhood*', *Hunger* (8 May 2015), my emphasis. Available at http://www.hungertv.com/feature/the-interview-celine-sciamma-girlhood/ (accessed 2 April 2017).
103. Ahmed, *Queer Phenomenology*; Freeman, *Time Binds*.
104. Sciamma, quoted in Mayer, '"She's getting back in the frame".

105. Ibid.
106. Davina Quinlivan, 'On how queer cinema might feel', *Music, Sound, and the Moving Image* 9/1 (2015), pp. 65–6.

Conclusion: Collectivities, the Familiar and (Un)Common Sense

1. Anu Koivunen, 'The promise of touch: turns to affect in feminist film theory', in L. Mulvey and A. Backman Rogers (eds), *Feminisms: Diversity, Difference and Multiplicity in Contemporary Film Cultures* (Amsterdam: Amsterdam University Press, 2015), p. 105; referencing Marks, *The Skin of the Film*.
2. Marks, *The Skin of the Film*, pp. 184–5, my emphasis.
3. Ahmed, *Queer Phenomenology*, p. 7.
4. Ibid., p. 11.
5. Marks, *The Skin of the Film*, p. 185.
6. There are notable links here with the arguments put forward by White and Whatling about the crucial role played by cinema in the formation of (public) lesbian identities in the 1930s and 40s, as discussed in Chapter 1.
7. Deleuze and Guattari, *Kafka*, p. 17; quoted in White, 'Lesbian minor cinema', p. 412, my emphasis.
8. A. Butler, *Women's Cinema*, p. 21, emphasis in original.
9. Farmer, 'Loves of Siam', p. 85.

Bibliography

Aaron, Michele, 'New queer cinema: an introduction', in M. Aaron (ed.), *New Queer Cinema: A Critical Reader* (New Brunswick: Rutgers University Press, 2004).

———, 'The new queer spectator,' in M. Aaron (ed.), *New Queer Cinema: A Critical Reader* (New Brunswick: Rutgers University Press, 2004).

Ahmed, Sara, *Queer Phenomenology: Orientations, Objects, Others* (Durham and London: Duke University Press, 2006).

———, *The Promise of Happiness* (Durham and London: Duke University Press, 2010).

Allen-Collinson, Jacquelyn, 'Running embodiment, power and vulnerability: notes towards a feminist phenomenology of female running', in E. Kennedy and P. Markula (eds), *Women and Exercise: The Body, Health and Consumerism* (London and New York: Routledge, 2010).

Allen-Collinson, Jacquelyn and Helen Owton, 'Intense embodiment: senses of heat in women's running and boxing', *Body and Society* 21/2 (2015), pp. 245–68.

Al-Saji, Alia, 'Bodies and sensings: on the uses of Husserlian phenomenology for feminist theory', *Continental Philosophy Review* 43/1 (2010), pp. 13–37.

Altman, Meryl, 'Teaching 70s feminism' (July 2001). Available at: https://userpages.umbc.edu/~korenman/wmst/70waves1.html (accessed 2 April 2017).

Altman, Rick, *The American Film Musical* (Bloomington: Indiana University Press, 1987).

Baker, Aaron, *Contesting Identities: Sports in American Film* (Chicago: University of Illinois Press, 2006).

Balázs, Béla, *Béla Balázs' Early Film Theory: Visible Man and the Spirit of Film*, trans. Rodney Livingston (New York: Berghahn, 1924/2010).

Barker, Jennifer, *The Tactile Eye: Touch and the Cinematic Experience* (Berkeley: University of California Press, 2009).

Bartky, Sandra Lee, 'Foucault, femininity and the modernization of patriarchal power', in I. Diamond and L. Quinby (eds), *Feminism and Foucault: Reflections on Resistance* (Boston: Northeastern University Press, 1988).

Berlant, Lauren, *Cruel Optimism* (Durham and London: Duke University Press, 2011).

Beugnet, Martine, *Cinema and Sensation* (Edinburgh: Edinburgh University Press, 2007).

Bibliography

Bollen, Jonathan, 'Queer kinesthesia: performativity on the dance floor', in J. C. Desmond (ed.), *Dancing Desires: Choreographing Sexualities On and Off the Stage* (Madison: University of Wisconsin Press, 2001).

Bolton, Lucy, *Film and Female Consciousness: Irigaray, Cinema and Thinking Women* (Basingstoke: Palgrave Macmillan, 2011).

——, 'Giggling girls and crackling crones: the phenomenology of women's laughter', Keynote *Film-Philosophy* Conference, Liverpool John Moores University (6–7 July 2011).

Bordwell, David and Kristin Thompson, *Film Art: An Introduction* (New York: McGraw-Hill, 2010).

Boyle, Raymond and Richard Haynes, *Power Play: Sport, the Media & Popular Culture* (Edinburgh: Edinburgh University Press, 2009).

Brace-Govan, Jan, 'Looking at bodywork: women and three physical activities', *Journal of Sport and Social Issues* 26/4 (2002), pp. 403–20.

Braidotti, Rosi, *Metamorphoses: Towards a Materialist Theory of Becoming* (Malden: Blackwell/Polity Press, 2002).

Brohm, Jean-Marie, *Sport: A Prison of Measured Time*, trans. Ian Fraser (London: Pluto Press, 1978).

Butler, Alison, *Women's Cinema: The Contested Screen* (London: Wallflower, 2002).

Butler, Judith, *Gender Trouble: Feminism and the Subversion of Identity* (New York: Routledge, 1990).

——, 'Athletic genders: hyperbolic instance and/or the overcoming of sexual binarism', *Stanford Humanities Review* 6/2 (1998). Available at: http://web.stanford.edu/group/SHR/6-2/html/butler.html (accessed 28 March 2017).

Chamarette, Jenny, *Phenomenology and the Future of Film: Rethinking Subjectivity Beyond French Cinema* (Basingstoke: Palgrave Macmillan).

Christiansen, Steen, 'Body refractions: Darren Aronofsky's *Black Swan*', *Academic Quarter* 3 (2011), pp. 306–15.

Clover, Carol J., *Men, Women and Chainsaws: Gender in Modern Horror Film* (Princeton: Princeton University Press, 1992).

Cohan, Steven, 'Introduction: musicals of the studio era', in S. Cohan (ed.), *Hollywood Musicals: The Film Reader* (New York: Routledge, 2002).

Colard, Jean-Max, '*Zidane, A Portrait du XXIème siècle* de Douglas Gordon et Philippe Parreno', *Les Inrockuptibles* 547 (2006), p. 54.

Collins, Robbie, '*Girlhood* review: "a coming-of-age classic"', *The Telegraph* (13 May 2015). Available at: http://www.telegraph.co.uk/film/girlhood/review/ (accessed 2 April 2017).

Creed, Barbara, *The Monstrous-Feminine: Film, Feminism, Psychoanalysis* (London: Routledge, 1993).

——, 'Lesbian bodies: tribades, tomboys and tarts', in J. Price and M. Shildrick (eds), *Feminist Theory and the Body: A Reader* (New York: Routledge, 1999).

Bibliography

Crenshaw, Kimberlé, *On Intersectionality: The Essential Writings of Kimberlé Crenshaw* (New York: Perseus, 2012).

Critchley, Simon, 'Humour as practically enacted theory, or why critics should tell more jokes', in R. Westwood and C. Rhodes (eds), *Humour, Work and Organization* (London and New York: Routledge, 2007).

Crossley, Nick, *The Social Body: Habit, Identity and Desire* (London: Sage, 2001).

Crosson, Seán, *Sport and Film*. (London: Routledge, 2013).

Csordas, Thomas, *Body/Meaning/Healing* (New York: Palgrave Macmillan, 2002).

Cvetkovich, Ann, 'White boots and combat boots: my life as a lesbian go-go dancer', in J. C. Desmond (ed.), *Dancing Desires: Choreographing Sexualities On and Off the Stage* (Madison: University of Wisconsin Press, 2001).

——, *An Archive of Feeling: Trauma, Sexuality and Lesbian Public Cultures* (London: Duke University Press, 2003).

D'Aloia, Adriano, 'Upside-down cinema', *Cinema: Journal of Philosophy and the Moving Image* 3 (2012), pp. 155–82.

——, 'Cinematic empathy: spectator involvement in the film experience', in D. Reynolds and M. Reason (eds), *Kinesthetic Empathy in Creative and Cultural Practices* (Bristol and Chicago: Intellect, 2012).

Daly, Ann, 'Classical ballet: a discourse of difference', in J. C. Desmond (ed.), *Meaning in Motion: New Cultural Studies of Dance* (Durham: Duke University Press, 1997).

Davis, Kathy 'Should a feminist dance tango? Some reflections on the experience and politics of passion', *Feminist Theory* 16/1 (2015), pp. 3–21.

Davis, Nick, *The Desiring-Image: Gilles Deleuze and Contemporary Queer Cinema* (New York: Oxford University Press, 2013).

de Lauretis, Teresa, *Alice Doesn't: Feminism, Semiotics, Cinema* (Bloomington: Indiana University Press, 1984).

del Rio, Elena, 'Rethinking feminist film theory: counter-narcissistic performance in Sally Potter's *Thriller*', *Quarterly Review of Film and Video* 21/1 (2004), pp. 11–24.

——, 'Film', in H. R. Sepp and L. Embree (eds), *Handbook of Phenomenological Aesthetics* (London and New York: Springer, 2010).

——, *Deleuze and the Cinemas of Performance: Powers of Affection* (Edinburgh: Edinburgh University Press, 2012).

Deleuze, Gilles and Félix Guattari, *Kafka: Towards a Minor Literature*, trans. Dana Polan (Minneapolis: University of Minnesota Press, 1986).

——, *What is Philosophy*, trans. Hugh Tomlinson (New York: Columbia University Press, 1994).

Desmond, Jane C., 'Making the invisible visible: staging sexualities through dance', in J. C. Desmond (ed.), *Dancing Desires: Choreographing Sexualities On and Off the Stage* (Madison: University of Wisconsin Press, 2001).

Bibliography

Doane, Mary Ann, 'Remembering women: psychical and historical constructions in film theory', in E. Ann Kaplan (ed.), *Psychoanalysis and Cinema* (London: Routledge, 1990).

Donaldson, Lucy, *Texture in Film* (Basingstoke: Palgrave Macmillan 2014).

Dyer, Richard, 'It's being so camp as keeps us going', in *The Culture of Queers* (London: Routledge, 1977/2005).

——, 'Entertainment and utopia', in R. Dyer (ed.), *Only Entertainment* (London: Routledge, 1992).

——, 'White', in *The Matter of Images: Essays on Representation* (London and New York: Routledge, 1993).

——, *White* (London and New York: Routledge, 1997).

Elsaesser, Thomas and Malte Hagener, *Film Theory: An Introduction Through the Senses* (New York and London: Routledge, 2010).

Epstein, Jean, '*Bonjour Cinema* and other writings', trans. Tom Milne, *Afterimage* 10 (1921/1981), pp. 8–39.

Farmer, Brett, 'Loves of Siam: contemporary Thai cinema and vernacular queerness', in P. A. Jackson (ed.), *Queer Bankok: Twenty-First-Century Markets, Media, and Rights* (Aberdeen and Hong Kong: Hong Kong University Press, 2011).

Fischer, Lucy, '"Dancing through the minefield": passion, pedagogy, politics and production in *The Tango Lesson*', *Cinema Journal* 43/3 (2004), pp. 42–58.

Fisher, Mark and Amber Jacobs, 'Debating *Black Swan*: gender and horror', *Film Quarterly* 65/1 (2011), pp. 58–62.

Foster, Susan Leigh, 'Dancing bodies', in J. C. Desmond (ed.), *Meaning in Motion: New Cultural Studies of Dance* (Durham: Duke University Press, 1997).

Freeman, Elizabeth, *Time Binds: Queer Temporalities, Queer Histories* (London: Duke University Press, 2010).

Friedberg, Anne, 'Identification and the star: a refusal of difference', *Star Signs: Papers from a Weekend Workshop* (London: BFI, 1982).

Fusco, Katherine, 'The actress experience: cruel knowing and the death of the picture personality in *Black Swan* and *The Girlfriend Experience*', *Camera Obscura* 82/1 (2013), pp. 1–35.

Gallese, Vittorio and Michele Guerra, 'Embodying movies: embodied simulation and Film Studies', *Cinema: Journal of Philosophy and the Moving Image* 3 (2012), pp. 183–210.

Garber, Marjorie, *Vested Interests: Cross-Dressing and Cultural Anxiety* (London: Penguin, 1993).

Garwood, Ian, *The Sense of Film Narration* (Edinburgh: Edinburgh University Press, 2013).

Gibson, Katie L. and Melanie Wolske, 'Disciplining sex in Hollywood: a critical comparison of *Blue Valentine* and *Black Swan*', *Women and Language* 34/2 (2011), pp. 79–96.

Bibliography

Gil, José, 'Paradoxical body', in A. Lepecki and J. Joy (eds), *Planes of Compositions: Dance, Theory and the Global* (London and New York: Seagull Books, 2009).

Ginsberg, Terri and Chris Lippard, *Historical Dictionary of Middle Eastern Cinema* (Toronto and Plymouth: The Scarecrow Press, 2010).

Graffy, Julian, 'A nation of two halves', *Sight & Sound* 16/6 (June 2006). Available online http://old.bfi.org.uk/sightandsound/review/3260 (accessed 2 April 2017).

Grant, Catherine, 'Secret agents: feminist theories of women's film authorship', *Feminist Theory* 2/1 (2001), pp. 113–30.

Grindon, Leger, *Knockout: The Boxer and Boxing in American Cinema* (Jackson: University Press of Mississippi, 2010).

Halberstam, Judith/Jack, *Female Masculinity* (London: Durham and London, 1998).

———, *In a Queer Time and Place: Transgender Bodies and Subcultural Lives* (New York: New York University Press, 2005).

———, *The Queer Art of Failure* (Durham and London: Duke University Press, 2011).

Haskell, Molly, *From Reverence to Rape: The Treatment of Women in the Movies* (Chicago: University of Chicago Press, 1974).

Hayward, Susan, *Cinema Studies: The Key Concepts* (London and New York: Routledge, 2000).

Heinämaa, Sara and Lanei Rodemeyer, 'Introduction', *Continental Philosophy Review* 43/1 (2010), pp. 1–11.

Hockey, John and Jacquelyn Allen-Collinson, 'Grasping the phenomenology of sporting bodies', *International Review for the Sociology of Sport* 42/2 (2007), pp. 115–31.

hooks, bell, *We Real Cool: Black Men and Masculinity* (New York and London: Routledge, 2004).

Ince, Kate, 'Bringing bodies back in: for a phenomenological and psychoanalytical film criticism of embodied cultural identity', *Film-Philosophy* 15/1 (2011), pp. 1–12.

———, 'Feminist phenomenology and the films of Sally Potter', in J. Boulé and U. Tidd (eds), *Existentialism and Contemporary Cinema: A Beauvoirian Perspective* (Oxford and New York: Berghahn, 2012).

Jagose, Annamarie, 'Queer Theory', *Australian Humanities Review* 4 (1996). Available at http://www.australianhumanitiesreview.org/archive/Issue-Dec-1996/jagose.html (accessed 2 April 2017).

———, *Queer Theory: An Introduction* (New York: New York University Press, 1997).

Jones, Amelia, 'Kinesthetic empathy in philosophical and art history: thoughts on how and what art means', in D. Reynolds and M. Reason (eds), *Kinesthetic Empathy in Creative and Cultural Practices* (Bristol and Chicago: Intellect, 2012).

Bibliography

Jones, Glen, 'In praise of an "invisible genre"? An ambivalent look at the fictional sports feature film', *Sport in Society: Cultures, Commerce, Media, Politics* 11/2–3 (2008), pp. 117–29.

Johnston, Claire, *Notes on Women's Cinema* (London: Society for Education in Film and Television, 1973).

Keeling, Kara, *The Witch's Flight: The Cinematic, the Black Femme and the Image of Common Sense* (Durham and London: Duke University Press, 2008).

Kheshti, Roshanak, 'Cross-dressing and gender (tres)passing: the transgender movie as a site of agentic potential in the New Iranian Cinema', *Hypatia: A Journal of Feminist Philosophy* 24/3 (2009), pp. 158–77.

Kohn, Eric, 'Cannes review: Céline Sciamma's *Girlhood* is one of the best coming of age movies in years', *Indiewire* (15 May 2014). Available at http://www.indiewire.com/article/cannes-review-celine-sciammas-girlhood-is-one-of-the-best-coming-of-age-movies-in-years (accessed 2 April 2017).

Koivunen, Anu, 'The promise of touch: turns to affect in feminist film theory', in L. Mulvey and A. Backman Rogers (eds), *Feminisms: Diversity, Difference and Multiplicity in Contemporary Film Cultures* (Amsterdam: Amsterdam University Press, 2015).

Laine, Tarja, *Feeling Cinema: Emotional Dynamics in Film Studies* (London: Bloomsbury, 2011).

———, *Bodies in Pain: Emotion and the Cinema of Darren Aronofski* (Oxford and New York: Berghahn, 2015).

Langer, Susanne, *Feeling and Form: A Philosophy of Art Developed from 'Philosophy in a New Key'* (London: Routledge and Keegan Paul, 1953).

Lindner, Katharina, '"In touch" with the female body: cinema, sport and lesbian representability', in K. Ross (ed.), *The Handbook of Gender, Sex and Media* (Oxford: Wiley-Blackwell, 2011).

———, 'Spectacular (dis-)embodiments: the female dancer on film', *Scope: An Online Journal of Film and Television Studies* 20 (2011), pp. 1–18.

———, 'Questions of embodied difference: film and queer phenomenology', *NECSUS European Journal of Media Studies* 1/2 (2012), pp. 199–217.

———, 'Corporeality and embodiment in the female boxing film', *Alphaville: Journal of Film & Screen Media* 7 (2014). Available at http://www.alphavillejournal.com/Issue7/HTML/ArticleLindner.html (accessed 2 April 2017).

———, 'Gender trouble in female sports films', in J. Hargreaves and E. Anderson (eds), *Routledge Handbook of Sport, Gender & Sexuality* (London and New York: Routledge, 2014).

———, 'Queering texture: tactility, spatiality and kinaesthetic empathy in *She Monkeys*', *Camera Obscura*, 32/3 (2017).

Mackay, Finn, *Radical Feminism: Feminist Activism in Movement* (Basingstoke: Palgrave Macmillan, 2015).

Bibliography

Manning, Erin, 'The elasticity of the almost', in A. Lepecki and J. Joy (eds), *Planes of Compositions: Dance, Theory and the Global* (London and New York: Seagull Books, 2009).

Marks, Laura U., *The Skin of the Film: Intercultural Cinema, Embodiment and the Senses* (London: Duke University Press, 2000).

Martin, Biddy, 'Extraordinary homosexuals and the fear of being ordinary', *Differences* 6 (1994), pp. 100–25.

——, 'Sexualities without genders and other queer utopias' *Diacritics* 24 (1994), pp. 104–21.

Mayer, So, *The Cinema of Sally Potter: A Politics of Love* (London : Wallflower Press, 2009).

——, ' "She's getting back in the frame": interview with Céline Sciamma', *The F Word: Contemporary UK Feminism* (5 May 2015). Available at http://www.thefword.org.uk/2015/05/celine_sciamma_interview/ (accessed 2 April 2017).

——, 'Uncommon sensuality: new queer feminist film theory', in L. Mulvey and A. Backman Rogers (eds), *Feminisms: Diversity, Difference and Multiplicity in Contemporary Film Cultures* (Amsterdam: Amsterdam University Press, 2015).

——, *Political Animals: The New Feminist Cinema* (London and New York: I.B.Tauris, 2016).

McKernan, Luke, 'Sport and the first films', in C. Williams (ed.), *Cinema: The Beginnings and the Future* (London: University of Westminster Press, 1996), pp. 107–16.

McLean, Adrienne L., *Dying Swans and Madmen: Ballet, the Body and Narrative Cinema* (New Jersey: Rutgers University Press, 2008).

——, 'If only they had meant to make a comedy: laughing at *Black Swan*', in M. Pomerance (ed.), *The Last Laugh: Strange Humors of Cinema* (Detroit: Wayne State University Press, 2013).

Medhurst, Andy, 'Camp', in A. Medhurst and S. R. Munt (eds), *Lesbian and Gay Studies: A Critical Introduction* (London: Cassell, 1997).

Meekums, Bonnie, 'Kinesthetic empathy and movement metaphor in dance movement psychotherapy', in D. Reynolds and M. Reason (eds), *Kinesthetic Empathy in Creative and Cultural Practices* (Bristol and Chicago: Intellect, 2012).

Mennel, Barbara, *Queer Cinema: Schoolgirls, Vampires and Gay Cowboys* (London: Wallflower, 2012).

Michotte, Albert, 'The emotional involvement of the spectator in the action represented in a film: toward a theory', in G. Thinès, A. Costall and G. Butterworth (eds), *Michotte's Experimental Phenomenology of Perception* (Hillsdale: Lawrence Erlbaum, 1953/1991).

Morris, Meaghan, *Too Soon Too Late: History in Popular Culture* (Bloomington: Indiana University Press, 1998).

Bibliography

Mottram, James, 'Céline Sciamma interview: step aside *Boyhood*, it's *Girlhood* time', *Independent* (24 April 2015). Available at: http://www.independent.co.uk/arts-entertainment/films/features/cline-sciamma-interview-step-aside-boyhood-its-girlhood-time-10199093.html (accessed 2 April 2017).

Mulvey, Laura, 'Visual pleasure and narrative cinema', *Screen* 16/3 (1975), pp. 6–18.

Naficy, Hamid, 'Veiled vision/powerful presences: women in post-revolutionary Iranian cinema', in M. Afkhami and E. Friedl (eds), *In the Eye of the Storm: Women in Post-Revolutionary Iran* (London and New York: I.B.Tauris, 1994).

——, 'Islamizing film culture in Iran: a post-Khatami update', in R. Tapper (ed.), *The New Iranian Cinema: Politics, Representation and Identity* (London and New York: I.B.Tauris, 2002).

Nastasi, Alison, '*Girlhood* director Céline Sciamma on reclaiming childhood, casting her girl gang, and how her film mirrors *Boyhood*', *Flavorwire* (30 January 2015). Available at http://flavorwire.com/502100/girlhood-director-celine-sciamma-on-reclaiming-childhood-casting-her-girl-gang-and-how-her-film-mirrors-boyhood (accessed 2 April 2017).

Niazi, Sarah, 'Urban imagination and the cinema of Jafar Panahi', *Wide Screen* 1/2 (2010). Available at http://widescreenjournal.org/index.php/journal/article/view/33/45 (accessed 2 April 2017).

O'Brien, Gabrielle, 'Mirror, mirror: fractured female identity in *Black Swan*', *Screen Education* 75 (2014), pp. 102–7.

Oksala, Johanna, 'A phenomenology of gender', *Continental Philosophy Review* 39/3 (2006), pp. 229–44.

Palmer, Tim, *Brutal Intimacy: Analyzing Contemporary French Cinema* (Middletown: Wesleyan University Press, 2011).

Panahi, Jafar and Maryam Maruf, 'Offside rules: An interview with Jafar Panahi', *Open Democracy* (6 June 2006). Available at https://www.opendemocracy.net/arts-Film/offside_3620.jsp (accessed 2 April 2017).

Parkinson, David, '*Offside* review', *Empire* (10 April 2006). Available at http://www.empireonline.com/movies/offside/review/ (accessed 2 April 2017).

Phillips, David, 'What's so queer here? Photography at the Gay and Lesbian Mardi Gras', *Eyeline* 26 (Summer 1994), pp. 16–19.

Pick, Anat, 'New queer cinema and lesbian films', in M. Aaron (ed.), *New Queer Cinema: A Critical Reader* (New Brunswick: Rutgers University Press, 2004).

Pomerance, Murray, 'The dramaturgy of action and involvement in the sports film', *Quarterly Review of Film and Video* 23 (2006), pp. 311–29.

Potter, Sally, 'Bruises and blisters', *Sight and Sound* 7/11 (1997) LFF supplement, pp. 4–7.

Potter, Susan, 'Mobilising lesbian desire: the sexual kinaesthetics of Dorothy Arzner's *The Wild Party*', *Screen* 52/4 (2011), pp. 442–60.

Probyn, Elspeth, *Outside Belongings* (London and New York: Routledge, 1996).

Bibliography

Quinlivan, Davina, 'On how queer cinema might feel', *Music, Sound, and the Moving Image* 9/1 (2015), pp. 63–77.

Reynolds, Dee, 'Kinesthetic empathy and the dance's body: from emotion to affect', in D. Reynolds and M. Reason (eds), *Kinesthetic Empathy in Creative and Cultural Practices* (Bristol and Chicago: Intellect, 2012).

——, 'Kinesthetic engagement: embodied responses and intersubjectivity', in D. Reynolds and M. Reason (eds), *Kinesthetic Empathy in Creative and Cultural Practices* (Bristol and Chicago: Intellect, 2012).

——, 'Mirroring movements: empathy and social interactions', in D. Reynolds and M. Reason (eds), *Kinesthetic Empathy in Creative and Cultural Practices* (Bristol and Chicago: Intellect, 2012).

Reynolds, Dee and Matthew Reason (eds), *Kinesthetic Empathy in Creative and Cultural Practices* (Bristol and Chicago: Intellect, 2012).

Rich, B. Ruby, 'New queer cinema', *Sight and Sound* 2/5 (1992), pp. 30–4.

——, 'Queer and present danger', *Sight and Sound* 10/3 (2000), pp. 22–5.

Romney, Jonathan, *'Offside'*, *Screen Daily* (17 February 2006). Available at http://www.screendaily.com/offside-sweden-2006/4026227.article (accessed 2 April 2017).

Rose, Ava and James Friedman, 'Television sports as mas(s)culine cult of distraction', in A. Baker and T. Boyd (eds), *Out of Bounds: Sports, Media, and the Politics of Identity* (Bloomington: Indiana University Press, 1997).

Rosen, Marjorie, *Popcorn Venus: Women, Movies and the American Dream* (New York: Coward, McCann & Geoghega, 1973).

Rossi, Jordan, 'The interview: Céline Sciamma – Girlhood', *Hunger* (8 May 2015). Available at http://www.hungertv.com/feature/the-interview-celine-sciamma-girlhood/ (accessed 2 April 2017).

Rowe, David, 'Time and timelessness in the sports film', *Sport in Society: Cultures, Commerce, Media, Politics* 11/2–3 (2008), pp. 146–58.

Rubin, Martin, 'Busby Berkeley and the backstage musical', in S. Cohan (ed.), *Hollywood Musicals: The Film Reader* (New York: Routledge, 1993/2002).

Saunders, Keeley, 'Gender-defined spaces, places and tropes: contemporary transgender representation in *Tomboy* and *Romeos*', *Journal of European Popular Culture* 5/2 (2014), pp. 181–93.

Sciamma, Céline, *Tomboy* DVD interview (2011).

Sedgwick, Eve Kosofsky, 'Paranoid reading and reparative reading; or, you're so vain, you probably think this introduction is about you', in E. K. Sedgwick (ed.), *Novel Gazing: Queer Readings in Fiction* (Durham: Duke University Press, 1997).

——, *Touching Feeling: Affect, Pedagogy, Performativity* (Durham and London: Duke University Press, 2003).

Shaviro, Steven, '*Black Swan*' (5 January 2011). Available at http://www.shaviro.com/Blog/?p=975 (accessed 2 April 2017).

Bibliography

Sheets-Johnstone, Maxine, *The Primacy of Movement* (Amsterdam and Philadelphia: John Benjamins, 2011).

Smelik, Anneke, 'Art cinema and murderous lesbians', in M. Aaron (ed.), *New Queer Cinema: A Critical Reader* (New Brunswick: Rutgers University Press, 2004).

Sobchack, Vivian, *The Address of the Eye: A Phenomenology of Film Experience* (Princeton: Princeton University Press, 1992).

——, *Carnal Thoughts: Embodiment and Moving Image Culture* (Berkeley: University of California Press, 2004).

Solnit, Rebecca, *River of Shadows: Eadweard Muybridge and the Technological Wild West* (New York: Viking, 2003).

Speed, Barbara, '*Girlhood* avoids easy answer in its portrayal of growing up in the Paris suburbs', *New Statesman* (12 May 2015). Available at http://www.newstatesman.com/culture/2015/05/girlhood-avoids-easy-answers-its-portrayal-growing-paris-suburbs (accessed 2 April 2017).

Stacey, Jackie, *Star Gazing: Hollywood Cinema and Female Spectatorship* (London: Routledge, 1994).

——, 'Wishing away ambivalence', *Feminist Theory* 15/1 (2014), pp. 39–49.

Stahl, Lynne, *Unhappy Medium: Filmic Tomboy Narrative and Queer Feminist Spectatorship*, PhD dissertation, Cornell University (2015).

Stam, Robert, 'Carnival, radical humor, and media politics', in R. Martin (ed.), *The Routledge Companion to Art and Politics* (New York and London: Routledge, 2015).

Stein, Edith, *On the Problem of Empathy*, trans. Waltraut Stein (Washington: ICS Publications, 1917/1989).

Straayer, Chris, *Deviant Eyes, Deviant Bodies: Sexual Re-orientation in Film and Video* (New York: Columbia University Press, 1996).

Streible, Dan, *Fight Pictures: A History of Boxing and Early Cinema* (Berkeley: University of California Press, 2008).

Talajooy, Saeed, 'Directors', in P. Jahed (ed.), *Directory of World Cinema: Iran* (Intellect: Chicago, 2012).

Tasker, Yvonne, *Spectacular Bodies: Gender, Genre and the Action Cinema* (London and New York: Routledge, 1993).

Theodore-Vachon, ReBecca, 'Interview: black women's lives matter in *Girlhood*', *RogerEbert.com* (7 February 2015). Available at http://www.rogerebert.com/interviews/interview-black-womens-lives-matter-in-girlhood (accessed 2 April 2017).

Thomas, Dori, 'A review of Céline Sciamma's *Girlhood*: an honest and emotionally powerful take on the coming-of-age genre', *Side B Magazine* (5 June 2015). Available at http://sidebmagazine.tumblr.com/post/120774164350/a-review-of-c%C3%A9line-sciammas-girlhood-an-honest (accessed 2 April 2017).

Toffoletti, Kim, 'Iranian women's sports fandom: gender, resistance, and identity in the football movie *Offside*', *Journal of Sport and Social Issues* 38/1 (2014), pp. 75–92.

Bibliography

Villarejo, Amy, *Lesbian Rule: Cultural Criticism and the Value of Desire* (London: Duke University Press, 2003).

Vincendeau, Ginette, 'Minority report', *Sight & Sound* 25/6 (2015), pp. 22–9.

Wacquant, Loïc, 'Carnal connections: on embodiment, apprenticeship, and membership', *Qualitative Sociology* 28/4 (2005), pp. 445–74.

Waldron, Darren, 'Embodying gender nonconformity in "girls": Céline Sciamma's *Tomboy*', *L'Esprit Créateur* 53/1 (2013), pp. 60–73.

Whannel, Garry, 'Winning and losing respect: narratives of identity in sports films', *Sport in Society: Cultures, Commerce, Media, Politics* 11/2–3 (2008), pp. 195–208.

Whatling, Clare, *Screen Dreams: Fantasising Lesbians in Film* (Manchester: Manchester University Press, 1997).

White, Patricia, *unInvited: Classical Hollywood Cinema and Lesbian Representability* (Bloomington: Indiana University Press, 1999).

——, 'Lesbian minor cinema', *Screen* 49/4 (2008), pp. 410–25.

Wiegman, Robyn, 'The times we're in: queer feminist criticism and the reparative "turn"', *Feminist Theory* 15/1 (2014), pp. 4–25.

Williams, Linda, 'Body genres: gender, genre, excess', *Film Quarterly* 44/4 (1991), pp. 2–13.

Young, Iris Marion, 'Throwing like a girl: a phenomenology of feminine body comportment, motility and spatiality', *Human Studies* 3/2 (1980), pp. 137–56.

Zaner, Richard, *The Problem of Embodiment: Some Contributions to a Phenomenology of the Body* (The Hague: Martinus Nijhoff, 1971).

Index

52 Tuesdays, 198

Aaron, Michele, 195
acrobat, 51–4, 96
Al-Saji, Alia, 64–5
Albert Nobbs, 176, 198
alienworld, 66
All About Eve, 118, 266n.145
Allen-Collinson, Jacqueline, 144, 148, 155, 158
An American in Paris, 107
apparatus (cinematic), 12, 76, 265n.100
auteur, auteurism, 17
authorship, 16–19 32, 86, 89–91, 226

backward (directionality, temporality), 8, 16, 86, 88–9, 93, 95, 100–2, 105, 172
   see also belatedness; drag
Balázs, Bela, 50
Ballet,
   ballet body, 74–5, 80, 116–17, 120–1, 127, 133–4
   ballet in cinema, 74, 118, 120–2
   gender in ballet, 116, 134
banlieu cinema, 224–5, 228
Barker, Jennifer, 5, 43–9, 52, 70, 110
   see also tactility (cinematic); textural analysis
Bazin, André, 42
Beau travail, 37
belatedness, 161–2, 171
   see also time, bad timing

Bend it Like Beckham, 144, 186
Berlant, Lauren, 151
   see also optimism
beside, besideness, 4–5
   see also paranoid reading; reparative reading; Sedgwick, Eve Kosofsky
Beugnet, Martine, 70, 147–8
body,
   body genres, 13, 119
      see also genre, horror; genre, melodrama; Williams, Linda; taste (bad)
   body of the dance, 77–8, 87, 115, 261n.6
   body of the film, 55, 78, 82, 125
   space of the body, 96–7, 108, 136
Bollen, Jonathan, 81–83
   see also queer, queer kinesthesia
Bolton, Lucy, 16, 70, 234, 237–8
Bourdieu, Pierre, 164
   see also habitus
boxing film, *see* genre, boxing film
Boyhood, 227
Boys Don't Cry, 197–8, 203, 210, 220–2
bracket, bracketing (in phenomenology), 42, 62, 64, 66, 103
Braidotti, Rosi, 4, 68, 103
breath, breathing, 78, 85, 94, 134–7, 154–9, 165, 168, 170, 171, 222, 240, 243–4
   see also respiration
Brother to Brother, 37

Index

But I'm a Cheerleader, 144
Butler, Alison, 15, 20, 36
Butler, Judith, 21, 26–8, 33, 61, 81–2, 87, 144, 150, 152–3, 156, 216–18, 220

Calamity Jane, 226
camp, 22, 118, 120
Campion, Jane, 16, 226
Carnal Thoughts, 67–8
  see also Sobchack, Vivian
Carrie, 118
Centre Stage, 118, 129
Chamarette, Jenny, 70, 253n.24
chase (cinematic), 47–8, 110
  see also handshake (cinematic)
Clover, Carol, 13
Cracks, 143
Creed, Barbara, 13
Critchley, Simon, 237
Cvetkovich, Ann, 2, 81
chrononormativity, 7, 11, 145, 151, 161–2, 164–5, 168
  see also Freeman, Elizabeth
Civil Rights, 23
close-up, 47, 49, 224
collectivity, collective, 8, 19–21, 25, 37, 68, 156, 183, 187, 191, 216, 230, 231, 232, 234, 235–40, 249
coming-of-age, 143, 194–5, 223, 225, 227–8
common sense, 34, 143, 195, 248–9
  see also familiarity; (un)common sense
Company, The, 75, 129
Critchley, Simon, 237
cross-dressing, 25, 34, 174–5, 178, 181–3, 190, 197–8, 200, 203
  see also disguise (gender); drag; temporary transvestite (film/trope)

D'Aloia, Adriano, 43, 46, 50–4, 133, 219
Dallas Buyers Club, 197
dance,
  body of the dance 77–8, 87, 115, 261n.6
    see also body
  dance film, see genre, dance film
  see also ballet; tango
Dancer, The, 75
Danish Girl, The, 197
Dasein, 59
Davis, Nick, 19, 35–7, 194–5
Davis, Kathy, 87, 110–11, 115
De Lauretis, Teresa, 15
Dead Ringers, 37
del Rio, Elena, 13–14, 39–41, 71–2, 85, 88, 92, 100, 114
Desmond, Jane C., 76, 78–81, 84, 143
discourse,
  cinematic discourse, cinema as discourse, 15, 17–18, 91
    see also authorship; enunciation; voice
  gender as discourse, 211
  and queer theory, 27–8
  women's discourse, 238
    see also speech
disguise (gender), 8, 146, 174–8, 180, 183, 204
  see also cross-dressing; rewind; transgender
Doane, Mary Ann, 12
double, doubling, 118–19, 121–6, 132–3, 136, 138, 167, 266n.145, 267n.151
  see also mirror, mirroring
Double, The, 119
drag,
  as cross-dressing, 11, 25, 192, 197, 200, 211, 219–20

Index

temporal drag, 11, 16
  see also backward; belatedness; Freeman, Elizabeth; time, bad timing
disorientation, 71, 90, 97, 100, 104, 248
  see also orientation; shattering
Donaldson, Lucy, 55
Dyer, Richard, 22, 70–1, 106–7, 230

Einfühlung, 52
empathy, 6–7, 44–6, 48–55, 77, 81–2, 108, 132, 206, 208, 214, 219
enunciation, cinematic, 6, 17–18, 91
  see also discourse; voice
enworldedness, 40–2
epistemology, 14, 58–9
  see also ontology
epoch, 64
Epstein, Jean, 50

face, facing, 11, 49, 90–1, 98–9, 101–2, 114, 191, 213–14, 253n.7
  see also orientation
familiarity, 47–8, 97, 99, 101–2, 105, 196, 201, 246–8
Farmer, Brett, 6, 248
Fischer, Lucy, 87, 130
Flat is Beautiful, 31
Foster, Susan Leigh, 128
Freeman, Elizabeth, 2, 7, 10–11, 16, 29, 145, 151, 160–2, 164
  see also chrononormativity; drag
Fried Green Tomatoes, 199
Fusco, Katherine, 122–3

Garwood, Ian, 55
Gay Liberation, 23–4
gaydar, 33–4
  see also lesbian, appearance

gender trouble, 25, 61, 138, 153
generation, generationality, 11, 29, 89, 145, 167
  see also genealogy of descent; lines; repronormative; waves
genealogy of descent, 11, 145, 151, 253n.1
  see also generation, generationality; lines; repronormative; waves
genre,
  boxing film, 141–2
  dance film, 3, 74–5, 80, 107, 118, 121, 128, 129, 131
  genre trouble, 142
  horror, 13, 118–20
  melodrama, 42–3, 118–20, 142
  sports film, 141–3, 146–9
  see also body genres
Gil, José, 96
Gold Diggers, The, 74
Grant, Catherine, 18
Gravity, 48
Grindon, Leger, 141–142
Gymnast, The, 143

habituation, habitual, 5, 47, 55, 81–2, 95–6, 148–9, 168
habitus, 164
  see also Bourdieu, Pierre
Halberstam, Judith/Jack, 2, 7, 145, 151, 160, 199, 204, 208–10, 221–2
handshake (cinematic), 44–6, 47
  see also chase (cinematic)
haptic, hapticity, 2, 5, 44, 79, 93–4, 113, 128, 135, 205, 207, 214, 245, 247–8
Heinämaa, Sara, 58–9
homeworld, 61–2, 66, 90

Index

hooks, bell, 151
 see also white supremacist capitalist patriarchy
horizon (bodily, perceptual, phenomenological), 5, 23, 25, 82, 94, 97–9, 114, 132, 139, 187, 191, 247, 249, 251
horror *see* genre, horror; body genres; genre
Husserl, Edmund, 42, 58–9, 61–5, 89

impression, 2, 97, 129, 138, 152, 166, 167–8, 193
 see also pressure; lines
Ince, Kate, 70, 85, 93–4
In the Cut, 16
In the Turn, 268n.13
intentionality, inhibited, 43, 95, 217
 see also 'Throwing like a girl'; Young, Iris Marion,
intercorporeality, 58, 217
intersubjectivity, 49, 51, 54, 58, 61–3, 66, 222
Irigaray, Luce, 16, 59, 103, 234, 238

Jagose, Annamarie, 25–7
Johnston, Claire, 15, 20
Jones, Amelia, 77
Juwanna Man, 176

Keaton, Buster, 45–6
Kheshti, Roshanak, 175, 177, 181–4
 see also (tres)passing
kinesis, 53

La Haine, 225–7
Laine, Tarja, 127–8, 134, 139
Langer, Susanne, 78
laughter, women's, 233–4, 237–40
lesbian

appearance, 33–4, 251n.2, 262n.22
 see also Villarejo, Amy
minor cinema, 32, 36
visibility, 24, 32–3, 143–4, 195, 199, 251n.2
liberation, *see* Gay Liberation; Women's Liberation Movement
lines (staying in line; crossing a/the line; straight lines; lining up) 10, 26, 151, 166, 178–9, 228 253n.1
 see also chrononormativity; genealogy of descent; pressure
lived-body, 14, 38, 41–3, 53, 55, 57, 60, 79, 127, 216, 233
liveness (of television/sport), 146, 180
Lost in Translation, 16

Manning, Erin, 110–11
 see also relational movement
Marks, Laura U., 2, 70, 85, 247
 see also skin of the film
Martin, Biddy, 83
Mayer, So, 85, 113, 194, 223, 267n.151, 268n.13
Medhurst, Andy, 22
melodrama, *see* genre; genre, body genre
Mennel, Barbara, 30
Merleau-Ponty, Maurice, 42, 46, 55, 59–60, 66, 81, 148, 153, 217
McLean, Adrienne L., 118, 120
Million Dollar Baby, 142–3
minor (literature, cinema), 6, 14, 19–21, 24, 31–2, 36–7, 248
mirror, mirroring, 49, 121, 124–9, 131, 132, 138, 167, 214–16, 267n.151
 see also double, doubling
morph, morphing (digital), 125–7, 132
Morris, Meaghan, 20
Morvern Callar, 16
motility, 42, 60

Index

Mrs Doubtfire, 175
Mulvey, Laura, 12–13, 15, 89, 117
musical, 74, 80, 106–7, 114, 118, 121, 230
musculature,
   cinematic musculature, 2, 5–6, 8, 41, 44–6, 49, 52, 55, 71, 76, 79–80, 86, 95, 97, 116, 120–1, 131, 137–9, 194, 205, 225–6, 229–31
   human musculature, 5, 7, 14, 44, 49, 52, 55, 75, 84, 120, 123, 131–2, 137–8, 161, 163, 214, 218, 237, 207, 213–18, 230–1, 237, 249
   muscular empathy, 6, 7, 44–6, 49, 77, 82, 214, 219
   muscular encounters, 2, 41, 44–7, 75, 107, 109–11, 134–5, 190–1, 214–15, 224, 242, 246–7
   see also chase (cinematic); handshake (cinematic)

Naficy, Hamid, 181
Naked Lunch, 37
neuro-phenomenology, 43
New Iranian Cinema, 176–8, 181–3
New Queer Cinema, 3, 23, 27, 29–30, 35, 195–6
   see also queer
noise, 231, 233–4

occupation, (un-/pre-)occupied, 90–1, 97, 99, 101–2, 105, 150, 169–70, 182, 184, 197–8, 219, 235–6
ocularcentrism, 34, 39, 117
Oksala, Johanna, 59–83
ontology, 14, 53, 57–9, 61–6, 77, 125, 129, 131–3, 136, 138, 182
   see also epistemology

orientation,
   cinematic orientation, 46–9
   phenomenological orientation, 51, 71, 82, 90–1, 97, 101, 104, 152–3, 197, 247–8
   see also disorientation; familiarity; spatiality (of gender); twist, twisted, twisting; zero point (of orientation)
Orlando, 74
optimism, 151
   see also Berlant, Lauren

Palmer, Tim, 201
paranoid reading, 4–5, 27, 204, 252n.12
   see also reparative reading
Personal Best, 143
Pick, Anat, 30–2
Pina, 75
Pomerance, Murray, 149–50
Portrait of a Young Girl at the End of the 60s in Brussels (*Portrait d'un jeune fille de la fin des années 60s à Bruxelles*), 31
post-phenomenology, 63, 65–7
Potter, Susan, 84–5
pressure, 7, 77, 96, 116–17, 133–6, 150, 154, 158–9, 162, 165–6, 168, 173, 201, 218, 230–1, 233–6, 240, 242, 249
   see also impression; lines
primordial experience, 52, 63, 99, 132–3
Probyn, Elspeth, 81
proprioception, 48–9, 130, 136
psychoanalysis, 12, 41–2

quasi (relations, experiences, bodies), 52–5

Index

queer
    failure, 7–8, 145, 150–1, 160–2, 174
        see also; success
    New Queer Cinema, 3, 23, 27, 29–30, 35, 195–6
    queer feminist archive, 3
        see also Wiegman, Robyn
    queer/feminist vernacular, 6, 248
    queer kinesthesia, 81
        see also Bollen, Jonathan
    queer theory and discourse, 27–8, 21
        see also discourse
    queer time, 165
    queer visibility, 9
Quinlivan, Davina, 245

Red Shoes, The, 118
reduction (phenomenological method), 59, 62–6
relational movement, 110–11
    see also Manning, Erin
reparative reading, 4–5, 16, 250, 252n.12
    see also paranoid reading
repronormative, 11
    see also chrononormativity; generation, generationality
Repulsion, 118
rewind (in transgender representation), 209
    see also disguise (gender); drag; temporary transvestite (film/trope); transgender
Reynolds, Dee, 51, 77–8
respiration, 155–8
    see also breath, breathing
Rich, B. Ruby, 29–30, 35
Rodemeyer, Lanei, 58–9, 65
roller derby, 144
Rosemary's Baby, 118
Rowe, David, 146–7, 154, 156

Saunders, Keeley, 197–8
Save the Last Dance, 129
scars, 152–3, 168
schema,
    corporeal, 148
    ontological, 61–6
    postural, 42
    temporal, 160
Sedgwick, Eve Kosofski, 4–5, 16
sense-ational, 5, 40
sensibility, sense-ibility, 3, 4, 21–2, 32, 40, 249
shattering, 104
    see also disorientation
Shaviro, Steven, 119–20
She Monkeys (Apflickorna), 143
She's the Man, 176–7
Sheets-Johnstone, Maxine, 93
Shortbus, 37
simulation (embodied), 44, 51
Singin' in the Rain, 107
skin of the film, 5, 52
    see also Marks, Laura U.
Smelik, Anneke, 30
Sobchack, Vivian, 2, 41–3, 49, 54, 56–8, 60, 67–70, 77, 85, 100
Some Like it Hot, 175
Something Must Break (Nånting måste gå sönder), 198
space of the body, 96–7, 108, 136
spatiality (of gender), 2, 5, 42–3, 60, 81–2, 115, 137, 143–5, 153, 184, 197, 231–2, 244, 247, 252n.22
    see also twist, twisted, twisting
speech,
    speech act, 81, 211
    women's speech, 13, 238
sports film,
    see genre, sports film
Stacey, Jackie, 13, 252n.12

Index

Stahl, Lynne, 199–200
Stam, Robert, 178–9, 192
Stein, Edith, 51–2, 59
Stella Dallas, 43, 56
stereotypes (critiques of), 12
Straayer, Chris, 175–7
　see also temporary transvestite (film/trope)
success, 7, 141–2, 150–1, 155, 160, 189, 246
　see also queer, failure
Swan Lake, 74, 117, 119, 121–4, 130

tables,
　round tables, 89, 100
　tables in/of philosophy, 89, 100–3
　writing tables, 89, 91, 97–105
tactility (cinematic), 44
　see also Barker, Jennifer
Talajooy, Saeed, 186–7
tango (and gender), 74, 80, 86–7
taste (bad), 119–20
　see also body genres
temporality, see backward; belatedness; time; rewind
temporary transvestite (film/trope), 175–7
　see also Straayer, Chris
textural analysis, 3, 5, 252n.7
　see also Barker, Jennifer
'Throwing like a girl', 60, 148
　see also intentionality (inhibited); Young, Iris Marion
time,
　bad timing, 145, 160, 161
　　see also belatedness
　film time, 147
　out of time, 109, 157, 161, 166
　queer time, 165
　sport time, 147

straight time, 7–8, 145, 166, 167
waste (of) time, 7, 164
　see also backward; belatedness; chrononormativity; drag
timelessness (in the sports film), 146
tomboy, tomboyism, 8, 37, 143, 161–2, 199–202, 208, 210, 220, 246
Toffoletti, Kim, 183
tools, 102–3
　see also tables
Tootsie, 175
transgender,
　transgender character/narrative, 182, 184, 200, 202, 204, 209, 222–3, 274n.30
　　see also *Boys Don't Cry*; cross-dressing; disguise (gender); drag; rewind; temporary transvestite (film/trope)
　transgender gaze, 205, 209–10
　　see also *Boys Don't Cry*
　transgender identity (politics), 34, 61, 199–202
　transgender move, 175, 182–4
　　see also Kheshti, Roshanak; (tres)passing
transcendental,
　ego, 42, 62, 65
　consciousness/subjectivity, 7, 59–63, 67
　phenomenology, 42, 58
Trapeze, 53–4
(tres)passing, 7–8, 37, 146, 175, 177–80, 182–4, 191–92
　see also Kheshti, Roshanak
trouble, see gender trouble; genre trouble; twist, twisted, twisting
twist, twisted, twisting, 5, 8, 252n.22
　see also gender trouble; spatiality (of gender)

Index

(un)common sense, 195, 246, 247–9
see also common sense

veiling (aesthetics of), 178, 180–1, 183
Velvet Goldmine, 37
vernacular (queer/feminist), 6, 248
Victor/Victoria, 175
Villarejo, Amy, 33–4, 201, 251n.2, 262n.22
see also gaydar; lesbian, appearance
Vincendeau, Ginette, 224–5
visibility,
   and identity, 21–2, 24–5, 144, 174–5, 200–2, 205, 224–5, 231
   and invisibility, 3, 15, 22, 33–4, 174–5, 178–9, 186, 196
   lesbian visibility, 24, 32–3, 143–4, 195, 199, 251n.2
   see also lesbian, appearance
   queer visibility, 9
   and representation/representability, 15, 21–2, 25, 34, 196, 199–200
   trans visibility, 195, 198, 209
voice,
   cinematic voice, 17–18, 91, 92
   see also discourse; enunciation
   (not) having a voice, 224, 231–4, 238
   see also speech

Waldron, Darren, 198–200, 202, 214
Water Lilies (*Naissance des pieuvres*), 194, 197, 212, 223, 143

Watermelon Woman, The, 37
waves, 10–11, 27, 29, 35, 89
   see also genealogy of descent; generations, generationality; lines
When Night is Falling, 143
Whatling, Clare, 22, 34, 199, 277n.6
White, Patricia, 22, 30–2, 34, 36, 199, 277n.6
white supremacist capitalist patriarchy, 151
   see also hooks, bell
Wiegman, Robyn, 3, 5
   see also archive (queer feminist)
Wild Party, The, 84–5
Williams, Linda, 13, 119
   see also body genres
Wrestler, The, 119
Women's Liberation Movement, 12, 23–4

Young, Iris Marion, 43, 60, 95, 102, 144, 148
   see also intentionality (inhibited); 'Throwing like a girl'

zero point (of orientation), 7, 51, 99, 111, 129, 137, 197
   see also orientation
Zidane: A 21st Century Portrait (*Zidane, un portrait du 21e siècle*), 147–8

www.ingramcontent.com/pod-product-compliance
Lightning Source LLC
Chambersburg PA
CBHW051804230426
43672CB00012B/2624